Lecture Notes in Computer Science 12338

More information about this series at http://www.springer.com/series/7411

Luigi Alfredo Grieco · Gennaro Boggia ·
Giuseppe Piro · Yaser Jararweh ·
Claudia Campolo (Eds.)

Ad-Hoc, Mobile, and Wireless Networks

19th International Conference on Ad-Hoc Networks
and Wireless, ADHOC-NOW 2020
Bari, Italy, October 19–21, 2020
Proceedings

Springer

Editors
Luigi Alfredo Grieco ⓘ
DEI
Polytechnic University of Bari
Bari, Italy

Gennaro Boggia ⓘ
DEI
Polytechnic University of Bari
Bari, Italy

Giuseppe Piro ⓘ
DEI
Polytechnic University of Bari
Bari, Italy

Yaser Jararweh ⓘ
Duquesne University
Pittsburgh, PA, USA

Claudia Campolo ⓘ
Mediterranea University of Reggio Calabria
Reggio Calabria, Italy

ISSN 0302-9743   ISSN 1611-3349 (electronic)
Lecture Notes in Computer Science
ISBN 978-3-030-61745-5   ISBN 978-3-030-61746-2 (eBook)
https://doi.org/10.1007/978-3-030-61746-2

LNCS Sublibrary: SL5 – Computer Communication Networks and Telecommunications

This Springer imprint is published by the registered company Springer Nature Switzerland AG
The registered company address is: Gewerbestrasse 11, 6330 Cham, Switzerland

Preface

The International Conference on Ad-Hoc Networks and Wireless (AdHoc-Now) is one of the most popular series of events dedicated to research on ad-hoc, mobile and wireless sensor networks, and computing. Since its inception in 2002, the conference has been held 18 times in 8 different countries, and the 19th edition was held in Bari, Italy, during October 19–21, 2020. Due to the COVID-19 outbreak, the conference was held virtually.

We wish to thank all of the authors who submitted their work. This year, AdHoc-Now received 39 submissions, and 23 papers were accepted for presentation after a rigorous review process involving the Technical Program Committee (TPC) members, some external reviewers, and the TPC chairs.

The AdHoc-Now 2020 program was organized in five sessions grouping the contributions into the following topics: Internet of Drones and Smart Mobility, Internet of Things and Internet of Medical Things, Intelligent, Programmable and Delay- and Disruption-Tolerant Networks, Secure Communication Protocols and Architectures, and Wireless Systems. In each of these sessions, new ideas and directions were discussed among attendees, thus providing an in-depth and stimulating view on the new frontiers in the field of mobile, ad hoc, and wireless computing.

We would like to thank all of the people involved in AdHoc-Now 2020. First of all, we are grateful to the TPC members and the external reviewers for their help in providing detailed reviews of the submissions; to Albert Bel Pereira, our submission and proceedings chair; to Giuseppe Piro, Yaser Jararweh, and Claudia Campolo, our TPC chairs; to Danda Rawat, Changqiao Xu, and Periklis Chatzimisios, our publicity chairs; to Pietro Boccadoro, our web chair; and to Simona Colucci, our local arrangement chair. We also thank the team at Springer for their great support throughout the entire process, from the submission phase until the proceedings production.

Finally, the organization was made possible through the strong help of our supporters: Springer and Springer's *Lecture Notes in Computer Science* (LNCS), Wiley *Internet Technology Letters (ITL)*, Consorzio Nazionale Interuniversitario per le Telecomunicazioni (CNIT), and Politecnico di Bari. A special thank you to all of them.

October 2020

Luigi Alfredo Grieco
Gennaro Boggia
Giuseppe Piro
Yaser Jararweh
Claudia Campolo

Organization

General Chairs

Luigi Alfredo Grieco   Politecnico di Bari, Italy
Gennaro Boggia   Politecnico di Bari, Italy

Technical Program Committee Chairs

Giuseppe Piro   Politecnico di Bari, Italy
Yaser Jararweh   Duquesne University, USA
Claudia Campolo   Università Mediterranea di Reggio Calabria, Italy

Publicity Arrangements Chairs

Danda Rawat   Howard University, USA
Changqiao Xu   Beijing University of Posts and Telecommunications, China
Periklis Chatzimisios   International Hellenic University, Greece

Submission and Proceeding Chair

Albert Bel Pereira   University Pompeu Fabra, Spain

Local Arrangement Chair

Simona Colucci   Politecnico di Bari, Italy

Web Chair

Pietro Boccadoro   Politecnico di Bari, Italy

Steering Committee

Evangelos Kranakis   Carleton University, Canada
Violet R. Syrotiuk   Arizona State University, USA
Michel Barbeau   Carleton University, Canada
Ionise Nikolaidis   University of Alberta, Canada

Program Committee

Amadeo Marica	Mediterranea University of Reggio Calabria, Italy
Andras Mora-Duplicada	University of Granada, Spain
Assis Flavio	Federal University of Bahia (UFBA), Brazil
Barcelo-Ordinas Jose M.	Polytechnic University of Catalonia, Spain
Bazzi Alessandro	University of Bologna, Italy
Boccadoro Pietro	Politecnico di Bari, Italy
Bogdan Groza	Politehnica University of Timisoara, Romania
Bramas Quentin	Université Pierre et Marie Curie, France
Bruneo Dario	University of Messina, Italy
Busnel Yann	IMT Atlantique, France
Calafate Carlos	Universitat Politècnica de València, Spain
De Paola Alessandra	University of Palermo, Italy
Di Maio Antonio	University of Luxembourg, Luxembourg
Dini Paolo	Centre Tecnològic de Telecomunicacions de Catalunya (CTTC), Spain
Dujovne Diego	Universidad Diego Portales, Chile
Elsts Atis	University of Bristol, UK
Fernando Velez	Universidade Beira Interior, Portugal
Fontes Ramon	Federal Institute of Bahia, Brazil
Iova Oana	INSA Lyon, France
Karyotis Vasileios	National Technical University of Athens, Greece
Klasing Ralf	CNRS and University of Bordeaux, France
Leone Pierre	University of Geneva, Switzerland
Liang Weifa	The Australian National University, Australia
Longo Francesco	University of Messina, Italy
Maillé Patrick	IMT Atlantique, France
Martinez Francisco J.	University of Zaragoza, Spain
Mavromatis Ioannis	University of Bristol, UK
Merlino Giovanni	University of Messina, Italy
Miozzo Marco	Centre Tecnològic de Telecomunicacions de Catalunya (CTTC), Spain
Mitton Nathalie	Inria, France
Montavont Julien	University of Strasbourg, France
Mosko Marc	Palo Alto Research Center, USA
Nardini Giovanni	University of Pisa, Italy
Pahl Marc-Oliver	Technical University of Munich, France
Palattella Maria Rita	LIST, Luxembourg
Papadopoulos Georgios	IMT Atlantique, France
Papagianni Chrysa	Nokia Bell Labs, Belgium
Papavassiliou Symeon	Institute of Communications and Computer Systems (ICCS), Greece
Postiglione Fabio	University of Salerno, Italy
Puliafito Carlo	University of Florence, Italy
Scarpa Marco	University of Messina, Italy

Sciancalepore Savio	Hamad Bin Khalifa University (HBKU), Qatar
Soua Ridha	University of Luxembourg, Luxembourg
Stea Giovanni	University of Pisa, Italy
Stefano Scanzio	CNR-IEIIT, Italy
Suresh Thanakodi	National Defence University of Malaysia, Malaysia
Syrotiuk Violet	Arizona State University, USA
Texier Geraldine	IMT Atlantique, France
Theoleyre Fabrice	CNRS, France
Tsiropoulou Eirini Eleni	University of New Mexico, USA
Turau Volker	Hamburg University of Technology, Germany
Valecce Giovanni	Politecnico di Bari, Italy
Vallati Carlo	University of Pisa, Italy
Vinel Alexey	Halmstad University, Sweden
Virdis Antonio	University of Pisa, Italy
Weis Frédéric	University of Rennes 1, France
Wrona Konrad	NATO Communications and Information Agency, The Netherlands
Xuan Liu	Southeast University, China
Zema Nicola Roberto	University of Paris-Saclay, France
Zorbas Dimitrios	Tyndall National Institute, Ireland

Contents

Intelligent, Programmable and Delay- and Disruption- Tolerant Networks

Dynamic Management of Forwarding Rules in a T-SDN Architecture with Energy and Bandwidth Constraints

Antonio Petrosino[1], Giancarlo Sciddurlo[1], Giovanni Grieco[1,2],
Awais Aziz Shah[1,2], Giuseppe Piro[1,2(✉)], Luigi Alfredo Grieco[1,2],
and Gennaro Boggia[1,2]

[1] Department of Electrical and Information Engineering (DEI), Politecnico di Bari,
Bari, Italy
{antonio.petrosino,giancarlo.sciddurlo,giovanni.grieco,awais.shah,
giuseppe.piro,alfredo.grieco,gennaro.boggia}@poliba.it
[2] CNIT, Consorzio Nazionale Interunivesitario per le Telecomunicazioni, Parma, Italy

Abstract. Telecom operators recently started to integrate Software-Defined Networking facilities for controlling and managing their optical transport networks. Here, the management of forwarding rules into the resulting Transport Software-Defined Networking (T-SDN) architecture has to be addressed by taking into account the energy and quality of service requirements. While the most of works in the literature studied these aspects separately, the few contributions that simultaneously take care of energy and quality of service requirements present latency, scalability, or control communication issues. Starting from these considerations, this paper formulates a novel methodology for the dynamic and reactive management of forwarding rules in a (potentially large-scale) T-SDN network, based on the knowledge of network topology, the power consumption of optical switches, the expected volume of traffic, and the variability of the actual traffic load. First, the expected volume of traffic and the estimated power consumption of optical switches are exploited to select the minimum number of nodes and transport links to activate, which enable the communication among any source and destination pairs declared within a given traffic matrix. Then, the bandwidth consumption of activated transport links is periodically monitored by a centralized controller and, in case of congestion, a new set of optical switches and transport links are quickly turned on for addressing the growth of the traffic load. The effectiveness of the proposed approach has been investigated through experimental tests and compared against another reference scheme which considers the energy issue only. Obtained results demonstrate its ability to offer higher levels of quality of service to end-users, at the expense of a limited decrease of the registered energy-saving.

Keywords: Software-Defined Networking · Transport network ·
Energy efficiency · Quality of service · Forwarding policies

L. A. Grieco et al. (Eds.): ADHOC-NOW 2020, LNCS 12338, pp. 3–15, 2020.
https://doi.org/10.1007/978-3-030-61746-2_1

1   Introduction

Transport networks are rapidly evolving towards flexible and controllable architectures able to dynamically manage the large heterogeneity of data flows [2]. For
this reason, telecom operators are revolutionizing their network infrastructures
by massively integrating Software-Defined Networking (SDN) facilities (i.e., separation of data and control planes, monitoring and configuration of networking
functionalities, and so on) [12]. In this context, the management of forwarding
rules in the resulting Transport-SDN (T-SDN) deployment is a very ambitious
task to accomplish. A challenging goal, in fact, is to reduce the power consumption of the operating network, while satisfying the requested levels of quality
of service (e.g., bandwidth consumption) [18,19]. At the same time, the high
variability of the traffic loads asking for quick, scalable, and easily deployable
strategies, makes things worse [3].

Several solutions in the current scientific literature address energy and bandwidth constraints almost separately [21]. From one hand, energy-efficient schemes
try to turn off as more optical switches and transport links as possible. Starting from the knowledge of network topology and the expected set of data flows
(declared through the so-called traffic matrix), available solutions configure forwarding rules by solving optimization problems [1,11,15,23,25] or by executing
heuristic algorithms [4–7,13,16]. With these mechanisms, most of the network
traffic is forwarded through a reduced set of links. Therefore, flow dynamics generally bring to network congestion issues. From another hand, the rest of contributions (see [20] and [22] for example) only targets quality of service requirements, while missing the energy constraints.

At the time of this writing, the energy consumption and bandwidth constraints are jointly considered in [8,10] and [24]. Specifically, [10] presents a
multi-objective algorithm that derives the set of links to disable, while fulfilling
the expected quality of service constraints. Here, forwarding rules are configured by one of the nodes of the network (acting as a controller) through in-
band communications. This, however, increases the latencies of the exchange of
control messages, as well as makes the resulting implementation infeasible in
large-scale scenarios. In fact, the in-band communication approach is optimal
in non-dynamic situations where it is not necessary to update the forwarding
rules every few seconds, but not for a dynamic environment because the benefits arising from the presence of a controller interacting with optical switches by
means of out-band communications are ignored during the in-band communication mode. The heuristic approach introduced in [24] configures forwarding rules
by creating spanning trees of nodes with assigned weights according to their
energy consumption. Unfortunately, it does not envisage to monitor the actual
traffic load, thus being unable to react to data flow dynamics and congestion
episodes. Finally, the work presented in [8] assumes to dynamically configure
forwarding rules by taking into account the expected traffic volume and by targeting the shutdown of as many transport links as possible. This solution surely
limits the energy consumption, but still lacks in reacting to the variability of the
actual traffic load.

In order to solve the issues characterizing the current state of the art, this paper proposes a novel methodology for the dynamic management of forwarding rules in T-SDN deployments. This is done by jointly considering the network topology, the power consumption of optical switches, the expected volume of traffic, and the variability of the actual traffic load. In particular, the proposed strategy starts by activating the minimum required nodes and transport links between the source and destination pair predefined within a given traffic matrix, based on the network topology and the estimated power consumption of the optical switches. Then, the bandwidth utilization of the activated transport links is periodically monitored by a centralized controller to recognize the actual traffic load. In case of congestion, new transport links and optical switches are activated to ensure the smooth running of the traffic inside the network. Experimental tests demonstrate the better trade-off between the power consumption and quality of service. The performance of the proposed approach has been experimentally investigated by emulating a T-SDN architecture within a desktop computer. The GÉANT[1] network topology, embracing 40 nodes, 58 bidirectional links, and an OpenDaylight controller, has been implemented within the Mininet environment. The actual traffic load is generated by activating a percentage of requests declared in a traffic matrix describing the data flows between up to 24 host pairs attached to the GÉANT topology. The collected results have been compared with the approach described in [16], which only reduce the energy consumption of the network. The produced results have been compared with the approach presented in [16], since it is a state of the art algorithm that achieves excellent energy savings. Indeed, the approach presented in this paper exhibits the lowest throughput degradation with respect to [16], thus demonstrating its successfully ability to redirect data flows across uncongested paths. Therefore, it is clear that the strategy presented in this paper provides a significant gain in terms of performance, at the expense a limited decrease of the registered energy-saving as compared to [16].

The rest of the paper is organized as follows: Sect. 2 presents the reference architecture. Section 3 describes the proposed algorithm. The description of the experimental testbed is presented in Sect. 4 along with the conclusion of the achieved results. Finally, Sect. 5 draws the conclusions and proposes future research activities.

2   The Reference Architecture and Main Assumptions

Figure 1 shows the reference T-SDN network considered in this work. According to the well-known SDN reference model, physical nodes and logical entities are grouped into three layers: infrastructure, control, and application [26]. The infrastructure layer embraces optical switches of the core network and edge routers. Optical switches forward data flows within the core network, according to the configured routing rules. Edge routers, instead, act as sources and destinations of data flows. Furthermore, a centralized controller monitors the

---

[1] https://www.geant.org/Networks (Accessed: 2020-03-15).

infrastructure layer and dynamically configures forwarding rules based on the outcomes of the routing algorithm working at the application layer.

Both Software-Defined Controller and optical switches implement the Open-Flow stack (southbound interface). The controller, implemented with OpenDay-light framework, periodically queries optical switches for collecting details about the network topology and the amount of bandwidth consumed by each physical port. When needed, it also delivers the new set of forwarding rules across the network. According to OpenFlow specifications, the communication in the southbound interface is managed by means of the REpresentational State Transfer (REST)CONF protocol [2]. The application entity implementing the routing algorithm and the controller interact with each other with RESTful Application Programming Interface (API)s [2]. In this case, the exchanged messages are encoded with the Yet Another Next Generation (YANG) data model (northbound interface) [17].

The design of the novel routing algorithm discussed herein grounds its roots on the following consideration. From one hand, the network operator knows the expected volume of traffic that can be generated between all possible pairs of source and destination edge routers. Such information is stored within the traffic matrix [26] and may vary during the time (e.g., the volume of traffic manageable by the T-SDN network in daily hours may be different from the one available during the night or weekend). On the other hand, the actual traffic load generated within the network may differ from the traffic matrix, spanning from a very limited percentage of the expected volume of traffic to its upper bound. This double level of dynamicity makes challenging the task performed by the routing algorithm. Indeed, the conceived methodology intends to configure the infrastructure layer by jointly considering information stored within the traffic matrix and the traffic load managed by optical switches during the time, periodically monitored by the controller.

A power model helps to estimate the amount of power consumed by optical switches belonging to the reference T-SDN network. Without loss of generality, this paper considers the model presented in [14], related to NEC PF 5240[2] OpenFlow switches. Here, the total amount of power consumed by an optical switch is given by five contributions:

- the amount of power required to keep the switch on, $P_{\text{base}} = 118.30\,\text{W}$;
- the amount of power needed to configure device settings and active ports, $P_{\text{conf}} = 0.52\,\text{W}$;
- the amount of power needed to install a new OpenFlow rule $P_{\text{flow-mod}} = 20.00\,\mu\text{W}$;
- the amount of power consumed for each control packet $P_{\text{packet}} = 711.00\,\mu\text{W}$;
- the amount of power consumption due to the processing of data flow $P_{\text{flow}} \ll 1\,\mu\text{W}$.

The analysis presented in [14] already demonstrated that the processing of data flows has a very minimal effect on the overall power consumption. Accord-

---

[2] https://www.necam.com/sdn/Hardware/PF5240Switch/ (Accessed: 2020-04-10).

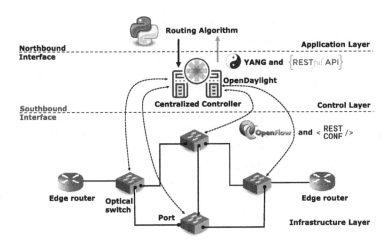

Fig. 1. Reference T-SDN network architecture.

ingly, it is possible to neglect the impact of P_{flow} and develop a strategy based on a traffic independent power model.

3   The Conceived Approach

The routing algorithm conceived in this paper periodically implements two different tasks. The first one provides an initial configuration of the T-SDN core network, based on the knowledge of the network topology and the expected volume of traffic declared by the traffic matrix. Therefore, it is executed only once, at the beginning of the validity period of the traffic matrix. The second task, instead, is implemented every congestion observation window and provides periodic updates of forwarding rules, based on the actual traffic load passing through the network. In order to effectively react to possible congestion episodes, the duration of the congestion observation window is much smaller than the validity period of the traffic matrix (i.e., tens of seconds instead of hours).

Initial Network Configuration Based on the Traffic Matrix (Task 1). It intends to reduce the overall power consumption by turning off as many devices and links as possible, while ensuring communication paths for any data flow reported in the traffic matrix. To this end, the network is modeled as an undirected graph G, where nodes represent optical switches and edges represent the transport links connecting optical switches. The set of demands D representing the traffic matrix is described by the pair of source node s and destination node t with their respective bandwidth demand d^{st}. Nodes belonging to the graph G are sorted according to their power consumption, from the most consuming device to the less consuming one. Links, instead, are randomly ordered. Then, an iteration on nodes is performed. At each iteration, the considered node in the ordered set and all of its links are tentatively turned off. Indeed, it is verified if at least one path exists for each traffic request declared in the traffic matrix. In the affirmative case, that node is removed from G since it is not necessary for the fulfillment of all traffic requests. Otherwise, the considered node and its links are left active into the network. Once the iteration on the nodes is completed, the same procedure is applied to the links. Also, in this case, the goal is to turn off unuseful or redundant links and leave active only a subset of links that guarantees the presence of communication paths for all data flows declared into the traffic matrix. A minimized graph G' is obtained at the end, which represents the network topology guaranteeing the greatest energy savings.

Given the minimized graph G', the shortest communication path for each data flow of the traffic matrix is identified according to the Dijkstra algorithm [9]. The calculated shortest paths are converted to forwarding rules and pushed on OpenFlow switches by the controller.

Redefinition of Forwarding Rules Based on Congestion Episodes (Task 2). In a dynamic environment where the actual traffic load changes, this task further adapts forwarding rules based on user demands and link capacity. To this end, the controller periodically sends OpenFlow messages to the switches, requesting information about the bandwidth consumption of their enabled ports. This helps to identify the activation of new flows that may congest transport links and provoke service degradation. This monitoring procedure allows to detect link congestion when the total bandwidth of the considered link is at least 90% occupied. Once detected the overloaded links, the data flows triggering that event are put within the congestion list. The recursive algorithm discussed before is implemented again over the network topology that excludes congested links. As a consequence, the algorithm will turn on transport links or optical switches that were turned off at the beginning. Then, a new shortest path is defined for each data flow in the congestion list, converted to forwarding rules, and pushed on OpenFlow switches. At the end of the congestion observation window, the network is configured as indicated by the first task. Therefore, congestion episodes are periodically managed, starting from a baseline network configuration.

To provide further insight, the pseudo-code describing the main functionalities of the conceived approach has been reported in Algorithm 1.

Algorithm 1. Pseudo code of the proposed methodology

Input: Graph G(nodes, links), set D of demand with traffic requirement d^{st} $\forall (s,t) \in D$
Output: Updated flow tables, Final graph
    TASK 1 (G, D):
1: $G' \leftarrow G$
    Nodes Optimization on G' ▷ *Nodes are sorted in a most power order.*
2: **for** $i \leftarrow 1\,to\,|\text{nodes}|$ **do**
3:     turn_off(nodes[i])
4:     **for all** $(s,t) \in D$ **do**
5:         **if** $!path\_exists(s,t)$ **then**
6:             turn_on(nodes[i])
7:         **end if**
8:     **end for**
9: **end for**
    Links Optimization on G' ▷ *Links are selected in random order.*
10: **for** $i \leftarrow 1\,to\,|\text{links}|$ **do**
11:     turn_off(links[i])
12:     **for all** $(s,t) \in D$ **do**
13:         **if** $!path\_exists(s,t)$ **then**
14:             turn_on(links[i])
15:         **end if**
16:     **end for**
17: **end for**
    Push Forwarding Rules
18: **for all** $(s,t) \in D$ **do**
19:     path$(s,t) \leftarrow Dijkstra\,algorithm$
20:     push_flow_rules()
21: **end for**
    # Controller monitors links bandwidth consumption.#
    TASK 2 (G, D):
22: **if** $congestion\_occurs$ **then**
23:     **Nodes Optimization**
24:     **Links Optimization**
25:     **for all** $(s,t) \in D$ **do**
26:         path$(s,t) \leftarrow Dijkstra\,algorithm$
27:         **for** $i \leftarrow 1\,to\,|\text{link\_in\_path}|$ **do**
28:             **if** $remaining\_link\_capacity < d^{st}$ and $link\_overloaded$ **then**
29:                 Congestion_list $\leftarrow (s,t)$
30:             **end if**
31:         **end for**
32:         **if** $!Congestion\_list.contains(s,t)$ **or**
    any path without overloaded links exists to satisfy (s,t) **then**
33:             update(remaining_link_capacity)
34:             push_flow_rules()
35:         **end if**
36:         $G'' \leftarrow remove\_overloaded\_links(G)$
37:         **if** $!Congestion\_list.empty()$ **then**
38:             Run **TASK 2**$(G''$, Congestion_list)
39:         **end if**
40:     **end for**
41: **end if**

4   Performance Evaluation

The performance of the proposed approach is experimentally investigated by emulating a T-SDN architecture within a desktop computer Intel Core i7–7700, RAM 16 GB, with Ubuntu 18.04 64-bit. Specifically, the GÉANT topology with 40 nodes and 58 bidirectional links is implemented with Mininet, since it allows to virtualize a network of OpenFlow switches with Open vSwitch kernel. The OpenDaylight framework is used as the network controller. The routing algorithm has been developed in Python. Without loss of generality, the conducted analysis considers transport links supporting 1 Gbps of bandwidth. A traffic matrix is arbitrarily created in order to describe the data flows expected between up to 24 host pairs randomly attached to the GÉANT topology. Each data flow in the traffic matrix presents a request rate of 400 Mbps. The actual traffic load is generated by activating a percentage of requests declared in the traffic matrix. To provide further insights, the performance of the proposed approach has been compared with respect to the algorithm presented in [16], which only tries to minimize energy consumption.

Figure 2 depicts a simplified example showing the ability of the conceived solution to successfully react to congestion episodes. The example considers three data flows, asking for 400 Mbps of bandwidth each, directed to the same destination. Figure 2a represents the network topology configured according to the algorithm presented in [16]. It is possible to observe that the link connecting node 32 to node 36, which only offers 1 Gbps of bandwidth, is congested. This means that the strategy presented in [16] is not able to fulfill the quality of service levels requested by the considered data flow. Note that the initial network configuration provided by Task 1 of the algorithm presented in Sect. 3 coincides with the one obtained through [16]. Differently, from [16], however, Task 2 implemented by the approach described in this paper adapts forwarding rules in reaction to congestion episodes. Figure 2b clearly shows how the path followed by Flow 3 is updated. Accordingly, the link between node 32 and node 36 in the example is not overloaded and the quality of service requested by all the three flows is achieved. Quantitative key performance indicators discussed below include the total power consumption of the T-SDN network, the percentage of deactivated links, and the percentage of throughput degradation registered by active data flows.

The total amount of power consumed by an operating T-SDN network is evaluated by considering 6 to 24 active data flows, generating 100% of the data rate declared in the traffic matrix (that is equal to 400 Mbps). In case, the network has all the optical switches and transport links turned on, the total power consumption is equal to 4792.32 W. This is reported in Fig. 3 as the peak value achievable in the absence of any energy-aware routing strategy. The other two curves reported in Fig. 3 shows the amount of power consumed by the considered T-SDN network as a function of the number of active data flows, when forwarding rules are set according to the algorithm presented in [16] and the solution conceived in this paper. As expected, results show that the increment of the number of active data flows always requires higher number of optical switches

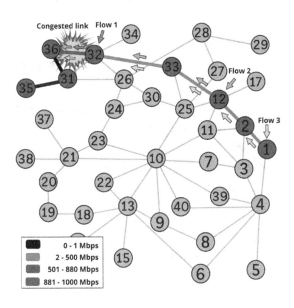

(a) Network configuration based on [16].

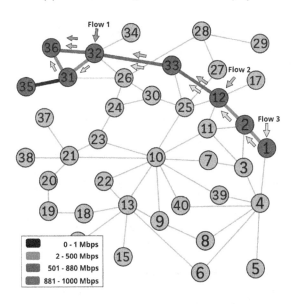

(b) Network configuration achieved with the proposed approach.

Fig. 2. Example showing the ability of the proposed approach to achieve energy and quality of service constraints.

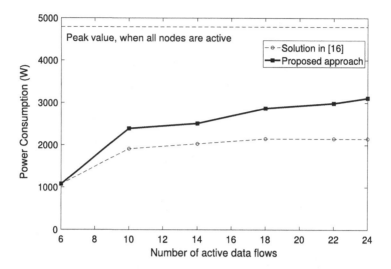

Fig. 3. Power consumption.

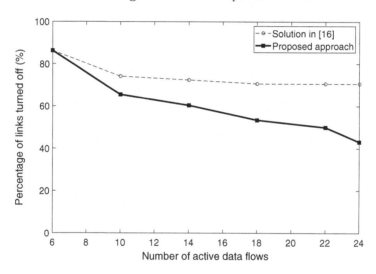

Fig. 4. Percentage of links turned off.

and links to activate in the network. This inevitably brings to an increment of the overall power consumption. It is also evident that the algorithm presented in [16] ensures the highest power saving, thanks to its ability to shut down as many optical switches and transport links as possible, without taking care of the quality of service level offered to end-users.   On the contrary, the methodology presented in the paper registers a slight increment of the power consumption due to the activation of more optical switches and links, triggered in answer to congestion events.

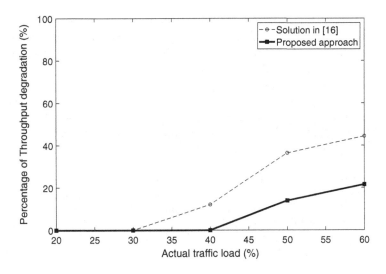

Fig. 5. Throughput degradation registered by active data flows

Figure 4, showing the percentage of deactivated transport links, fully confirms the aforementioned discussion: the proposed solution forwards data flows through a higher number of uncongested paths. It is also possible to observe that the difference between the two investigated approaches becomes more evident when the number of active data flows increases. In this case, in fact, the higher the bandwidth requirement, the higher the number of paths to activate for avoiding network congestion.

The real effectiveness of the conceived solution is highlighted in Fig. 5, which reports the degradation of the throughput registered by active data flows due to bandwidth constraints, measured as a function of the traffic load (expressed as a percentage of the bandwidth requirement declared in the traffic matrix). Since [16] does not apply any re-routing strategy after the congestion, a large traffic load seriously degrades network performance. The approach presented in this paper exhibits the lowest throughput with respect to [16], thus demonstrating its successful ability to redirect data flows across uncongested paths. From these considerations, it is evident that the strategy presented in this paper provides a significant gain in terms of performance at the expense of a limited decrease of registered energy-saving as compared to [16].

5   Conclusions

This paper focuses on T-SDN networks and formulated a novel methodology for the dynamic management of forwarding rules in the presence of energy and bandwidth constraints. The conceived approach configures communications paths and decides optical switches and transport links to be activated by jointly considering the network topology, the power consumption of optical switches, the expected volume of traffic, and variability of the actual traffic load. Experimental tests demonstrate its ability to achieve the best compromise between the power consumption of the overall network and the quality of service offered to end-users. Future research activities will analyze the complexity and investigate the behavior of the considered solution in complex and large scale network while considering realistic traffic matrix and flow generation statistics. Moreover, it will also investigate its adoption in hierarchical T-SDN deployments, based on two layers of controllers introduced to improve scalability and provide a comprehensive comparison with the other available state of the art approaches.

Acknowledgment. This work was mainly supported by the Apulia Region (Italy) Research project INTENTO (36A49H6). It was also partially supported by the PRIN project no. 2017NS9FEY entitled "Realtime Control of 5G Wireless Networks: Taming the Complexity of Future Transmission and Computation Challenges" funded by the Italian MIUR and by the Italian MIUR PON projects Pico&Pro (ARS01 01061), AGREED (ARS01 00254), FURTHER (ARS01 01283) and RAFAEL (ARS01 00305).

References

1. Al Mhdawi, A.K., Al-Raweshidy, H.S.: iPRDR: intelligent power reduction decision routing protocol for big traffic flood in Hybrid-SDN architecture. IEEE Access **6**, 10944–10955 (2018)
2. Alvizu, R., et al.: Comprehensive survey on T-SDN: software-defined networking for transport networks. IEEE Commun. Surv. Tutorials **19**(4), 2232–2283 (2017)
3. Arif, M., Wang, G., Geman, O., Bala, V.E., Tao, P., Brezulianu, A., Chen, J.: SDN-based vanets security attacks applications and challenges. Appl. Sci. **10**(9), 3217 (2020)
4. Assefa, B.G., Ozkasap, O.: Link utility and traffic aware energy saving in software defined networks. In: Proceedings of IEEE International Black Sea Conference on Communications and Networking, pp. 1–5 (2017)
5. Assefa, B.G., Ozkasap, O.: A novel utility based metric and routing for energy efficiency in software defined networking. In: Proceedings of International Symposium on Networks, Computers and Communications, pp. 1–4 (2019)
6. Assefa, B.G., Ozkasap, O.: RESDN: a novel metric and method for energy efficient routing in software defined networks. IEEE Trans. Network Serv. Manage. 1 (2020)
7. Awad, M.K., Rafique, Y., Alhadlaq, S., Hassoun, D., Alabdulhadi, A., Thani, S.: A greedy power-aware routing algorithm for software-defined networks. In: Proceedings of IEEE International Symposium on Signal Processing and Information Technology (ISSPIT), pp. 268–273 (2016)
8. Ba, J., Wang, Y., Zhong, X., Feng, S., Qiu, X., Guo, S.: An SDN energy saving method based on topology switch and rerouting. In: NOMS 2018–2018 IEEE/IFIP Network Operations and Management Symposium, pp. 1–5 (2018)
9. Deng, Y., Chen, Y., Zhang, Y., Mahadevan, S.: Fuzzy dijkstra algorithm for shortest path problem under uncertain environment. Appl. Soft Comput. **12**(3), 1231–1237 (2012)
10. Fernández-Fernández, A., Cervelló-Pastor, C., Ochoa-Aday, L.: A multi-objective routing strategy for QoS and energy awareness in software-defined networks. IEEE Commun. Lett. **21**(11), 2416–2419 (2017)

11. Giroire, F., Moulierac, J., Phan, T.K.: Optimizing rule placement in software-defined networks for energy-aware routing. In: Proceedings of IEEE Global Communications Conference, pp. 2523–2529 (2014)
12. Goransson, P., Black, C., Culver, T.: Software Defined Networks: A Comprehensive Approach. Morgan Kaufmann, Burlington (2016)
13. Heller, B.et al.: Elastictree: saving energy in data center networks. In: 7th USENIX NSDI, p. 17 (2010)
14. Kaup, F., Melnikowitsch, S., Hausheer, D.: Measuring and modeling the power consumption of openflow switches. In: Proceedings of 10th International Conference on Network and Service Management (CNSM) and Workshop, pp. 181–186 (2014)
15. Li, H., Jiang, G., Chai, R.: Energy consumption optimization based joint routing and flow allocation algorithm for software defined networking. In: Proceedings of 19th International Symposium on Wireless Personal Multimedia Communications (WPMC), pp. 311–316 (2016)
16. Maaloul, R., Taktak, R., Chaari, L., Cousin, B.: Energy-aware routing in carriergrade ethernet using SDN approach. IEEE Trans. Green Commun. Network. **2**(3), 844–858 (2018)
17. Parladori, G., Gasparini, G., Ruggi, F., Broi, A.D., Simone, V., Nicassio, F.: YANG modelling of optical nodes. In: Proceedings of 20th Italian National Conference on Photonic Technologies (Fotonica 2018), pp. 1–4 (2018)
18. Polese, M., Chiariotti, F., Bonetto, E., Rigotto, F., Zanella, A., Zorzi, M.: A survey on recent advances in transport layer protocols. IEEE Commun. Surv. Tutorials **21**(4), 3584–3608 (2019)
19. Rehmani, M.H., Davy, A., Jennings, B., Assi, C.: Software defined networks-based smart grid communication: a comprehensive survey. IEEE Commun. Surv. Tutorials **21**(3), 2637–2670 (2019)
20. Sathyanarayana, S., Moh, M.: Joint route-server load balancing in software defined networks using ant colony optimization. In: Proceedings of International Conference on High Performance Computing Simulation (HPCS), pp. 156–163 (2016)
21. Shah, A.A., Piro, G., Grieco, L.A., Boggia, G.: A review of forwarding strategies in transport software-defined networks. In: 2020 22nd International Conference on Transparent Optical Networks (ICTON), pp. 1–4. IEEE (2020)
22. Stefano, A.D., Cammarata, G., Morana, G., Zito, D.: A4SDN - adaptive alienated ant algorithm for software-defined networking. In: Proceedings of 10th International Conference on P2P, Parallel, Grid, Cloud and Internet Computing (3PGCIC), pp. 344–350 (2015)
23. Vasić, N., Bhurat, P., Novaković, D., Canini, M., Shekhar, S., Kostić, D.: Identifying and Using Energy-Critical Paths. In: Proceedings of the Seventh Conference on emerging Networking Experiments and Technologies, pp. 1–12 (2011)
24. Wang, H., Li, Y., Jin, D., Hui, P., Wu, J.: Saving energy in partially deployed software defined networks. IEEE Trans. Comput. **65**(5), 1578–1592 (2016)
25. Wu, Z., Ji, X., Wang, Y., Chen, X., Cai, Y.: An energy-aware routing for optimizing control and data traffic in SDN. In: Proceedings of 26th International Conference on Systems Engineering (ICSEng), pp. 1–4 (2018)
26. Xia, W., Wen, Y., Foh, C.H., Niyato, D., Xie, H.: A survey on software-defined networking. IEEE Commun. Surv. Tutorials **17**(1), 27–51 (2015)

Towards Named AI Networking: Unveiling the Potential of NDN for Edge AI

Claudia Campolo[1]([⊠]), Gianmarco Lia[1], Marica Amadeo[1], Giuseppe Ruggeri[1], Antonio Iera[2], and Antonella Molinaro[1]

[1] University Mediterranea of Reggio Calabria, Reggio Calabria, Italy
{claudia.campolo,gianmarco.lia,marica.amadeo,giuseppe.ruggeri,
antonella.molinaro}@unirc.it
[2] University of Calabria, Rende, Italy
antonio.iera@dimes.unical.it

Abstract. Thanks to recent advancements in edge computing, the traditional centralized cloud-based approach to deploy Artificial Intelligence (AI) techniques will be soon replaced or complemented by the so-called *edge AI* approach. By pushing AI at the network edge, close to the large amount of raw input data, the traffic traversing the core network as well as the inference latency can be reduced. Despite such neat benefits, the actual deployment of edge AI across distributed nodes raises novel challenges to be addressed, such as the need to enforce proper addressing and discovery procedures, to identify AI components, and to chain them in an interoperable manner. Named Data Networking (NDN) has been recently argued as one of the main enablers of network and computing convergence, which edge AI should build upon. However, the peculiarities of such a new paradigm entails to go a step further. In this paper we *disclose the potential of NDN to support the orchestration of edge AI.* Several motivations are discussed, as well as the challenges which serve as guidelines for progress beyond the state of the art in this topic.

Keywords: Edge computing · Information centric networking · Named Data Networking · Internet of Things · Artificial Intelligence · Edge AI

1 Introduction

The research interest in Artificial Intelligence (AI) was recently boosted by the advancements in cloud computing and the massive deployment of Internet of Things (IoT) devices. Indeed, several IoT applications, such as video surveillance, autonomous driving, smart home appliance and industrial automation, greatly benefit from the use of AI capabilities, including data, image, audio, and video analysis. Among AI algorithms, Deep Learning (DL) methods consist of two phases: *training phase* and *inference phase*. The first one has the

© Springer Nature Switzerland AG 2020
L. A. Grieco et al. (Eds.): ADHOC-NOW 2020, LNCS 12338, pp. 16–22, 2020.
https://doi.org/10.1007/978-3-030-61746-2_2

purpose to set, according to input data, the weights of the Artificial Neural Network (ANN) by which, during the second phase, decisions (e.g., classification, recognition) are taken. Such operations are memory- and power-hungry. Hence, typically, resource-constrained IoT devices just send the data streams they collect/sense to the remote cloud. Mega-scale data-centers, with their virtually unlimited capabilities, are then responsible for processing raw data and deriving knowledge to be sent back to requesting devices/users. The emergence of the edge computing paradigm, by bringing computing resources closer to devices, paves the way for re-engineering the way in which AI solutions are deployed. If DL services are deployed at the edge, close to where input data are produced and likely consumed, the latency and cost of sending data to the cloud for model training/inference will be reduced, while also offloading the core network [1].

Following the groundbreaking paradigm pushing AI to the edge, referred to as *edge AI*, the AI model training and inference tasks can be performed across several edge nodes, such as base stations, backhaul nodes, and IoT gateways. The cloud data center capabilities are used whenever additional processing power is needed and trained models are to be stored.

Despite the numerous literature works targeting the orchestration of edge computing resources to tackle the placement of generic computing tasks, several peculiar issues arise when dealing with the orchestration of AI workloads. First, placement decisions should be taken not only to ensure that data collection latencies, computation times and/or energy consumption are minimized, but also to provide the needed inference accuracy of trained ANNs. Heterogeneous devices may provide inference results with different accuracy levels, e.g., according to their computing capabilities. Second, similarly to contents, AI inference results, once computed, could serve different requests. Finally, another issue for distributed AI at the edge, unlike in centralized AI deployments, is the lack of interoperability due to fragmented and mainly application-specific solutions [2]. Hence, it is crucial to identify and discover AI components to build intelligent applications upon them, while efficiently using network and computing resources.

In this paper we promote the usage of the Named Data Networking (NDN) paradigm (https://named-data.net/) to deal with the aforementioned issues. Originally conceived as an innovative content delivery solution, NDN has been more recently overhauled to deal with edge computing [3–6], as scanned in Sect. 2. Its native in-network caching capability coupled with the semantic-rich naming scheme would play a crucial role in facilitating the deployment of edge AI solutions, as we discuss in Sect. 3. To the best of our knowledge, this is the first work that discloses the potential of NDN for orchestrating edge AI.

2   From Named Contents to Named Services

NDN [7] implements name-based consumer-driven communication based on the exchange of two packets types, *Interest* and *Data*, originally used to request and provide authenticated contents, respectively. One Data packet exactly consumes one Interest packet. Both packets carry hierarchical Uniform Resource Identifier (URI)-like names which uniquely identify the content. There are no specific restrictions in the way name components can be defined. Data packets also piggyback the publisher's signature and other authentication information to enable per-packet security. By design, NDN provides in-network caching and multicast support. Each node maintains a Content Store (CS) to cache incoming Data packets according to local storage policies. This allows intermediate nodes to satisfy future requests and speed up data retrieval, while reducing the amount of traffic crossing the network. A Pending Interest Table (PIT) and a Forwarding Information Base (FIB) are maintained to, respectively, record the pending requests that wait to be consumed by Data packets and identify the outgoing interfaces (and relevant attributes, e.g., latency) to forward the Interests.

Recently, the NDN logic has been extended to complement data retrieval by data processing. According to the pioneering vision in [8], referred to as Named Function Networking (NFN), an NDN name can be used to identify contents, processing functions and/or a combination of them. A consumer can request a named function to be applied over a content (e.g., video compression), and the network uses advanced routing-by-name mechanisms to discover both the content and the node in charge of executing that function and returning the processed content. This output can be cached to satisfy future requests without the need of performing the computation again. NFN was extended in [3] to tackle wireless edge domains, where mobile consumers broadcast requests to offload a computing service to a more powerful node in the neighbourhood. The Interest packet is extended to carry the name of the processing function and a set of attributes that describe the consumer's demands, e.g., maximum tolerated latency, to allow a potential provider to self-candidate for the task execution. A smart deferral scheme is defined that lets the best provider (i.e., the one that executes the service in the shortest time) answer first. Therefore, on receiving the first response, the consumer immediately offloads the task to that node. The work in [5] identifies two distinct mechanisms to enable computing services via NDN in a wired edge domain. In the proactive approach, edge nodes periodically advertise the functions they support and their resource utilization (e.g., CPU, storage) by piggybacking this information in the routing protocol messages. Vice versa, in the reactive approach, the information is transmitted at the reception of the service request from the consumer. In both cases, the node with the lowest resource utilization is selected as the executor in such a way as to guarantee the fair distribution of computation efforts. Conversely, in [6], an orchestration scheme is defined aiming at guaranteeing the lowest service execution time. It accounts for two terms: (i) the time needed to collect the data to be processed, which depends on the network status and the proximity to the data, and (ii) the processing time, which depends on the local available resources and the demands of the service. The selection of the executor is performed in a reactive way: at the Interest reception, each node computes its own service execution cost and the one with the lowest cost is selected as the executor. Different policies may be flexibly enforced by applying the same distributed orchestration logic.

3   Why NDN for Edge AI?

In edge AI every edge node can contribute to the AI workflow by playing different roles. For instance, a node can provide the computing capabilities to run a specific ANN, although initially not locally available. Another one can own the trained ANN model itself and perform the inference whenever requested and also cache it. Nodes can also contribute to partial local model training in the case of Federated Learning (FL) [9]. In such a challenging and dynamic context, NDN can play a crucial role to properly identify AI components, route requests towards the discovered ones, by accounting for their requirements, and also chain them. In the following, the motivations for the evolution of edge AI towards a *named AI networking* paradigm will be discussed, by also treasuring previous NDN literature and its consolidated extensions to support edge computing.

Naming and Discovery. An addressing scheme is needed to identify all available AI components, i.e., models, model parameters, inference results, in the edge domain. This facilitates the discovery for subsequent composition of the intelligent service (set of services) exploiting the AI components. The semantic-rich NDN naming well suits the aforementioned need. Unique expressive NDN names can adequately identify input data and inference results as piece of contents. In addition, names can request the retrieval of a ANN model and/or its execution as well as the ANN weights. AI components can be definitely treated as first class citizens, similarly to contents in the vanilla NDN. They can be referred directly by their name, regardless of the identity of the node where they are actually hosted. For instance, the name */recognition/AlexNet/w* would allow a node to download the weights of the specific Convolutional Neural Network (CNN) model to be used for image recognition. The usage of well-known namespaces can facilitate AI interoperability, overstepping the current difficulties in letting fragmented AI applications and components interact.

Caching. AI inference results, once computed, can be reused and serve requests from different applications. For instance, a co-located group of tourists in a museum may need the same output from an object recognition module of an Augmented Reality (AR) application. Caching inference results can be highly helpful *(i)* to save valuable computing resources, *(ii)* to avoid the redundant input data exchange, and *(iii)* to reduce the inference latency [1]. The caching decision also applies to ANN models which a node can decide to keep locally. Implementing caching at the network layer, as foreseen by NDN, can be fast and flexible. Moreover, thanks to the Interest aggregation in the PIT, if multiple nodes need the same computation/model, only one request is forwarded towards the potential cacher, and the replies are sent in multicast saving network resources. Caching and replacement decisions can be taken by accounting for the popularity of the model/parameter/inference, but also for their temporal validity, not to waste the limited storage resources at the edge. Applications must have the capability to specify the *freshness* with which they want to receive a given inference result, similarly to what suggested in [10] for IoT contents.

In-network Processing. Building upon the NDN/NFN philosophy, decisions about where to place AI components and how and which components to reach and chain (e.g., computational resources, cached inference results, ANN models, input data, weights) can be taken *in-network*. Specifically, an edge node can either reply to a request for a named inference result if it is eligible to satisfy it, or it can route the request towards a node which already stores the output, to save processing resources. The latter case is depicted in Fig. 1. Instead, it may autonomously decide to execute it, if the latency to reach the cached inference (as tracked in the FIB) is higher than the one needed to retrieve the input data through Interest/Data packets exchange and locally perform the inference. Context-rich attributes can be used to specify the demands for AI components, e.g., the desired inference accuracy and latency, and help the decision about which components to reach and activate. An Interest with name */recognition/cars/Rome/intersection32/4June/11:12* coupled with an attribute specifying *acc >80* can be sent to request the recognition of cars passing by intersection 32 in the city of Rome on June 4th, between 11:00 and 12:00, with an accuracy higher than 80%. Only those nodes providing such feature could reply with Data packets. Attributes can also facilitate the discovery of clients (e.g., mobile devices) in charge of locally training a model in FL procedures. Such devices are typically randomly selected [9]. An NDN Interest-driven discovery solution like the one devised in [3] could make the selection smarter. An Interest can be sent which specifies the requested type of learning task and also related parameters through attributes. Then, candidate task executors reply according to their capabilities. Instead of receiving the first reply only, multiple replies can be collected with a single request, e.g., if the Long Lived Interest option is leveraged [11], to discover the best contributors.

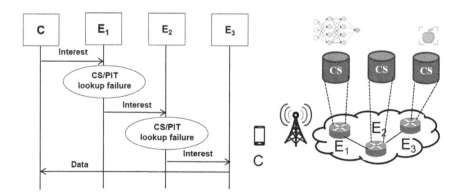

Fig. 1. Named AI networking workflow. C requests an inference result; E_1 hosts the ANN model but it routes the request towards a cached inference result provided by E_3, which replies with a Data packet.

Security. Authentication for input contents as well as for models/inference to be transferred into Data packets is natively ensured in NDN. Indeed, such packets are digitally signed with a signature which is part of the Data Packet itself. Additional security countermeasures are needed; some of them have been investigated in the literature extending NDN for edge computing [6,12], e.g., signed Interest packets, mutual consumer-provider authentication to verify the requester for an AI task is legitimate and the node providing the AI component is authorized. On top of them, traditional solutions, like encryption and differential privacy mechanisms may be required for privacy preservation whenever sensitive data are exchanged for training/inference purposes [1].

Table 1. Matching between the main edge AI needs and NDN features.

Edge AI needs	NDN features
Discovery and addressing of distributed and application-specific AI components	Well-known semantic-rich namespace
Reuse of inference results	In-network caching, request aggregation and multicast delivery
Placement, reachability and chaining of AI components	In-network processing, context-rich attributes, Long Lived Interests
Security	Data packet authentication, signed Interests

4 Conclusions

In this paper we have proposed NDN, and its extensions, as an enabler of the transition from centralized AI to distributed edge AI, which well addresses its peculiarities (as summarized in Table 1). As a future work we plan to provide the algorithmic design of the NDN components and to quantitatively assess their benefits in orchestrating edge AI.

Acknowledgments. This work has been partially supported by the A COGnItive dynamic sysTem to allOw buildings to learn and adapt' (COGITO) project, funded by the Italian Government (PON ARS01_00836).

References

1. Wang, X., et al.: Convergence of edge computing and deep learning: a comprehensive survey. IEEE Commun. Surv. Tutorials **22**(2), 869–904 (2020)
2. Ramos, E., et al.: Distributing intelligence to the edge and beyond. IEEE Comput. Intell. Mag. **14**(4), 65–92 (2019)
3. Amadeo, M., et al.: NDNe: enhancing named data networking to support cloudification at the edge. IEEE Commun. Lett. **20**(11), 2264–2267 (2016)

4. Scherb, C., et al.: Resolution strategies for networking the IoT at the edge via named functions. In: 2018 15th IEEE CCNC, pp. 1–6 (2018)

5. Mtibaa, A., et al.: Towards edge computing over named data networking. In: 2018 IEEE International Conference on Edge Computing (EDGE), pp. 117–120 (2018)

6. Amadeo, M., et al.: IoT services allocation at the edge via named data networking: from optimal bounds to practical design. IEEE Trans. Netw. Serv. Manage. **16**(2), 661–674 (2019)

7. Zhang, L., et al.: Named data networking. ACM SIGCOMM Comput. Commun. Rev. **44**(3), 66–73 (2014)

8. Tschudin, C., Sifalakis, M.: Named functions and cached computations. In: IEEE CCNC, pp. 851–857 (2014)

9. Wang, X., Han, Y., Wang, C., Zhao, Q., Chen, X., Chen, M.: In-edge AI: intelligentizing mobile edge computing, caching and communication by federated learning. IEEE Network **33**(5), 156–165 (2019)

10. Quevedo, J., et al.: Consumer driven information freshness approach for content centric networking. In: 2014 IEEE INFOCOM Workshop, pp. 482–487 (2014)

11. Carzaniga, A., et al.: Content-based publish/subscribe networking and information-centric networking. In: ACM SIGCOMM Workshop on Information-centric Networking, pp. 56–61 (2011)

12. Amadeo, M., et al.: Securing the mobile edge through named data networking. In: 2018 IEEE WF-IoT, pp. 80–85 (2018)

Fast and Cost-Efficient Virtualized Network Function Placement Algorithm in Wireless Multi-hop Networks

Zahra Jahedi and Thomas Kunz[(⊠)]

Carleton University, Ottawa, ON K1S 5B6, Canada
zahrajahedi@cmail.carleton.ca, tkunz@sce.carleton.ca

Abstract. Network Function Virtualization (NFV) can lower the CAP-EX and/or OPEX for service providers and allows the deployment of services quickly. The main challenge in the use of Virtualized Network Functions (VNF) is optimally placing them in the physical network in terms of deployment cost and resource consumption. The critical problem of VNF placement is inherently NP-hard and the available optimal solutions do not scale with respect to the network size. The problem of NFV placement is even more challenging in wireless networks as we are facing the issue of scarcity of BW due to the presence of interference. Therefore, this paper aims to solve the problem of VNF placement in wireless multi-hop networks by considering BW limitations and scalability. We tackle both issues at once by limiting the search space to the shortest paths. We search for the placement solution along shortest paths to minimize the BW consumption and at the same time reduce the search space to the nodes and links along the shortest path. The results are compared to a mathematical optimization model and a comparable heuristic model. They show that our proposed heuristic greatly decreases the execution time in comparison to the mathematical model and the alternative heuristic while keeping the acceptance ratio close to the optimal solution.

Keywords: Network function virtualization · Wireless multi-hop network · Network function placement · Integer linear programming

1 Introduction

Network Function Virtualization (NFV) brings new opportunities and challenges. One of the main challenges is the optimized placement of the virtualized functions based on the characteristics and available resources of the network [6]. Placement of Network Functions (NF) can affect the path traffic flows take and consequently bandwidth usage in the network [8]. A chain of NFs with predefined parameters is referred to as a Service Graph (SG). The placement of all NFs of an SG is a Network Function Embedding Problem (NFEP): mapping the Virtual Network Functions (VNF) and the links between them to the physical

© Springer Nature Switzerland AG 2020
L. A. Grieco et al. (Eds.): ADHOC-NOW 2020, LNCS 12338, pp. 23–36, 2020.
https://doi.org/10.1007/978-3-030-61746-2_3

network [6]. NFEP can be modeled as a mathematical optimization problem that can be solved using different Linear Programming (LP) solvers/tools [6]. Mathematical optimization models are proven to be NP-hard and are not scalable. The solution for this issue is to design a heuristic with lower complexity that can provide a near-optimal solution. In this paper we propose a Fast And Cost-Efficient (FACE) heuristic that achieves two key objectives: minimizing the consumption of network resources while at the same time accepting as many placement requests as possible.

Compared to wired networks, multihop wireless networks such as MANETs, VANETs, or wireless sensor networks suffer from severe bandwidth (BW) limitations. That is due to a number of reasons: typical wireless technologies operate at lower transmission rates, compared to wired technologies such as Ethernet, etc. Also, when multihop wireless networks are built up from devices using a single radio, flows interfere with themselves (a node that is a relay between source and destination can only either receive or transmit, but not both at the same time). Finally, wireless technologies typically experience significant interference (either from other flows or due to the above self-interference), significantly lowering the available BW for each link. Our designed heuristic is based on solving the problem of NF placement faster than the optimization models while minimizing the BW consumption. Limiting our search to the shortest paths between the source and destination of the request will lower the size of the search space, which reduces the execution time while reducing the BW consumption.

We use a Breadth First Search (BFS) method to calculate all shortest paths for all possible pairs of nodes in the network prior to running the placement algorithm. Upon the arrival of a request we extract these pre-computed shortest paths based on the request's source and destination. Among all shortest paths we start with the one that increases the chance of successful placement of the request. Then the NF that has the fewest options for placement will be chosen (based on the nodal resources of nodes along the shortest path and the resource request of that NF). We will then iteratively place other NFs, backtracking if necessary when an unfeasible solution is encountered. The process will be repeated until all NFs are being placed.

We compare our results against a mathematical optimization model and a similar heuristic. The collected results show the effectiveness of our approach in lowering the execution time and providing near-optimal acceptance ratio. It can be seen from the comparisons that although the execution time has been decreased drastically, the acceptance ratio is close to the acceptance ratio of the optimal approach. The recorded results shows that FACE can solve the placement problem much faster than either the optimization model or the alternative heuristic. Due to these properties, FACE is particularly able to solve the NFEP in larger networks in real-time, compared to the alternatives.

The remainder of this paper is organized as follows: Section 2 discusses some of the most recent related work on NFEP and the characteristics of the heuristics in the related papers. Section 3 introduces our heuristic model and its different stages. Section 4 describes the modeling environment and results. We conclude the work in Section 5.

2   Related Work

The amount of work on NFEP is considerable. This problem can be modeled by using mathematical methods or by designing a heuristic algorithm. The mathematical methods will provide optimal results (based on a defined objective function) but are proven to be NP-hard. They are not applicable to large scale networks and it is common to develop a heuristic algorithm. The mathematical methods for solving the optimization problem can be different forms of Linear Programming (LP), Non-Linear Programming (NLP), etc. Constraints can be defined based on the limitations of the physical network, and NFs, and objectives are defined to minimize one or multiple parameters.

There are various optimization models proposed for placement in wired and wireless networks. As our aim here is to provide a fast and cost-efficient heuristic applicable to wireless multi-hop networks, we focus our review on heuristic algorithms and only briefly introduce the optimization model we employ to compare the performance of our heuristic model. In our previous work [5] we proposed a mathematical optimization model for placement of the SGs in wireless multi-hop networks. That model uses Integer Linear Programming (ILP) to place a chain of NFs and includes interference as a BW constraint. The objective of the optimization model is to minimize the mapping cost based on the requirements of the NFs and available resources in the network. We use the interference model introduced in [5] and considered the effect of interference in calculating BW consumption by the request placement. As our results showed, the solution time for even smaller networks grew fast, making this approach not attractive for larger scenarios. However, for smaller networks we can use the results from this model to evaluate the performance of any proposed heuristic.

Designing a heuristic algorithm can be an alternative solution for NFEP in wired and wireless networks with less computational demand and near optimal performance. Here we review the recent proposed heuristics that took unique approaches and provided novel methods for mapping SGs' NFs to a physical network.

The authors of [2] broke the problem of an SG placement into sub-problems of placing each NF of an SG and the link connected to the NF. The authors showed that the multi-stage algorithm can reduce the execution time in comparison to the optimization model. However the lower execution time is reached by sacrificing the number of accepted requests. As the placement problem is being broken into smaller parts, the proposed algorithm does not have information about the whole problem. It optimizes placement of each NF, not the whole SG. [3] uses Dynamic Programming (DP) to organize the problem into smaller interdependent sub-problems of placing each VNF and the virtual link connected to it towards the next VNF. The solutions for the sub-problems are then aggregated to compose the overall chain placement. [3] compared its method of dynamic programming with the multi-stage method. They showed that both methods' execution times are similar, since both can find solutions in polynomial time. The proposed heuristic in [3] only optimizes the placement of each NF, not the whole SG, which lowers the execution time and also decreases the number of accepted requests.

The proposed heuristic in [11] consists of 3 parts. First, it computes the list of physical node candidates for each VNF, then sorts them based on the number of physical node candidates for placement in increasing order. In the last step, the heuristic computes the placement cost of that VNF and its virtual link to the physical network and chooses the one with the lowest cost. Prioritizing the placement of NFs with lower options for placement will improve the acceptance ratio, but lack of considering the whole SG during the placement is a shortcoming of this method. [12] places NFs one by one based on their order in the SG. [12] exploits the intuition of finding the nearest server which supports the first NF in the chain of NFs for each flow. After this step, the algorithm removes the VNF under consideration from the chain and finds the nearest server that supports the next VNF of the chain and so on. The proposed heuristic in [12] is fast and simple but only considers optimization for each NF not the whole SG.

Some heuristics, such as the one proposed in [9], focus on designing an algorithm which can be combined with the optimization model to reduce the execution time of the model. A sampling-based Markov approximation (MA) approach is proposed in [9] to solve the NP-hard problem which requires a long convergence time. The method begins with a random feasible solution, and iterates the process of transformation from the current solution to another feasible solution until the steady-state distribution of the Markov chain appears. To reduce the execution time, the solution space is reduced to a subset of randomly chosen nodes that satisfy the resource demands of a request. It is been stated that the problem can be solved in polynomial time but the execution time of the algorithm is not being mentioned or compared with other proposed heuristics with similar time complexity.

[10] narrows the target search space of VNF placement by introducing a smaller accessible scope where the locations of VNFs are confined. The requests are categorized based on their source and destination. The nodes with lowest sum of distance from source and destination are in the accessible scope of the request. The size of each accessible scope for each set of requests is proportional to the total traffic volume of those request. It is shown in [10] that the size of the accessible scope will impact the time efficiency and performance of the NF placement. Considering all nodes to be in the accessible scope will not reduce the execution time but will provide the acceptance ratio of the optimization model. On the other hand, a very small accessible scope will decrease the execution time but also the acceptance ratio. This approach, unlike the previous heuristics, considers the whole SG and its source and destination. In the design of our heuristic we adopted this idea to narrow the search space, discussed in more detail in the next section.

In the design of a heuristic model for wireless networks, the scarcity of bandwidth should be considered and given priority. We saw that many heuristics first place the NFs and then connect them, which is not efficient in terms of bandwidth consumption. Keeping a balance between reducing the execution time and increasing the acceptance ratio is another factor that should be considered. We can not oversimplify our heuristic model and select nodes randomly without considering its impact on future requests and expect to achieve a high acceptance ratio. One of the interesting methods we reviewed here was the one proposed in [10]. We will be using the idea behind their heuristic in our design to reduce the search space for the nodes that are along shortest paths between the source and destination of a request. This reduction in the search space will decrease the execution time. At the same time, it constrains the placement of NFs to be on paths that minimize BW consumption. We believe it is beneficial to give priority to those NFs that have lower number of candidates for placement, as discussed in [11], and will consider this factor in our placement too.

3 Fast and Cost-Efficient(FACE) Heuristic Model

As we mentioned earlier, some methods use a reduced search space idea. For example, we could consider only nodes that are on the shortest path, easily identified by the fact that the sum of their distance from source and destination equals the hop count of the shortest path(s). However, we also need to identify the links over which the data will flow, and not all links among this subset of nodes will be links that belong to the shortest paths. We therefore explicitly look for all shortest paths between the source and destination of the request and limit our search for an efficient placement to these paths. With the use of a shortest path, we are reducing the BW consumption and at the same time reducing the execution time of the placement algorithm. The placement algorithm starts with searching for all possible shortest paths between all possible source-destination pairs in the network. Requests arrive one at a time and our algorithm will attempt to place them. As a request arrives, the shortest paths will be extracted based on the request's source and destination and the search for a cost-efficient placement will be limited to these shortest paths. The requests have BW demand and nodal resource requirements for each NF. The physical network consists of nodes that have nodal resource and links that have available BW.

In this section, we provide a detailed description of the algorithm that searches for all shortest paths and then will provide a detailed description of the placement algorithm.

3.1 Search for All Shortest Paths

The placement algorithm starts with searching for all possible shortest paths between all possible pairs of source and destination in the network. We use a search method similar to Breadth First Search (BFS). Assume the physical network is a graph where its nodes are the vertices of the graph and the links are the edges. The BFS explores the edges of the graph to discover the vertex that is reachable from the source node. It computes the shortest distance from the source to each reachable vertex in the graph. We made some changes to the BFS to start from the source and end when it reaches the destination node. Also, in addition to the distance, we record the shortest paths themselves. In our search for shortest paths we define one array and one matrix for each node u in the physical network:

- $dist_u$: An array that represents the shortest distance in terms of the number of hops from the source node.
- $nodes_u$: A matrix which records nodes involved in each different shortest paths found from source node to node u.

The initial value of $dist$ for all nodes is infinity, except for the source node which is equal to 0. The initial matrix of $nodes$ for all nodes is empty. The search algorithm starts traversing the physical network graph and while visiting neighbor y of node x it compares the value of $dist_y$ with $dist_x + 1$. If $dist_y$ is greater than $dist_x + 1$ it means that $dist_y$ describes a path longer than the shortest path. So we decrease $dist_y$ to $dist_x + 1$ and assign $nodes_x$ to $nodes_y$. If $dist_y = dist_x + 1$ then it means we found another shortest path to node y. In this case $nodes_y$ is the union of $nodes_x$ and $nodes_y$. The pseudo-code of this search algorithm is presented in Algorithm 1. This algorithm can find all possible shortest paths for all pairs of nodes. The output of the algorithm is p, which is a set of shortest paths p_{ij} for each pair of nodes in the physical network.

Algorithm 1: Finding all shortest paths

Result: $nodes_{dest}$ that contains all shortest paths
x is the source node;
y are the neighbors of node x;
while $y \sim destination$ **do**
    if $dist_y > dist_x + 1$ **then**
        $dist_y \leftarrow dist_x + 1$;
        $nodes_y \leftarrow nodes_x$;
    else if $dist_y = dist_x + 1$ **then**
        $nodes_y \leftarrow [nodes_y; nodes_x]$;
    $x \leftarrow y$;
    $y \leftarrow neighbors - of - y$;
end

The following example demonstrates how we update the parameters of each node during the search for all shortest paths. As it is shown in Fig. 1, we consider a network of 6 nodes and want to find all shortest paths from node 1 to 6. In the first stage, we update the parameters of the source node's neighbors, which are nodes 2 and 3. Figure 1a shows the second stage and updated parameters of the neighbors of node 2 and Fig. 1b shows the third stage, after we updated the parameters for neighbors of node 3. In the third stage, when processing node 5, $dist_5 = dist_3 + 1$. So we update $nodes_5$ to the union of $nodes_3$ and $nodes_5$. Figure 1c shows the final stage and all shortest paths from 1 to 6 can be found in $nodes_6$.

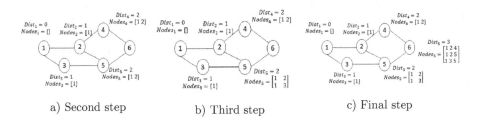

a) Second step   b) Third step   c) Final step

Fig. 1. Second, third, and final stages of finding all shortest paths.

3.2 Placement Algorithm

The requests arrive one at a time and are placed separately. Each request has a duration, once an accepted request expires, it will be removed from the network and the associated used resources will be released. Our placement algorithm can be divided into three main parts.

1. Selecting a candidate shortest path.
2. Selecting the NF to place.
3. Selecting the node for NF placement.

Select a Candidate Shortest Path. To keep our algorithm fast and eliminate the shortest paths with insufficient resources, we first check the availability of bandiwdth (BW) and nodal resources. To check the availability of BW in shortest paths L_p we consider the BW consumption by virtual links and the effect of interference. We use the protocol interference model widely used in the literature [4] and our own prior work [5] which defines an interference set for each link in the physical network. The interference set for each link consists of all the links that are connected to the nodes in the transmission range R of the sender or receiver. $d_{u'u}$ represents the distance between node u and u'. The $intset_{E_{uv}}$ captures that transmission on the link (E_{uv}) between node u and v will affect the BW usage of all the links whose transmitter is within the transmission range of the sender u or the receiver v.

$$\forall E_{uv} \in L_p :$$

$$intset_{E_{uv}} = \{E_{u'v'} | d_{u'u} \vee d_{v'v} \vee d_{v'u} \vee d_{u'v} \leq R\}$$

The BW check limits the search to the shortest paths with sufficient available BW. The nodal resource check depends on the placement but we perform an easy check to eliminate the shortest paths that cannot be used for the placement of the SG. We consider the case for the placement of the most problematic NF, which is the one with the highest nodal resource demand. If we cannot find any node along the shortest path with enough nodal resource to place that NF, that shortest path will be eliminated.

To choose the shortest path which is more likely to have sufficient nodal resources, we sort the shortest paths based on their minimum nodal resources in decreasing order. The shortest path with the maximum-minimum nodal resource will be chosen for the placement. If the placement at any stage was not successful, we return to this list and choose the next shortest path with maximum-minimum nodal resource. At every stage of our placement algorithm, we give priority to the options that increase the probability of successful placement in order to place as many requests as possible in a speedy manner.

Select a NF to Place. Now that we have chosen a candidate shortest path we can start placement of the NFs along the path. We start from the NF that is hardest to place. The NFs are sorted based on the number of possible candidate nodes in increasing order. A candidate node parameter $candid_{f_i}$ is defined for each NF of the SG and is equal to the number of nodes along the shortest path that can be used for the placement of that specific NF. In choosing the nodes along the shortest path we consider two parameters: a node has to provide sufficient nodal resources, and the NFs that previously were placed. The order of the NFs in the SG is fixed and we can not re-order them. Furthermore, we do not want to have a placement that passes a physical link more than once. E.g. if the third NF of the SG is being placed in the second node of the shortest path, subsequent NFs in the SG can not be placed in the first node. The candidate nodes are being chosen based on the placement of previous NFs to avoid loops and backtracking in the placement. If there are no candidate nodes for any of the NFs at any stage of placement, the chosen path is infeasible and the placement process will choose the next shortest path with maximum-minimum nodal resource and repeat the process of NF placement.

Select a Node for Placement. To place the chosen NF in one of the nodes along the shortest path we sort its candidate nodes based on their index difference and choose the node with the lowest index difference. The index of the nodes along the shortest path is equal to their order in the shortest path e.g. the source node's index is one. The index of a NF is equal to its order in the SG, e.g. the index of the first NF of the SG is one and the index of second NF is two. We compare the index of the chosen NF with the index of the candidate nodes and choose the one with the minimum index difference with the chosen NF. In the end, the available resources of the nodes, BW of the links, and the list of candidate nodes for the remaining NFs will be updated.

4 Modeling Environment and Results

Two platforms are being used to solve the placement problems: MATLAB to implement our heuristic algorithm, and AMPL to solve the mathematical optimization model and the alternative heuristic proposed in [10]. AMPL is a modeling language designed to be used for solving optimization problems such as linear and non-linear programming problems [1]. We used AMPL to solve the optimization model and the compared heuristic as it works with a wide range of solvers. We used BARON for solving our optimization model in AMPL as described in more detail in [1]. Unlike AMPL, which is designed for solving optimization models, MATLAB allows us to develop our heuristic algorithm for VNF placement.

The wireless topologies are generated with the use of the method proposed in [7]. where the nodes are randomly deployed in a square area, based on a uniform distribution. We generate topologies with 20, 30, and 40 nodes, the network area grows with the number of nodes. We keep the average node density constant, consequently the network size ranges from $490 * 490\,\mathrm{m}^2$ for the 20 node network to $980 * 980\,\mathrm{m}^2$ for the 40 nodes network [7]. Nodes in the wireless network are directly connected if their distance is less than or equal to the transmission range of the nodes. This transmission range is constant for all nodes and we verified that all of the generated topologies are connected.

We used the same parameter value as [6] in order to be able to compare our results. Nodal resources of nodes and the bandwidth of links are values uniformly distributed between 100 and 150 in all network scenarios. The flows arrive over time following a Poisson process with an average rate of four flows per 100 time units. Each flow has a lifetime, exponentially distributed with an average of $\mu = 500$ time units and is accompanied by a SG, defining the required NFs and their interconnection to handle this flow. There are 6 NFs per request. The nodal resource demands of each NF follows a uniform distribution between 1 and 20. The bandwidth requirement of all links of the request is the same and chosen uniformly from between 1 and 50 units.

4.1 Measurement Metrics

To measure the performance of our proposed heuristic and compare its performance with the other models we used the following parameters.

- Acceptance ratio: The total number of accepted requests divided by the total number of requests.
- Average BW Cost: Average of the BW units used for the deployed requests that are not expired. Note that this includes the bandwidth of links actually used by flows, as well as the bandwidth consumed on adjacent links due to interference.
- Execution time: The total time that it takes to place all requests in the course of an experiment simulation 20,000 s.

4.2   Results

We applied our heuristic model to wireless multi-hop networks of increasing size to evaluate its performance in terms of the time it takes to solve the placement problem and its success in placing the requests. To benchmark our results, we applied the Integer Linear Programming (ILP) model for wireless multi-hop networks introduced in [6] to the same topologies and the same set of requests as our heuristic model. Finally, we compared our results with the accessible scope heuristic proposed in [10] that we reviewed earlier.

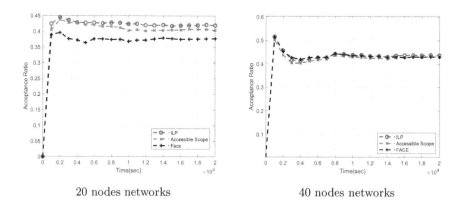

20 nodes networks   40 nodes networks

Fig. 2. Comparing acceptance ratios of three models, 20 and 40 nodes network.

Table 1. Execution times in seconds for networks of different size

Network size	20	30	40	100
ILP model	142.6	427.3	967.22	–
The accessible scope heuristic	49.9	66.5	96.80	–
FACE	5.70	6.4	10.3	143.82

Figure 2 shows the acceptance ratios recorded for wireless networks of 20 and 40 nodes for all three approaches. It can bee seen from Fig. 2a that our heuristic model's acceptance rate is lower than the recorded acceptance ratios for both the ILP model and the accessible scope heuristic model for networks of 20 nodes. We expected to have a lower number of accepted requests than the other models as we strictly limit our search space to the shortest paths between source and destination of the request. The accessible scope heuristic imposes fewer limitation on its search space than ours and considers all the nodes that are involved in the shortest paths, which provide more options for placement of SGs than our model. Figure 2b shows the acceptance ratios recorded for all three models for larger networks of 40 nodes. It can be seen from the figures that the recorded acceptance ratios of all three models become closer to each other as the size of networks grows (a trend we also observed with the intermediate network size of 30 nodes, not shown here for space reasons). As shown in Fig. 2b, for wireless networks of 40 nodes, the acceptance ratio of all three models are less than 1% apart. As our goal is to apply the placement method to larger networks, our heuristic seems to successfully provide a performance similar to the mathematical model for such networks.

The advantage of our model is that it can provide an acceptance ratio close to the mathematical model in a timely manner. Table 1 shows the average recorded execution time of the three models for different size networks. The recorded time of our heuristic model includes the time it takes to find all shortest paths and the time consumed for providing a placement solution for all requests, while the other models' execution time only measures the time it takes to provide a placement solution for all requests. Putting strict limitations on the search space resulted in the low execution time for our model. It can be seen that, for 20 node networks, the execution time of our model is a few seconds, whereas the execution time of the ILP model is in the order of 100 s. The execution time of the accessible scope heuristic is lower than the ILP model but still much higher than our model's execution time as it is using an ILP for finding an optimal placement for a SG, constrained to a smaller subnetwork. By considering the recorded acceptance ratios and the execution times we can see that in networks of 40 nodes our proposed heuristic can solve the placement problem much faster than the other two (by one or two orders of magnitude) while accepting almost the same number of requests as the optimal model. Table 1 also shows that the proposed heuristic model can be applied to much larger networks of 100 nodes and provides solutions in a timely manner. As we run the experiment for 20,000 s and 4 requests arrive per 100 s, all models processed a total of 800 requests. If it takes on average 143 s for the complete run in wireless network of 100 nodes, we can place a single request in approximately 0.17 s (some of the 143 s is taken up with the pre-processing, determining all shortest paths). Which implies that we can provide a placement solution almost in real-time, something neither of the other two approaches are able to. The mathematical optimization model and the accessible scope heuristic take hours to solve the problem and provide an optimal placement solution.

We recorded the average BW cost for placement of requests. Figure 3 shows the recorded average BW cost of the FACE heuristic model for 20, 30, and 40 nodes networks. The average BW cost increases as the size of networks grows. That is expected as larger networks have a bigger diameter and therefore longer shortest paths between randomly selected source-destination pairs, consuming more BW. Figure 4a and Fig. 4b compare average BW costs recorded for the FACE heuristic model and the ILP model for networks of 20 and 40 nodes respectively. The lower average BW cost achieved by the ILP model is due to the fact that the ILP explicitly considers the impact of interference, and so would choose, among available placements, not only the one that minimizes the BW

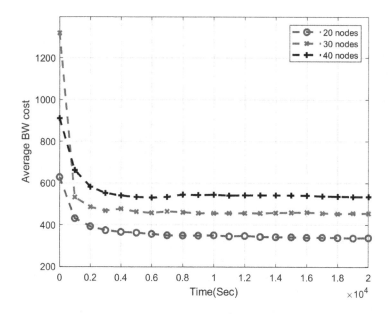

Fig. 3. FACE average BW cost for different size wireless networks

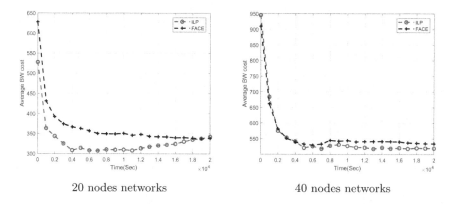

20 nodes networks   40 nodes networks

Fig. 4. Comparing average cost of FACE and ILP, 20 and 40 nodes networks

along that path, but also the one that reduces interference on neighboring links. Our proposed heuristic does not explicitly model this cost, using interference primarily to exclude certain candidate paths. However we can see that the difference between the recorded average cost of both models again seems to be bigger for the smaller network. For the network of 40 nodes, the difference is substantially reduced, again indicating that, for larger networks, the performance of FACE approaches that of the optimal solution.

5   Conclusion

The main challenge in the use of NFVs is optimally mapping the SG requests to the physical network. The placement problem is more challenging in wireless multi-hop networks as we are facing the problem of interference between wireless links, which causes higher BW consumption. As optimal placement methods are NP-hard and can not be applied to large size networks, we provide the FACE heuristic algorithm that can find a placement for SGs with low execution time. The FACE heuristic model minimizes BW consumption and provides solutions in a timely manner.

We compared our results with a similar heuristic and an optimization model, formulated as an ILP. The results show that the proposed heuristic reduces the execution time in comparison to the ILP model dramatically while it does not have a great impact on the number of accepted requests, especially for larger size networks. We can see from the results that although the accessible scope heuristic can provide better acceptance ratio in smaller networks, its execution time is much higher than FACE and it can not be applied to larger size networks.

In the future, we will more thoroughly study the performance benefits of the proposed FACE heuristic. For example, while we consider interference, the evaluations here only consider a fixed network density. We will explore whether the explicit considerations of interference in the placement decisions will be important for varying network densities. We also will vary the request arrival rate and/or the availability of network resources, to explore how the heuristic performs in networks that are more lightly of highly loaded.

In our previous work [6] we already showed that placing requests one at a time is not optimal and we may do better by selecting, among multiple possible choices, a solution that increases the chances of placing future requests. Our goal is to incorporate the factors we identified in [6] in making decision between multiple shortest paths and the process of placing NFs through the chosen shortest path.

Finally, one insight from this work is that a relatively simple heuristic can perform quite competitively, in terms of costs, with more complex heuristics or solving the embedding problem in an optimal manner, while providing answers/solutions to placement requests almost in real-time. We will therefore explore how far we can simplify the heuristic without sacrificing placement performance.

References

1. AMPL: a modeling language for large-scale optimization. OR/MS Today **36**(2), 68 (2009)
2. Bari, F., Chowdhury, S.R., Ahmed, R., Boutaba, R., Duarte, O.C.M.B.: Orchestrating virtualized network functions. IEEE Trans. Netw. Serv. Manage. **13**(4), 725–739 (2016)
3. Ghribi, C., Mechtri, M., Zeghlache, D.: A Dynamic Programming Algorithm for Joint VNF Placement and Chaining, pp. 19–24. ACM (2016)

4. Gupta, P., Kumar, P.R.: The capacity of wireless networks. IEEE Trans. Inf. Theory **46**(2), 388–404 (2000)

5. Jahedi, Z., Kunz, T.: Virtual network function embedding in multi-hop wireless networks. In: Proceedings of the 15th International Joint Conference on e-Business and Telecommunications, ICETE 2018 - vol. 1: DCNET, ICE-B, OPTICS, SIGMAP and WINSYS, Porto, Portugal, July 26–28, 2018. pp. 199–207 (2018). https://doi.org/10.5220/0006887401990207

6. Jahedi, Z., Kunz, T.: Optimal VNF placement: addressing multiple min-cost solutions. In: Obaidat, M.S. (ed.) ICETE 2018. CCIS, vol. 1118, pp. 1–23. Springer, Cham (2019). https://doi.org/10.1007/978-3-030-34866-3_1

7. Kunz, T., Mahmood, K., Li, L.: Broadcasting in multihop wireless networks: the case for multi-source network coding. In: IEEE International Conference on Communications (ICC), pp. 5157–5162. IEEE (2012)

8. Mohammadkhan, A., Ghapani, S., Liu, G., Zhang, W., Ramakrishnan, K.K., Wood, T.: Virtual function placement and traffic steering in flexible and dynamic software defined networks. vol. 2015, pp. 1–6. IEEE (2015)

9. Pham, C., Tran, N.H., Ren, S., Saad, W., Hong, C.S.: Traffic-aware and energy-efficient vnf placement for service chaining: joint sampling and matching approach. IEEE Trans. Serv. Comput. **13**(1), 172–185 (2020)

10. Qi, D., Shen, S., Wang, G.: Towards an efficient vnf placement in network function virtualization. Comput. Commun. **138**, 81–89 (2019)

11. Riggio, R., Bradai, A., Rasheed, T., Schulz-Zander, J., Kuklinski, S., Ahmed, T.: Virtual Network Functions Orchestration in Wireless Networks, pp. 108–116. IFIP (2015)

12. Tajiki, M.M., Salsano, S., Chiaraviglio, L., Shojafar, M., Akbari, B.: Joint energy efficient and qos-aware path allocation and VNF placement for service function chaining. IEEE Trans. Network Serv. Manage. **16**(1), 374–388 (2019)

Evaluation of DTN Routing Algorithms in Scheduled Public Transport Networks

José Irigon de Irigon[✉], Felix Walter[✉], and Thomas Springer[✉]

Faculty of Computer Science, Computer Networks Group,
Technische Universität Dresden, Dresden, Germany
{jose.irigon,felix.walter,thomas.springer}@tu-dresden.de

Abstract. Public transport networks (PTN) can serve as a basis to establish low-cost communication solutions by using Delay- and Disruption-tolerant Networking (DTN) technologies. Since vehicles move according to a schedule, DTN protocols able to leverage topological information are expected to perform well in such a setup. Anyway, it has not been evaluated, if deterministic protocols perform best or if opportunistic protocols like PRoPHET or Spray and Wait can outperform them in some scenarios if appropriate parameter tuning is performed. In this paper, the performance of state-of-the-art DTN routing protocols, namely Epidemic Routing, Spray and Wait, PRoPHET, MaxProp, and CGR is compared with respect to their use in PTN. The performance comparison takes delivery probability, average latency, buffer utilization, and network overhead into account. The ONE was extended to simulate vehicle movement according to tracks and the schedule of the PTNs of Helsinki, Freiburg, and Prague. Our evaluation results demonstrate that protocol parameters should be selected carefully to achieve the best performance in different scenarios. The most efficient parameterization of protocols is described, and their influence on different performance metrics is discussed.

Keywords: DTN · Routing · Public transport systems · Performance evaluation

1 Introduction

Delay- and Disruption-tolerant Networking (DTN) enables *store-carry-forward* data transmission in *challenged networks*, which may face disrupted end-to-end paths or vast delays on individual links. For that purpose, application data are encapsulated in *bundles* and routed via the DTN overlay network. Applications for DTN explored in research are Interplanetary Internet, underwater networks, wireless sensor networks, and vehicular networks. Disruption-tolerant vehicular networks have been explored for various use cases to either enable connectivity in disconnected areas or to establish decentralized and cost-efficient communication alternatives in urban settings. In this work we focus on urban public transport

© Springer Nature Switzerland AG 2020
L. A. Grieco et al. (Eds.): ADHOC-NOW 2020, LNCS 12338, pp. 37–52, 2020.
https://doi.org/10.1007/978-3-030-61746-2_4

systems (PTS). PTS vary with respect to covered area, topology, number of lines, stop density, route length, trip frequency and number of used vehicles. As a result, the frequency of contacts and potential paths is highly dependent on the PTS topology and setup. Consequently, the characteristics of each PTS might influence which DTN protocol and parameter setup performs best. Even if deterministic DTN protocols can exploit PTS schedules to derive a contact graph and, thus, be expected to perform best, opportunistic approaches may outperform them due to parameterization, replication control and buffer management that might address specific PTS characteristics better.

In this paper we explore the performance of five DTN protocol versions in three urban public transport systems based on simulations with the ONE simulator [19]. The contribution of the paper is twofold. First, we examine parameter settings for each protocol to identify which protocol setup works best in each of the three urban PTS. Second, we compare the best performing setup of all five DTN protocols to identify the DTN protocol that works best in each PTS. For both series of experiments we investigate a set of performance metrics, namely delivery probability, latency and buffer utilization. The goal is to identify relations between these metrics and maximize one metric over others.

The paper is organized as follows: in Sect. 2 an overview about classes of DTN routing protocols and their major characteristics is given followed by a rationale for the selection of the particular protocols explored in this paper. As related work, DTN protocol performance evaluations are discussed in Sect. 3 with a focus on DTN over PTS. Section 4 introduces the approach for investigating the selected DTN protocols in three urban PTS. The evaluation results are discussed in Sect. 5. The paper concludes with a summary of our results and an outlook to future research in the field of DTN over PTS.

2   Background

Due to the inherent disruptions and delays in challenged networks, DTN routing algorithms are fundamentally different from those leveraged in IP networks. They may employ different levels of knowledge concerning the network topology. While some *opportunistic* algorithms perform reactive decisions based only on current connectivity, others estimate a utility metric from the history of contacts, which may also be exchanged transitively. *Deterministic* algorithms, such as Contact Graph Routing (CGR), leverage a schedule of future episodes of connectivity (*contacts*), which has to be provided in advance. In this paper, we compare the performance of five routing algorithms that make different assumptions of the application scenario and the provided information.

Epidemic Routing [27] is an opportunistic routing protocol often used as a baseline for comparison. The algorithm replicates messages to all reachable nodes, as long as they do not already carry a copy of the message. The latter is determined by the regular exchange of *summary vectors* containing unique message identifiers. Though the authors propose to enforce a maximum hop count, the number of replicas is not limited.

In contrast, *Spray and Wait* [26] limits the number of message replicas to a fixed value. Every time a message is forwarded, the algorithm decreases the number of copies in the buffer by the transmitted number of copies. The authors propose two techniques for calculating the latter; by setting it to half of the copies in the local buffer (*Binary* Spray and Wait) or always transmitting only a single copy (*Source* Spray and Wait).

The *Probabilistic Routing Protocol using History of Encounters and Transitivity* (PRoPHET) is specified in an IRTF Internet Draft [1]. Its forwarding decisions are based on the *delivery predictability* metric, which is derived for every known node from the history of encounters. During a contact, the value is adjusted due to the expectation of reaching the corresponding neighbor again. An aging factor is employed to decrease the metric over time if no further contacts are observed. Additionally, the delivery predictability values are disseminated to other nodes, allowing for transitive estimations. This way, bundle replication can focus on neighbors with a high probability to reach the destination. After a bundle has been delivered, acknowledgments are spread throughout the network, allowing nodes to clear their buffers of the bundle.

MaxProp [4] applies a similar transitive probability estimation technique as well as acknowledgments. Further, it extends the buffer management and queuing order by prioritizing messages based on their age and the number of traversed hops. This way, messages newly-introduced into the network are disseminated faster than older messages which were already forwarded via several hops.

The deterministic approach taken by *Contact Graph Routing* (CGR) [5] is vastly different: A *contact plan* has to be provided to the algorithm in advance, from which a *contact graph* is derived. This representation of the time-varying topology is used to calculate routes to every destination via a shortest-path algorithm. For every bundle, a viable route is selected and the bundle is proactively scheduled for transmission to the next node on the path. The implementation used in this work follows the standard recommended by the consultative committee for space data systems's (CCSDS), Schedule-aware bundle routing (SABR) [6].

The goal of our work was to find the most suitable routing algorithm for PTNs. By our selection, we expect to get an overview of the performance of approaches based on different levels of topological information: While Epidemic Routing as well as Spray and Wait rely solely on properties of the messages, PRoPHET and MaxProp leverage historical data and transitive information for their utility metrics, and sCGR calculates routes using a schedule provided in advance. Although the latter can exploit PTN schedules and, thus, is expected to perform well in scheduled networks, we perform parameter tuning of the opportunistic protocols with the goal to analyze whether they can compete with or even outperform the deterministic approach that needs an increased amount of initial information.

3   Related Work

Public Transport Systems have been proposed as disruption-tolerant data carrier in rural areas to provide educational means [16,25], economic development [13] and latency insensitive connectivity [17,22,25]; in urban areas they have been additionally proposed to offload traffic from mobile networks [14,20] and environmental monitoring [7,15]. Simulation is commonly used to estimate the performance of proposed routing algorithms in those scenarios. The faithful reproduction of the target mobility is essential to produce useful results. However, the accurate reproduction of complex scenarios is challenging, computationally intensive, and requires proper parameterization.

An extensive survey of tools and models for opportunistic networks is found in [9]. In the attempt to reproduce mobility faithfully, a set of available traces have been recurrently used to assess the performance of novel routing algorithms. However, traces are rarely available for each desired scenario; they are expensive to produce, inflexible (regarding to scaling and parameterization), and cannot be used in scenarios that do not yet exist. We could identify a few works in the DTN literature that, based on open data information, were able to create realistic PTN scenarios and compare their routing performance:

The *Routing in Urban Public Transport Systems* (RUTS) [10] reproduced the bus network of Braunschweig based on geographical information from OpenStreetMap [24] and exporting it to the *Simulation of Urban MObility* (SUMO) [21] to be combined with line definition and stop locations. The authors used a custom micro-mobility simulator to make a synthetic trace later imported to the ONE simulator. Based on the information extracted from timetables, a routing algorithm was proposed that forwards messages according to the encounter likelihood. In RUTS, differently from the current approach, buses are not assigned to a specific route and may serve a different line at every shift. As we notice in the evaluation, this difference seems to cause a considerable difference in routing algorithms based in contact history.

The *Urban Routing Backbone Simulator* (URBeS) [12] proposed the use of an open data provider (Google Transit Feeds - GTFS) in the creation of realistic scenarios. However, the authors do not make it clear whether the real trajectory between bus stations is considered since this information is optional and missing in most GTFS feeds. URBeS proposes a probabilistic routing algorithm based on the number of encounters to exchange messages from buses to a destination bus line (instead of a specific bus). In its evaluation, a period of 10 h is considered (8 a.m. to 6 p.m.); Epidemic Routing achieves the highest delivery ratio, but it was considered unsuitable due to the number of replicas per message.

Zimmermann *et. al* provide behavioral analysis of the bus network in Aachen through a simulated scenario created with the support of the transportation provider and technical operator. [28] The simulation considers the time-span of six hours from 7:30 to 13:30 on Mondays; besides, they assume that every bus and bus stop (station) are equipped with an 802.11 module, allowing bus-to-bus as well as bus-to-station communication. The paper highlights the impact of infrastructure elements to the number of contacts. Unfortunately, only Epidemic Routing was considered, ignoring the influence of those elements in the determinism of future contacts and the ability of different routing algorithms to explore this information. Different use-cases that use static communication modules to support communication over vehicles with opportunistic mobility have been mentioned in [2], but we could not find a performance assessment of DTN routing algorithms in a PTN network that allow vehicle-to-vehicle and vehicle-to-station communication. Finally, [23] highlights that the performance of a routing algorithm is highly dependent on its parameterization. Unfortunately, novel routing algorithms are often compared to inappropriate algorithms using only standard parameterization.

4   Methodology and Evaluation Setup

We use a simulation approach based on a mobility model that reproduces the vehicle motions in PTN. To get a performance overview in distinct networks, we selected PTNs that vary in terms of the number of traffic lines and stations as well as the covered area. As a first step, the parameters of *PRoPHET* and *Spray and Wait* were tuned to identify those versions that perform best in the three PTNs. In addition, we explored if a single parameter setup performs best in all three PTNs or if parameters should be tuned for every scenario. As a second step, we compared the performance of the best performing versions of the five selected routing protocols to explore which of them performs best in the selected PTNs and if there is a single protocol that performs best in all PTNs or if the results differ in the three PTNs. In the following, we describe the selected PTN, preparation of scenario data, and the simulation setup.

For the evaluation, we selected three PTSs with different characteristics, which are illustrated in Fig. 2. The metro network of Prague, with three traffic lines serving 61 stations, is the smallest with respect to traffic lines and stations but covers the largest area of 230 km². The tram network of Freiburg and Helsinki cover smaller areas (63 km² in Freiburg and 43 km² in Helsinki) but contain a larger number of traffic lines and stations. Table 1 illustrates the parameters of the three PTS scenarios.

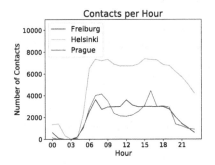

Fig. 1. Contacts over time

Table 1. Evaluated scenarios

	Prague Metro	Freiburg Tram	Helsinki Tram
GTFS Version	23.03.20	01.08.19	21.03.20
Area (km²)	230	63	43
# Stations	61	89	213
# Traffic Lines	3	5	9
# Sim. Vehicles	106	117	116
# Trips in a day	1550	1458	2262

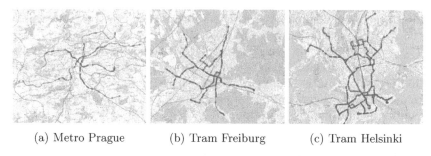

(a) Metro Prague   (b) Tram Freiburg   (c) Tram Helsinki

Fig. 2. Scenarios

Our scenario data is based on the General Transit Feed Specification (GTFS) and extended with geographic information from Open Street Maps with support of the map matching tool Pfaedle [3]. Route descriptions with station coordinates and vehicle schedules for each transit line were extracted and translated to a format suitable to feed the mobility model of the simulation tool. We used the ONE extended by a mobility model that reproduces real vehicle movement in PTN to generate scenario data for the simulations.

A trip represents the movement of a vehicle along a route of a particular traffic line according to a given timetable. It is defined by its departure time, departure station and arrival station. Usually, two stations are repeatably used as departure and arrival stations for a traffic line. However, routes vary in real PTNs. In [12], Gaito et. al. proposes the exclusion of all routes that are not *closed*, i.e., trips served by vehicles departing from or arriving at stations other than the first or the last of a route taken as a model. Based on the selected scenarios, we verified that the exclusion of those routes causes a considerable change in the network capacity. The metro line A of Prague, for example, defines 140 trips (70 in each direction) in a day whose route ends one station earlier. In this work, we propose the concept of *reference route* as a list of stations to be used as a model. Trips are defined as a pair of indices to the reference route and departure time. Only routes whose head or tail is not contained in the reference route are ignored. The number of routes represented depends on the proper choice of the reference route. Considering any route from the timetable as a candidate, we defined the reference route as the candidate capable of representing the greatest number of trips. Our simulation was able to represent over 95% of all trips defined in the schedule by using reference routes.

As the simulation starts, the mobility model instantiates a scheduler that is responsible for assigning trips to vehicles according to the timetable. Every vehicle queries the scheduler for its first trip, setting its location to the departure station. From this moment on, a vehicle must be located at the departure station at the departure time in order to be assigned to a trip (there are no jumps between stations or vehicular relocation). The scheduler works as follows: at startup, it reads from the disk all trips based on the timetable. Then, it chooses a vehicle V that has no trips assigned and adds it to the list of trips to serve, calculating its arrival time (AT) and arrival station (AS). Next, it selects the first trip departing from AS after AT, repeating this process for all trips V is able to serve. Finally, the next idle vehicle is chosen, and the process starts over until all trips are served.

At depart time, a vehicle calculates the speed using the expected time and distance to the next station as defined in the trip received by the scheduler and starts moving at a constant speed. At each station, it waits a configurable amount of time. In our experiments, a random waiting time between 10 and 15 s is used. As a vehicle arrives at the end of a trip, a vehicle queries the scheduler for the next available trip. If no further trips are defined, or in case the vehicle has to wait longer than 20 min, it turns off its radio.

In this work, both vehicle-to-vehicle and vehicle-to-station communication is considered. However, only stations are chosen as source and destination of bundles. Bundles are created at a constant pace; when a bundle is created, two stations are randomly chosen as source and destination. We assume that every vehicle and station is equipped with an 802.11p module. The amount of time a vehicle stops at a station is a configuration parameter. Our evaluation considers a stopping time of 30 s and a communication range of 80 m line of sight. In our evaluation we varied the message size and transmission capability, since they are application dependent and vary greatly depending on the use-case. Our evaluation considered two message sizes (1 MB and 5 MB) and transmission speed of 8 Mbps and 40 Mbps.

Due to the lack of information on vehicle reallocation, some lines end up with a disproportionate number of vehicles. On the one hand, the creation messages for vehicles that are out of service masks the evaluation of the routing protocol. A similar effect occurs in choosing vehicles serving their last trip as the bundle destination. On the other hand, ignoring the message creation when the chosen vehicle is out of service changes the frequency with which messages are created across simulation runs.

5   Evaluation

For the evaluation of different routing algorithms and metrics, we defined three classes of network load: a *low load* class with bundle size of 1 MB, 12 bundles created per minute and transmission speed of 40 Mbps; an *average load* class with bundle size of 1 MB, 20 bundles created per minute and transmission speed is 8 Mbps; finally, a *high load* class with 5 MB bundles created at every second and transmission speed of 8 Mbps.

5.1   Defining the Simulation Period

To deal with the known limitations of the ONE simulator's scalability, we first explore in two experiments whether an eight-hour period is capable of producing usable results.

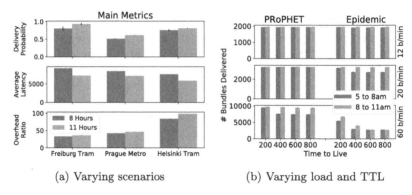

(a) Varying scenarios   (b) Varying load and TTL

Fig. 3. Setting simulation period (Color figure online)

In the first experiment, we measured the performance of PRoPHET Routing in different scenarios for the early eight and eleven hours of a day to verify whether the different setups produce comparable results. 10 runs for every city were performed varying β from 0.1 to 1.0 in steps of 0.1. Figure 3a contains the measured values for delivery probability, average latency, and overhead ratio. The increase in simulation time shows a consistent rise in delivery probability and overhead ratio, and a decrease in average latency. In the second experiment, we compared the number of delivered bundles for PRoPHET and Epidemic in the same periods simulating the PTS of Freiburg, while varying bundle time to live (TTL) and network load. The goal of this experiment was to verify the influence of the warm up time on probabilistic routing performance. The results of three runs are presented in Fig. 3b. On top, a low load variation that creates 12 bundles every minute is shown; in the middle the average load variation is presented, that creates 20 bundles per minute; at the bottom, in the high load variation, a bundle is created every second. We ran every routing algorithm with four different TTLs varying from 200 to 800 min, as specified in the x axis. The bars represent the absolute number of messages delivered in two consecutive periods separately: from 5 a.m. to 8 a.m. (blue) and from 8 a.m. to 11 a.m. (orange).

Under *low load* (left), there is a minimal difference in the number of delivered bundles between the two periods observed for TTL equal to or higher than 400. This difference increases considerably for Epidemic under *average load*. During the first hours of the day, bundles are generated at a constant pace but cannot be exchanged due to the lack of vehicular mobility. During the first trips, vehicles collect and distribute bundles stored along the route. Epidemic Routing is the most affected since PRoPHET can better utilize the contact time by avoiding the waste of contact time with bundles with low delivery probability. A further increase in the transmission load eventually reaches the limits of PRoPHET routing that starts to present a similar tendency, even though being able to cope with congestion better than Epidemic. The second experiment shows that

Epidemic had an increasing number of delivered bundles in the second period, similarly to PRoPHET.

This result excludes the assumption that the improvement over time noticed in the first experiment was caused (at least exclusively) by the learning process. The tendencies observed in the main performance metrics were consistent, and the congestion effects were noticeable in both periods. Therefore, we conclude that the outcome of simulation realized in those scenarios during the first eight hours of a week-day are able to produce meaningful material to the performance assessment of different DTN routing algorithms. Consequently, in the following experiments the first eight hours of a week-day are simulated.

5.2   Spray and Wait: *Binary* vs. *Source*

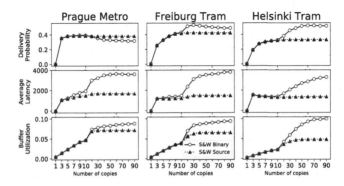

Fig. 4. Spray and wait average load: 1 MB size, 20 bundles/min, 8 Mbps

Spray and Wait Routing assumes that the highest possible delivery likelihood is achieved by Epidemic, at the price of energy and latency. The goal of this section is threefold: first, verify whether these assumptions hold for public transportation systems; second, assess the importance of the right parameterization as well as the factors that affect its performance; third, compare both spray variations (*Binary* vs. *Source*) to verify whether one of them is more suitable for public transport systems. Spray and Wait variants have a single parameter: the number of replicas. In our experiments, we vary this number from one to nine in steps of two and from 10 to 90 in steps of 10 s. We analyzed the results for delivery probability, average latency, and buffer utilization for the three scenarios. Figure 4 illustrates the behavior for a network configuration under *average load*. Average latency represents the period between message creation and delivery. Figure 4 depicts the average latency based on bundles created after 5 a.m. Buffer utilization is presented in percentage of the total storage capacity. Our experiments utilized 1 TB storage, excluding congestion due to lack of storage. However, we consider storage occupancy an important metric, since proposed use cases frequently consider limited storage capabilities.

In *average load* and *lower load* scenarios, *Binary* spray performed better than *Source* with respect to delivery probability (DP). However, the observed gain in DP in the city of Freiburg and Helsinki comes at the cost of latency and buffer utilization (caused by an increasing number of transmissions). For example, in the city of Freiburg, a simulation with 30 copies achieved the highest DP (53%), 23.5% better than the result obtained using ten copies. However, this performance improvement also increases the average latency in 110% and buffer utilization in 178.5%. In the *high load* scenario, an increase in the number of bundles also decreases DP due to congestion. The use of 30 copies in our experiments caused 45% DP lost in Prague, 50% in Freiburg, and 56% in Helsinki with the best number of copies three (Prague), three (Freiburg), and five (Helsinki). In general, *Source* Spray and Wait is not the right candidate for complex PTS. It only forwards one bundle at a time to be delivered directly to the destination. Since, in our scenarios, bundles are created exclusively by stations, they are only delivered if the destination is reachable in two hops. However, in *high load* scenarios, *Source* Spray performed similarly to *Binary* spray, sometimes slightly better. Based on these results, only *Binary* Spray and Wait is used in the assessment of different DTN routing protocols in Subsect. 5.4

5.3   PRoPHET

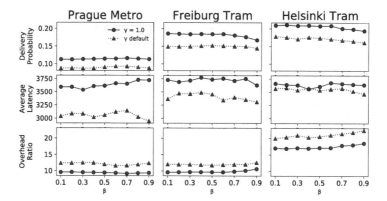

Fig. 5. Tuning PRoPHET

PRoPHET is a probabilistic routing algorithm that maintains a table with the predictable likelihood of future encounters to each neighbor. It has two parameters: γ defines how fast the expected probability decreases over time (aging); β defines a reducing factor to the expected probability at each extra hop (transitivity). In this section, we analyze the importance of the right tuning for PRoPHET, i.e., how aging and transitivity affect the performance of different configurations and how the design of the simulation framework may affect the outcome of the routing algorithm. We performed an initial set of runs varying γ and verified that, as long as the schedule is respected, the best outcome is achieved, ignoring the aging factor ($\gamma = 1.0$). This behavior is understandable since vehicles visit the same set of stations with high likelihood. Moreover, when aging is taken into account, the lack of communication during the night affects the first morning trips negatively, since vehicles suppose that future communications are rare, based on the nocturnal behavior. For each scenario and parameterization set (low, average, and high load), two sets of 10 experiments were performed: in one set, γ was set to its default value (0.999885791), and in the other set γ was set to 1.0. In each set, we varied β from 0.1 to 1.0 in steps of 0.1. The result for the *high load* run is illustrated in Fig. 5. Setting the γ to 1 increased the delivery probability in every scenario for all βs and caused a decrease in the overhead ratio, i.e., the number of copies per message delivered. Although an increase in average latency seem to be associated with an increase in DP, experiments show that *average load* configurations still achieve better DP (70% for γ of 1 against 64% for default value, while a similar average latency was achieved. In Helsinki, tuning the right β resulted in an increase of 12% in DP, showing the importance of the proper routing parameterization in PTS scenarios, as Oliveira et al. have shown for opportunistic networks in [23].

Finally, the chosen routing algorithms takes into account vehicles (tram, bus) instead of lines. We believe that a small modification in the routing algorithm that decide based on the line identifier (instead of device identifier) and to learn about the line statistics could overcome the effects of the lack of knowledge about the device behavior between trips. Consequently, we identified nine individual setting for β and γ for each of the three scenarios and network load options that produced the best performance results. These settings will be used in the comparative evaluation of DTN protocols.

5.4 Performance Comparison Between Different Routing Algorithms

This section compares the performance of the routing algorithms Epidemic, Binary Spray and Wait, PRoPHET, MaxProp, and CGR. An extensive tuning for MaxProp, as we have done for PRoPHET and Spray and Wait, was not performed because the simulation of MaxProp is computing-intensive and time-consuming. Instead, we used the default configuration for MaxProp for all simulation runs. A second challenge was to simulate CGR in the ONE. The ONE has known scalability limitations [9], and our implementation was not able to simulate the tram network of Helsinki. Our approach to circumvent this problem was to export the trace generated by the ONE as input for the *aiodtnsim*, an asyncio-based DTN simulator [11] to simulate CGR in each scenario. *aiodtnsim* was validated against the ONE and produced comparable results for Epidemic and Spray and Wait. Figure 6 summarizes the results of each routing algorithm under different loads. Under *low load*, all routing algorithms with exception to Spray and Wait presented high delivery probability and similar outcome (all results were within 0.8% of their mean in each scenario). Spray and Wait did not perform better because the maximum number of copies was limited to 90.

Increasing this number should allow Spray and Wait to have a DP similar to Epidemic.

Under *average load*, CGR presented the highest DP in each scenario, followed by PRoPHET; additionally, CGR achieved the least average latency in Freiburg and Helsinki. An attentive reader might find curious the fact that the buffer utilization of Spray and Wait changes drastically. Notice that the illustrated bar corresponds to the best parameterization (number of copies) per scenario: 9 copies in Prague, 30 in Freiburg, and 90 in Helsinki. The lowest DP was achieved by Epidemic routing in the three scenarios. Although MaxProp does not stand out for a high DP, its drop policy's effect is perceptible in the resulting buffer utilization, especially in Freiburg and Helsinki.

In *high load* scenarios, DP values are much lower for all protocols than in low and *average load* scenarios. In Prague and Freiburg the highest DPs were achieved with *Binary Spray and Wait*: 16.72% and 19.15% respectively; the downside is that in Prague, it also had the second-highest average latency. The second highest DP had CGR with 12.06% and 18.37%. In Helsinki, CGR achieved the highest DP (31.41%) and the least latency, followed by PRoPHET and Spray and Wait with 21% DP. MaxProp and Epidemic achieved the lowest DP.

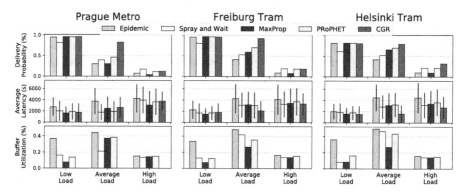

Fig. 6. Routing algorithm comparison

Epidemic Routing, despite its simplicity, was able to achieve high DP in the three scenarios under *low load*, but DP falls rapidly as soon as load increases. Besides, it presented the highest latency and buffer utilization through all experiments. Spray and Wait achieved an overall low latency, but also low DP for *low* and *average load*; in *high load* scenarios it stand out, given that it is configure with the right number of copies. The maximum DP under low load was achieved with the maximum number of copies (90 in our experiments); under *average load*, the highest DP was achieved with 9, 30, and 60 copies in Prague, Freiburg, and Helsinki respectively; finally, under *high load* the number of copies fall to 3, 3, and 5. Despite using its default configuration, MaxProp achieved the highest DP in all cities under *low load* (Prague: 96.11%, Freiburg: 96.5% and Helsinki:

82.01%), the lowest latency in Prague and Freiburg, and the second least buffer requirements, due to its ability to delete acknowledged messages and buffer management. PRoPHET was among the three highest DPs in each scenario and stood out in scenarios for the *average load* without the requirement of a precise contact plan, as in CGR. It stands in the average regarding average latency and buffer utilization. Finally, CGR achieved the highest DP in general, especially under *average load*: 82.74%, 92.40%, and 0.7963% compared to 45.93%, 70.41%, and 70.46% achieved by the second-highest DP (PRoPHET) in the cities of Prague, Freiburg and Helsinki, respectively. Additionally, the average latency of CGR was the lowest in Freiburg and Helsinki for average, and *high load* and its buffer utilization was the least in each experiment since it is a single copy approach.

Considering another perspective, it is possible to classify the routing algorithms according to the amount of information they exchange to support the routing algorithm. The most straightforward algorithm is Epidemic, which does not need to change any information. It is a good choice if resources are abundant and the load remains low; however, regardless of the load, Epidemic presents the highest average latency and buffer utilization in all scenarios. Besides, PD of the Epidemic declines rapidly as the load increases, due to congestion. Therefore, our experiments lead to the conclusion that the Epidemic should be avoided whenever resources are limited, or there is no guarantee that the load will remain low. Spray and Wait control the number of replicas to minimize congestion; our experiments show that this approach can effectively increase the DP and decrease latency, especially under *high load*. However, defining the number of replicas is challenging: it is statically configured in Spray and Wait, but the right number depends on the communication and mobility behavior. We tested all variations in our experiments and chose the best outcome, but this cannot be done in reality. An alternative is to exchange information at runtime to adapt the number of replicas, as proposed in [8]. MaxProp's buffer management and acknowledgments proved to be effective in reducing buffer utilization. Additionally, it takes into account the delivery likelihood based on transitive information about contact opportunities exchanged at runtime. Its DP was, in average, lower than PRoPHET, but we must consider that it used its default configuration. PRoPHET has achieved in average the second highest DP routing exclusively based on information about contact opportunities, which seems to be an effective routing strategy in PTS networks. This assumption is reinforced by the result of CGR that reached the highest PD and the lowest storage usage based on precise information about contact opportunities. These results lead us to believe that the theoretical results presented by Jain et al. [18] are valid to a scheduled scenario as PTS, reaffirming the premise that algorithms capable of exploiting the environmental information accurately are expected to achieve higher performance. A detailed study to consider the effects of delays and unexpected route modifications caused by accidents or disasters in the outcome of those routing algorithms is proposed as future work.

6 Conclusion and Future Work

In this paper, the performance of five DTN routing protocols was explored in three urban public transport networks, namely the metro network in Prague, and the tram networks in Freiburg and Helsinki. We incorporated route information and time tables from real public transport networks in the ONE simulator. In the first simulation step, we identified the time period of the first 8 h of a weekday as sufficient for our simulations. Next, a comparison between Source and Binary Spray and Wait shows that the latter variant is more appropriate for this setup. We highlighted the importance of proper parametrization and its trade-offs, based on an extensive set of runs with Spray and Wait and PRoPHET Routing. Finally, we compared the performance of five selected DTN protocols. Simulations revealed that the protocol performance was highly dependent on the network load. Epidemic Routing obtained poor performance metrics under average and high loads. Binary Spray and Wait was able to improve DP, reduce average latency and buffer utilization given that it used the right parameterization. MaxProp's approach to exchange acknowledgements and buffer management based on transitive probabilities exchange was able to achieve the second best performance in buffer utilization. PRoPHET achieved the second highest DP in average, behind CGR that, in general achieved the best overall performance. Since the right parametrization depends on the network load, our results lead to the conclusion that information about the network behavior at runtime should be taken into account. The communication behavior (creation of messages) in this work remained constant, and mobility respected the schedule. The assessment of the above mentioned protocols under variable load and unexpected mobility are planned as future work.

Acknowledgement. This work is partially funded by the German Research Foundation (DFG) within the Research Training Group Role-based Software Infrastructures for continuous-context-sensitive Systems (GRK 1907).

References

1. Lindgren, A., Doria, E.D.S.G.: Probabilistic Routing Protocol for Intermittently Connected Networks. Internet Engineering Task Force, October 2011. https://tools.ietf.org/html/draft-irtf-dtnrg-prophet-09. Experimental
2. Baron, B., Spathis, P., De Amorim, M.D., Viniotis, Y., Ammar, M.H.: Mobility as an alternative communication channel: a survey. IEEE Commun. Surv. Tutor. **21**(1), 289–314 (2019)
3. Bast, H., Brosi, P.: Sparse map-matching in public transit networks with turn restrictions. In: GIS: Proceedings of the ACM International Symposium on Advances in Geographic Information Systems, pp. 480–483 (2018)
4. Burgess, J., Gallagher, B., Jensen, D., Levine, B.N.: MaxProp: routing for vehicle-based disruption-tolerant networks. In: Proceedings of the IEEE INFOCOM, May 2006
5. Burleigh, S., et al.: Contact graph routing in DTN space networks: overview, enhancements and performance. IEEE Commun. Mag. **53**(3), 38–46 (2015)

6. CCSDS members: schedule-aware bundle routing (2019). https://public.ccsds.org/Pubs/734x3b1.pdf
7. Christodoulou, S., Gizas, A., Asimakopoulos, G.: Dynacargo routing subsystem and its algorithms for efficient urban waste collection. In: Proceedings of the 11th International Conference on Practice and Theory of Automated Timetabling (PATAT-2016), Udine, Italy, pp. 45–61 (2016)
8. Cui, J., Cao, S., Chang, Y., Wu, L., Liu, D., Yang, Y.: An adaptive spray and wait routing algorithm based on quality of node in delay tolerant network. IEEE Access **7**, 35274–35286 (2019)
9. Dede, J., et al.: Simulating opportunistic networks: survey and future directions. IEEE Commun. Surv. Tutor. **20**(2), 1547–1573 (2018)
10. Doering, M., Pögel, T., Wolf, L.: DTN routing in urban public transport systems. In: Proceedings of the 5th ACM Workshop on Challenged Networks - CHANTS 2010, p. 55. ACM Press, New York (2010)
11. Walter, F.: A minimal framework for performing DTN simulations based on Python 3.7 and asyncio (2020). https://gitlab.com/d3tn/aiodtnsim
12. Gaito, S., Maggiorini, D., Rossi, G.P.: Leveraging Bus Mobility to Enable Communications in Urban Areas. Wired, p. 14 (2011)
13. Galati, A., Sazonovs, A., Olivares, M., Mangold, S., Gross, T.R.: Delay tolerant networking for the socio-economic development in rural South Africa. In: Gaggi, O., Manzoni, P., Palazzi, C., Bujari, A., Marquez-Barja, J.M. (eds.) GOODTECHS 2016. LNICST, vol. 195, pp. 195–202. Springer, Cham (2017). https://doi.org/10.1007/978-3-319-61949-1_21
14. Gao, Z., Meng, J., Wang, Q., Yang, Y.: Data offloading for deadline-varying tasks in mobile edge computing. In: Proceedings of the 2018 IEEE SmartWorld, Ubiquitous Intelligence and Computing, Advanced and Trusted Computing, Scalable Computing and Communications. Cloud and Big Data Computing, Internet of People and Smart City Innovations, SmartWorld/UIC/ATC/ScalCom/CBDCo, pp. 1479–1484 (2018)
15. Giannini, C., Calegari, P., Buratti, C., Verdone, R.: Delay tolerant network for smart city: exploiting bus mobility. In: AEIT 2016 - International Annual Conference: Sustainable Development in the Mediterranean Area, Energy and ICT Networks of the Future, pp. 1–6 (2016)
16. Grasic, S., Lindgren, A.: Revisiting a remote village scenario and its DTN routing objective. Comput. Commun. **48**, 133–140 (2014)
17. Guo, S., et al.: Very low-cost internet access using KioskNet. Comput. Commun. Rev. **37**(5), 95–100 (2007)
18. Jain, S., Fall, K., Patra, R.: Routing in a delay tolerant network. ACM SIGCOMM Comput. Commun. Rev. **34**(4), 145 (2005)
19. Keränen, A., Ott, J., Kärkkäinen, T.: The ONE simulator for DTN protocol evaluation. In: Proceedings of the Second International ICST Conference on Simulation Tools and Techniques (2009)
20. Komnios, I., Tsapeli, F., Gorinsky, S.: Cost-effective multi-mode offloading with peer-assisted communications. Ad Hoc Netw. **25**(PB), 370–382 (2015)
21. Lopez, P.A., et al.: Microscopic traffic simulation using sumo. In: The 21st IEEE International Conference on Intelligent Transportation Systems. IEEE (2018)
22. Naidu, S., Chintada, S., Sen, M., Raghavan, S.: Challenges in deploying a delay tolerant network. In: Proceedings of the Annual International Conference on Mobile Computing and Networking, MOBICOM, pp. 65–71 (2008)

23. de Oliveira, E.C.R., et al.: Context-aware routing in delay and disruption tolerant networks. Int. J. Wireless Inf. Netw. **23**(3), 231–245 (2016). https://doi.org/10.1007/s10776-016-0315-2
24. OpenStreetMap contributors: planet dump (2017). https://planet.osm.org, https://www.openstreetmap.org
25. Pentland, A., Fletcher, R., Hasson, A.: DakNet: rethinking connectivity in developing nations. Computer **37**(1), 78–83 (2004)
26. Spyropoulos, T., Psounis, K., Raghavendra, C.S.: Spray and wait : an efficient routing scheme for intermittently connected mobile networks. In: SIGCOMM, pp. 252–259 (2005)
27. Vahdat, A., Becker, D.: Epidemic Routing for Partially-Connected Ad Hoc Networks. Technical Report CS-200006. Department of Computer Science, Duke University (2000). http://issg.cs.duke.edu/epidemic/epidemic.pdf
28. Zimmermann, T., Wirtz, H., Punal, O., Wehrle, K.: Analyzing metropolitan-area networking within public transportation systems for smart city applications. In: 2014 6th International Conference on New Technologies, Mobility and Security - Proceedings of NTMS 2014 Conference and Workshops, pp. 1–5 (2014)

Internet of Drones and Smart Mobility

Geocaching-Inspired Navigation for Micro Aerial Vehicles with Fallible Place Recognition

Michel Barbeau[1], Joaquin Garcia-Alfaro[2(✉)], and Evangelos Kranakis[1]

[1] Carleton University, Ottawa K1S 5B6, Canada
[2] Institut Polytechnique de Paris, SAMOVAR, Telecom SudParis, Palaiseau, France
jgalfaro@ieee.org

Abstract. This paper extends an existing decisional framework for the navigation of Micro Aerial Vehicle (MAV) swarms. The work finds inspiration in the geocaching outdoor game. It leverages place recognition methods, information sharing and collaborative work between MAVs. It is unique in that a priori none of the MAVs knows the trajectory, waypoints and destination. The MAVs collectively solve a series of problems that involve the recognition of physical places and determination of their GPS coordinates. Our algorithm builds upon various methods that had been created for place recognition. The need for a decisional framework comes from the fact that all methods are fallible and make place recognition errors. In this paper, we augment the navigation algorithm with a decisional framework resolving conflicts resulting from errors made by place recognition methods. The errors divide the members of a swarm with respect to the location of waypoints (i.e., some members continue the trip following the proper itinary; others follow a wrong one). We propose four decisional algorithms to resolve conflicts among members of a swarm due to place recognition errors. The performance of the decisional algorithms is modeled and analyzed.

Keywords: Micro aerial vehicle · Drone formation control · Drone swarm · Goal location · Quadcopter · Information sharing · Localization · Path planning · Navigation · Place recognition

1 Introduction

Recent developments in MAV technologies enable several applications such as inspection of infrastructures [1], parcel delivery [2] and search and rescue operations [3]. Modern MAVs are equipped with cameras, GPS and various sensors. We focus our attention on the navigation problem for a swarm of MAVs. Navigation involves the planning of a path. Existing path planning approaches use results from the robotics literature such as artificial potential function [4], random tree [5] and Voronoi diagram [6]. Specific related issues have been addressed such as obstacle avoidance [7] and embedding of computational intelligence [8].

© Springer Nature Switzerland AG 2020
L. A. Grieco et al. (Eds.): ADHOC-NOW 2020, LNCS 12338, pp. 55–70, 2020.
https://doi.org/10.1007/978-3-030-61746-2_5

In this paper, we extend a decentralized path planning algorithm for MAV swarms, originally published in [9]. This algorithm is one of a kind. At the start, the MAVs do not know the trajectory they have to follow. Each MAV is given some information that enables the recognition of places along the way. While they proceed along a path, the MAVs cooperate and determine the GPS coordinates of a series of landmarks. The MAVs use their on-board cameras and other sensors, such as microphones, to collect observational data to recognize places and determine their GPS locations. They exchange together these locations to solve simple geometric problems, that is, determination of circle foci and line and perimeter intersections. The recognition of places and resolution of geometric problems determine the waypoints and how they are related. There are numerous methods available for place recognition, including navigation systems, visual recognition, environmental sound and thermal infrared imaging (cf. [10–14] for further details). However, none of them is perfect. They all make errors. The presence of errors misleads the members of a swarm with respect to the waypoint locations. In this paper, we address the problem of conflict resolution due to place recognition errors in the context of the swarm navigation algorithm originally presented in [9].

We create a decisional framework to resolve conflicts due to errors that occur during waypoint recognition. We propose four conflict resolution algorithms assembling the replies returned by place recognition queries executed by the MAVs. In four different ways, they apply the majority rule. The first algorithm establishes a baseline and formalizes what is done originally in [9]. The second algorithm leverages the availability of multiple place recognition methods. It is a two-level process. Within each MAV, the available place recognition methods are applied. The majority's decision of the methods applied by an individual MAV is selected. Individual decisions are exchanged among the members of a swarm. The final decision is the majority's decision of the swarm. The third algorithm is a flat process. Each MAV applies all available place recognition methods. All results are exchanged with all members of a swarm. The final result is the majority's decision of all individual results obtained by all applications of the methods in a swarm. The fourth algorithm is similar to the second one, but it captures with a threshold the idea that some place recognition methods might not be even capable of producing results due to non favorable conditions (e.g., due to a high number of failures). We demonstrate through error probabilistic models that the second, third and fourth algorithms improve the performance of the baseline algorithm.

Section 2 surveys related work. Section 3 reviews the algorithm originally presented in [9]. Section 4 describes the decisional framework details of our algorithms and provides simulation results. Section 5 concludes the paper.

2   Related Work

Path planning for a swarm of MAVs involves collective movement of the ensemble from one waypoint to another, while at the same time avoiding intermediate obstacles and possibly according to a pattern. There is extensive scientific literature on the subject. Radmanesh et al. [7] made a survey on path planning with obstacle avoidance. Otto et al. [15] are concerned with path planning with a coverage goal, while Zhao et al. [8] surveyed path planning involving computational intelligence. Several path planning approaches are inspired from ideas developed for classical robotics. For example, some of these use artificial potential functions [4], random trees [5] and Voronoi diagrams [6]. Path planning may be combined with team work and formation control [16]. Some approaches have been adapted to quadcopters [17]. Similarly to other path planning algorithms, the MAVs have a common goal, i.e., a location or coverage of an area. In contrast to the others, in our algorithm the MAVs do not know what the exact goal is, i.e., the covered area or final location, until the very end.

For landmark recognition, several authors use machine learning. Maravall et al. [18,19] use probabilistic knowledge-based classification and learning automata for the recognition of patterns associated to visual landmarks. In [20], classification rules are associated to probability weights that are adapted dynamically using supervised reinforcement learning. There is an adaptation process that is conducted using a two-stage learning procedure. In the first stage, a series of variables are associated to each rule, e.g., the variables associated to the construction of a landmark recognition classifier are constructed using images' histogram features, such as standard deviation, skewness, kurtosis, uniformity and entropy. In the second stage, a series of weights is associated to every variable whereby the weights are obtained by applying a reinforcement algorithm, i.e., incremental R-L [19,20], over a random environment. This results in a specific image classifier for the recognition of landmarks, which is then loaded to the MAVs.

Related to MAV formation control, [21] assumes that the signal propagation model of a MAV has the shape of a sphere and analyzes network capacity allocation in a MAV-based network infrastructure. Furthermore, it proposes a formation algorithm that determines the 3D geographic location of each MAV. In [22], it is shown how to operate a swarm by human piloting a MAV (the leader) while the remaining followers are autonomous. A solution is proposed to synchronize and orchestrate a swarm of MAVs, based only on ad hoc communications to position MAVs. Finally, in [23], the authors formulate the multi-UAV formation reconfiguration problem as an optimal control problem with dynamical and algebraic constraints. They provide a hybrid particle swarm optimization and genetic algorithm.

The approach presented in [9] uses an information sharing path planning algorithm for MAV swarms. The swarm is expected to conduct a mission, whose final destination and entire path are unknown to the MAVs in the swarm. In order to complete the mission, MAVs are requested to cooperate and exchange information to compute and determine a series of intermediate steps by resolving a discrete localization problem. At each step, the MAVs execute a geocaching-like algorithm using navigational devices (e.g., GPS receivers) and visual references to landmarks to unravel trajectory waypoints. Together, the MAVs build a shared-information path planning process. The information sharing approach in [9] has been extended in [24] by adding research ideas inspired from search with advice over graphs [25], rings and complete network [26].

3 Incremental Path Construction Algorithm

We have introduced a navigation algorithm for a swarm of n MAVs, where n is a positive integer greater than or equal to three [9]. The algorithm is one of its kind in that it adopts an information sharing and collaborative model. It also finds inspiration in the geocaching outdoor recreational activity. We describe in the sequel its main characteristics.

3.1 Constructing a Path

A navigation path is defined by a sequence of waypoints. At the start, each individual MAV does not know what the waypoints are and what the path consists of, although every MAV in the swarm is seeded with some information. While, they progress from the origin to the destination, each MAV in the swarm has specific tasks to achieve. The completion of each of these tasks provides complementary information. The MAVs share their information with the other members of the swarm. Together, they uncover the location of each waypoint of the path.

Formally, a path consists of k waypoints $p_0, p_1, \ldots, p_{k-1}$, where k is a positive integer. The swarm starts from the point p_0. Intermediate and the final waypoints $p_1, p_2, \ldots, p_{k-1}$ are initially unknown and determined one by one. For $i = 1, \ldots, k-1$, the MAVs collectively resolve a localization challenge. For each instance of this challenge, for $j = 1, \ldots, n$, the jth MAV finds the position of a reference point q_j. Determining the reference point requires finding the precise location of a place. For instance, such a place can be a building with specific architectural characteristics, e.g., a church with a double bell tower. Before starting, the MAV is seeded with visual clues about that place. Using its camera, observational data is collected. Using this data, place recognition methods and a GPS, the precise position of the place is computed. The resulting position is a point q_j. Every MAV exchanges the location of q_j with the other members of the swarm.

Assuming the recognition of the places has been correctly conducted, all the reference points sit on the perimeter of an imaginary circle, see Fig. 1(a). The centre of this circle is set as the origin of a unit vector v. The waypoint p_i is determined by the intersection of the supporting line of v and perimeter of the circle, see Fig. 1(b). Using waypoint p_i as reference, the MAVs head in a direction defined by a direction vector d to find the reference points of the next waypoint, see Fig. 1(c). A path is a succession of "chained" waypoints, see Fig. 1(d). Before the start of the procedure, for every waypoint, every MAV receives information that will be used to recognize its reference points, such as physical characteristics. The MAV is also given the vectors v and d, for every waypoint. At each step, there is a unique circle determined by three reference points or more. The representation of vector v finds its inspiration in an outdoor recreational game called geocaching. It is hidden within the circle. An example is pictured in Fig. 2. The origin of v is located at the focus of the circle. In this example, the orientation of v is revealed by the upstream flow of the river, a clue given beforehand to the MAVs.

This navigation algorithm requires recognition of places, such as buildings and rivers. For this aspect, we depend on the research about place recognition [12,13]. Several methods have been developed, including approaches specific to building recognition [27] and applicable to recognition from the air [11,28]. While many techniques are resting on visual data, place recognition can also rely on environmental sound [10] such as flowing water, vehicular traffic or school yard. Each of the place recognition methods is fallible and has a degree of precision. It is determined empirically through testing and experimentation. In [12], precision is defined as the ratio of true positives over the sum of true positives plus the false positives. For a given method, we define the error probability as one minus its precision. This leads to a fault model for our algorithms detailed in the next sub-section.

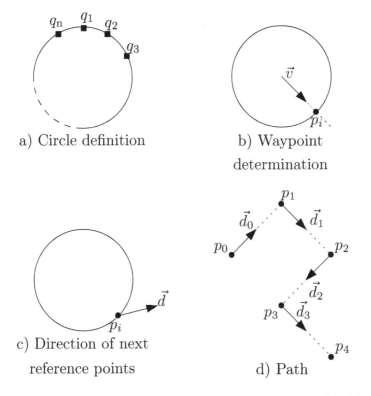

a) Circle definition

b) Waypoint
determination

c) Direction of next
reference points

d) Path

Fig. 1. Incremental path construction algorithm illustrated. Pictures (a), (b), and (c) constitute steps required to determine the next waypoint, while picture (d) depicts a resulting path.

Fig. 2. Representation of vector $\boldsymbol{v}$.

3.2   Fault Model

The algorithm originally presented in [9] solves failures in a partial manner. For instance, assume the two scenarios depicted in Fig. 3. Figure 3(a) consists of an arrangement of 11 MAVs with three faulty MAVs. Black dots represent reliable MAVs and black squares faulty MAVs. In this situation, the two non-faulty MAVs at the intersection of the two circles wrongly determine circle S' instead of circle S. If the decision to pick S or S' is according to the majority rule

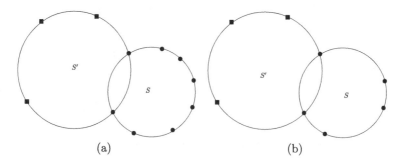

Fig. 3. Black dots represent reliable MAVs and black squares unreliable MAVs. (a) An arrangement of $n = 11$ MAVs with $f = 3$ faulty MAVs. (b) An arrangement of $n = 8$ MAVs with $f = 3$ faulty.

(six MAVs), then the whole swarm makes a correct decision (circle S).
Figure 3(b) consists of an arrangement of eight MAVs with three faulty MAVs.
Two circles are determined S and S'. The former being correct while the latter
is incorrect. Two non-faulty MAVs, at the intersection of the two circles, are
deceived by the three faulty MAVs. They participate to the determination of
the incorrect circle (S' instead of S). If the decision to pick S or S' is according to the majority rule (five MAVs), then the whole swarm makes an incorrect
decision (S').

In this paper, we address situations such as the ones depicted in Fig. 3.
The goal is to increase the probabilities that a swarm of MAVs makes correct
choices, accomplishes its mission and reaches the final destination. Errors are
due to failures to recognize places correctly by each of the different methods.
We assume that MAVs have the capability to concurrently apply several place
recognition methods. The results of the applications of the different methods by
the MAVs can be assembled together through communications and improved the
decisional procedure. Building upon the algorithm introduced in [9] and place
recognition methods, we introduce new algorithms. The recognition methods can
be faulty. Hence, the MAVs can make errors and pick wrong reference points.
For a given waypoint, they must compute together the center of a circle. In
multiple-circle situations, ambiguity is resolved using a voting procedure and
majority rules. Once a circle is determined and chosen, the swarm computes the
center and waypoint. When a waypoint is correctly computed, the MAVs in the
swarm makes a right move. In the following section, we formalize these ideas.

4   Decisional Framework

The MAVs of a swarm co-operate to accomplish a mission that consists of following a path with several waypoints. The discovery of each waypoint is achieved
using a combination of visual and sound clues, observational data, place recognition methods and GPS information. This means that the MAVs process queries
about place locations. The obtained replies are exchanged among the swarm
members. Due to place recognition errors, replies may be inconsistent. Based on
majoritarian rule, the replies are assembled together to determine a waypoint.
This procedure is repeated for each step until the destination is reached. The
resulting sequence of waypoints forms a path. In the sequel, we describe details
of the decisional framework taking into account place recognition errors and
disagreement between among swarm members.

4.1   Queries and Indicators

Let $N = \{1, 2, \ldots, n\}$ denote the set of MAVs navigating a terrain. Let $I = \{1, 2, \ldots, m\}$ be a set of indicators. Every indicator $i \in I$ may correspond to a
place recognition method.

The MAVs need to navigate a terrain. They query available indicators. At
a given location within the terrain, and for each MAV-indicator pair (u, i) a

query $Q(u, i)$ is made by MAV u. The obtained reply may be the precise GPS coordinates of a place. Besides, each reply may be wrong with probability p or correct with probability $1 - p$. The probability p may depend on the MAV u and/or indicator i being used. Further, we assume that the queries, and replies, are independent of each other, across the MAVs.

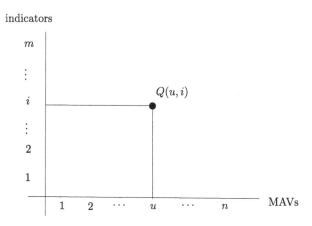

Fig. 4. Query $Q(u, i)$ made by a MAV u to indicator i.

As shown in Fig. 4, it is convenient to depict the query system in the (u, i) coordinate system with the u-axis representing the MAVs $u \in N$ and the i-axis the indicators $i \in I$. The place recognition methods associated with indicators may vary and depend on sensing and computing capabilities of the MAVs. In the sequel, it is assumed that all MAVs $u \in N$ may query exactly the same set of indicators, I.

4.2   Distributed Majority

There are two basic ways to reach a decision. Either every MAV processes queries individually or MAVs process queries together as a group. In the first way, all MAVs query a single indicator, say $i \in I$, corresponding to a single place recognition method. The MAVs exchange their replies, i.e., the reference points $q_1, q_2, \ldots, q_n$, resulting from the application of the place recognition method. The replies may be inconsistent and define several circles. To resolve conflicts, the MAVs use a majoritarian rule to select a single circle focus. This decisional process is captured in Algorithm 1.

Algorithm 1. Single Indicator

1: Every MAV $u \in N$ queries a single indicator, resulting into points $q_1, q_2, \ldots, q_n$.
2: MAVs exchange reference points $q_1, q_2, \ldots, q_n$
3: All MAVs adopt the outcome of the swarm majority, resulting into a circle focus.

Let $p_n(i)$ denote the error probability of Algorithm 1, for n MAVs all using a single common indicator $i \in I$. It is given by the following formula.

$$p_n(i) = 1 - \sum_{l=\lceil n/2 \rceil}^{n} \binom{n}{l} [1 - p(i)]^l \, p(i)^{n-l}, \tag{1}$$

where $p(i)$ is the probability that a reply to a query is correct and $1 - p(i)$ that it is wrong, for the indicator i, for all MAVs $u \in N$. Algorithm 1 corresponds to the decisional logic in [9]. However, one can go beyond a single indicator. When all MAVs use all indicators in I, then they may exchange their individual majority decisions obtained across all indicators and follow the resulting swarm majority.

In a second individualistic approach, every single MAV in N uses all available indicators in I. It applies the standard majority rule to select a reply, i.e., a reference point. The reference points are exchanged among the MAVs. The group selects the circle determined by the majority of the MAVs. The decisional process is captured in Algorithm 2.

Algorithm 2. Multiple Indicators Hierarchical

1: Every MAV $u \in N$ queries all its indicators.
2: Every MAV determines the indicator majority point q_u, $u \in 1, 2, \ldots, n$.
3: MAVs exchange reference points $q_1, q_2, \ldots, q_n$
4: All MAVs adopt the outcome of the swarm majority, resulting into a circle focus.

Let p_m denote the error probability of the majority rule for a single MAV using all m indicators,

$$p_m = 1 - \sum_{k=\lceil m/2 \rceil}^{m} \binom{m}{k} (1 - p)^k p^{m-k}, \tag{2}$$

where p is the probability that a reply to a query is correct and $1 - p$ that it is wrong, assuming that it is the same across all place recognition methods. We can also derive an equation without this assumption, indexing the probabilities over the indicators. Each MAV makes a decision independently querying all available indicators. The MAVs exchange their decisions and follow the resulting group majority. Assuming independence, the error probability of Algorithm 2 is given by the following formula.

$$p_{m,n} = 1 - \sum_{l=\lceil n/2 \rceil}^{n} \binom{n}{l} (1 - p_m)^l p_m^{n-l}, \tag{3}$$

In retrospect, there are advantages and drawbacks in Algorithms 1 and 2. On the one hand, in either case they are flexible in that one may select the indicators used in the majority decision and which are more suited to the terrain being navigated or available communication possibilities and thus save in energy and communication costs, say. On the other hand, it should be emphasized that some indicators may not be available for querying to all MAVs because of environmental conditions, say, throughout the entire waypoint navigation process. This in turn may cause additional overhead on the MAVs that are required to maintain a database of active indicators per waypoint depending on environmental conditions.

Algorithm 3 combines Algorithms 1 and 2 in a comprehensive manner in that it adjusts and updates its set of MAVs and set of indicators employed in each waypoint. As such, it may yield more accurate results. A selected subset $N' \subseteq N$ of MAVs may query a selected subset $I' \subseteq I$ of indicators. They exchange all their replies. Because place recognition methods may disagree, a single MAV may generate several reference points. The circle determined by the majority of the replies is chosen.

Algorithm 3. Multiple Indicators Flat

1: All MAVs in N' query all indicators in I', resulting into points $q_1, q_2, \ldots, q_{|N'| \cdot |I'|}$.
2: MAVs exchange reference points $q_1, q_2, \ldots, q_{|N'| \cdot |I'|}$
3: All MAVs $u \in N'$ pick the majority among all outcomes, result is a circle focus.

Let $n' = |N'|$ and $m' = |I'|$. Let $p_{m',n'}$ denote the error probability of the majority rule for MAVs in N' and indicators in I'. It is given by the following formula.

$$p_{m',n'} = 1 - \sum_{r=\lceil m'n'/2 \rceil}^{m'n'} \binom{m'n'}{r} (1-p)^r p^{m'n'-r}, \tag{4}$$

where p is the probability that a reply to a query is correct and $1 - p$ that it is wrong, for all the MAVs and all indicators. Note that Eq. (4) is the most general, for a fixed p. It subsumes Eqs. (1) and (2), as this can be seen by choosing $N' = N, I' = \{i\}$ and $N' = \{u\}, I' = I$, respectively.

An interesting point to make here is that the quality of the assembled answers depend on the reliability of the communications between the MAVs. Algorithm 3 is the most complete but also the most demanding in communication overhead while Algorithms 1 and 2 depend on more local conditions, to a certain extent.

4.3   Majority with a Threshold

The validity of Algorithms 1 and 2, and their generalization presented as Algorithm 3, hinges on the assumption that all the participating MAVs get replies to their queries. It may be the case that replies to queries are not obtained by a MAV due to harsh signal conditions (see Fig. 5). In this approach, a MAV participates in the majority algorithm when the number of obtained replies exceeds a certain predetermined threshold value.

Indicators

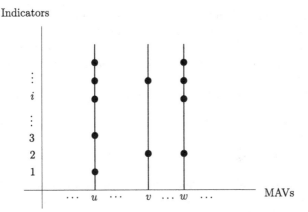

Fig. 5. Certain MAVs may not necessarily get replies for all the queries made. The MAVs u, v, w depicted are the ones for which the number of obtained replies exceeds a certain predefined threshold value.

More formally, for each MAV u let I_u be a random variable that counts the number of indicators in I that replied to a query made by u. It is natural to assume that I_u is a binomial random variable $B(q, m)$ with parameters q $(0 < q < 1)$ and m, the number of indicators. The value of q may well depend on conditions of the environment as the MAVs are navigating waypoints. The binomial random variable $B(q, m)$ could be approximated with a Poisson random variable having arrival rate $\lambda = mq$ and probability of k arrivals equal to $\frac{\lambda^k}{k!} e^{-\lambda}$, where $m \to \infty$, $q \to 0$ and $mq \to \lambda$.

We now require that the vote of a MAV u counts towards the computation of the majority if $I_u > t$, where t is a fixed predetermined threshold value. Evidently in this counting, MAVs that obtain low numbers of replies are not taken into account in the final computation of the majority. The algorithm parametrized with a threshold value t generates a set of VOTERS, namely the set of MAVs that pass the threshold t. It is formalized as Algorithm 4.

Algorithm 4. Threshold Majority (t)

1: All MAVs in N query all indicators in I.
2: MAVs with number of received replies exceeding threshold t become $VOTERS$.
3: $VOTERS$ exchange reference points.
4: Majority decision is decided among $VOTERS$.

Algorithm 4 has the advantage that it takes into account only the MAVs that have the potential to provide the most accurate majorities based on the number of reliable indicators. Ultimately, it is a MAV that judges the appropriateness of a reply or even if a reply by a particular indicator is feasible given geometric and other communication factors. However, the choice of the threshold value t may be critical. If it is too high, then the opinion of a large number of MAVs is excluded while if it is set too low the majority is cluttered with inaccurate answers. We can derive estimates on the threshold t using Chernoff bounds (see [29]). For example, we know that for $t > \lambda$, then we may have the formula.

$$\Pr[I_u > t] \leq \left(\frac{e\lambda}{t}\right)^t \cdot e^{-\lambda} \tag{5}$$

4.4   Numeric Results

Next, we discuss the numeric evaluation of Algorithms 1, 2, 3, and 4. Figure 6 have been obtained with implementation of the equations associated to each algorithm, Eqs. (1) to (5), using representative ranges of parameters. The x-axis represents a range for the indicator error probability. The y-axis plots the resulting error probability, for every algorithm. Variable m corresponds to the number of indicators. Variable n indicates the number of MAVs in the swarm. For Algorithm 4, variable v indicates the number of MAVs participating to the voting

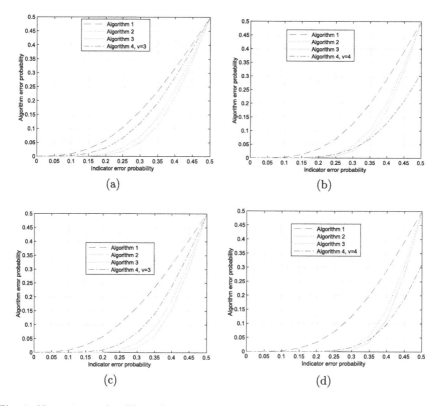

Fig. 6. Numeric results. Plots depict error probabilities, assuming (a) $m = 3$, $n = 5$; (b) $m = 3$, $n = 7$; (c) $m = 5$, $n = 5$; and (d) $m = 3$, $n = 5$.

process. The parameters associated to the indicators of each equation are based on experimental values reported in the literature, such as failure ratios expected from navigation systems, visual recognition, environmental sound and thermal infrared imaging [10–14]. As we can appreciate with the results, Algorithm 1 is always worst than all the others. For low indicator error probability, Algorithms 2, 3, and 4 have similar performance. The curves also indicate that a higher number of participating MAVs reduces the probability of errors. The same is true for the number of indicators.

4.5 Simulation Results

The numeric results reported in the previous section are extended in this section. We have implemented our decisional framework and algorithms in Java and conducted Monte Carlo simulations. In Fig. 7, the x-axis represents the number of members in a swarm. We show simulation results in which all four algorithms involve an incremental number of MAVs (from 10 to 90 MAVs), randomized failure ratios reported in the literature of navigation systems, visual recognition, environmental sound and thermal infrared imaging. The simulation aims at evaluating the chances of mission success of a swarm. Each simulation consists

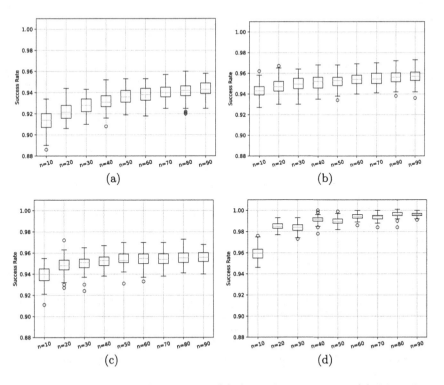

Fig. 7. Monte Carlo simulations results. (a) Algorithm 1, $m = 1$. (b) Algorithm 2, $m = 5$. (c) Algorithm 3, $m = 7$. (d) Algorithm 4, $m = 10$.

of 1000 iterations per x-axis value. The y-axis represents the success rate, i.e., number of successful iterations per x-axis value. Additional results are available in a companion website, online at github.[1]

5 Conclusion

This paper has extended an existing path planning algorithm for MAV swarms. The revisited approach assumes that MAVs collectively work to determine and solve a discrete location problem, in order to discover initially unknown intermediate landmarks. By collectively determining and sharing the landmark locations, the MAVs are able to complete their mission and reach their final destination. We assume that the process is prone to random failures. The original algorithm fails at handling situations where a series of faulty MAVs disrupt the collective procedure. It may affect the remaining MAVs to complete their mission. The new algorithms presented in this paper improve the original work. They are resilient to random failures.

The methodology proposed offers potential for additional research, exploration and testing more sophisticated majority strategies based on probability distributions that are realistic in that they are sensitive, for example to geographic location, proximity to base station and/or landmarks and available energy of the drones.

Acknowledgments. We acknowledge the financial support from the Natural Sciences and Engineering Research Council of Canada (NSERC), the European Commission (H2020 SPARTA project, under grant agreement 830892), and the SAMOVAR research laboratory of Télécom SudParis.

References

1. Aerial Robots for Sewer Inspection, "ARSI". http://echord.eu/essential_grid/arsi/. Accessed 2019
2. DHL: "DHL's Parcelcopter: changing shipping forever". http://bit.ly/2WV7KcO. Accessed 2019
3. Altigator: "Drones for search and rescue missions". https://altigator.com/drones-for-search-rescue-missions/. Accessed 2019
4. Khatib, O.: Real-time obstacle avoidance for manipulators and mobile robots. Int. J. Robot. Res. **5**(1), 90–98 (1986)
5. LaValle, S.M.: Rapidly-exploring random trees: A new tool for path planning, Department of Computer Science, Iowa State University, Technical report (1998)
6. LaValle, S.: Planning Algorithms. Cambridge University Press, New York (2006)
7. Radmanesh, M., Kumar, M., Guentert, P.H., Sarim, M.: Overview of path-planning and obstacle avoidance algorithms for UAVs: a comparative study. Unmanned Syst. **06**(02), 95–118 (2018)

---

[1] https://github.com/jgalfaro/mirrored-geomav.

8. Zhao, Y., Zheng, Z., Liu, Y.: Survey on computational-intelligence-based UAV path planning. Knowl. Based Syst. **158**, 54–64 (2018)
9. Barbeau, M., Garcia-Alfaro, J., Kranakis, E.: Geocaching-inspired resilient path planning for drone swarms. In: IEEE Conference on Computer Communications (IEEE INFOCOM 2019) Workshops, pp. 620–625, April 2019. https://doi.org/10.1109/INFCOMW.2019.8845318
10. Chu, S., Narayanan, S., Kuo, C.J.: Environmental sound recognition with time-frequency audio features. IEEE Trans. Audio Speech Lang. Process. **17**(6), 1142–1158 (2009)
11. Gehrig, M., Stumm, E., Hinzmann, T., Siegwart, R.: Visual place recognition with probabilistic voting. In: IEEE International Conference on Robotics and Automation (ICRA 2017), pp. 3192–3199 (2017)
12. Lowry, S., et al.: Visual place recognition: a survey. IEEE Trans. Robot. **32**(1), 1–19 (2016)
13. Galvez-López, D., Tardos, J.D.: Bags of binary words for fast place recognition in image sequences. IEEE Trans. Robot. **28**(5), 1188–1197 (2012)
14. Spaan, D., et al.: Thermal infrared imaging from drones offers a major advance for spider monkey surveys. Drones **3**(2), 34 (2019)
15. Otto, A., Agatz, N., Campbell, J., Golden, B., Pesch, E.: Optimization approaches for civil applications of unmanned aerial vehicles (UAVs) or aerial drones: a survey. Networks **72**(4), 411–458 (2018)
16. Turpin, M., Michael, N., Kumar, V.: Capt: concurrent assignment and planning of trajectories for multiple robots. Int. J. Robot. Res. **33**(1), 98–112 (2014)
17. Rizqi, A.A.A., Cahyadi, A.I., Adji, T.B.: Path planning and formation control via potential function for UAV quadrotor. In: 2014 International Conference on Advanced Robotics and Intelligent Systems (ARIS), pp. 165–170, June 2014
18. Maravall, D., de Lope, J., Fuentes Brea, J.P.: A vision-based dual anticipatory/reactive control architecture for indoor navigation of an unmanned aerial vehicle using visual topological maps. In: Ferrández Vicente, J.M., Álvarez Sánchez, J.R., de la Paz López, F., Toledo Moreo, F.J. (eds.) IWINAC 2013. LNCS, vol. 7931, pp. 66–72. Springer, Heidelberg (2013). https://doi.org/10.1007/978-3-642-38622-0_7
19. Maravall, D., de Lope, J., Fuentes, J.: Navigation and self-semantic location of drones in indoor environments by combining the visual bug algorithm and entropy-based vision. Front. Neurorobot. **11**, 46 (2017)
20. Narendra, K., Thathachar, M.: Learning Automata: An Introduction. Courier Corporation (2012)
21. Park, S., Kim, H., Kim, K., Kim, H.: Drone formation algorithm on 3d space for a drone-based network infrastructure. In: IEEE 27th Annual International Symposium on Personal, Indoor, and Mobile Radio Communications (PIMRC), pp. 1–6, September 2016
22. Shrit, O., Martin, S., Alagha, K., Pujolle, G.: A new approach to realize drone swarm using ad-hoc network. In: 2017 16th Annual Mediterranean Ad Hoc Networking Workshop (Med-Hoc-Net), pp. 1–5, June 2017
23. Duan, H., Luo, Q., Shi, Y., Ma, G.: Hybrid particle swarm optimization and genetic algorithm for multi-UAV formation reconfiguration. IEEE Comput. Intell. Mag. **8**(3), 16–27 (2013)
24. Barbeau, M., Garcia-Alfaro, J., Kranakis, E., Santos, F.: Quality amplification of error prone navigation for swarms of micro aerial vehicles. In: 2019 IEEE Globecom Workshops (GC Wkshps), pp. 1–6. IEEE (2019)

25. Kranakis, E., Krizanc, D.: Searching with uncertainty. In: 6th International Colloquium on Structural Information & Communication Complexity, SIROCCO 1999, Lacanau-Ocean, France, 1–3 July 1999, pp. 194–203 (1999)
26. Kirousis, L.M., Kranakis, E., Krizanc, D., Stamatiou, Y.C.: Locating information with uncertainty in fully interconnected networks. In: Herlihy, M. (ed.) DISC 2000. LNCS, vol. 1914, pp. 283–296. Springer, Heidelberg (2000). https://doi.org/10.1007/3-540-40026-5_19
27. Farfan-Escobedo, J.D., Enciso-Rodas, L., Vargas-Muñoz, J.E.: Towards accurate building recognition using convolutional neural networks. In: 2017 IEEE XXIV International Conference on Electronics, Electrical Engineering and Computing (INTERCON), pp. 1–4 (2017)
28. Mur-Artal, R., Tardós, J.D.: ORB-SLAM2: an open-source slam system for monocular, stereo, and RGB-D cameras. IEEE Trans. Robot. **33**(5), 1255–1262 (2017)
29. Mitzenmacher, M., Upfal, E.: Probability and Computing: Randomization and Probabilistic Techniques in Algorithms and Data Analysis. Cambridge University Press, New York (2017)

A Dual-Stack Communication System for the Internet of Drones

Pietro Boccadoro[1,2(✉)], Alessandro Santorsola[1], and Luigi Alfredo Grieco[1,2]

[1] Department of Electrical and Information Engineering (DEI),
Politecnico di Bari, Bari, Italy
{pietro.boccadoro,alessandro.santorsola,luigi.Alfredo.grieco}@poliba.it
[2] CNIT, Consorzio Nazionale Interuniversitario per le Telecomunicazioni,
Politecnico di Bari, Bari, Italy

Abstract. The Internet of Drones (IoD) is an emerging network architecture that leverages bidirectional communications between Unmanned Aerial Vehicles (UAVs) and a ground infrastructures. Given its versatility, the IoD is a key enabler for the evolution of sophisticated verticals, thus including Smart Cities, Industry 4.0 and Smart Transportation, to name a few. As a matter of fact, a swarm of drones can carry out real-time data gathering, industrial plants monitoring and wide area surveying. Since drones are battery-supplied systems, energy efficiency, communication reliability, and flight formation management routines become critical aspects of the IoD design. This work discusses the communication facets in a swarm of drones, leveraging the joint adoption of Bluetooth and Millimeter-Wave technologies. The proposal enables the exchange of heterogeneous data with a ground infrastructure while facilitating coordinated flight of the swarm. The resulting dual mode system optimizes energy resources, while maximizing reliability and effectiveness of drones' communications.

Keywords: IoD · Bluetooth · mmWave · 5G

1 Introduction

Unmanned Aerial Vehicles (UAVs), also known as drones, are emerging in many applications thanks to advanced sensing capabilities and wireless technologies [1,2], thus granting data gathering [3] and/or provisioning [4,5]. Furthermore, drones are characterized by a high mobility at variable altitude, which qualifies their employability in several operating scenarios, thus including delivery systems, real-time traffic monitoring and city surveillance, infrastructure inspection, search and rescue, service provisioning, and smart agriculture [2,3,6–10]. In addition, multiple UAVs can be used to assist 5G & beyond cellular systems to empower network performance toward reliable video streaming, massive data transmission and additional coverage ranges [11]. Despite this flourishing perspectives, drones require a very careful integration and optimization of computation and communication technologies to prolong battery lifetime while fulfilling service requirements.

© Springer Nature Switzerland AG 2020
L. A. Grieco et al. (Eds.): ADHOC-NOW 2020, LNCS 12338, pp. 71–83, 2020.
https://doi.org/10.1007/978-3-030-61746-2_6

The present work aims at modeling a thorough communication system for the IoD that addresses (i) reliable communication, (ii) group flight, (iii) route planning, and (iv) event management [1]. To this aim, the proposal is based on a Dual-Stack Communication System, that uses both Bluetooth and Millimeter-Wave technologies for short-range and mid-range communications, respectively. In addition, an asynchronous event management protocol has been proposed to achieve at runtime continuous route and resource optimization. To thoroughly characterize the communication performances of the swarm, several performance indexes are considered, such as the degree of message fragmentation, the duty cycle, and the waiting time. As an outcome, the performance level of the swarm has been discussed as the trade-off between the number of drones within the swarm, their contribution to the overall network traffic, as well as the mean waiting time experienced by each of them. To the best of authors' knowledge, this is the first contribution that systematically approaches the IoD to functionally design communications among drones in a swarm and to/from the ground network using these communication technologies.

This work is organized as follows: Sect. 2 presents the technological background and provides motivations for the work. Section 3 discusses the details of the proposal. Section 4 evaluates the performance of swarm communications. Section 5 concludes the work and draws future perspectives.

2 Motivations and Background

Communications in an IoD architecture are hereby classified in two different categories: (i) data exchanged for flight control purposes within the swarm (i.e., short-range communications), and (ii) information exchange between drones and the ground infrastructure (i.e., mid-range communications). To sum up, most of the relevant works already proposed by the scientific literature [2,4–10] deal with the problem connected to Ait-to-Air (A2A) and Ait-to-Ground (A2G) communications (e.g., Quality of Service (QoS)), relying on one of the following approaches:

i Only one communication technology for both A2A and A2G is considered for messages exchange [4,5,8].
ii Cellular network technologies and IEEE 802.11x are jointly adopted to improve connectivity, coverage area, and reachability [9,10].
iii Connection issues are completely neglected [2,6,7] and design efforts are devoted to advanced application layer solution for improving/enriching the set of operations and tasks that a drone can carry out.

In the first approach, no need arises to modify and/or adapt the chosen technology. Unfortunately, the choice may not simply fit all the application requirements/functions and it could be not trivial to tailor its primitives to the needs of IoD. The integration proposed in the second approach aims at capitalizing the pros of cellular networks and Wi-Fi, while counteracting their cons. In the third approach, instead, all the involved technologies underlying the application layer are left unspoken, which does not necessarily implies that implementation can be straightforward. It is worth remarking that most of these approaches do not include security-by-design, thus leaving both short-range and mid-range communications vulnerable to potential attacks in both Line of Sight (LoS) and Non Line-of-Sight (NLoS) conditions.

The communication system proposed herein deals with diversified communication technologies at design level in both A2A and A2G messages exchange. The A2A type involves drones flying together at a distance that is usually lower than 10 m. Here, the Bluetooth [12] technology, with specific reference to the Bluetooth Low Energy (BLE) version, can be a winning solution. Bluetooth uses Ultra High Frequency (UHF) in the Industrial, Scientific and Medical (ISM) Band, spanning from 2.4 to 2.485 GHz, and it is specifically designed for Personal Area Networks (PANs). Bluetooth has a high spectral efficiency, thanks to the Gaussian Frequency Shift Keying (GFSK) modulation and to the Frequency Hopping Spread Spectrum (FHSS), which are of great interest in a number of operating scenarios, such as, industrial automation [13] and drone-based ones [14]. The basic network topology can be defined as a collection of slaves operating with one master, which goes under the name of *Piconet*. Bluetooth also supports synchronized transmission from one master to multiple slaves, which may be useful for flight control messages exchange within the swarm. BLE proposes dedicated optimizations in terms of energy consumption, which can be very useful in the context of energy constrained UAVs.

On the other hand, each drone must exchange messages with the reference ground infrastructure. To enable these A2G communications, the 5G technological landscape proposes several interesting candidates and, among them, Millimeter-Waves (mm-Waves) technology seems to be the most promising [5]. In fact, it grants the efficient support of billions of users leveraging seamless connectivity with high traffic volumes support (i.e., multi-gigabit data-rate) with very low latencies. mmWave accounts for massive connectivity, high throughput and spectral efficiency, thanks to new modulation and multiple access schemes [15]. In particular, the frequency range in the Extremely High Frequency (EHF) 24–28 GHz bands [5] will be considered because propagation-related problems and variable channel response will be negligible [15–17] in the reference applications [11,16].

Considering all of the above, 5G mmWave-based communications are hereby proposed for a joint adoption with Bluetooth.

3   The Proposed Approach

The reference IoD scenario (as depicted in Fig. 1) involves a swarm of drones with a given mission plan which goes from a starting point (i.e., point A) to an ending one (i.e., point B). To reach the destination, the drones will cross a certain number of way-points indicated as Global Position System (GPS) coordinates.

During the mission, each UAV in the swarm carries out a number of georeferenced *Basic Queries*, with several purposes (e.g., collecting images, video

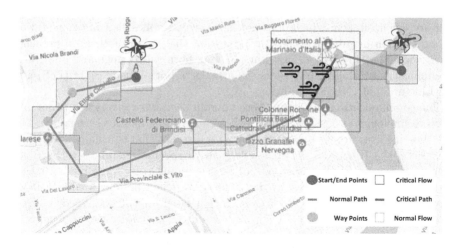

Fig. 1. Mission example with details on the flight plan.

streams or gathering data from sensor networks). Information retrieval is carried out through on-board or ground sensors [2,18]. Additional information are linked to drones' management, e.g., battery status, mission status updates, and presence of obstacles, if any. Drones are also exchanging information related to their GPS positions, Roll-Pitch-Yaw (RPY) angles, battery status, and a timestamp. The whole set of data is represented as an informational vector, i.e., $\overline{V}$. To associate each information to a specific drone, the Medium Access Control (MAC) address can be used as ID.

The message exchange is made by: (i) communications within the swarm, and (ii) from drones to the ground infrastructure. In the first case, slave drones send information to the master-drone with periodicity $\bar{t}$ (in seconds). Data acquired during the mission by each slave (i.e. images, video and sensors data) are sent autonomously, according to a specific decision algorithm, to the ground infrastructure. In this way, all data coming from each drone in the swarm can be sent to the ground infrastructure, without specifically requiring messages aggregation. To identify both the source and the exact location, the ID of the drone must be included, as well as the GPS-related information. In the second, instead, the master-drone sends the $N-1$ information vectors $\overline{V}$, composing the so-called Table of References (ToR), to a ground infrastructure (as in [4]), a task that is accomplished at regular time intervals, namely Δ ($\sim$60 s), being $\bar{t} < \Delta$. This value can be fine-tuned on the basis of the information of interest (e.g., positions and angles). It is worth noting that time synchronization can be easily achieved thanks to time information within GPS data. The overall message exchange in the reference IoD architecture is depicted in Fig. 2 and the described dataset is summarized in Table 1.

In real scenarios, adverse weather conditions may arise while the mission is ongoing. Once detected, and suddenly communicated to the ground management infrastructure, a new path will be calculated for each drone to avoid the critical flight zone. As a result, a certain number of *Enforced Queries* can be carried out by drones in an asynchronous way. Once the critical event is no longer threatening the mission, the *Basic Queries* can be restored.

To monitor the status of the mission, it is herein proposed an Event Management System (EMS), which is acting as a task scheduler and process flow control algorithm. In particular, the Finite State Machine (FSM) (see Fig. 3a) models a process that starts from the situation in which, while on-the-fly, the drone keeps its attitude toward destination. Once an event of interest, i.e., *trigger event*, is detected the EMS handles the upload of a new route coming from the ground infrastructure and then the system moves to the *Restart* state. During this state the previous operations that have been stopped will be resumed. From this point on, the mission may start back again from where the mission plan was interrupted.

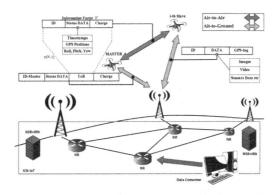

Fig. 2. Messages exchange among entities.

Table 1. Table of data-related notations and communication direction.

Name	Symbol	Unit	A2A	A2G
Reference time instant	$\bar{t}$	[s]	✓	✓
Position over x-axis (i.e., Longitude)	x_i	Degree	✓	
Position over y-axis (i.e., Latitude)	y_i	Degree	✓	
Position over z-axis (i.e., Altitude)	z_i	[m]	✓	
Initial drones position vector in $\bar{t}$	$P_{\bar{t}}$	$\mathbb{R}$	✓	
Average number of expected movements	j	$\mathbb{Z}$		✓
Distance covered during the j-th movement	D_j	[m]	✓	✓
Drone speed over the j-th movement	v_j	m/s	✓	✓
Energy intake over D_j for the i-th drone	E_j^{i-th}	[J]	✓	✓
Overall energy intake for the i-th drone	E^{i-th}	[J]	✓	✓
Mission duration	T	[s]		✓
Speed of a drone	v	[km/h]		✓
Information vector	$\overline{V}$	(Tuple) Angles		✓

3.1   Energy Efficiency

While drones are moving, distances among them may vary, frequently and suddenly. The energy intake minimization is referred to the movements within a certain reference area, subdivided with an $x \times y$ grid structure (see Fig. 3b). To identify obstacles, or no-flying zones, each intersection (i.e., GPS point) can be marked as variable or not.

Let be $P_{\bar{t}}$ a vector of drones' (initial) positions at time $\bar{t}$, and $P_{\bar{t}+1}$ the vector at time $\bar{t} + 1$, with $\bar{t} \in [0, +\infty[$. In a swarm of N drones, it is possible to identify their positions in a three-dimensional space thanks to the triple (x_i, y_i, z_i), where (x_i, y_i) represent longitudinal and latitudinal coordinates while z_i represents the altitude (i.e., the quota). The energy consumption for the i-th drone, with $i \in \{1, 2, ...N\}$, can be expressed as a function of the distance D_{ij} between two consecutive points and the speed v_{ij}. Let S be the estimated number of movements that are needed to reach the destination position for each drone, $j \in \{1, 2, ..., S\}$. The energy consumption for the i-th drone over the distance D_{ij} can be expressed as a function of the power $p(v_{ij})$ over time:

$$E_{ij}(D_{ij}, v_{ij}) = \int_{t=0}^{t=(\frac{D_{ij}}{v_{ij}})} p(v_{ij}) \, dt = \frac{p(v_{ij})}{v_{ij}} D_{ij} \tag{1}$$

Since the maximum battery capacity for each drone is fixed to C, the overall energy expenditure for the i-th drone is: $E_i = \sum_{j=1}^{S} E_{ij}(D_{ij}, v_{ij}) \leq C$. To find the minimum path it is necessary to minimize E_i.

A possible solution to the problem is proposed in Algorithm 1. It is assumed to be executed by the ground infrastructure and is used to create an oriented cyclic graph in which each node represents a possible position (i.e., a waypoint in the mission plan). The algorithm iteratively detects all the nodes close to the current one. For each of them, D_{ij} and E_{ij} will be computed to state which of the nodes will be the following one in the path. The values of D_{ij} and E_{ij} for the new node are stored and associated to the path between the two nodes. The procedure is iterated until either (i) the mission is over, and hence destination is reached, or (ii) an emergency landing is triggered.

3.2   Swarm Formation

The flight of a swarm can be considered as a two-folded problem. First, keeping/changing attitude over time can be referred to the mechanics of the flight. Second, the underlying criteria could be due to topological control and effective data communications. In fact, the constant update of the respective positions of drones in a swarm may have a non negligible impact on data rates, latencies and QoS. Without loss of generality, this work assumes a sphere as the reference geometry, with the master-drone in the center and the slave-drones displaced as shown in Fig. 4. Under these conditions, all drones will be placed at constant distance from the master-drone without influencing each other. 2-D circular geometries for the formation of swarm of robots represent a winning

---

Algorithm 1: Minimum-Energy Path Algorithm

Input : Geographical Zone G
Output: Minimum-Path Vector P

1 *Subdivide G in a $X \times Y$ grid;*
2 *Mark each point as Not-Available, if any;*
3 SET Start.Pos $\leftarrow$ *Position A;*
4 SET End.Pos $\leftarrow$ *Position B;*
5 SET drone speed to v;
6 **foreach** *Drone* **do**
7   SET $P_{\bar{t}}[i]$=Start.Pos ;
8   INSERT Root.Node $\leftarrow$ [Start.Pos,ID.rootnode];
9   INSERT End.Node $\leftarrow$ [End.Pos,ID.endnode];
10   **foreach** *Node l of z* **do**
11   **while** $P_{\bar{t}}[i]$ *is not End.Pos* **do**
12   *Identify $P_{\bar{t}+1}[i]$ and $P_{\bar{t}}[i]$ closer to End.Pos;*
13   **if** $P_{\bar{t}+1}[i]$ *is available* **then**
14   SET Candidate.Pos[k] $\leftarrow$ $P_{\bar{t}+1}[i]$
15   **foreach** *element of Candidate.Pos* **do**
16   *Calculate:*
17                 $D_{ij}(Candidate.Pos[k], P_{\bar{t}}[i]);$
18                 $E_{ij}(D_{ij}, v);$
19   **if** *Position Candidate.Pos[k] has been already considered* **then**
20   ADD Link [E_{ij}, ID.parentnode];
21   l++;
22   **else**
23   INSERT Leaf.Node s.t. :
24   Leaf.Node.$P_{\bar{t}}[i]$ = Candidate.Pos[k];
25   SET ID.leafnode ;
26   Create LinkTAB ;
27   ADD Link [E_{ij}, ID.parentnode];
28   z++ ;
29   l++;
30   P $\leftarrow$ Route(ID.rootnode, ID.endnode);
31   Calculate E_i;
32   **if** $E_i < C$ **then**
33   P is admissible
34   **else**
35   P is not admissible since the solution does not respect the energy constraint

---

strategy in symmetric contexts [19]. Hence, the sphere can be considered as the most straightforward solution for UAVs, since they are capable of moving in a 3-D space.

3.3   Link Analysis

To provide a dedicated link analysis, the following assumptions are done: (i) the N drones are identical, (ii) the real-time management of the mission is carried out by the ground infrastructure, (iii) positions and status data of each drone are communicated to ground by the master-drone, and (iv) each drone sends images, videos and sensors data to the ground-base independently. Table 2 summarized all the entities and symbols used hereby.

Table 2. Summary of notation.

Name	Symbol	Domain	Unit
Number of frames	F	$\mathbb{N}$	#
Transmission time	T_f	Time	s
Interframe time	T_IF	$\{150 \times 10^{-6}\}$	s
Total transmission time	T_{FS}	Time	s
Number of timeslots	N_{TS}	$\{1,3,5\}$	#
Master-slave transmission time	T_{M-S}	Time	s
Service time	T_S	Time	s
Slot probabilities	p_1, p_3, p_5	[0,1]	#
Packet arrivals rate	λ	$\mathbb{N}$	Packets/Slot
Average waiting time	$\bar{W}$	Time	s
Average packet length	L	$\mathbb{N}$	Bit
GPS message dimension	γ	$\mathbb{N}$	Byte
Minimum number of detections	m	$\mathbb{N}$	/
Minimum number of GPS positions	α	$\mathbb{N}$	/
Number of sensors	β	$\mathbb{N}$	/
RPY data	RPY	$\mathbb{R}$	Degree

5G links are proposed to be used by master-drone and slave-drones to send information to ground; this is motivated by the fact that they offer multi-gigabit data-rate and low latencies, thus allowing huge transmission in extremely brief time. In a single detection, assuming to use double-type attributes, with β sensors that carry out m surveys, there will be $8\beta m$ bytes to be transmitted for each drone. Of course, images and videos are far bigger when compared to sensors data (e.g., $10-100$ MB for images, and ~ 1 GB for video). In Table 3, the whole set of information to be communicated via 5G link from the swarm to the ground infrastructure is summarized.

In A2A communications, instead, the exchange of information vectors V_i takes place for each slave $i \in [0, N-2]$, toward the master (see Table 4). The master and the slaves are in communication using a time-slotted Symmetric Piconet and the polling scheme is a standard Time Division Duplex (TDD)

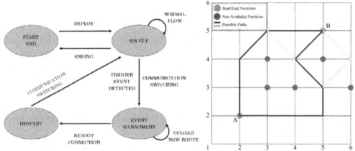

(a) Finite State Diagram of the EMS. (b) Examples of reference grid.

Fig. 3. Mission plan handling, via the proposed (a) EMS, and (b) a concrete example of possible updates.

Table 3. Details on data types (and estimated size) handled by the slaves and the master in the swarm and associated to A2G communications.

	Slaves			Master
Type of data	*Sensors Data*	*Images*	*Videos*	*Table of References Master Data (M-BS)*
Size [B]	$\sim GB$			132 N m +14

Table 4. Details on the information (and estimated size) within messages flowing from the master drone to the slave ones, and viceversa, in A2A communications.

	Slaves to master	Master to slaves
Type of data	*ID Positioning Data Battery StatusRPY DataTimestamp*	*Control Data*
Size [B]	132 m + 14	(N-1) α (γ + 6 + Int + RPY)

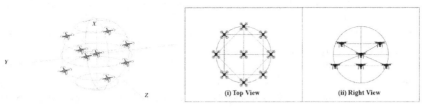

(a) Swarm Formation in 3D.   (b) (i) (YZ plane), (ii) (XZ plane).

Fig. 4. The proposed swarm formation.

multiplexing [20]. The master-drone sends a *Data Request Packet* every $k \in \{1, 3, 5\}$ timeslots to each slave. Once a *Data Request Packet* is received, each slave sends its V_i.

Considering that slaves-to-master communications are based on GPS messages γ of about 100 B, each V_i is composed by $m\gamma$ bytes, where m represents the number of surveys needed to create the mission plan. Similar considerations can be done for the data communicated by the drones, i.e., battery status. Assuming to map these information with a double-type attribute, there will be (i) $8m$ B, (ii) 6 B for the Drone ID (MAC Address Network Card), (iii) 24 B for the RPY, and (iv) 8 B for the timestamp.

As for master-to-slaves communications, instead, collision avoidance must be considered as a priority. Similarly, the presence of obstacles or adverse weather conditions, must be handled at runtime. In this case, the master has to communicate to each slave a set of GPS positions describing the new route. Here, α is the minimum number of GPS points needed to avoid an obstacle, while satisfying the battery optimization criterion. Therefore, a total of $(N-1)\alpha(\gamma+6+Int)B$ will be sent. It is worth specifying that Int represents an integer value used by the EMS to trigger route changes. Similarly, there will also be a total of $(N-1)\alpha RPY$ for attitude correction. Bluetooth channels use a Frequency-Hop/Time-Division-Duplex (FH/TDD), with 625 μs-long time slots [12,20].

For the sake of simplicity, it is assumed that each slave drone has infinite buffer and that packets are generated according to a *Poisson Arrival Process*. The arrival rate to each active queue is λ *packets/slot* and service time is a discrete random variable k that can assume values in the range $\{1, 3, 5\}$ with probability $p_k = 1/3$. Further, the inter-arrival time is exponential and there's only one server (i.e., the channel). Hence, the queue can be modeled as an $M/G/1$. Hence, each slave will be characterized by a certain waiting time with non-negligible impact on network performance.

4   Performance Evaluation

The reference technologies have different network performance, e.g., latencies and data-rates, in both uplink and downlink. In particular, since the BLE technology is extremely constrained when compared to mmWave 5G (i.e., 2 Mbps for BLE and 2 Gbps for 5G), the attention is focused on the achievable network performance in the uplink phase in the swarm. The solution can be characterized in terms of degree of message fragmentation, duty cycle, and waiting time.

The degree of fragmentation depends on (i) the amount of data to be transmitted, and (ii) the number of surveys (i.e., m) carried out by the drones. Since each Bluetooth frame has a 255 B payload [12], sending each information vector V_i may take F frames. Even assuming an *Uncoded* Bluetooth frame, that has a size of 264 B, more than one frame is needed to send a single vector V_i. The time taken for sending a frame can be expressed as a function of the amount of data to be transmitted. The total transmission time will be $T_{FS} = FT_f + (F-1)(T_{IF})$. It is observed that the larger the frame number, the longer the overall time taken to complete data transmission. As a side-effect, more energy is needed for a complete transmission to take place. It is worth noting that, in real cases, the probability of filling the non-infinite buffer on each drone is higher. Without loss of generality, it is herein assumed that the control on transmission errors (due to packet collisions, interference and propagation errors), and re-transmissions are demanded to upper layer functionalities.

The active period of each slave, i.e., the time period during which the slave sends data to the master, can be defined in terms of duty cycle and waiting time. The *Duty Cycle* δ can be expressed as: $\delta = \frac{T_{FS}}{T_{tot}} = \frac{T_{FS}}{(N-1)T_{FS}+T_{M-S}+T_{M-BS}}$ where T_{M-BS} is the time taken by the master-drone to send the ToR and its status data with a 5G link. Figure 5a shows the *Duty Cycle* as a function of the swarm population. δ decreases as α (hence, the number of GPS positions required) increases. This is motivated by the fact that the term T_{M-S} becomes dominant. It clearly results that m and α are design parameters can be fine tuned to address specific requirements and/or QoS criteria. The service time T_S is modeled as $T_S = x_k = k \times 625\,\mu s$. Given a probability value for the slot length $p_k = 1/3$, the mean service time results to be $E[T_S] = \sum_{k=1}^{3} x_k p_k$ and the mean waiting time is: $\bar{W} = E[T_S]\left(\frac{(E[T_S]^2+V[T_S])}{2E[T_S]^2}\frac{\bar{\rho}}{1-\bar{\rho}}\right)$, where $\bar{\rho}$ represents the mean uplink load. For the sake of simplicity, the value of α is kept constant, and a mean value for δ is considered to average all the possible values of m surveys. In Fig. 5b, the mean waiting time is represented as a function of the uplink load. Assuming a fixed value for α, it results that the higher the number of GPS coordinates sent, the higher the mean waiting time. At the same time, $\bar{W}$ increases with the swarm population. To sum up, it has been verified that a 9% variation of the mean waiting time is observed as the population increases by 35%. Given a value for the uplink load, instead, the waiting time is sensibly (i.e., 57%) reduced when the population of the swarm drops from 8 to 5 slaves.

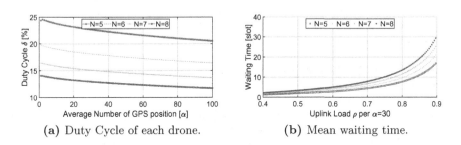

(a) Duty Cycle of each drone.   (b) Mean waiting time.

Fig. 5. Performance evaluation of Slave-to-Master communications.

5   Conclusions

This work proposed a Dual-Stack Communications system, based on mmWave and Bluetooth, for the emerging IoD network infrastructure. The proposal is strengthened by an EMS that solves viability problems and optimizes trajectories, thus limiting energy expenditures. Further, a criteria has been derived to trade-off between duty-cycling and mean waiting time in drones' swarms. Despite the discussed assessments, in the future, the assumed upper-bound to drones' population should be exceeded. At the same time, different geometries may be evaluated. Among the major stakeholders for future researches there are control and management mechanisms for flight coordination and trajectory correction. Machine learning could be used to dynamic formation handling. To reach these ambitious goals, dedicated network and system level simulation tools will be involved [21].

Acknowledgments. This work was partially supported by the Italian MIUR PON projects Pico&Pro (ARS01 01061), AGREED (ARS01 00254), FURTHER (ARS01 01283), and RAFAEL (ARS01 00305), by the PRIN project no. 2017NS9FEY entitled "Realtime Control of 5G Wireless Networks: Taming the Complexity of Future Transmission and Computation Challenges" funded by the Italian MIUR, and by the Apulia Region (Italy) Research projects INTENTO (36A49H6).

References

1. Gharibi, M., Boutaba, R., Waslander, S.L.: Internet of drones. IEEE Access **4**, 1148–1162 (2016)
2. Motlagh, N.H., Taleb, T., Arouk, O.: Low-altitude unmanned aerial vehicles-based internet of things services: comprehensive survey and future perspectives. IEEE Internet Things J. **3**(6), 899–922 (2016)
3. Mozaffari, M., Saad, W., Bennis, M., Nam, Y.-H., Debbah, M.: A tutorial onuavs for wireless networks: applications, challenges, and open problems. IEEE Commun. Surv. Tutor. **21**(3), 2334–2360 (2019)
4. Boccadoro, P., Losciale, M., Piro, G., Grieco, L.A.: A standard-compliant and information-centric communication platform for the internet of drones. In: European Wireless 2018; 24th European Wireless Conference, May 2018, pp. 1–6 (2018)
5. Gapeyenko, M., Petrov, V., Moltchanov, D., Andreev, S., Himayat, N., Koucheryavy, Y.: Flexible and reliable UAV-assisted backhaul operation in 5G mmWave cellular networks. IEEE J. Sel. Areas Commun. **36**(11), 2486–2496 (2018)
6. Sayler, K.: A world of proliferated drones: a technology primer, a world of proliferated drones series. Arms Control Today **45**, 7 (2015)
7. Hall, R.J.: An internet of drones. IEEE Internet Comput. **20**(3), 68–73 (2016)
8. Rahman, M.A.: Enabling drone communications with wimax technology. In: IISA 2014, The 5th International Conference on Information, Intelligence, Systems and Applications, July 2014, pp. 323–328 (2014)
9. Alzenad, M., Shakir, M.Z., Yanikomeroglu, H., Alouini, M.: FSO-based vertical backhaul/fronthaul framework for 5G+ wireless networks. IEEE Commun. Mag. **56**(1), 218–224 (2018)
10. Lin, X., et al.: The sky is not the limit: LTE for unmanned aerial vehicles. IEEE Commun. Mag. **56**(4), 204–210 (2018)
11. Meng, S., Su, X., Wen, Z., Dai, X., Zhou, Y., Yang, W.: Robust drones formation control in 5g wireless sensor network using mmWave. Wirel. Commun. Mob. Comput. **2018**, 1–7 (2018)
12. Bluetooth, Bluetooth Core Specification v5.0, 06 December 2016. https://www.bluetooth.com/specifications/bluetooth-core-specification

13. Frotzscher, A., et al.: Requirements and current solutions of wireless communication in industrial automation. In: IEEE International Conference on Communications Workshops (ICC), June 2014, pp. 67–72 (2014)
14. Shin, H., Choi, K., Park, Y., Choi, J., Kim, Y.: Security analysis of FHSS-type drone controller. In: Kim, H.-W., Choi, D. (eds.) WISA 2015. LNCS, vol. 9503, pp. 240–253. Springer International Publishing, Cham (2016). https://doi.org/10. 1007/978-3-319-31875-2_20
15. Cai, Y., Qin, Z., Cui, F., Li, G.Y., McCann, J.A.: Modulation and multiple access for 5G networks. IEEE Commun. Surv. Tutor. **20**(1), 629–646 (2018)
16. Khawaja, W., Ozdemir, O., Guvenc, I.: UAV air-to-ground channel characterization for mmWave systems. In: 2017 IEEE 86th Vehicular Technology Conference (VTC-Fall), September 2017, pp. 1–5 (2017)
17. Marcano, A.S., Christiansen, H.L.: Performance of non-orthogonal multiple access (NOMA) in mmwave wireless communications for 5g networks. In: International Conference on Computing, Networking and Communications (ICNC), January 2017, pp. 969–974 (2017)
18. Orsino, A., et al.: Effects of heterogeneous mobility on D2D-and drone-assisted mission-critical MTC in 5G. IEEE Commun. Mag. **55**(2), 79–87 (2017)
19. Xue, Z., Zeng, J.: Circle formation control of large-scale intelligent swarm systems in a distributed fashion. In: Yu, W., He, H., Zhang, N. (eds.) ISNN 2009. LNCS, vol. 5552, pp. 1105–1115. Springer, Heidelberg (2009). https://doi.org/10.1007/978-3-642-01510-6_125
20. Zussman, G., Segall, A., Yechiali, U.: On the analysis of the bluetooth time division duplex mechanism. IEEE Trans. Wirel. Commun. **6**(6), 2149–2161 (2007)
21. Grieco, G., Artuso, R., Boccadoro, P., Piro, G., Grieco, L.: An open source and system-level simulator for the internet of drones. In: Proceedings of IEEE International Workshop on Internet of Mobile Things (IoMT), in conjunction with PIMRC 2019, Istanbul, Turkey, September 2019

Consensus-Based Algorithms for Controlling Swarms of Unmanned Aerial Vehicles

Raffaele Carli[1] , Graziana Cavone[1] , Nicola Epicoco[2(✉)] ,
Mario Di Ferdinando[2] , Paolo Scarabaggio[1] , and Mariagrazia Dotoli[1]

[1] Department of Electrical and Information Engineering,
Polytechnic of Bari, Bari, Italy
{raffaele.carli,graziana.cavone,paolo.scarabaggio,
mariagrazia.dotoli}@poliba.it
[2] Center of Excellence DEWS, Department of Information Engineering,
Computer Science and Mathematics, University of L'Aquila, L'Aquila, Italy
{nicola.epicoco,mario.diferdinando}@univaq.it

Abstract. Multiple Unmanned Aerial Vehicles (multi-UAVs) applications are recently growing in several fields, ranging from military and rescue missions, remote sensing, and environmental surveillance, to meteorology, logistics, and farming. Overcoming the limitations on battery lifespan and on-board processor capabilities, the coordinated use of multi-UAVs is indeed more suitable than employing a single UAV in certain tasks. Hence, the research on swarm of UAVs is receiving increasing attention, including multidisciplinary aspects, such as coordination, aggregation, network communication, path planning, information sensing, and data fusion. The focus of this paper is on defining novel control strategies for the deployment of multi-UAV systems in a distributed time-varying set-up, where UAVs rely on local communication and computation. In particular, modeling the dynamics of each UAV by a discrete-time integrator, we analyze the main swarm intelligence strategies, namely flight formation, swarm tracking, and social foraging. First, we define a distributed control strategy for steering the agents of the swarm towards a collection point. Then, we cope with the formation control, defining a procedure to arrange agents in a family of geometric formations, where the distance between each pair of UAVs is predefined. Subsequently, we focus on swarm tracking, defining a distributed mechanism based on the so-called leader-following consensus to move the entire swarm in accordance with a predefined trajectory. Moreover, we define a social foraging strategy that allows agents to avoid obstacles, by imposing on-line a time-varying formation pattern. Finally, through numerical simulations we show the effectiveness of the proposed algorithms.

This work received funding from the Italian University and Research Ministry under project RAFAEL (National Research Program, contract No. ARS01_00305) and from the European Union's Horizon 2020 programme under project Comp4Drones (ECSEL Joint Undertaking RIA-2018, grant agreement No. 826610).

L. A. Grieco et al. (Eds.): ADHOC-NOW 2020, LNCS 12338, pp. 84–99, 2020.
https://doi.org/10.1007/978-3-030-61746-2_7

Keywords: Unmanned Aerial Vehicles · Swarm intelligence · Trajectory control

1   Introduction

In the last decade, there has been an increasingly research interest in developing control techniques for Unmanned Aerial Vehicles (UAVs), thanks to their capability to perform complex tasks in dangerous situations where the human intervention is prevented.

UAVs vary in weight, size, type, altitude, payload, and many other factors (see [9]). One of the most common UAV, extensively used in practical applications, is the quadcopter (see, for instance, the work in [10]). Many control strategies have been proposed in the literature concerning the position control of UAVs, and particularly of quadcopters (see, for instance, the earlier contributions in [3,13,21]). In particular, one of the main investigated topics is the path planning strategy, which is often used to implement a collision avoidance behavior (see, for instance, [11,14,22]).

More recently, inspired by the flocking behavior of several animal species (such as birds, fishes, and insects), and thanks to the development of new technologies, many results concerning the formation control of large numbers of UAVs have been provided (see, [6] and the comprehensive introduction in [2]).

The great interest on this topic is mainly due to the fact that the demand for the use of swarms of UAVs is recently growing in several field, such as military and rescue missions, remote sensing and environmental surveillance (including farming applications), logistics, as well as traffic surveillance, civil infrastructure inspection, weather forecasting, hazardous cleanup, etc. In effect, it is well-known that a swarm of agents, in which each agent locally interacts with the other agents and the environment, is able to perform complex tasks which are not achievable by the use of a single agent.

Therefore, the use of multiple UAVs as an organized swarm can significantly increase the performances of the single UAV, as well as of the overall group [1,7, 10,23]. Indeed, each agent of the swarm is allowed to make use of the resources and capabilities of other agents through communication and/or coordination, and provide it with extra capabilities. On the other hand, this framework clearly requires the use of more than one sensor, actuator, or payload.

A fundamental coordination problem in swarms of UAVs is the formation control problem, whose objective is to continuously maintain, in the most optimal way, the desired formation while the team motion proceeds. Indeed, in common applications, it is often required that agents are arranged in a suitable shape in order to perform the desired task. In addition, multi-agents perform best when kept in a fixed formation relative to one another, which ensures an intelligent path planning and avoids collisions when the swarm moves from the initial location to a specified destination [17,26].

Many approaches to the formation control problem of UAVs have been presented in the literature, among which, the most commonly adopted are the following:

- the consensus approach (see, e.g., the contributions in [4,5,8,16,24–29]), where each agent updates its state based on the communication with its neighbor agents, and finally achieves the consistency of all agents states;
- the leader-follower approach (see, e.g., [20,31]), whose aim is to select one of the agents as the leader (who tracks the predefined trajectories), while the others agents are the followers (who track the leader according to a given scheme);
- the virtual structure approach (see, for instance, [12,30]), which is based on the assumption that agents represent the vertices of a rigid virtual structure, and as such each agent only needs to track the virtual point on this virtual structure. Although this approach can ensure a high precision, it requires high communication and computing power;
- the behavior-based approach (see [15]), which is inspired by the behavior of biological groups, requiring the definition of several basic control behaviors of agents, and the definition of formation control instructions for each agent, defined by a weighted average of the desired behaviors.

It is to be noticed that the above methodologies can be combined each other. In particular, a consensus between agents can be reached even when a leader-follower approach, a virtual structure, or a behavior-based approaches are first applied. Therefore, consensus has received a great attention in the recent years. In effect, it has a distributed nature (which stands out with the aim of achieving a common objective by using local information [19]) and therefore it does not require the acquisition of the entire information on the formation, thus reducing computational costs as well as the required communication bandwidth [18]. Moreover, through a consensus approach, the damage or destruction of individuals has little effect on the overall formation, which makes the consensus algorithm robust, adaptable, and expandable [29].

Among the already recalled contributions on consensus-based formation control of multi-UAVs systems, the work in [24] proposes a consensus-based feedback linearization method to design a leaderless formation control law for quadrotors, such that a desired time-varying formation can be achieved. The consensus problem in the case of time-delay systems is studied in [28], showing that a leader-follower consensus approach can efficiently compensate both delays and disturbances. Experiments concerning the outdoor time-varying formation flight for multi-quadrotor systems are shown in [4]. In [5], second-order multi-agent systems for multi-quadrotors with switching interaction topologies are analyzed for the case where the states of the followers form a predefined time-varying formation while tracking the state of the leader. A distributed linear-quadratic regulator controller based on the consensus approach is proposed in [16] to control heterogeneous multi-agent systems (i.e., quadrotors and two wheeled mobile robots) so that they cooperatively accomplish some tasks. In [26] a decentralized hybrid swarm control mechanism for quadrotor helicopters is presented, showing that, through the decentralized approach, a group of agents is able to successfully achieve the desired formation and follow predefined paths without any collision. Finally, in [29], a distributed control law based on the consensus approach is designed for multi-quadrotor systems.

Table 1 summarizes the recalled state of the art on multi-UAVs. In particular, for each of the above contributions, Table 1 shows the approach adopted to solve the formation control problem (columns from 2 to 5) and the main features (columns from 6 to 9).

Table 1. Literature contributions on multi-UAVs: adopted approaches for the formation control and addressed features.

	Approach adopted for the formation control problem				Addressed features			
	Consensus	Leader-follower	Virtual structure	Behaviour based	Time-varying formation	Switching topology	Collision avoidance	Additional features
[4]	X				X			
[5]	X	X			X	X		
[12]			X		X			
[15]				X			X	
[16]	X				X	X		
[20]	X	X						
[26]	X				X	X		
[25]	X	X			X			
[26]	X						X	
[27]	X							Input-delay
[28]	X	X						Disturbances Input-delay
[29]	X	X						
[30]	X	X	X		X		X	
[31]	X	X					X	

By analyzing Table 1, it is evident a lack of literature contributions that simultaneously allow to take into account a time-varying formation and a switching topology, while ensuring the collision avoidance of multi-UAVs. Therefore, in order to overcome the encountered limitations of the recalled literature contributions, in this paper we propose a distributed control strategy for swarms of UAVs based on the leader-follower consensus approach under a time-varying topology. More in detail, the dynamics of each UAV is modeled by a discrete-time integrator to analyze the main swarm intelligence strategies in terms of flight formation, swarm tracking, and social foraging. First, we define a distributed control strategy for steering the agents of the swarm towards a collection point. Then, we cope with the formation control defining a procedure to arrange agents in a family of geometric formations, where the distance between each pair of UAVs is predefined. Subsequently, we focus on the swarm tracking defining a distributed mechanism based on the so-called leader-follower consensus to move the entire swarm in accordance with a predefined trajectory. Moreover, we define a social foraging strategy that allows agents to avoid obstacles, by imposing on-line a time-varying formation pattern. We finally perform some numerical simulations to show the effectiveness of proposed algorithms.

We highlight that, with respect to the current state of the art in the field of control techniques for multi-UAVs, in this work we simultaneously address a challenging time-varying distributed set-up characterized by the following features:

- each UAV has limited resources in terms of communication coverage, so that it can only receive information locally from a time-varying subset of the swarm;
- the UAVs are required to dynamically avoid obstacles by imposing on-line a time-varying formation pattern;
- both the topology of communication and the configuration of leader and followers are time-varying.

The paper is organized as follows. Section 2 presents some preliminaries on the addressed swarm control problems. In Sect. 3 we discuss the system model and we present the distributed algorithms for controlling swarms of UAVs. In Sect. 3 the results obtained from the numerical experiments are illustrated and analyzed. Lastly, conclusions and remarks for future work are presented in Sect. 4.

2   Preliminaries on Swarm Control Problems

Getting inspiration from the behavior of swarms in nature provides several advantages to researchers that focus on modeling and controlling multi-agent systems, such as multiple UAVs. For example, considering the behavior of animals or insects, these are generally organized such that decisions of an individual depend on the behavior of other members: each individual acts as a data harvester from the surrounding environment, so that the whole swarm can make the right decision. Sometimes it is possible that the whole swarm is dependent on the decisions of a single leader. Several swarming intelligence strategies are indeed adaptable to multi-UAVs applications, while being nowadays characterized by low cost and acceptable implementation complexity. The increasing attention towards mechanisms aimed at enabling a large number of UAVs to operate semi-autonomously is also due to the recent rapid development of communication network infrastructures (e.g., 5G) that allow data exchange in a faster and more efficient way. At the same time, the computational capability in autonomous vehicles has grown too, thus allowing the use of increasingly complex algorithms.

In the sequel we describe the main mechanisms performed by components in a swarm, namely aggregation, flight formation, social foraging, and swarm tracking [1].

- **Aggregation**. Aggregation is the basic mechanism performed by swarms. It corresponds to the ability of a swarm to work and organize itself, moving towards a specific target point, while avoiding collisions among components of the same swarm and obstacles that may be present along the way. From a theoretical point of view, all the components could converge in a single point. Obviously, this is not feasible in real applications, where a safety inter-distance between components must be ensured to avoid collisions.

- **Flight formation**. Flight formation consists in the ability of the components of a swarm to comply with a predefined geometric pattern starting from an initial disordered configuration. In a typical formation task, the scale of the given geometric pattern (i.e., the relative distances between the nodes in the geometric pattern indicating the desired final positions of the swarm components) may or may not be specified. In this work, we address the problem of formation stabilization and achievement of a predefined geometric shape with a-priori known node inter-distances.
- **Swarm tracking**. Swarm tracking consists in the union of aggregation and flight formation. It is the ability of all the components of a swarm to follow a given path, while maintaining the formation configuration. Keeping a swarm formation is an important task for many aspects. For example, squadrons of military planes can save fuel by flying in a V-formation, and migrating birds are supposed to do the same. Furthermore, in several applications it is required to reduce the size of the formation during the flight, and this can only be done by adopting specific geometrical patterns.
- **Social foraging**. Social foraging is aimed at increasing the probability of success for the single components in the swarm. For swarm motion, the emergent behavior is significantly affected by the interactions of the swarm members with their environment. This interaction is commonly modeled by the ability to discriminate favorable and dangerous transit areas in the surrounding environment. From a practical perspective, a favorable region can represent a target to be reached, and a dangerous one can be an obstacle to be avoided. In general, this behaviour is achieved through several mechanisms. For instance, when the so-called leader-following approach is applied, the entire swarm follows a particular member (i.e., the leader), who exactly knows where the favorable area or the target point is located.

3   The Proposed Distributed Control Algorithms

In this section we present a set of distributed control algorithms to allow multiple UAVs to perform the basic swarm tasks, namely aggregation, flight formation, social foraging, and swarm tracking. The proposed approach is based on a multi-agent framework, where the leader-following consensus mechanism under a time-varying topology is used to steer all the UAVs strategies to achieve a common goal. More in detail, we assume that each UAV updates its position gathering the information about the position of its own neighbors, that is, a subset of the entire UAVs swarm that is connected to the given UAV. Note that a connection between two UAVs exist if the distance between them is lower than their communication range.

3.1   Model of Multi-UAVs

First, we model the swarm of UAVs by a direct graph $\mathcal{G} = (\mathcal{N}, \mathcal{E})$, where $\mathcal{N} = \{1, \ldots, N\}$ is the set of nodes (or agents) with cardinality $N = |\mathcal{N}|$ representing the UAVs, and $\mathcal{E} \in \mathcal{V} \times \mathcal{N}$ is the set of edges describing the communication link between pairs of UAVs. In the sequel, we refer to agents and edges, putting aside the explicit reference to UAVs and link connections. During the movement of the swarm, the corresponding graph may change. If there is an agent without edges (because it is too far from anyone else in the swarm), the task cannot be successfully completed for the entire swarm. The same happens if the agent positions produce two or more isolated graphs. Therefore, in the sequel we assume that the swarm is represented by a connected graph, meaning that there is always at least a direct path between every pair of agents.

Second, we model the dynamics of each agent as a discrete-time single integrator:

$$x_i(k+1) = x_i(k) + u_i(k), \quad i \in \mathcal{N} \tag{1}$$

where $x_i(k) \in \mathbb{R}^3$ represents the state -in terms of position in a three-dimensional space- of agent i at time k and $u_i(k)$ denotes the control input of agent i at time k.

Finally, we assume that an agent is represented by a fictitious sphere, whose radius ϵ_r identifies the coverage range of the embedded proximity sensor that is used to detect free path and avoid potential collisions with other agents and obstacles.

3.2 Aggregation Control

A solution to the aggregation problem is found straightforward by the consensus algorithm, which is commonly used in a distributed framework, where each agent is allowed to communicate with a subset of all the remaining ones. The consensus problem deals with achieving an agreement among a group of processes connected by an unreliable communications network. In particular, the consensus is achieved if the differences between the values shared by members of the swarm are as close as possible to a given parameter.

Preliminarily, we respectively denote as $l(k)$ and $\mathcal{N}_f(k) = \mathcal{N} \setminus \{l(k)\}$ the identifier of the leader agent (referred to as leader in the sequel) and the set of follower agents (referred to as followers in the sequel). Given the initial known locations $x_i(0)$ $(i \in \mathcal{N})$ of agents, the position $x_i \in \mathbb{R}^3$ of agent i is updated in accordance with the consensus algorithm for time-varying topologies [19], defined as follows:

$$x_i(k+1) = x_i^*(k+1), \quad i = l(k) \tag{2}$$

$$x_i(k+1) = x_i(k) - \frac{\sum_{j \in \mathcal{M}_i(k)}(x_i(k) - x_j(k))}{|\mathcal{M}_i(k)|}, \quad i \in \mathcal{N}_f(k) \tag{3}$$

where $x_i^*(k)$ denotes the known position of the leader at time k and $\mathcal{M}_i(k)$ is the set of neighbors j related to agent i, which is time-varying according to the topology of the graph at time k. We remark that equations in (2)–(3) represent a simple implementation of the consensus algorithm. Also note that the time-varying graph is not required to be connected at each time instant. Indeed, it can be demonstrated that the consensus iterations are convergent if the union of the time-varying graphs over a finite time horizon is connected [19].

3.3   Formation Control

The flight formation principle relies on defining polynomial potential functions for each agent such that targets and forbidden locations (i.e., obstacles) constitute the zeros of these functions. An iterative algorithm is used to update the position of each follower and impose the predefined distance between each pair of agents (including the leader) based on the negative and positive gradient between the target and obstacle function, respectively. The control of flight formation is composed by three main steps, simultaneously performed by each agent:

– 1) defining the desired position of all the followers related to the neighbors positions, according to the formation geometric pattern;
– 2) defining the target and obstacle polynomial potential functions for all the followers, according to the target and obstacles positions;
– 3) updating the follower position by using Newton's iterative method.

Preliminarily, given the predefined formation pattern, we denote the desired inter-distance between agents i and j as $d_{ij} = ||x_i - x_j||$. The target set for follower i is defined as the set of points whose distance from all the other agents $j \neq i$ (i.e., including the leader) is equal to d_{ij}:

$$\mathcal{H}_i^T(k) = \bigcup_{j \in \mathcal{N} \backslash \{i\}} \mathcal{H}_{ij}^T(k), \quad i \in \mathcal{N}_f(k) \tag{4}$$

where $\mathcal{H}_{ij}^T(k)$ is the target set when only agent j is assumed to be present:

$$\mathcal{H}_{ij}^T(k) = \left\{ x_j(k) + d_{ij} \frac{x_i(k) - x_j(k)}{||x_i(k) - x_j(k)||} \right\}, \, i \in \mathcal{N}_f(k), \, j \neq i. \tag{5}$$

Given the target set $\mathcal{H}_i^T(k)$ for agent i, the corresponding attraction potential function $F_i^T : \mathbb{R}^3 \to \mathbb{R}^3$ is defined at time k such that the following condition is satisfied:

$$F_i^T(t_i(k)) = 0, \quad t_i(k) \in \mathcal{H}_i^T(k), \quad i \in \mathcal{N}_f(k). \tag{6}$$

For a given agent i it is more convenient to define an attraction potential function $F_{ij}^T(\cdot)$ for each of the other agents $j \neq i$, rather than leveraging only on $F_i^T(\cdot)$ that holistically takes all the target point into account. For the sake of simplicity, we only show the formulation of $F_{ij}^T(\cdot)$ in the case of a two-dimensional space. Assuming that the position of the target and agent i at time k are $t_{ij}(k) = [t_{1j}(k) \ \ t_{2j}(k)]^\top$ and $x_i(k) = [x_{1i}(k) \ \ x_{2i}(k)]^\top$, respectively, the potential attraction function is:

$$F_{ij}^T(x_i(k)) = \begin{cases} x_{1i}(k)x_{2i}(k) - x_{1i}(k)t_{2j}(k) + x_{1i}(k) - x_{2j}(k) \\ x_{2i}(k) - t_{2j}(k) \end{cases}, i \in \mathcal{N}_f, j \neq i. \tag{7}$$

It is apparent that it holds that $F_{ij}^T(x_i(k)) = 0$ if $x_i(k) = t_{ij}(k)$.

Assuming there are no obstacles, the zero of $F_i^T(\cdot)$ can be determined by Newton's method:

$$x_i(k+1) = x_i(k) + \lambda \Delta x_a(k), \quad i \in \mathcal{N}_f(k) \tag{8}$$

where λ is a step size representing the attraction coefficient. The step vector $\Delta x_{ai}(k)$ is computed as follows:

$$\Delta x_{ai}(k) = \sum_{j \in \mathcal{N} \setminus \{i\}} \frac{A_{ij}(k)}{||A_{ij}(k)||}, \quad i \in \mathcal{N}_f(k) \tag{9}$$

where:

$$A_{ij}(k) = -[\nabla F_{ij}^T(x_i(k))]^{-1} F_{ij}^T(x_i(k)), \ i \in \mathcal{N}_f(k), \ j \neq i. \tag{10}$$

Analogous considerations can be used to avoid collisions between agents [6]. Indeed, the avoidance of collisions between agents is guaranteed if agents $j \neq i$ (i.e., including the leader) are considered as obstacles by follower i. Hence, the obstacle set for agent i is defined as follows:

$$\mathcal{H}_i^O(k) = \bigcup_{j \in \mathcal{N} \setminus \{i\}} \mathcal{H}_{ij}^O(k), \ i \in \mathcal{N}_f(k) \tag{11}$$

where $\mathcal{H}_{ij}^O(k)$ contains only agent j as obstacle:

$$\mathcal{H}_{ij}^O(k) = \{x_j(k)\}, \ i \in \mathcal{N}_f(k), \ j \neq i. \tag{12}$$

Given the target set $\mathcal{H}_i^O(k)$ for agent i, the corresponding repulsion potential function $F_i^O : \mathbb{R}^3 \rightarrow \mathbb{R}^3$ is defined to take the position of all other agents $j \neq i$ into account. Similarly to the previous case, it is more convenient to define a repulsion potential function $F_{ij}^O(\cdot)$ for each other agent $j \neq i$. here again, for the sake of simplicity, we show the formulation of $F_{ij}^O(\cdot)$ in the case of a two-dimensional space. Assuming that the position of the obstacle is $o_{ij}(k) = [o_{1j}(k) \ o_{2j}(k)]^\top$, the repulsion potential function is:

$$F_{ij}^O(x_i(k)) = \begin{cases} x_{1i}(k)x_{2i}(k) - x_{1i}(k)o_{2j}(k) + x_{1i}(k) - o_{1j}(k) \\ x_{2i}(k) - o_{2j}(k) \end{cases}, \ i \in \mathcal{N}, \ j \neq i. \tag{13}$$

Having defined a repulsion potential function, the computation of the position of follower i in (8) is consequently updated as follows:

$$x_i(k+1) = x_i(k) + \lambda(\Delta x_a(k) + \Delta x_r(k)), \ i \in \mathcal{N}_f(k) \tag{14}$$

where the position variation takes also the repulsion step $\Delta x_{ri}(k)$ into account. This step is computed as summation of terms $\bar{R}_{ij}(k)$ related to the repulsion from single agent $j \neq i$:

$$\Delta x_{ri}(k) = \sum_{j \in \mathcal{N} \setminus \{i\}} \bar{R}_{ij}(k), \ i \in \mathcal{N}_f(k). \tag{15}$$

The repulsion step $\Delta x_{ri}(k)$ related to presence of agent $j \neq i$ is computed as follows:

$$\bar{R}_{ij}(k) = \begin{cases} \frac{1}{(1+(\frac{||R_{ij}(k)||}{C_r})^\mu)||R_{ij}(k)||^3} R_{ij}(k) - \frac{\epsilon_r}{(1+(\frac{\epsilon_r}{C_r})^\mu)\epsilon_r^3}, ||x_i(k) - x_j(k)|| \leq \epsilon_r \\ 0, ||x_i(k) - x_j(k)|| > \epsilon_r \end{cases},$$

$$i \in \mathcal{N}_f(k),\ j \neq i. \tag{16}$$

where C_r and μ are two coefficients of the repulsion component, ϵ_r denotes the safety inter-agent distance and it holds:

$$R_{ij}(k) = +[\nabla F_{ij}^O(x_i(k))]^{-1} F_{ij}^O(x_i(k)),\ i \in \mathcal{N}_f(k),\ j \neq i. \tag{17}$$

In order to improve the convergence of the flight formation mechanism, the step size λ in (14) can be replaced by an adaptive step size $\lambda_i(k)$ at time k for each follower i. By defining the relative error between the desired inter-distance and the actual one at time k:

$$\zeta_i(k) = \frac{\sum_{j \in \mathcal{M}_i(k)} ||d_{ij} - (x_i(k) - x_j(k))||}{|\mathcal{M}_i(k)|},\ i \in \mathcal{N}_f(k) \tag{18}$$

the adaptive step size shape is defined as:

$$\lambda_i(k) = p\, e^{c_i(k)},\ i \in \mathcal{N}_f(k) \tag{19}$$

where p is a tuning coefficient and $c(k)$ is the error variation:

$$c_i(k) = \zeta_i(k) - \zeta_i(k-1),\ i \in \mathcal{N}_f(k). \tag{20}$$

3.4   Trajectory Tracking and Collision Avoidance

The problems related to the trajectory tracking and collision avoidance can be addressed by leveraging on the concepts shown in the previous sections.

As for trajectory tracking, the first step consists in selecting a leader between the agents and considering the remaining ones as followers. Subsequently, on the one hand the attraction potential function of the leader is set to be coincident with the points of a known trajectory that ends in the destination point:

$$\mathcal{H}_i^T(k) = \{x_i^*(k)\},\quad i = l(t) \tag{21}$$

Note that the leader is not required to be the same agent through the whole path towards the target. Indeed, it can be demonstrated that the leader-following consensus iterations are convergent even if the leader role switches from one agent to others, which is an important feature from a practical point of view (e.g., in case a failure occurs to the leader). On the other hand, thanks to (4) all the followers are required to maintain the flight formation until the destination is reached.

As for the collision avoidance, this task is simultaneously performed by all the agents. Specifically, all obstacles and no-fly zones are associated with the repulsion function, whilst all the remaining zones are assumed to be free-flight space. This ensures that during the flight path the entire swarm tries to maintain the formation, while this is unavoidably modified due to any obstacles present along the way. Preliminarily, we denote the obstacle set for no-fly zones as dynamic set $\mathcal{H}^{\text{nofly}}(k)$. Hence, the definition of the obstacle set for followers in (11) is modified to take the presence of no-fly zones into account:

$$\mathcal{H}_i^O(k) = \mathcal{H}^{\text{nofly}}(k) \cup \bigcup_{j \in \mathcal{N} \setminus \{i\}} \mathcal{H}_{ij}^O(k), \ i \in \mathcal{N}_f(k). \tag{22}$$

Finally, we introduce a repulsion potential function also for the leader such that the leader is able to avoid no-fly zones:

$$\mathcal{H}_i^O(k) = \mathcal{H}^{\text{nofly}}(k), \ i = l(k). \tag{23}$$

4   Numerical Experiments

In this section we show the results of the application of the distributed control technique for aggregation and flight formation, swarm tracking, and social foraging of multi-UAVs to a set of selected numerical experiments. In particular, we consider a fleet of four UAVs, which is a common fleet dimension in multi-UAVs applications, for which the communication system has a connected graph configuration and each UAV can communicate with a set of neighbors of the fleet. Since in this article we use a leader-following based algorithm, only one UAV (i.e., the leader) knows the position of the destination and this information is shared with all the remaining UAVs of the fleet through consensus mechanism.

First, we test the aggregation and flight formation control method by considering three types of geometric formations, i.e., snake, triangular, and square. For all the formation configurations we consider a minimum inter-agent distance between a generic pair of neighboring UAVs equal to $d_{ij} = 2$ ($i \in \mathcal{N}, j \neq i$). The initial coordinates of the UAVs in the xyz-space are randomly generated. The leader is randomly switched between different UAVs along the path of the mission, and, at each change of the leader, the information relating to the target destination is also communicated. Note that this choice relies on the need to keep limited the computational effort. Nonetheless, without loosing in generality, other choices are also possible.

In all the configurations the UAVs are imposed to reach a planar formation. As an example, in Fig. 1 we report the graphical results in the xyz-space of the aggregation and formation control for the square configuration. The blue stars represent the initial position of the UAVs, and the orange squares their final positions. The trajectory of the four UAVs is represented by dashed colored lines. The shape of the formation is described by the light red square that has the four UAVs at its vertices. In Fig. 2 we show the evolution of the mean error of the UAVs positions with respect to the final configuration formation. It can be observed that the error lowers under 20% after 20 iterations and reaches the zero value after 50 iterations.

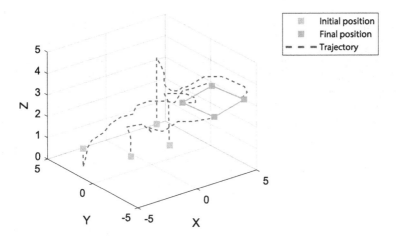

Fig. 1. Aggregation and formation control for a square formation configuration. (Color figure online)

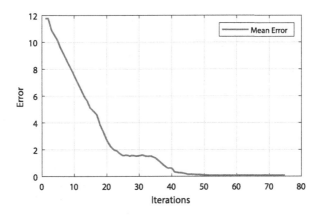

Fig. 2. Evolution of the mean position error of UAVs with respect to the final configuration.

The swarm tracking is then tested with various trajectories (i.e., linear, sawtooth, and sinusoidal), which are assigned to the leader of the fleet. In Fig. 3 the trajectory of the controlled fleet in case of a sinusoidal target and a square formation is shown. The four UAVs move from their initial to their final positions following the leader. The initial location of the UAVs is represented by green small squares, while the final position is represented by red green squares, except from the leader, which is identified by a yellow circle. The leader moves along a predefined sinusoidal trajectory, represented by a yellow dashed line, and completes its mission. It is to be noticed that the fleet formation control ensures the four UAVs to keep their square configuration throughout the whole mission. Finally, we show the results of the UAVs control obtained in presence of obstacles along the path of the mission. As shown in Fig. 4, the four UAVs start their mission by reaching the square formation, the initial positions are represented by a yellow square for the leader and green squares for the followers. The leader knows the final target but does not have a predefined trajectory to follow. The UAVs need to pass through a narrow corridor (e.g., a restricted flight zone) that does not allow to keep the square formation. The distributed control of the fleet allows the avoidance of the obstacle and the achievement of the final target by the leader. Note that, immediately after overcoming the barriers, the fleet returns in a square formation, which further proves the effectiveness of the formation and trajectory control.

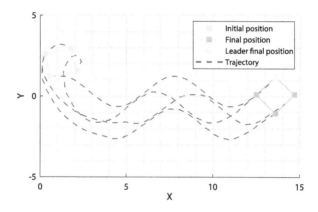

Fig. 3. Control of the UAVs trajectories with a sinusoidal target movement. (Color figure online)

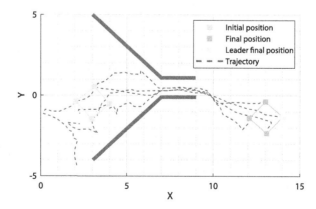

Fig. 4. Control of the UAVs trajectories in a narrow corridor. (Color figure online)

5   Conclusions

This work presents a distributed control approaches for the deployment of multi-UAV systems based on the joint application of the leader-following consensus theory and swarm intelligence paradigm. On the one hand, the proposed approach fills a gap in the existing literature, where there is a lack of investigations on distributed set-ups where the topology of communication, configuration of leader and followers, and formation pattern are typically time-varying. On the other hand, the application to numerical experiments highlights the effectiveness of the proposed control strategy in solving the main problems related to swarm behaviours, such as aggregation, formation control, swarm tracking, and social foraging under time-varying scenarios.

Future research will be focused on extending the proposed algorithms to agents having a double integrator behavior. We will also integrate additional objective functions and constraints into the system dynamics in order to model UAVs in a more realistic fashion. Finally, future work will be devoted to perform a comparison with some more mature methods and assess the scalability of the algorithms in larger-scale scenarios, and modeling uncertainty sources that may affect decision parameters.

References

1. Bandala, A., Dadios, E., Vicerra, R., Lim, L.G.: Swarming algorithm for unmanned aerial vehicle (UAV) quadrotors: swarm behavior for aggregation, foraging, formation, and tracking. J. Adv. Comput. Intell. Intell. Inform. **18**(5), 745–751 (2014)
2. Barabasi, A.L.: Taming complexity. Nat. Phys. **1**(2), 68–70 (2005)
3. Colorado, J., Barrientos, A., Martinez, A., Lafaverges, B., Valente, J.: Mini-quadrotor attitude control based on Hybrid Backstepping & Frenet-Serret theory. In: Proceedings of the IEEE International Conference on Robotics and Automation (ICRA) (2010)
4. Dong, X., Yu, B., Shi, Z., Zhong, Y.: Time-varying formation control for unmanned aerial vehicles: theories and applications. IEEE Trans. Contr. Syst. Techn. **23**(1), 340–348 (2015)
5. Dong, X., Zhou, Y., Ren, Z., Zhong, Y.: Time-varying formation tracking for second-order multi-agent systems subjected to switching topologies with application to quadrotor formation flying. IEEE Trans. Ind. Electron. **64**(6), 5014–5024 (2016)
6. Gazi, V., Passino, K.: Swarm Stability and Optimization. Springer, Heidelberg (2011). https://doi.org/10.1007/978-3-642-18041-5
7. Gioioso, G., Franchi, A., Salvietti, G., Scheggi, S., Prattichizzo, D.: The flying hand: a formation of UAVs for cooperative aerial telemanipulation. In: Proceedings of the IEEE International Conference on Robotics and Automation (ICRA), p. 4335–4341 (2014)
8. Gu, Z., Shi, P., Yue, D., Ding, Z.: Decentralized adaptive event-triggered h_∞ filtering for a class of networked nonlinear interconnected systems. IEEE Trans. Cybern. **49**(5), 1570–1579 (2018)
9. Indu, C., Singh, R.: Trajectory planning and optimization for UAV communication: a review. J. Discret. Math. Sci. Cryptog. **23**(2), 475–483 (2020)

10. Kushleyev, A., Mellinger, D., Powers, C., Kumar, V.: Towards a swarm of agile micro quadrotors. Auton. Robots **35**(4), 287–300 (2013)
11. Lee, H., Kim, H., Kim, H.: Path planning and control of multiple aerial manipulators for a cooperative transportation. In: Proceedings of the IEEE/RSJ International Conference on Intelligent Robots and Systems (IROS) (2015)
12. Low, C.: A dynamic virtual structure formation control for fixedwing UAVs. In: Proceedings of the 9th IEEE IEEE International Conference on Control and Automation (ICCA), pp. 627–632 (2011)
13. Magnussen, O., Ottestad, M., Hovland, G.: Experimental validation of a quaternion-based attitude estimation with direct input to a quadcopter control system. In: Proceedings of the International Conference on Unmanned Aircraft Systems Unmanned Aircraft Systems (ICUAS) (2013)
14. Mellinger, D., Michael, N., Kumar, V.: Trajectory generation and control for precise aggressive maneuvers with quadrotors. Exp. Robot. **79**, 361–373 (2014)
15. Monteiro, S., Bicho, E.: A dynamical systems approach to behavior-based formation control. In: Proceedings of the IEEE International Conference on Robotics and Automation (ICRA), pp. 2606–2611 (2002)
16. Mu, B., Shi, Y.: Distributed LQR consensus control for heterogeneous multiagent systems: theory and experiments. IEEE/ASME Trans. Mech. **23**(1), 434–443 (2018)
17. Nathan, P., Almurib, H., Kumar, T.: A review of autonomous multi-agent quadrotor control techniques and applications. In: Proceedings of 4th International Conference on Mechatronics (ICOM) (2011)
18. Pantelimon, G., Tepe, K., Carriveau, R., Ahmed, S.: Survey of multi-agent communication strategies for information exchange and mission control of drone deployments. J. Intell. Robot. Syst. **95**, 779–788 (2019)
19. Ren, W., Beard, R.: Distributed Consensus in Multi-vehicle Cooperative Control - Theory and Applications. Springer, London (2008). https://doi.org/10.1007/978-1-84800-015-5
20. Roldo, V., Cunha, R., Cabecinhas, D., Silvestre, C., Oliveira, P.: A leader-following trajectory generator with application to quadrotor formation flight. Robot. Auton. Syst. **62**(10), 1597–1609 (2014)
21. Sa, I., Corke, P.: Estimation and control for an open-source quadcopter. In: Australian Conference of Robotics and Automation (ACRA) (2011)
22. Saska, M., et al.: Autonomous deployment of swarms of micro-aerial vehicles in cooperative surveillance. In: Proceedings of the International Conference on Unmanned Aircraft Systems (ICUAS) (2014)
23. Saska, M., Vakula, J., Preucil, L.: Swarms of micro aerial vehicles stabilized under a visual relative localization. In: Proceedings of the IEEE International Conference on Robotics and Automation (ICRA), pp. 3570–3575 (2014)
24. Seo, J., Ahn, C., Kim, Y.: Controller design for UAV formation flight using consensus based decentralized approach. In: Proceedings of the AIAA Infotech@Aerospace Conference (2009)
25. Song, Z., Duan, C., Wang, J., Wu, Q.: Chattering-free full-order recursive sliding mode control for finite-time attitude synchronization of rigid spacecraft. J. Franklin Inst. **356**(2), 998–1020 (2019)
26. Toksoz, M., Oguz, S., Gazi, V.: Decentralized formation control of a swarm of quadrotor helicopters. In: Proceedings of the IEEE 15th International Conference on Control and Automation (ICCA) (2019)

27. Wang, C., Tnunay, H., Zuo, Z., Lennox, B., Ding, Z.: Fixed-time formation control of multirobot systems: design and experiments. IEEE Trans. Ind. Electron. **66**(8), 6292–6301 (2019)
28. Wang, C., Zuo, Z., Qi, Z., Ding, Z.: Predictor-based extended-state-observer design for consensus of MASs with delays and disturbances. IEEE Trans. Cybern. **49**(4), 1259–1269 (2009)
29. Wang, J., Zhou, Z., Wang, C., Shan, J.: Multiple quadrotors formation flying control design and experimental verification. Unmanned Syst. **7**(1), 47–54 (2019)
30. Zhao, S.: Affine formation maneuver control of multi-agent systems. IEEE Trans. Autom. Contr. **63**(12), 4140–4155 (2018)
31. Zhao, S., Dimarogonas, D., Sun, Z., Bauso, D.: A general approach to coordination control of mobile agents with motion constraints. IEEE Trans. Automat. Contr. **63**(5), 1509–1516 (2018)

STOP: A Location Spoofing Resistant Vehicle Inspection System

Henrique F. Santos[1], Rui L. Claro[1]([⊠]), Leonardo S. Rocha[2],
and Miguel L. Pardal[1]

[1] INESC-ID, Instituto Superior Técnico, Universidade de Lisboa, Lisbon, Portugal
{hfigueiredosantos,rui.claro,miguel.pardal}@tecnico.ulisboa.pt
[2] Universidade Estadual do Ceará, Fortaleza, Brazil
leonardo.sampaio@uece.br

Abstract. An effort is being made by authorities worldwide to improve
the safety of the transportation of goods while preserving efficiency. Vehicle inspections are important for safety but not very frequent. When
they do happen, vehicles are selected on the roadside and authorities
spend a long time retrieving the relevant information while the vehicle
is stopped. In this paper, we present and evaluate STOP, a road transportation vehicle inspection support system with tamper-proof records
to prevent location spoofing attacks. To the best of our knowledge, it
is the first such system described in literature. The STOP system uses
mobile devices and a central server to allow authorities to select and
notify vehicles for inspection while retrieving the needed information to
prepare the procedure beforehand. The location chain for each vehicle
can be verified and signed by the inspectors. We implemented a prototype in the Android platform and tested it with real users. We evaluated
the system's location retrieval accuracy, response times, and Bluetooth
communication during inspection.

Keywords: Smart mobility · Transportation · Mobile applications ·
Location spoofing prevention · Location proofs

1 Introduction

The frequent inspection of road transportation can bring several positives outcomes, such as improved safety for drivers, vehicles, and goods, along with
decreased environmental impact and significant savings. At an inspection site,
an inspector orders incoming transportation vehicles to stop to conduct an
inspection, with no previous knowledge of what these vehicles are transporting. Depending on the type or size of freight, the inspector has to adapt the
procedure to the situation, possibly requesting assistance from colleagues. Naturally, these manual steps can take a long time. If the selection and notification
of vehicles for inspection could be done beforehand, inspectors would then have
additional time to prepare the inspection procedure until the vehicle arrives.

© Springer Nature Switzerland AG 2020
L. A. Grieco et al. (Eds.): ADHOC-NOW 2020, LNCS 12338, pp. 100–113, 2020.
https://doi.org/10.1007/978-3-030-61746-2_8

This can improve efficiency and reduce the duration of inspections. By leveraging location-based services (LBS), it is possible to enable location reporting of transportation vehicles to authorities. As such, it is possible to know the ongoing transportation and what vehicles are close to the inspection site. A simple mobile device with Internet connection can be used by the inspector to retrieve the documentation beforehand and to create a checkpoint. Additionally, inspectors can submit inspection outcome reports digitally.

In this paper, we present and evaluate STOP, a novel road transportation vehicle inspection support system using location proofs. Its main goal is to validate location chains, one for each vehicle, allowing information critical to the inspection process to be stored and validated in tamper-proof records.

The paper is organized as follows: Section 2 presents the background and related work; Sect. 3 presents the STOP system in detail; Sect. 4 presents the experimental evaluation that was done; and Sect. 5 completes the document with a summary of the contributions and opportunities for future work.

2 Background and Related Work

The location reporting of each vehicle enables the selection of vehicles and the consecutive preparation of inspections. Therefore the proposed system needs reliable location reporting. This section provides background on location systems, with an emphasis on systems that are able to provide location proofs.

2.1 GPS-Based Location Systems and Applications

The Global Positioning System (GPS) is composed by a set of 31 operational satellites that emit radio signals that a GPS receiver can use to determine its position on Earth [1,6]. The receiver locks to the signal of at least 4 satellites and calculates its position, taking into account the current time and the known coordinates of the satellites. Each GPS satellite continually broadcasts a signal that includes a pseudo-random code known to the receiver and a message that includes the time of transmission of the code and the satellite position at that time.

Location Tracking Systems. A GPS tracker is a device that enables real time position tracking of attached objects [9]. This device continuously retrieves its location by retrieving satellite signals from GPS. Currently transportation companies use *fleet management systems* that receive and gather data from the trackers inside vehicles to present real time information of the vehicles to the users. These solutions allow companies to monitor their fleet, ensuring secure transportation and reporting the delivery to a client as it happens. The device transmits the collected information through Global System for Mobile Communications (GSM) cellular network to the servers of the provider, which is presented through a web portal or computer software.

Use of Location by Mobile Applications. GPS location is widely used across the majority of mobile devices in use today. Two of the most common uses are road navigation and ride-sharing [4,14]. These mobile applications rely on the location reported by devices to guide users to their destination for example.

Navigation applications have also been used in the transportation sector [11]. Every carrier wants to decrease route times and reduce costs with fuel consumption and vehicle maintenance. Therefore it is important to dynamically change routes according to traffic information. The use of a mobile application provides a low cost integration with any road route navigation system through mobile data.

Security. Despite being widely used, GPS is not considered fully secure [12,13]. A GPS spoofing attack aims to deceive GPS receivers by broadcasting incorrect signals. These are structured to resemble a set of normal GPS signals and they can be modified to cause the receiver to estimate its position where desired by the attacker. Inexpensive GPS spoofing devices are available in the market [7], therefore an attacker can easily purchase such devices. It is then possible to deceive mobile devices running road navigation applications [17], air drones [8], ships [16] and working vehicles [3].

2.2   Location Certification

A *location proof*, as defined by Saroiu and Wolman, is a mechanism to allow mobile devices to prove their location to applications and services [15]. The authors considered that a component of an existent wireless infrastructure such as Wi-Fi Access Points and cellular towers can issue metadata containing location information. A device can request a location proof from the infrastructure and this proof can be sent to applications with the intent of proving the location of the mobile device. There have been several systems that allow the creation of location proofs, namely, Saroiu and Wolman's work, APPLAUS [18], CREPUS-COLO [2] and SureThing [5]. In these systems, a Prover broadcasts a location proof request through wireless communication to nearby devices. The witness creates a proof and signs it with its private key. The proof contains the observation made by the witness that can also contain additional data, such as specific secret code sequences being transmitted at the location, and pictures from a surveillance camera, that further prove that the prover device was at that location at the time. The Location Proof Server can later verify the proof.

Zhu and Cao proposed a location proof system called APPLAUS using only Bluetooth enabled mobile devices [18], using five entities: *Prover*, the mobile device who collects proofs from neighbors, *Witnesses*, untrusted mobile devices that generate location proofs, *Location Proof Server*, to store proofs, *Certificate Authority*, to store and validate public keys, and *Verifier*, that verifies submitted proofs. The system does not use an existent wireless infrastructure. It uses pseudonyms for each Prover and Witness to prevent device tracking.

Canlar et al.[2] created CREPUSCOLO to address both the *neighbor-based* type of proof-based solutions, where nearby mobile devices create proofs, and the *infrastructure-based* type, where location proofs are acquired from trusted infrastructure elements, such as Wi-Fi Access Points. The system uses the same entities of APPLAUS with the addition of the *Token Provider*, a trusted entity placed at a strategic location that generates a proof, called *token*, that may contain an object, such as a picture from a surveillance camera, that proves the device was at that location. Location proofs are exchanged and created like in APPLAUS, with the addition of a nonce in the proof request and in the associated location proof, to prevent replay attacks. The Token Provider is used to mitigate attacks where one device may broadcast messages from another device located at a different site and therefore witnesses may create proofs of the prover located at a different place.

SureThing [5] aims to provide correct location proofs to other applications and services, indoors or outdoors, using as motivation improving the APPLAUS and CREPUSCOLO works. It uses multiple entities similar to the ones in the two previous works presented, *Prover*, *Witness*, *Verifier* and *Certification Authority*, and it also uses geographical coordinates, Wi-Fi fingerprinting and Bluetooth beacons as location proof techniques. Ferreira and Pardal introduced two methods for collusion avoidance, to prevent colluding devices to create incorrect location proofs. The *Witness Redundancy* mechanism forces the Prover to gather proofs from more than one Witness and chooses the number of witnesses according to the level of service possible. Each proof has a different trust value according to the number of witnesses used. *Witness Decay* ensures that if a Prover is getting proofs from the same Witness, they gradually become less valuable and the Verifier will not validate the location if the Prover can not gather proofs with enough value.

3   The STOP System

We present a road transportation inspection support solution named STOP: Secure Transport lOcation Proofs. Its main goal is to provide and register the accurate location information for inspectors and drivers, by using mobile devices. STOP has security mechanisms to prevent and mitigate malicious intents. The system is owned by an *Authority* responsible for the rules for vehicle selection and goods inspection. It audits the system and validates every procedure. It also keeps the history of each participant, and can use it to handle exceptions, like equipment or inspector failures.

The system uses *pseudonyms* instead of the real identities of the participating entities as it does not need this information to operate.

3.1   Inspection Process

A transportation starts with a company registering the freight information with the competent authorities. A carrier or the company itself performs the transportation, which can be inspected by authorities at any point of the route. The on-board device retrieves its location and uploads it at a system-defined rate. The process is finished when the goods are delivered to the reported receiver.

An inspector arrives at an inspection site, starts the application, logs in and creates a *checkpoint*. The inspector defines the *selection range*, a perimeter from inspection sites where all vehicles inside are considered for selection. The *selection rule* is applied, and, for example, a vehicle is chosen at random from inside the selection range. At this time, the on-board device of the selected vehicle retrieves the checkpoint information, which is presented to the driver. When the vehicle arrives at the checkpoint, the Transport device communicates with the Inspect device and inspection starts. The inspector checks the system records and the vehicle and freight documentation. The inspector can register additional information in form of text, pictures or audio. When all of the inspection information is complete, it can be reviewed and approved.

The *Location Chain* needs to be valid. The chain represents the positions of the vehicle during the transportation of goods, in chronological order. A location chain item is either a *Location Point* or *Location Proof*, as illustrated in Fig. 1. Both contain the signature of the previous item. A local copy of the location chain is kept by the Transport device so that the system can operate even when an Internet connection is not available.

A location point contains the geographic coordinates retrieved by the transporter device GPS, at a time point of the trip. A location proof contains the geographic and time coordinates retrieved by an inspector device at a checkpoint along with the additional collected evidence.

The location chain is protected by the chain of signatures. Each item signs the previous one, including the signature. This way, it is possible to verify if the previous item is modified or missing, providing protection against record tampering. It is also possible to check whether the location data from the previous items is consistent with the inspection being actually carried out on site. The location tracking and the inspection data is intertwined, and, as a result, both are strengthened: the location points have to be consistent with the itinerary until the inspection, and the inspection data is reinforced to have happened at the time and place, following the itinerary.

3.2 Localization

The STOP system uses the *Google Play services location* API, which allows to program constant location retrieval. We use this to obtain the most accurate location positions possible for small time intervals (1 s). These intervals are still subject to fluctuations, due to battery optimization or poor connectivity of the device.

Device localization has changed in recent Android versions. Location retrieval is no longer tied only to GPS tracking, as devices also use additional information from nearby Wi-Fi networks, from GSM networks and other device sensors[1]. We discuss the impact of the usage of multiple sources of localization in our evaluation, in Subsect. 4.1.

---

[1] https://policies.google.com/technologies/location-data.

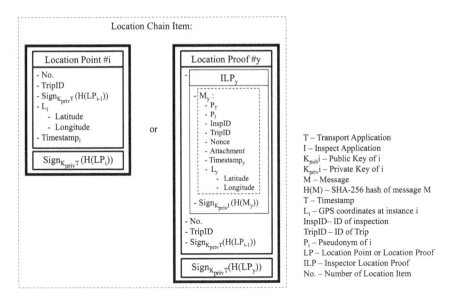

Fig. 1. Types of location chain item.

3.3 Architecture

The STOP system is structured in three tiers: Presentation, Logic and Data, as shown by Fig. 2. This allows for integration of new components such as different storage systems and user interfaces.

The main components of the system are the Central Ledger, the Transport and Inspect mobile applications. The *Central Ledger* is a central server that receives transportation and inspection records. All communication with the Central Ledger is done through a Representational State Transfer (REST)ful Application Programming Interface (API). A detailed description of the interface was done in *OpenAPI* description language format. The records are kept in a database for concurrency control, load balancing, and increased availability, with multiple servers.

The *Transport* mobile application runs on a mobile device inside of the vehicle transporting the reported goods in a device with an active Internet connection during the transportation process.

The *Inspect* mobile application is used by the inspector on a mobile device at an inspection location. After a vehicle is selected, the application presents the respective transportation information for the inspector to analyze while the vehicle reaches the checkpoint. The application communicates with the device inside of an inspected vehicle via short-range communication. A location proof is generated at the end of the inspection procedure. The proof contains pseudonyms of the *Transport* and *Inspect* devices, a trip identifier, and a random nonce generated by the Central Ledger for the occasion. This proof can replace any

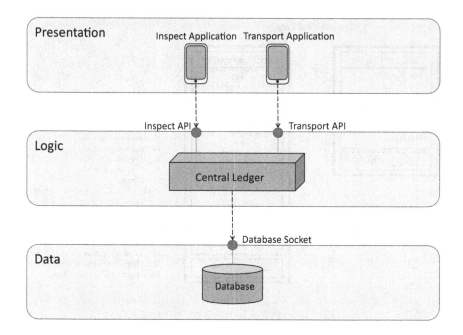

Fig. 2. STOP system architecture.

paper report done by the inspector, as it proves the inspection was conducted and contains the relevant evidence.

3.4   Communication Protocol

The *remote* communication between the applications and the Central Ledger is done through the provided REST API web service via cellular network. This API uses standard HTTP over TLS[2] to protect the messages [10].

The Central Ledger acts, effectively, as a Certification Authority (CA) for the public keys. An external CA can also be used.

The *local* communication between devices is done using Bluetooth. As a close proximity communication protocol, it is ideal for the inspection process, and acts as a location spoofing countermeasure.

Figure 3 shows the interaction when a vehicle is selected for inspection. The *Inspect* and *Transport* devices obtain the public key certificate of the other device from the central ledger, along with a nonce and a pseudonym for each device. This is necessary to encrypt the Bluetooth communication between these devices and to prevent replay, eavesdropping and tampering attacks.

---

[2] https://tools.ietf.org/html/rfc8446.

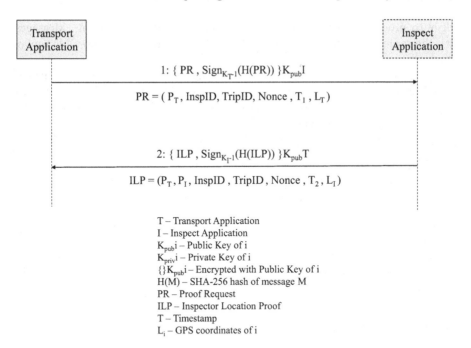

Fig. 3. Inspection protocol.

When the vehicle arrives to the checkpoint, the *Transport* application starts searching for the Bluetooth device announcing as device name the pseudonym of the device of the inspector. When found, the transporter device starts the communication by broadcasting a proof request. The broadcast message is encrypted with the public key of the inspector to guarantee that it can only be decrypted by the inspector. The broadcast message contains the proof request, represented in the figure as PR, and the signature of the hash of the proof request, made with the private key of the transporter, to guarantee that the proof request was created by the transporter. The proof request contains pseudonyms of the devices, the identifiers of the inspection and trip, the nonce generated by the central ledger, the timestamp of the transporter device and its GPS coordinates.

When the inspector device receives a message from a device with the pseudonym of the transporter device, it validates if it is a proof request and, if correct, notifies the inspector to conduct the inspection. When the inspection is done, the outcome is reported in a message containing the proof, represented in the figure as proof, signed by the inspector. The message is encrypted with the public key of the transporter. The message is then sent through the established Bluetooth socket to the transporter device. The inspector device additionally sends a copy of the proof to the central ledger. The transporter device receives the proof, decrypts and validates it, adds the signature of the previous location item and sends it to the central ledger. If the transporter device did not receive the proof after successfully sending a proof request, it will request the central ledger to produce a new nonce and pseudonym for that inspection. Messages with the same nonce, pseudonyms and identifiers are rejected as possible replay attacks.

Every message or object requires a digital signature to be considered authentic. A signature is computed by calculating the hash value of the object with the *SHA-256* algorithm. It is then encrypted with the RSA algorithm using the private key of the device that created the message.

4   Evaluation

The evaluation of the system focused on the following subjects:

- Are the location coordinates retrieved from Android mobile devices accurate enough for the system procedures?
- What are the best parameters for the selection of vehicles for inspection?
- Is the designed interaction protocol suitable for Bluetooth communication in an inspection scenario?

4.1   Location Accuracy

As the system uses the latest reported location from the on-board device of a vehicle, it is important to determine if mobile devices are capable of retrieving accurate location points. We set out two courses done with the STOP Transport application with different users. Course I was done using a mobile device inside of a automobile. Course II was done with 3 groups of two users, each one with a mobile device and each group traveling in a different bus. Having the users traveling through Course II in groups of two allowed us to assess possible discrepancies between devices performing the same route.

Upon visualizing the reported location points throughout the different courses, it is possible to detect some anomalies, but overall location points are close to the real trajectory. One of the performed courses contains a section inside of a tunnel and the mobile device that performed this course did not report any location point in this section. Figure 4 shows this anomaly, as the sections of the course that do not contain red dots are the sections inside the tunnel.

Another performed course has tall buildings in its surroundings which is known to affect GPS signal. Upon visualizing the several reported user trajectories in this course, we noticed moments where the location coordinates reported were in buildings. Although we cannot confirm it, we suspect, as Android also uses Wi-Fi fingerprint for location retrieval, that the devices might have detected known SSIDs and BSSIDs of Wi-Fi networks in these buildings. With a poor GPS connectivity, the devices might have calculated their positions inside of the building, taking into account the Wi-Fi networks detected.

Although visual analysis helps recognizing and understanding some issues, it does not gives us the overall accuracy levels of the reported location points. Therefore we have performed calculations on the retrieved location information

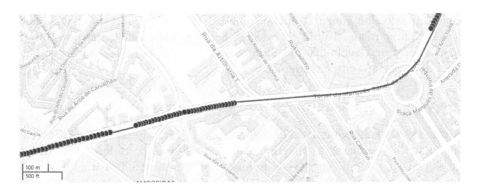

Fig. 4. Location detection issues inside of a tunnel.

Table 1. Location retrieval accuracy results.

User	No. points	Average distance (m)
A	1244	4.64
B	1673	5.57
C	832	7.32
D	1375	8.19
E	1376	8.94
F	1820	18.97
G	1885	7.51

of the devices. Table 1 shows the average distance between the reported and the exact trajectories of each user.

User A performed a course that was primarily highway courses with occasional city sections, while the rest of the users performed the same city course. The average distance of user A is lower than 5 m, which we consider tolerable as the vehicle was mainly traveling between 90 Km/h and 120 Km/h and the city sections of the course were not surrounded by tall buildings and did not include narrow roads. With the rest of the users, we conclude that accuracy in a complete city environment is not as good as in a highway. Vehicle speeds are lower but the average distance was higher. All users of this course, except user F, had an average distance to the real trajectory between 5 and 9 m. User F reported that his device may have a GPS malfunction because previous usages of navigation applications showed incorrect location positions. We conclude that this malfunction justifies the substantial average distance to the real trajectory, as user F always traveled with user G and this user had an overall average similar to the other users.

This accuracy assessment allows us to determine where the optimal location for a inspection site is. Inspectors should assess if the area inside the selected inspection selection range is not surrounded by tall buildings and does not include narrow roads. To our knowledge, heavy road vehicle inspections often occur in location that fulfills this requirement, as most of these vehicles do not travel in a constant city environment.

4.2 Vehicle Selection

We consider that the parameters defined in our architecture and by the Authority user should be evaluated as they influence the selection procedure. As vehicles will be traveling at different speeds and we want to have an efficient application, we want to assess if a fixed location retrieval rate should be implemented or not, taking into consideration that a higher location retrieval rate requires more processing from the mobile device and Central Ledger. The highest location retrieval rate possible will ensure the system has the most recent location of each vehicle, however it will demand more processing from the components. Before assessing this parameter, we wanted to confirm if the location retrieval rates defined in the Android implementation were in fact being fulfilled. Figure 5 illustrates the reported location retrieval rates. The horizontal axis represents the number of the reported location point and the vertical axis represents the time interval the location point took to be retrieved.

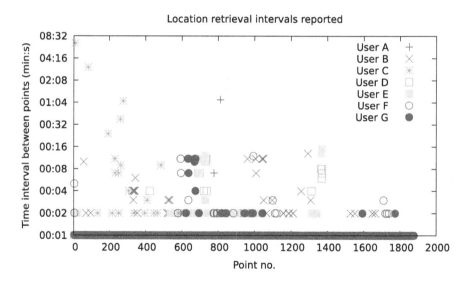

Fig. 5. Location retrieval intervals reported.

For all users, which had a 1 s rate set, there were some points with a substantial interval, however most of the points are in the exact 1 s mark. This showcases why the average rate is above one second but the percentage of points that have not fulfilled the set rate is minimal. We presume that a substantial location retrieval interval occurs when the GPS signal is not satisfactory, the device cannot use mobile data or the device is optimizing the battery consumption.

Results show that it is possible to have a one second retrieval rate, therefore we conclude that we can rely on the location retrieval rate defined on Android systems. However as mentioned, having a one second retrieval rate would create a considerable demand from the device and Central Ledger, despite guaranteeing that the system would have the most possible up-to-date location. We suggest that the location retrieval rate should be variable considering the speed of the vehicle. The device would constantly change its location retrieval rate to adapt to the speed at which the vehicle is moving. Speed can be calculated with the already retrieved points or with a specialized Android location tool-kit method[3].

We also performed inspection selection tests simultaneously with 6 users. Two Inspect users were at one checkpoint each and the distance between the two checkpoints was higher than the defined inspection selection range of 500 m. The six Transport users started the course and the Inspect users were at the corresponding checkpoint, requesting an inspection every minute until the request was fulfilled. Inspection protocols would be performed with the two devices side-by-side.

Out of the inspections performed, there was an occasion where a user that had just been inspected was again selected for inspection. The issue occurred because the user was stopped due to traffic near the checkpoint, therefore he was eligible for selection due to the defined rule in the prototype. One improvement that could prevent this situation is to establish a minimum selection range, i.e., vehicles too close to the checkpoint would not be considered for inspection and there would not be any risk of a vehicle being selected and not being able to stop on time. The rest of the inspections performed did not have any anomalies.

4.3   Bluetooth Inspection Interaction

We replicated an inspection area with a metal container similar to ones that carry goods in transportation vehicles. A Samsung Galaxy S9 device running Android 8 was used as the Transport device and a Nokia 8 device running Android 9 was used as the Inspect device. Both devices have Bluetooth 4.0. We positioned the Transport device in front of the container and proceeded to request an inspection in the Inspect device. The Transport device was selected.

In a typical inspection scenario, an inspector might move around the container and our architecture considers that a Bluetooth connection is maintained during this procedure. However a metal container might interfere with the Bluetooth connection. Therefore we performed several movements around the container to test if the connection was maintained.

The inspector was able to walk around the container and approve the inspection near the Carrier user. This procedure was done successfully 3 times. This did not happen when the inspector would stop for more than 5 s behind the

---

[3] https://developer.android.com/reference/android/location/Location#getSpeed().

container, the connection would be lost. Therefore we conclude that the Bluetooth inspection protocol cannot consider that a Bluetooth connection is fully maintained during an inspection process, while the inspector moves to perform the inspection. A possible change to the protocol would be to divide it in two phases. After ending the inspection procedure, the inspector heads towards the driver and approves the inspection to send the proof.

4.4 Discussion

We evaluated important features of Android devices used for our prototype, specifically location retrieval and Bluetooth communication. We concluded that in a highway course location points are accurate. Inside tunnels, however, devices cannot retrieve location information because they cannot receive signal from the GPS satellites. In a city course we concluded that GPS signal strength varies and the device may report location points outside of roads for example because of the obstructions caused by buildings, for example. The system will operate better on roads outside of cities or in locations without GPS obstacles.

Regarding the location retrieval rate, we found the results to be satisfactory as the Android devices were able to report most of the location points at the defined location rate. We suggest a variable location retrieval rate for better device optimization.

Upon testing the initial selection rules implemented, we proposed that the selection rule should be composed of maximum and minimum inspection selection range and a estimated time of arrival with a route planning procedure. This allows vehicles to be notified on time and guarantees that a selected vehicle does not need to change its route to reach the checkpoint.

As a result of the Bluetooth experiments, we redesigned the protocol to be divided in two phases, with separate Bluetooth connections, one for the start and another for the completion of the inspection.

5   Conclusion

This paper described the architecture, implementation and evaluation of the STOP system. The system uses the location from on-board mobile devices to track incoming vehicles to inspection sites and location proofing to digitally certify the location chain and the inspection data. The evaluation of the prototype provided insights regarding the feasibility of this type of system and the location retrieval features of Android devices.

Acknowledgements. This work was supported by national funds through FCT, Fundação para a Ciência e a Tecnologia, under project UIDB/50021/2020 and through project with reference PTDC/CCI-COM/31440/2017 (SureThing).

References

1. Bajaj, R., Ranaweera, S.L., Agrawal, D.P.: GPS: location-tracking technology. Computer **35**, 92–94 (2002)
2. Canlar, E.S., Conti, M., Crispo, B., Di Pietro, R.: CREPUSCOLO: a collusion resistant privacy preserving location verification system. In: 2013 International Conference on Risks and Security of Internet and Systems (CRiSIS) (2013)
3. CBS: N.J. Man In A Jam, After Illegal GPS Device Interferes With Newark Liberty Operations (2013). https://newyork.cbslocal.com/2013/08/09/n-j-man-in-a-jam-after-illegal-gps-device-interferes-with-newark-liberty-operations/
4. eMarketer: Maps and Navigation Apps: Discovery, Exploration Features Open Up Ad Opportunities (2018). https://www.emarketer.com/content/maps-and-navigation-apps
5. Ferreira, J., Pardal, M.L.: Witness-based location proofs for mobile devices. In: 17th IEEE International Symposium on Network Computing and Applications (NCA) (November 2018)
6. GPS.gov: GPS space segment (2019). https://www.gps.gov/systems/gps/space/
7. Hill, K.: Jamming GPS Signals Is Illegal, Dangerous, Cheap, and Easy (2017). https://gizmodo.com/jamming-gps-signals-is-illegal-dangerous-cheap-and-e-1796778955
8. Humphreys, T.: Statement on the vulnerability of civil unmanned aerial vehicles and other systems to civil GPS spoofing. The University of Texas at Austin, Technical report (2012)
9. Hynes, M., Miller, B., Barrett, M.: GPS Tracker US Patent (2003)
10. Krawczyk, H., Paterson, K.G., Wee, H.: On the security of the TLS protocol: a systematic analysis. In: CRYPTO 2013: Advances in Cryptology, pp. 429–448 (2013)
11. Loten, A.: Life on the Road Gets a Little Easier as Truckers Adopt Digital Technology (2019). https://www.wsj.com/articles/life-on-the-road-gets-a-little-easier-as-truckers-adopt-digital-technology-11559727001
12. Narain, S., Ranganathan, A., Noubir, G.: Security of GPS/INS based on-road location tracking systems. In: 2019 IEEE Symposium on Security and Privacy (SP) (2019)
13. Onishi, H., Yoshida, K., Kato, T.: GNSS vulnerabilities and vehicle applications. In: 2016 13th Workshop on Positioning, Navigation and Communications (WPNC) (2016)
14. Ridester: Inside the Ridesharing Revolution, 2018 Edition (2018). https://www.ridester.com/2018-rideshare-infographic/
15. Saroiu, S., Wolman, A.: Enabling new mobile applications with location proofs. In: ACM Proceedings of the 10th Workshop on Mobile Computing Systems and Applications, p. 9 (2009)
16. The University of Texas at Austin: UT Austin Researchers Successfully Spoof an $80 million Yacht at Sea (2013). https://news.utexas.edu/2013/07/29/ut-austin-researchers-successfully-spoof-an-80-million-yacht-at-sea/
17. Zeng, K., Shu, Y., Liu, S., Dou, Y., Yang, Y.: A practical GPS location spoofing attack in road navigation scenario. In: ACM Workshop on Mobile Computing Systems and Applications (HotMobile) (2017)
18. Zhu, Z., Cao, G.: APPLAUS: a privacy-preserving location proof updating system for location-based services. In: IEEE Conference on Computer Communications, INFOCOM 2011 (2011)

A Simulation Framework for QoE-Aware Real-Time Video Streaming in Multipath Scenarios

Manlio Bacco[1(✉)], Pietro Cassarà[1], Alberto Gotta[1], and Massimo Puddu[2]

[1] Institute of Information Science and Technologies (ISTI),
National Research Council (CNR), Pisa, Italy
{manlio.bacco,pietro.cassara,alberto.gotta}@isti.cnr.it
[2] University of Pisa, Pisa, Italy
massimo.puddu5@studenti.unipi.it

Abstract. This work presents the ongoing development of a simulation/emulation framework for real-time multimedia transmissions in multi-channel scenarios. The proposed software engine can be used to simulate the aggregation of multiple network links delivering a video flow from a video source, such as a camera mounted on-board an Unmanned Aerial Vehicle (UAV), to the indented receiver, such as the pilot on the ground. The software engine can also be used in real testbeds exploiting multiple physical links, such as 4G/5G cellular connections. The main aim of this novel software framework is to support the design, development, and test of different scheduling strategies to achieve real-time, good quality and fluidity, energy-efficient multimedia transmissions, by selecting the optimal subset of network channels able to meet the target Quality of Experience (QoE) at the receiver.

Keywords: Video quality · PSNR · Simulator · Scheduling · Multipath

1 Introduction

UAVs are attracting the attention of both the scientific community and the industrial world. Their use in science is mainly directed to UAV-assisted base-station nodes [1] in 5G networks or more complex heterogeneous networks such as space information networks [2]. In civil applications, UAVs are nowadays employed in a variety of application scenarios, thanks to the versatility and low cost. Application fields of interest vary from supervising danger situations in smart environments, remote monitoring of buildings and infrastructures, treatments in precision agriculture, rescue procedures, etc.[3–5]. In those scenarios, an UAV can provide both a fast deployment and a live visualization to remote operators through on-board cameras [6]. The advantage of having a reliable live video-feedback from an UAV is twofold: on the one hand, it opens to the use of Augmented Reality (AR)/Virtual Reality (VR) techniques to support operators;

L. A. Grieco et al. (Eds.): ADHOC-NOW 2020, LNCS 12338, pp. 114–121, 2020.
https://doi.org/10.1007/978-3-030-61746-2_9

on the other hand, it enables the remote management of the UAV. Indeed, remote piloting leverages Global Navigation Satellite System (GNSS)-based services through way-points, which trace a route to the destination. However, remote visual feedback for the pilot is a requirement to perform adjustment and emergency maneuvers, thus constantly monitoring the surrounding environment and avoiding possible accidents. The extreme heterogeneity of conditions, such as time- and space-varying channels characteristics, require very careful testing of the communication subsystem, and real testbeds are both costly and risky. For this reason, a simulation/emulation tool is an effective solution in this regard. To fill the gap between a simulation platform and a real environment, we propose in this work an emulation tool, able to reproduce the communication chain between a remote UAV and a visualization interface used by the pilot. Both simulated and real links between the transmitter and the receiver can be used and tested. The proposed tool differs from other renowned ones, like EvalVid [7], because it aims at designing and implementing multipath scheduling policies; for instance, exploiting multiple cellular connections jointly, so meeting the requirement of a minimum QoE [8] (measured according to the Mean Opinion Score (MOS)) when subject to real or simulated Quality of Service (QoS) parameters, such as Packet Loss Rate (PLR), jitter, and delay. Furthermore, the emulation tool will implement a man-in-the-loop feedback chain to allow the end-user (e.g. the pilot) to provide subjective feedback (e.g. perceived QoE) to the scheduler. The feedback provided by the end-user can be used jointly with objective feedback metrics (e.g. QoS), such as Peak Signal-to-Noise Ratio (PSNR). This additional subjective feedback can be leveraged through a reinforcement approach to map QoE onto QoS in different scenarios, also opening to the use of proactive [9] and reactive coding [10,11] to counteract impairments.

In Sect. 2, we present a brief survey of analytical models to map QoS onto QoE. In Sect. 3, the proposed simulator framework is presented. The conclusions and the future works are in Sect. 4.

2 QoE Models for Video Quality Assessment

As mentioned in Sect. 1, reliable video feedback from an UAV to a remote operator on the ground allows developing real-time remote command and control systems for UAVs. In this scenario, quantifying the feeling of the operator about the received video, in terms of QoE, becomes crucial to design a control system adapting the video transmission to the quality of the network links, expressed in terms of QoS. Appropriate metrics are then needed to evaluate the mapping of the variations of the QoS parameters into the user-level QoE perception. Once done, such a mapping can be used by a control system to keep the user-perceived quality above an acceptable threshold. A reference metric used to measure the feeling of a user about a video is the MOS [8]. MOS evaluation is performed using the statistical inference on the opinion scores, usually within a five-point interval. For the scope of this work, both video quality and video fluidity are considered, thus entailing the need for control policies. Video artifacts, missing frames, poor fluidity, and so on, mainly depend from QoS parameters such as packet loss, delay, jitter, or reordering.

Several works in the literature, e.g. [12–14], faced with the definition of mapping QoS onto QoE. In [13,14], the authors discuss learning approaches for both online and offline mapping. All the proposed mappings build on quality comparisons between the undistorted video and the received video, namely *reference* and *outcome*, respectively. The quality of the outcome can be rated in terms of MOS using the reference. Whether the reference is available or not defines the following types of metrics: Full Reference (FR), No Reference (NR), and Reduced Reference (RR). In the case of FR, subjective and objective comparisons of the outcome with the reference can be performed, because both are available at the receiver. Hence, an accurate metric can be derived, performing the offline estimation of the model parameters. Offline estimations can be very precise, but also rather complex and strictly dependant from the considered settings. In the case of NR, a quality score must be derived directly from the outcome, because no reference video is available at the receiver. An alternative comes from online estimations of QoE, for instance through the end-user's feedback. NR-based metrics lack the possibility of discerning between quality issues and disturbance due to the network [13,14]. On the one hand, the latter cannot be precisely captured; on the other hand, obtained metrics are rather simple (low complexity) and thus suitable for online use in resource-constrained and/or real-time settings. In the case of RR, man-in-the-loop techniques are used, thus users' feedback is collected at the sender in addition to network statistics. Such a feedback can be used to evaluate the perceived QoE and consequently mapped onto QoS. The estimation of the mapping parameters can be performed using online approaches [14]. Also, the RR metric is rather simple, thus opening to its use in resource-constrained and/or real-time settings, as in our reference scenario [6].

Figure 1 shows a qualitative mapping between QoE (y-axis) and QoS (x-axis); QoS degrades when moving from QoS_1 to QoS_2. The first region, to the left of the threshold QoS_1, represents the case of a slight degradation of QoS with negligible effects on the QoE. When the QoS degradation falls within $[QoS_1, QoS_2]$ (i.e., the second region), the QoE start decreasing and, as the line color turns from green to orange, it increasingly becomes uncomfortable for end-users. After the threshold QoS_2 (third region), QoE can be considered as unacceptable, with end-users potentially giving up on the service. In [15,16], the authors discuss the results of a metric having a similar trend to that in Fig. 1. They show that a model based on Eq. (1) is suitable for a scenario using cellular networks.

$$QoE = k_1 - \frac{k_2}{(1 + \frac{k_3}{QoS^{k_4}})^\eta} \tag{1}$$

The maximum value of QoE is imposed through the parameter $k1$. Instead, the parameters $\{k2, k3, k4, \eta\}$ depend on the network and on the video codecs used for the video streaming, and must be evaluated empirically. The model in Eq. (1) is also adopted in [17] to analyze the mapping between QoE and QoS, taking into account the correlation of both PLR and packet size. The authors use those

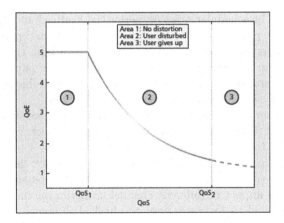

Fig. 1. Quantitative trend of the QoE vs QoS parameter (Color figure online)

two parameters to evaluate the theoretically expected Decodable Frame Rate. Q can be defined as the fraction of the decodable frame rate, i.e., the ratio of the number of theoretically expected decodable frames to the total number of frames sent by a video source. Then, the authors rewrite the model in Eq. (1) as a function of Q with values ranging within $[0, 1]$, also providing an estimation for the set of parameters $\{k1, k2, k3, k4, \eta\}$. The estimation in [17] is a good match for our reference scenario [6] because the cross-layer approach proposed therein puts the network parameters, i.e., QoS, in relation with the perceived QoE. In details, the latter is influenced by the packet error rate, in turn affecting the decoding rate of video frames (I, P, and B frames).

3   The Novel Software Tool

The logical architecture of the tool proposed in this work can be seen in Figs. 2 and 3. Three main blocks can be identified: sender, channel, and receiver. The sender side takes a video stream as input, captured through the use of the PCAP interface (e.g., employing *tcpdump/libpcap*). The input video flow must be a RTP/UDP stream, which is then sent to a TEE[1] module (see Fig. 2) responsible for the creation of N copies of the stream, with N being the instantiated source modules, corresponding to N physical channels. Each source module src_i is responsible for delivering the video to the corresponding receiver module dst_i via the physical channel ch_i. Thus, the multimedia stream to be delivered can be replicated up to N times. The logical multipath channel is composed of N physical channels, jointly used to meet the desired QoE. The scheduler module is responsible for implementing the scheduling policy, exploiting periodic feedbacks. In fact, the transmission probability pt_i is estimated by the scheduler per source module by applying a strategy aiming at maximizing the QoE of the

---

[1] Name inspired by the Gstreamer *tee* module performing the same function.

multimedia flow. The scheduler relies on periodical feedback to adjust the transmission probability per channel according to the implemented policy, which uses the QoS parameters (see Sect. 2) as inputs. In more words, the copies of each packet of the stream are sent (or not) on the corresponding physical channel ch_i according to its transmission probability pt_i; thus, it is possible to finely control the use of each physical channel, ranging from 0% to 100%.

In order to better understand how the simulator works, we should distinguish between the use of simulated physical channels (see Subsect. 3.1) and real ones (see Subsect. 3.2). In fact, each source element src_i opens a network socket to send data to the corresponding socket dst_i at destination: thus, it is alternatively possible to: (i) rely on the simulated channel implementation we developed to assess the impact of different channel statistics on the perceived QoE; (ii) use a custom tool to simulate/emulate physical channels, such as NetEm[2]; (iii) transmit the video via real physical channels. At this time, options (i) and (ii) are under testing, and (iii) under active development. The destination side is described in Sectsect. 3.3.

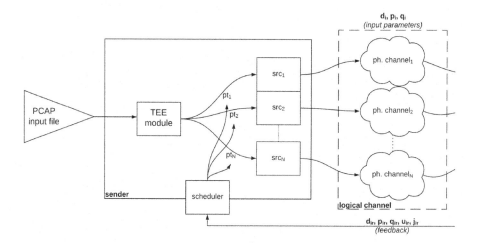

Fig. 2. Sender side and channel

3.1   Simulated Physical Channels

When multiple physical channels are simulated, it is possible to set the channel statistics by means of an external configuration file. Three parameters must be set: the delay d_i introduced by each channel; the average rate of loss events p_i, and the average rate of packet losses q_i per channel. In more words, each time a loss event is triggered according to the rate p_i, the number of lost packets within the loss event is governed by the rate q_i, thus accounting for bursty losses. The parameters d_i, p_i, and q_i must be provided for each channel as a tuple (α_i, β_i), representing shape and scale of a Gamma distribution $\Gamma_i(\alpha_i, \beta_i)$.

---

[2] Details at http://man7.org/linux/man-pages/man8/tc-netem.8.html.

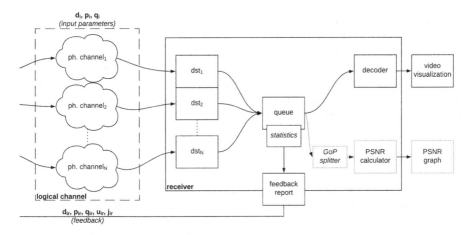

Fig. 3. Channel and receiver side

3.2   Real Physical Channels

If a real testbed is considered, then the video is sent to a receiver running on another machine. In the case of emulated channels, external tools can be exploited (e.g. NetEm). In both cases, the configuration parameters presented in Subsect. 3.1 are ignored. Thus, actual delay, rate of loss events, and average rate of packet losses depend on external parameters or factors.

3.3   Destination Side

At the destination side, each module dst_i receives the packet stream on the listening socket and forwards them to the queue module. The latter is responsible for aggregating the N flows and calculating per-flow statistics. The tuple of values that provides the per-flow statistics are: (i) the average delay d_{ir}; (ii) the average rate of loss events p_{ir}; (iii) the average rate of packet losses q_{ir}; (iv) the average rate of out-of-order packets u_{ir}; (v) and the jitter j_{ir}. A feedback report is built by concatenating the N tuples, and then the report is sent to the scheduler module at the sender side. The queue module forwards the received stream to the video decoder, then to a video player. We assume real-time video, i.e., a maximum overall delay of $m = 200$ [ms] as in [6]. A Gstreamer-based[3] pipeline is used for playing the video, composed of the following ordered Gstreamer plugins: `udpsrc | rtpbin | rtph264depay | h264dec | audiovideosink`. Such a solution can be substituted by other solutions taking an UDP/RTP stream as input.

In the case of emulated/simulated channels with both sender and receiver running on the same machine, the three modules in dotted squares in Fig. 3, i.e. the Group of Pictures (GoP) splitter, the PSNR calculator, and the PSNR graph, are automatically enabled. The GoP splitter recognizes the end of a H.264

---

[3] Details at https://gstreamer.freedesktop.org.

GoP, then it waits additional m [ms] to account for delayed or out-of-order packets, and finally writes to disk the still images (video frames) composing the GoP. Assuming that still images, representing the original video sequence, are also available at the sender side (or in a local directory whose path is set in the configuration file), PSNR can be computed. The resulting data series is then graphically visualized in the *PSNR graph* module, providing a real-time objective evaluation of the received video.

4   Conclusions

We plan to conclude soon the development and test phases of the proposed software tool, which will be freely released as open source code to the scientific community. Future works see the development of a web interface to test and use the simulator, along with the possibility of providing subjective feedback to the scheduler as regards the perceived video quality. Multiple scheduling strategies will be designed, developed, and tested, taking into account video quality, video fluidity, channels use, and energy efficiency.

References

1. Li, B., Fei, Z., Zhang, Y.: UAV communications for 5G and beyond: recent advances and future trends. IEEE IoT J. **6**(2), 2241–2263 (2018)
2. Bacco, M.: IoT applications and services in space information networks. IEEE Wirel. Commun. Mag. **26**, 31–37 (2019)
3. Bacco, M.: UAVs and UAV swarms for civilian applications: communications and image processing in the SCIADRO project. In: Pillai, P., Sithamparanathan, K., Giambene, G., Vázquez, M.Á., Mitchell, P.D. (eds.) WiSATS 2017. LNICST, vol. 231, pp. 115–124. Springer, Cham (2018). https://doi.org/10.1007/978-3-319-76571-6_12
4. Bacco, M., Delmastro, F., Ferro, E., Gotta, A.: Environmental monitoring for smart cities. IEEE Sens. J. **17**(23), 7767–7774 (2017)
5. Bacco, M., et al.: Monitoring ancient buildings: real deployment of an IoT system enhanced by UAVs and virtual reality. IEEE Access **8**, 50:131–50:148 (2020)
6. Bacco, M., Cassará, P., Gotta, A., Pellegrini, V.: Real-time multipath multimedia traffic in cellular networks for command and control applications. In: Vehicular Technology Conference (Fall), Honolulu, Hawaii, USA, pp. 1–5. IEEE (September 2019)
7. Klaue, J., Rathke, B., Wolisz, A.: EvalVid – a framework for video transmission and quality evaluation. In: Kemper, P., Sanders, W.H. (eds.) TOOLS 2003. LNCS, vol. 2794, pp. 255–272. Springer, Heidelberg (2003). https://doi.org/10.1007/978-3-540-45232-4_16
8. ITU-T, REC-P.800.2 SERIES P: Terminals and Subjective and Objective Assessment Methods (July 2016). www.itu.int/rec/T-REC-P.800.2/en
9. Wu, M., Makharia, S., Liu, H., Li, D., Mathur, S.: IPTV multicast over wireless LAN using merged hybrid ARQ with staggered adaptive FEC. IEEE Trans. Broadcast. **55**(2), 363–374 (2009)

10. Celandroni, N., Gotta, A.: Performance analysis of systematic upper layer FEC codes and interleaving in land mobile satellite channels. IEEE Trans. Veh. Technol. **60**(4), 1887–1894 (2011)
11. Gotta, A., Barsocchi, P.: Experimental video broadcasting in DVB-RCS/S2 with land mobile satellite channel: a reliability issue. In: International Workshop on Satellite and Space Communications, pp. 234–238. IEEE (2008)
12. Engelke, U., Zepernik, H.-J.: Perceptual-based quality metrics for image and video services: a survey. In: Next Generation Internet Networks Conference, pp. 190–197. IEEE (May 2007)
13. Alreshoodi, M., Danish, E., Woods, J., Fernando, A., De Alwis, C.: Prediction of perceptual quality for mobile video using fuzzy inference systems. Trans. Consum. Electron. **61**, 546–554 (2015)
14. Riker, E.A.A., Mu, M., Zeadally, S.: Real-time QoE prediction for multimedia applications in wireless mesh networks. In: IEEE International Conference on CCNC 2012, pp. 592–596 (January 2012)
15. Poncella, J., Gomez, G., Hierrezuelo, A., Lopez-Martinez, F.J., Aamir, M.: Quality assessment in 3G/4G wireless networks. Bus. Media Wirel. Pers. Commun. **76**, 363–377 (2014)
16. Monteiro, V.F., Sousa, D.A., Maciel, T.F., Lima, F.R.M., Rodrigues, E.B., Cavalcanti, F.R.P.: Radio resource allocation framework for quality of experience optimization in wireless networks. Network **29**, 33–39 (2015)
17. Sidibe, M., Koumaras, H., Kofler, I., Mehaoua, A., Kourtis, A., Timmerer, C.: A novel monitoring architecture for media services adaptation based on network QoS to perceived QoS mapping. Sig. Image Video Process. **2**, 307–320 (2008)

Internet of Things and Internet of Medical Things

Image-Based Mobility Assessment in Elderly People from Low-Cost Systems of Cameras: A Skeletal Dataset for Experimental Evaluations

Laura Romeo[✉], Roberto Marani, Antonio Petitti, Annalisa Milella,
Tiziana D'Orazio, and Grazia Cicirelli

Institute of Intelligent Industrial Technologies and Systems
for Advanced Manufacturing, National Research Council, Bari, Italy
laura.romeo@stiima.cnr.it

Abstract. In recent years, the scientific community has found increasing interest in technological systems for the evaluation of the mobility performance of the elderly population. The reduced quantity of dataset for gait and balance analysis of elderly people is a serious issue in studying the link between cognitive impairment and motor dysfunction, particularly in people suffering from neurodegenerative diseases. In this context, this work aims to provide a dataset with skeletal information of people aged 60 years and older, while they perform well-established tests for stability assessment. 27 healthy people and 20 patients affected by neurodegenerative diseases, housed at two different nursing institutes, have been selected for the stability analysis. Subjects have been observed and evaluated by clinical therapists while executing three motion tests, namely balance, sit-to-stand and walking. The stability postural and gait control of each subject has been analyzed using a video-based system, made of three low-cost cameras, without the need for wearable and invasive sensors. The dataset provided in this work contains the skeletal information and highly-discriminant features of the balance, sit-to-stand and walking tests performed by each subject. To evaluate the efficiency of the balance dataset, the estimated risk of fall of the subjects has been processed considering the extracted features, and compared with the expected one. Final results have proven a good estimation of the risk of fall of the people under analysis, underlining the effectiveness of the dataset.

Keywords: Skeletal dataset · Neurodegenerative diseases · Low-cost cameras · OpenPose

1 Introduction

It has been shown that there is a strict link between cognitive impairment and motor dysfunction such as deficits in gait and balance [6,9]. Furthermore, func-

© Springer Nature Switzerland AG 2020
L. A. Grieco et al. (Eds.): ADHOC-NOW 2020, LNCS 12338, pp. 125–130, 2020.
https://doi.org/10.1007/978-3-030-61746-2_10

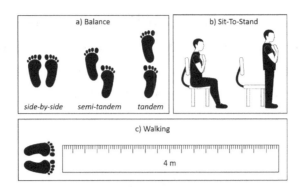

Fig. 1. SPPB tests: a) Balance test, which is composed of three exercises where the patient has to stand with the feet in side-by-side, then in semi-tandem and finally tandem positions; b) Sit-To-Stand test, which consists in sitting and standing up 5 times while keeping the arms crossed on the chest; c) Walking test, which consists in the patient covering a path of 4 m.

tional assessment measure protocols can help to qualify gait and posture of the patients. In this scenario, the Short Physical Performance Battery (SPPB) represents a well-established means to assess physical performance status and evaluate functional capabilities [3], to monitor and prevent the risk of falls. Such functional assessment measure is composed of three tests to assess lower body function, namely Balance Test (BT), Sit-To-Stand Test (STST) and Walking Test (WT), which instructions are represented in Fig. 1.

The risk of fall is qualitatively evaluated by expert clinical personnel with respect to the execution of the SPPB tests, in agreement with the medical protocols. Despite the high professional competence of the operators, the need for developing innovative technological systems is of great interest, since human-based assessment can be susceptible to drifts and biases. For this purpose, the need for datasets containing physical performance status information is becoming an issue of increasing interest, as the development of new technological systems that can support clinical personnel strictly depends on both the quality and quantity of available data.

In literature, various datasets related to the evaluation of the motion skills of elderly people are presented [1,5,7], yet none of them gives skeletal information specifically to the SPPB protocol. Most of the datasets outlined in literature provide information only regarding the static analysis of the patient, without releasing information about the dynamic aspect, which is fundamental in evaluating the risk of falls. Moreover, even when the patient's skeleton is analyzed, the dataset often concerns only a singular type of exercise, thus producing a non-heterogeneous amount of data.

This work provide a complete dataset of age, sex and skeletal information of people aged 60 years and older, while they perform all the three tests included in the SPPB protocol. A complete vision-based system, made of three low-cost cameras, has been developed for accurately measuring stability postural control,

Table 1. Classification method for each test. Each exercise is assessed based on its duration.

Test	0	1	2	3	4
Balance	*Side-by-side*	0–9 s	0–2 s	3–9 s	10 s
		semi-tandem	*tandem*	*tandem*	*tandem*
Sit-To-Stand	*Incapable*	>7.5 s	7.4–5.4 s	5.3–4.1 s	<4.1 s
Walking	*Incapable*	>16.6 s	16.6–13.7 s	13.6–11.2 s	<11.2 s

without the need for wearable and invasive sensors. The exercise videos, grabbed from two nursing institutes, have been normalized and synchronized to extract the most significant features from the skeletons, which carry information about balance, gait, and strength, to properly evaluate the risk of falls. Such features, along with sex, age, and the skeletal information of the patient itself, have been added to the dataset. The reliability of the dataset has been tested using the features extracted in the BT as input of a classifier [8]. Final results have proven a good estimation of the risk of fall of people under analysis.

The paper is structured as follows. Section 2 defines the tests included in the SPPB protocol. In Sect. 3 the developed methodology is defined, along with the video pre-processing and the feature extraction for the provided dataset. Section 4 draws the evaluation of the dataset, highlighting its efficiency. Finally, the conclusions are presented in Sect. 5.

2 Tests Definition

The proposed paper aims to establish the risk of fall of elderly people and patients affected by neurodegenerative diseases, through the analysis of the tests included in the SPPB. Several patients, housed at the two nursing institutes of the study, have been selected for the postural and stability analysis. Each patient has been instructed to perform first the BT, then the STST, and finally the WT. For each test, a specialized therapist observes the patients and measures their time execution using a stopwatch. Such tests are then evaluated following an appropriate score system, shown in Table 1.

In the following, the SPPB tests are defined:

- **Balance Test:** The test of standing balance includes side-by-side, semi-tandem and tandem positions. The patient is instructed to maintain each position for 10 s, measured by a clinical therapist. If a patient fails to complete the test within ten seconds, the elapsed time is measured anyway.
- **Sit-To-Stand Test:** The STS test consists of sitting and rising from a chair placed against the wall for safety purposes. The patient is asked to fold her/his arms across her/his chest, and to stand up and sit down from the chair 5 times. A clinical therapist times the exercise starting from the initial sitting position to the final standing position.

- **Walking Test:** During the walking test, the patient is instructed to follow a path of 4 m with no obstructions. A clinical therapist is in charge of timing the exercise.

3 Methodology

3.1 Camera Setup and Video Pre-processing

The whole setup consists of three low-cost cameras, namely the HIKVision [4], usually used for video-surveillance. The three cameras have been installed in fixed position, along the sides of a volume of interest. As stated previously, two setups have been designed and installed in two nursing homes, under different condition of lighting, acquiring 720 × 480 resolution videos.

As the output videos are not suitable for image processing in their raw form, a pre-processing phase is mandatory to prepare the videos to the following feature extraction procedure. In detail, the pre-processing stage is a sequence of selection and conversion algorithms, namely:

- **Frame per second (FPS) conversion:** As the videos from the three cameras have variable framerates, the lowest framerate among the three videos has been selected, projecting the time axes on a common reference, sampled with a unique framerate to achieve uniformity.
- **Video shifting:** A start signal, given the clinical therapists with a remote control, triggers the three video acquisitions, which however start with non-negligible relative delays. To overcome such issue, the early-started videos are shifted of a number of frames equal to the relative delays.
- **Video trimming:** As most of the videos are long streams, the input streams are trimmed in exercise-related sub-videos.
- **Video Calibration:** As the videos suffer from image distortion, the extrinsic parameters have been extracted from the cameras of both setups to properly calibrate them.

3.2 Features Extraction

The complete knowledge of the position in space, or equivalently in the image plane, of the skeletal joints of the patients is enough to infer postural information. For this reason, the feature extraction process starts with the detection of the skeleton of the patients under analysis.

Skeleton detection is performed by means of the OpenPose library [2], which gives a real-time multi-person 2D pose estimation, aiming to represent both position and orientation of human limbs. For this work, the COCO training model has been implemented. It allows the identification of 18 skeletal joints from each person.

Different features have been chosen depending on the type of exercise, aiming to extract the most relevant information according to the test under analysis. As a matter of fact, each test provides different, yet relevant information regarding

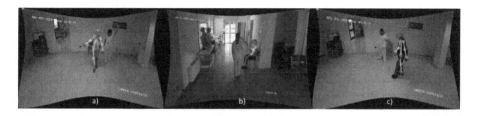

Fig. 2. SPPB tests performed by different patients. Namely, a) Balance Test, b) Sit-To-Stand Test, and c) Walking Test.

the posture and stability of the patient. Therefore, it reveals to be fundamental to properly select the highly-discriminant features with respect to each test, in order to suitably gather an amount of information about the patient as heterogeneous as possible.

4   Dataset Evaluation

The proposed paper has been developed to provide sex, age, skeleton information and highly-discriminant features of patients performing SPPB tests. 20 patients suffering from a neurodegenerative disease and 27 healthy people perform the tests.

As a first step, all the acquired videos of the exercises performed by the patients have been studied, to evaluate their validity. Then, the preprocessing phase has been carried out to prepare the videos for the skeleton and features extraction, via the application of the OpenPose library. Finally, the dataset is completed with a vector of evaluation scores given by clinical therapists for each test.

Examples of patients performing BT, STST, and WT are shown in Fig. 2. To properly evaluate the efficiency of the dataset[1], the information grabbed from patients performing BTs are considered. The highly-discriminant features extracted from the skeletons are used to feed a decision tree classifier, which has been trained to label patients into 5 classes of increasing risk of falls, shown in Table 1. The final score given by clinical therapists has been compared to estimated one [8]. The good accuracy of the system (equal to 79.1%) shows the effectiveness of the provided dataset.

5   Conclusions

In this paper, a complete dataset composed of sex, age, skeletal information and relevant features of elderly people performing SPPB protocol has been presented. Subjects have been grabbed by a system of three low-cost surveillance cameras. Then, proper video processing techniques have been used to highlight

---

[1] The dataset will be shortly uploaded on the website: http://cms.stiima.cnr.it/isp/.

the skeletal joints of the subjects and to extract highly-discriminant features. It has been proved the high efficiency of the proposed dataset in the assessment of the patient's stability and posture skills, and their consequent risk of fall.

In the future, further semantic analysis of the videos will be investigated, to analyze more relevant features to be extracted from the skeletons, and to assess the progress of the neurodegenerative disease of patients observed during long periods.

Acknowledgement. The authors thank Michele Attolico and Giuseppe Bono for their technical and administrative support.

References

1. Auyeung, T.W., Arai, H., Chen, L., Woo, J.: Normative data of handgrip strength in 26344 older adults-a pooled dataset from eight cohorts in Asia. J. Nutr. Health Aging **24**(1), 125–126 (2020)
2. Cao, Z., Hidalgo, G., Simon, T., Wei, S.E., Sheikh, Y.: OpenPose: realtime multi-person 2D pose estimation using Part Affinity Fields. arXiv preprint arXiv:1812.08008 (2018)
3. Guralnik, J.M.: A short physical performance battery assessing lower extremity function: association with self-reported disability and prediction of mortality and nursing home admission. J. Gerontol. **49**(2), M85–M94 (1994)
4. HIKVision: Products and solution. https://www.hikvision.com/en/
5. Nguyen, T.N., Meunier, J.: Walking gait dataset: point clouds, skeletons and silhouettes. DIRO, University of Montreal, Technical report, p. 1379 (2018)
6. Pavasini, R.: Short physical performance battery and all-cause mortality: systematic review and meta-analysis. BMC Med. **14**(1), 215 (2016)
7. Perkin, O., McGuigan, P., Stokes, K.: Dataset for 'exercise snacking to improve muscle function in healthy older adults: A pilot study' (2019)
8. Romeo, L., Marani, R., Lorusso, N., Angelillo, M.T., Cicirelli, G.: Vision-based assessment of balance control in elderly people. In: 2020 IEEE International Symposium on Medical Measurements and Applications, MeMeA 2020, Bari, Italy (May 2020)
9. Schlicht, J., Camaione, D.N., Owen, S.V.: Effect of intense strength training on standing balance, walking speed, and sit-to-stand performance in older adults. J. Gerontol. Ser. A Biol. Sci. Med. Sci. **56**(5), M281–M286 (2001)

Energy Saving in TSCH Networks by Means of Proactive Reduction of Idle Listening

Stefano Scanzio$^{(\boxtimes)}$ ⓘ, Gianluca Cena ⓘ, Adriano Valenzano ⓘ, and Claudio Zunino ⓘ

National Research Council of Italy (CNR-IEIIT),
Corso Duca degli Abruzzi 24, 10129 Turin, Italy
{stefano.scanzio,gianluca.cena,adriano.valenzano,
claudio.zunino}@ieiit.cnr.it

Abstract. Conserving energy is probably the most important requirement in wireless sensor networks. In TSCH, this goal is obtained by subdividing time into slots, and by switching the communication interface of Internet of Things devices (frequently referred to as motes) off when, at any given time, neither transmissions nor receptions are scheduled for them. Nevertheless, in this kind of networks a considerable amount of energy may still be wasted due to idle listening. This occurs every time a cell is scheduled for frame reception but no transmissions are performed in the related slot and channel.

In this paper, Proactive Reduction of Idle Listening (PRIL) techniques are introduced, which aim at lowering the energy wasted because of the above phenomenon. In particular, here we focus on a simplified mechanism that only considers the first hop (PRIL-F). A relevant feature of this kind of techniques is that they cannot worsen performance in any way. On the contrary, in those cases where they can be applied, they may only bring benefits. Results obtained through a simulation campaign show a tangible reduction in energy consumption, especially for periodic traffic generation, in application contexts based on either a star topology (wireless sensor and actuator networks) or a two-level topology (wireless sensor networks).

Keywords: Time Slotted Channel Hopping · TSCH · Wireless sensor networks · Wireless sensor and actuator networks · Power saving · Energy consumption · Idle listening · PRIL · PRIL-F

1 Introduction

The Time Slotted Channel Hopping (TSCH) operating mode of the IEEE 802.15.4 [1] standard is an established technique that permits to save energy through traffic scheduling [2], increasing at the same time determinism in channel access [3]. In TSCH, motes are time-synchronized, time is divided into discrete time slots, and each mote knows the set of slots it is involved in, during

© Springer Nature Switzerland AG 2020
L. A. Grieco et al. (Eds.): ADHOC-NOW 2020, LNCS 12338, pp. 131–144, 2020.
https://doi.org/10.1007/978-3-030-61746-2_11

which the circuitry of its wireless interface must be on. Additionally, TSCH relies on channel hopping, which dynamically selects the transmission channel on a slot-by-slot basis by means of a pseudo-random function. This improves communication resilience against narrow-band disturbance and interference. In optimized implementations, a mote switches off its radio module every time no transmissions or receptions are scheduled for it, which results in a consistent amount of energy being saved. In many typical application contexts, a residual, non-negligible amount of energy may nevertheless be wasted due to idle listening. This occurs when a receiver mote switches on its wireless interface because a reception is scheduled, but no frame is actually sent by the transmitting mote, simply because in its transmission queue there is no frame ready to be sent.

The basic idea proposed in this paper, which was named PRIL, is to dynamically (and temporarily) turn the wireless interface in receivers off in those cells where idle listening is expected for sure. A relevant feature of PRIL techniques is that they cannot worsen network behavior, e.g., in terms of performance indices like reliability and power consumption (i.e., PRIL only provides benefits). In particular, the focus of this paper is on PRIL-F, which is a PRIL technique that is specific for the first hop, i.e., which has effect on the hop between the source mote and the next mote in the path to the destination, which is optimized for wireless sensors and actuator networks (WSAN) with star topologies and wireless sensor networks (WSN) with two-level topology. These two latter network configurations are really common in practice.

Results about the PRIL-F technique, obtained through discrete-event simulation, highlighted a tangible reduction in energy consumption. Other ways to lower the energy wasted for idle listening when overprovisioning is exploited to increase capacity on some links, maintaining at the same time the required level of service, are described in [4,5]. However, those techniques are quite specific and, in general, not as effective as PRIL, because they operate on an intra-slotframe basis and are only intended to minimize the effects on consumption of overprovisioning. On the contrary, PRIL techniques operate on an inter-slotframe basis and take full advantage from the traffic characteristics. Interestingly, intra- and inter-slotframe approaches can be adopted at the same time.

This paper has the following structure. In the next Sect. 2 the PRIL and PRIL-F techniques will be introduced. Section 3 describes the experimental environment and the discrete-event simulator, which are used in Sect. 4 to obtain experimental results. Finally, Sect. 5 draws some conclusions and sketches our future work.

2 Proactive Reduction of Idle Listening (PRIL)

In some real implementations, the energy E_{listen} consumed by a mote for *idle listening*, i.e., to listen to the channel for the reception of a single frame in the case that the frame does not arrive, can be more than half the energy spent to actually send (E_{tx}) or receive (E_{rx}) a frame. For instance, for OpenMoteSTM devices [6], when the maximum dimension for confirmed frames is taken into account (whose size is 127 B), the values for energy are $E_{rx} = 651.0\,\mu J$, $E_{tx} = 485.7\,\mu J$ and $E_{listen} = 303.3\,\mu J$ (see Table 1 and Subsect. 3.1 for more details). The latter two contributions, i.e., E_{tx} and E_{rx}, refer to essential operations performed by the mote for communicating, which are directly related to the transmission of a piece of data over the network between given source and destination devices. However, it is worth remembering that in all the cells scheduled for reception (RX) in the TSCH matrix, the mote must have its receiving apparatus on. When no data is received in these cells, the energy required to wake up the mote and perform channel sensing should be considered as wasted from the application point of view.

Actually, the portion of energy consumed for idle listening with respect to the other two contributions (i.e., transmission and reception) is not fixed, but depends on the average generation period of frames by the application and the characteristics of the channel. For instance, as a simple but representative example of the problem, let us consider an application that needs to transmit a packet every $T_{S \to D} = 60\,s$ between two neighbor motes M_S and M_D separated by one hop, and that one cell is reserved for this exchange every 2 s. This means that, if the transmission succeeds at the first attempt, just one every 30 cells will be actually used by the transmitter. In other words, 96.6% of the times the cell remains unused and energy is consequently wasted on the receiver due to idle listening. If channel errors are considered, the fraction of slots wasted for idle listening decreases because of retransmissions performed by the Automatic Repeat reQuest (ARQ) mechanism [7] exploited to increase reliability.

The ability to lower, if not completely eliminate, the contribution of idle listening would significantly reduce energy consumption and lead to a substantial increase of battery lifetime. The idea proposed in this paper, referred to as PRIL, relies on the definition of a new Media Access Control (MAC) `sleep` command. When a mote receives a sleep command, it suspends listening in the given cell for the amount of time specified in the command. Possibly, inhibition of listening can be addressed to other cells defined in the TSCH matrix of the receiving mote and, by exploiting additional mechanisms, even to subsequent motes in the path to the destination. This latter option, which would make the technique more flexible, was not evaluated in this work, and was left for future investigations.

In order to reduce power and bandwidth consumption, the sleep command can be embedded right into the data frames sent by M_S to M_D, exploiting *information elements*. This command includes suitable parameters that specify for how long listening must stay disabled in one (or more) motes in the path between M_S and M_D. Such duration can be expressed in either relative or absolute terms. In the former case, the number of slots (or slotframes) is given for which listening is suspended. In the latter case, instead, an Absolute Slot Number (ASN) is provided that represents the slot when listening must be re-enabled. The best option, in order to achieve a compact encoding, is certainly to specify the relative number of slotframes, because it just requires a few bits, the exact number depending on the maximum time for which listening can be disabled. A more complex encoding should instead be selected in the case the sleep command refers to more than one cell and mote.

An important property of PRIL that is worth remarking is that the destination mote continues to behave according to its normal operation in the case the sleep command, for any reason, is not received. Losing a sleep command is typically a rare event, because the maximum number of allowed attempts per frame ranges, depending on the implementation, between 4 and 16. However, in the case it gets lost, the network keeps working exactly in its usual way, just without any of the improvements provided by PRIL. Returning to PRIL-enabled operation occurs as soon as a subsequent frame including a new sleep command is received.

In this paper, a simple but effective PRIL technique will be presented and evaluated, which operates in a simplified way and targets quite common contexts. We named it Proactive Reduction of Idle Listening at the First hop (PRIL-F).

2.1   PRIL-F

The PRIL-F technique just acts on the first hop in a path connecting a source mote M_S and a destination mote M_D. Let $M_S, M_1, M_2, \ldots, M_D$ be the path between M_S and M_D. The sleep command is included in the frame sent by mote M_S, and it has effect only on mote M_1, i.e., energy saving regards only M_1.

The sleep command, which is encoded as an *information element*, contains the time T_{next} (expressed in terms of the related ASN) in which listening in the cell must be reactivated again. Although ASN is actually a relative time, as it represents the number of timeslots since network startup, it can be considered as an absolute time from the PRIL point of view. In fact, whenever the value of ASN is reset to zero as a consequence of a network reconfiguration, the internal state of PRIL (i.e., sleeping cells) is also reset. In this paper, using an absolute time (like the ASN) or a relative time (based on a number of slots or slotframes) is equivalent, because we did not model the additional energy spent to send the information element containing T_{next}. In practical implementations, this contribution can be often considered negligible when compared with the energy spent for sending the whole frame. As an example, for the confirmed transmission of a packet with a 30 B payload, the overhead due to the physical layer (6 B), the medium access control layer (23 B), and the confirmation provided by the related ACK frame (33 B) have to be also considered in TSCH. Overall, the amount of data transmitted on the wireless medium is 92 B. For encoding the sleep command in an information element (e.g., in a specific *header information element*), both its prefix (length and element ID, 2 B) and the related ASN (5 B) have to be taken into account. As a consequence, the overhead caused by adding T_{next} to frames is below 10%.

An example of the PRIL-F technique, which holds also for more complex PRIL versions when the computation of T_{next} is possible, is reported in Fig. 1. To better highlight the behavior of the technique, we set the maximum number of transmission attempts a packet can undergo before being discarded to $N_{tries} = 2$ (i.e., the initial attempt plus one retry) and the size of the slotframe to $N_{slot} = 2$. The generation period on the sender is equal to 3 slotframes. Boxes with red dashed lines denote periods where listening is suspended. In the figure, three situations are reported: in the first, the frame containing $T_{next} = 109$ is received by the destination mote, and the effect of PRIL-F is that idle listening is prevented in two cells; in the second, both frames containing the sleep command $T_{next} = 115$ are lost, and PRIL-F has no effect; in the third, the frame containing $T_{next} = 121$ arrives to the destination at the second attempt, and idle listening is saved in one slot.

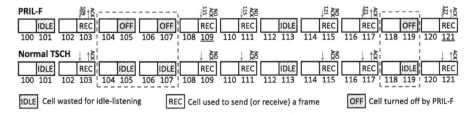

Fig. 1. Example of PRIL-F/PRIL operation and comparison with conventional TSCH.

Clearly, so that PRIL-F can correctly work the sending mote M_S must have the ability to compute the value T_{next} (that depends on the time of the immediately following transmission), so that it can be embedded in the current outgoing frame. In several application contexts of WSNs, this requirement can be easily meet. In particular, in many sensing and control applications packets are sent cyclically [8] and, since the transmission period is known in advance, the computation of T_{next} is quite trivial. This is the case, e.g., of most industrial contexts [9]. In other kinds of applications, a value can be determined for T_{next} that does not worsen transmission latency only when a lower bound exists on the intertime between two adjacent packet transmissions (sporadic generation) or in those cases where it is possible to conceive some algorithm that foresees the next transmission time. The latter aspect is certainly an interesting research topic, but it is out of the scope of the current work, which more pragmatically aims at evaluating the effects of PRIL on the energy consumption of real motes. As long as T_{next} can be correctly determined (in some way) PRIL-F never worsens performance, in the sense that reliability and latency remain unchanged (in some conditions they can be also computed analytically [10]), while power consumption typically decreases by a tangible amount.

The PRIL-F technique is intended for WSNs where paths include very few hops. As we will see in experimental results, this technique mostly suits networks with either a star or a two-level tree topology. On the contrary, if applied to very deep network architectures, the saved energy decreases as the number of levels increases. Analyzing more in detail some relevant scenarios, the star topology is quite common in many practical applications devoted to control and sensing. Some examples are in-vehicle networks [11], most wireless solutions conceived for industrial systems [12], and wireless body area networks (WBAN) [13]. In

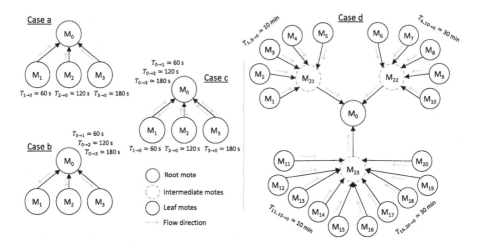

Fig. 2. Experimental configurations for single-level star topology (cases *a*, *b*, and *c* on the left) and two-level topology (case *d* on the right).

the case of a star topology, PRIL-F proves to be optimal, i.e., it ensures the best results concerning the saving related to the energy wasted for idle listening.

For multi-level architectures the situation is slightly different. The application for which the PRIL-F technique provides the best results is sensing, where communication takes place between leaves and the root in the upward direction. In the case of two-level networks, thanks to PRIL-F intermediate motes turn their receiving interface on at runtime only when needed, i.e., when a packet will be certainly transmitted by a leaf mote. In this configuration, the root mote is unable to selectively switch off listening in cells so as to prevent idle listening, because it is two hops away from leaves. However, this is typically irrelevant, since this device is customarily connected to an external power source. When the number of levels is higher than two, only the intermediate mote that communicates directly with the source benefits from PRIL-F. It is worth pointing out that, for upward transmission (related to sensing), leaf motes turn on their radio module only when they effectively have some data to send, and consequently no optimization that involves disabling the cells subject to idle listening is possible at that level. In addition, motes close to the root are sometimes provided with an external power supply, in which case energy saving techniques are not necessary.

Below, some of the previously described network architectures will be analyzed in detail by means of an extensive experimental campaign based on simulation.

3   Experimental Setup

The following simulation analysis was carried out to compare the performance of the proposed PRIL-F technique with a conventional TSCH implementation. A number of relevant cases were taken into account, which are reported in Fig. 2. The first three configurations, which are identified in the figure as *case a*, *b*, and *c*, refer to networks with a star topology. They are related to systems where the network traffic consists only of upward communications from leafs to the root (*case a*), only of downward communication from the root to leafs (*case b*), and of both upward and downward communications (*case c*). For these configurations we defined flows with three distinct periods, namely 60.04 s for flows directed to (or coming from) mote M_1, 120.06 s for flows involving M_2, and 180.10 s for flows involving M_3. We selected periods that are not exactly multiples so as to model tolerances in real oscillators and, in particular, to take into account the fact that time slotting in a TSCH network exploits time synchronization among motes [14], but the generation of packets by applications is triggered by the local time sources, which are not synchronized in any way. The reason behind this decision is to add some randomness on the order with which packets of each flow are queued in motes. Each flow is characterized by the source and destination motes. In detail: flows $\tau_{0 \to 1}$ and $\tau_{1 \to 0}$ refer to mote M_1, $\tau_{0 \to 2}$ and $\tau_{2 \to 0}$ to mote M_2, and $\tau_{0 \to 3}$ and $\tau_{3 \to 0}$ to mote M_3.

The last configuration in Fig. 2 (*case d*) includes 24 motes, and is representative of larger networks made up of two levels. Below the root, at the first level, three intermediate motes (M_{21}, M_{22}, and M_{23}) act as relays for three distinct sets of leaf motes. In the first set ($\tau_{1 \dots 5 \to 0}$), which is connected to M_{21}, each mote generates a periodic flow whose period is about 10 min. Also in this case periods were selected so that they are not exactly the same. A second set of flows ($\tau_{6 \dots 10 \to 0}$) was defined for the five motes connected to M_{22}, and the generation period was set to about 30 min. Finally, the 10 motes from M_{11} to M_{20} are connected to mote M_{23}. In this case, half of the motes have generation periods equal to about 10 min, while for the other half generation periods are about 30 min.

More details about the simulator and the most important configuration parameters used in experimental campaigns are provided below.

3.1   The Simulator

A streamlined, custom simulator has been purposely implemented, with the aim to have available a tool for analyzing specific aspects of TSCH, which is simpler and more flexible than existing full-fledged simulators. It eases development and experimentation of new techniques related to, e.g., power saving, including those relying on idle listening prevention. In addition, this approach allowed us to focus on the most relevant details related to the effectiveness of PRIL techniques, by implementing only those parts of the protocol that are strictly required for our analysis.

Many simulators exist for TSCH, and some of them deal specifically with the IPv6 over the TSCH mode of IEEE 802.15.4 (6TiSCH) [15] protocol. Although in this paper motes based on 6TiSCH were taken as reference for modeling power consumption, the presented techniques can be applied to every protocol based on TSCH, and more in general to those relying on time slotting and Time-Division Multiple Access (TDMA). The most popular network simulator for 6TiSCH is

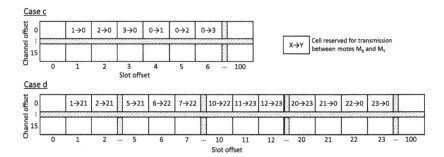

Fig. 3. Configuration of the matrices defining the global schedule for experimental conditions in cases c and d .

probably *6TiSCH simulator* [16]. Compared with 6TiSCH simulator, our simulator is noticeably simpler. In particular, it only permits a static configuration of the TSCH schedule, it does not allow the definition of shared cells, and it does not model the transmission of control messages. Moreover, it supports only static network topologies (i.e., the RPL protocol was not implemented,) and does not take into account the application layer and the related protocols.

Our simulator is implemented as a discrete-event one, and is based on the SimPy framework, which is written in the **python** programming language. The TSCH matrices that define the schedule were statically configured as follows: starting from slot offset 1, we firstly placed the cells associated to upward flows, and then those regarding downward flows. For configurations with more than one level, like *case d* in Fig. 2, we scheduled the transmissions between leafs and intermediate motes before the transmissions between intermediate motes and the root.

Channel hopping was implemented in the simulator but, for the sake of simplicity, the same frame error probability $\epsilon = 0.2$ (which is a plausible value for real setups [10]) was selected for all links and channels. This means that, due to retries, the number of frames transmitted on air is about 25% higher than generated packets. The configurations of the matrices defining the global schedule for the experimental conditions in cases c and d are reported in Fig. 3. The simulator makes it possible to easily configure the number of slots within the slotframe (N_{slot}), the duration of a slot (T_{slot}), the maximum number of transmission attempts per frame (N_{tries}), and the frame error probability for every link.

The energy model used by the simulator is the one reported in [6] for Open-MoteSTM devices equipped with a STM32F103RB 32-bit microcontroller and the Atmel AT86RF231 radiochip, and executing the OpenWSN operating system. Measures of energy consumption for other kinds of motes can be found in [17,18]. Starting from [6], and multiplying the values reported in that work (which are expressed in coulombs) by the typical supply voltage of these motes (3 V), we obtained the energy (expressed in joules) to transmit (E_{tx}) and receive (E_{rx}) a confirmed frame with size 127 B, as well as the energy wasted for idle listening (E_{listen}). In the analysis reported in this paper, only the energy consumed by the network component has been taken into account. In this context, the energy related to computation is mostly irrelevant, because it is not affected by PRIL techniques. The main configuration parameters we used in the simulator, including those related to energy consumption, are listed in Table 1.

Table 1. Most relevant simulation parameters.

Quantity	Description	Typical value
N_{slot}	Number of slots within the slotframe	101
T_{slot}	Duration of a slot	20 ms
N_{tries}	Maximum number of tries	16
ϵ	Frame error probability	0.2
E_{tx}	Energy to transmit a DATA frame and receive the ACK	485.7 μJ
E_{rx}	Energy to receive a DATA frame and transmit the ACK	651.0 μJ
E_{listen}	Energy wasted for idle listening	303.3 μJ

In order to provide statistics related to power consumption, the simulator counts the number of cells in the experiment actually used to transmit and receive confirmed frames, and those in which idle listening occurs. Starting from these counters, it computes the rates at which each one of the previous operations takes place (f_{tx}, f_{rx}, and f_{listen}, respectively), and then the power consumption (P_{tx}, P_{rx}, and P_{listen}, respectively). All these quantities represent average values evaluated over the whole experiment.

4   Results

The first experimental campaign was aimed to assess the effectiveness of PRIL-F for cases a, b, and c of Fig. 2 (i.e., for a star topology). In all the experiments, unless otherwise specified, we used the parameters reported in Table 1 and the generation periods, for each flow, reported in Fig. 2. The simulated duration of each experiment was set to 1 year, which consists in 15.6 millions of slotframe repetitions.

As highlighted in the results reported in Table 2, in these experimental conditions power consumption was reduced by one order of magnitude. For instance, in *case c* it decreased from 964.48 μW to 86.76 μW. As stated above, PRIL-F provides the best results with a one-level star topology. In all conditions (i.e., *cases a*, *b*, *c*), the rate f_{listen} with which idle listening events occur decreases from relatively high values (e.g., f_{listen} = 5209 slots/h for M_0 in configurations *case a* and *c*) to practically 0 (f_{listen} = 0.0206 slots/h, again for M_0 in *case a* and *c*). It did not reach exactly 0 for two main reasons: firstly, during network startup, before the first sleep command (i.e., a frame containing T_{next} encoded

Table 2. Comparison between conventional TSCH and the PRIL-F techniques for network architectures based on a star topology .

Cond.	Mote	T_{app} [s]	Conventional TSCH					PRIL-F				
			f_{tx}	f_{rx}	f_{listen}	P_{listen}	P	f_{tx}	f_{rx}	f_{listen}	P_{listen}	P
			[slots/hour]			[µW]		[slots/hour]			[µW]	
Case a	M_0	-	-	137.38	5209	438.86	463.70	-	137.38	0.0206	0.00174	24.85
	M_1	60	74.90	-	-	-	10.11	74.90	-	-	-	10.11
	M_2	120	37.50	-	-	-	5.06	37.50	-	-	-	5.06
	M_3	180	24.98	-	-	-	3.37	24.98	-	-	-	3.37
	All motes		137.38	137.38	5209	438.86	**482.24**	137.38	137.38	0.0206	0.00174	**43.38**
Case b	M_0	-	137.38	-	-	-	18.54	137.38	-	-	-	18.54
	M_1	60	-	74.90	1707	143.82	157.36	-	74.90	0.0034	0.000287	13.55
	M_2	120	-	37.50	1745	147.02	153.80	-	37.50	0.0069	0.000581	6.78
	M_3	180	-	24.98	1757	148.03	152.55	-	24.98	0.0103	0.000868	4.52
	All motes		137.38	137.38	5209	438.86	**482.24**	137.38	137.38	0.0206	0.00174	**43.38**
Case c	M_0	-	137.36	137.41	5209	438.86	482.24	137.36	137.41	0.0206	0.00174	43.38
	M_1	60	74.89	74.92	1707	143.82	167.47	74.89	74.92	0.0034	0.000287	23.65
	M_2	120	37.52	37.45	1745	147.02	158.85	37.52	37.45	0.0069	0.000581	11.84
	M_3	180	25.00	25.00	1757	148.03	155.92	25.00	25.00	0.0103	0.000868	7.90
	All motes		274.77	274.78	10418	877.72	**964.48**	274.77	274.78	0.0412	0.00347	**86.76**

as an information element) is sent, listening was not disabled; secondly, for packets that went lost (i.e., for which N_{tries} transmission attempts were performed without success) the receiving mote did not go to sleep (until T_{next}) because the sleep command is not received (see Fig. 1). As expected, the PRIL-F technique had no effect on f_{tx} and f_{rx}, which are directly related to the slots actually used to transmit data frames.

The power consumption P is computed by the simulator using the following formula:

$$P = f_{tx} \cdot E_{tx} + f_{rx} \cdot E_{rx} + \underbrace{f_{listen} \cdot E_{listen}}_{P_{listen}} \tag{1}$$

It must be noted that frequencies reported in Table 2 have to be transformed in hertz (Hz) dividing them by 3600. Results show that the contribution $P_{listen} = f_{listen} \cdot E_{listen}$ is practically reduced to 0 by PRIL-F.

Concerning *cases b* and *c*, where downward flows are also considered, the overall power consumption with conventional TSCH is practically the same for motes M_1, M_2, and M_3, whereas it is proportional to the sending period T_{app} when PRIL-F is exploited, which is exactly the desired behavior.

Results for the two-level network (*case d*) are reported in Table 3. In this case the network is used only for sensing, and leaf motes (from M_1 to M_{20}) are configured so that they do not perform any reception of packets (at least, those involved in applications). For this reason, no energy saving can be obtained for them with PRIL techniques. Similarly, PRIL-F has no effect on mote M_0, because it is more than one hop away from packet sources, which for sensing applications are usually leaf motes. Only in the case intermediate relay motes (M_{21}, M_{22}, and

Table 3. Comparison between conventional TSCH and PRIL-F techniques for a WSN architecture with two levels (*case d*).

Mote	Conventional TSCH					PRIL-F				
	f_{tx}	f_{rx}	f_{listen}	P_{listen}	P	f_{tx}	f_{rx}	f_{listen}	P_{listen}	P
	[slots/hour]			[μW]		[slots/hour]			[μW]	
M_0	-	99.93	5247	442.06	460.13	-	99.93	5247	442.06	460.13
M_1 (10 min)	7.49	0.0	0.0	0.0	1.01	7.49	0.0	0.0	0.0	1.01
M_6 (30 min)	2.51	0.0	0.0	0.0	0.34	2.51	0.0	0.0	0.0	0.34
M_{21}	37.53	37.50	8873	747.55	759.40	37.53	37.50	0.170	0.0143	11.86
M_{22}	12.51	12.51	8898	749.66	753.61	12.51	12.51	0.509	0.0429	3.99
M_{23}	49.90	49.96	17772	1497.29	1513.06	49.90	49.96	0.678	0.0571	15.82
Relays	99.94	99.97	35543	2994.50	**3026.06**	99.94	99.97	1.357	0.114	**31.68**
All motes	199.90	199.90	40790	3436.56	**3499.68**	199.90	199.90	5248	442.14	**505.26**
All without M_0	199.90	99.97	35543	2994.50	**3039.55**	199.90	99.97	1.357	0.114	**45.16**

M_{23}) as well perform sensing on a cyclic basis, some improvements on energy consumption can be achieved for the root mote M_0. However, in most real WSNs the root is connected to a wired power supply.

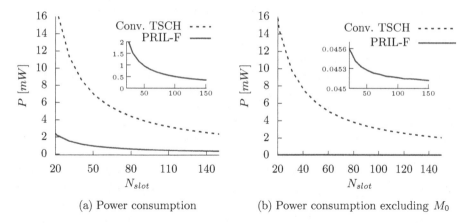

(a) Power consumption   (b) Power consumption excluding M_0

Fig. 4. Power consumption in conventional TSCH and PRIL-F vs. N_{slot}, including (on the left) and excluding (on the right) the root mote (gateway). Zoomed out portions of interest are also included as subplots.

On the contrary, the energy saved by intermediate motes thanks to PRIL-F is considerable. In particular, in the proposed experimental condition, the overall power consumption of intermediate motes (row labeled "Relays" in the table) is reduced by two orders of magnitude, from 3026.06 μW to 31.68 μW. Considering such motes individually, the one with the highest power consumption is M_{23}, which relays the traffic of 10 leaves. For this mote, energy consumption decreases from 1513.06 μW to 15.82 μW when PRIL-F is exploited, which is more close to leaf motes (even though still one order of magnitude larger).

A beneficial effect of PRIL-F in this configuration is to balance the power consumed by distinct motes of the network, by bringing relief to intermediate

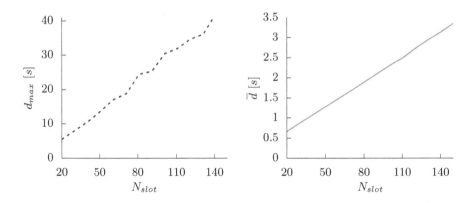

Fig. 5. Maximum (d_{max}, on the left) and average ($\overline{d}$, on the right) latency vs. N_{slot}.

motes, which are typically the most energy-hungry. Consequently, this increases the overall network lifetime in those cases where planned maintenance foresees that battery replacement is carried out on all motes at the same time. The decrease in power consumption is noticeable also when the network is considered as a whole. Excluding mote M_0, which typically is not powered on batteries, overall consumption decreases from $3039.55\,\mu$W to $45.16\,\mu$W.

A final set of experiments was performed to evaluate the effect of N_{slot} (i.e., the number of slots in one slotframe) on power consumption and transmission latency. In particular, the same experiment of *case d* was repeated 15 times, by varying N_{slot} from 11 to 151 with a step equal to 10 slots. Plots related to the power consumption for both conventional TSCH and PRIL-F are reported in Fig. 4. In particular, the plot in Fig. 4a refers to the whole network, while the plot in Fig. 4b shows the same data, but excluding the contribution of the root mote M_0. As expected, in both cases power consumption decreases quickly when the width of the slotframe increases. The PRIL-F technique outperforms conventional TSCH, especially when mote M_0 is excluded from the computation of the power consumption. In the latter case, the actual value chosen for N_{slot} is practically irrelevant, i.e., it ranges from $46.09\,\mu$W when $N_{slot} = 11$ to $45.12\,\mu$W when $N_{slot} = 151$ (see the zoomed out portion in the subplot of Fig. 4b).

The relationship between N_{slot} and the transmission latency is linear, as highlighted by plots in Fig. 5, which refer to the maximum (d_{max}) and average ($\overline{d}$) values of latency, respectively.

In conclusion, in the typical operating conditions considered in this paper, the adoption of PRIL-F, when feasible, permits real motes to save a tangible amount of energy. Moreover, by configuring smaller values for N_{slot} (or when more than one cell is scheduled for communication between pairs of motes) it enables smaller cycle times without impacting in a tangible way on power consumption. This implies shorter latency and improved real-time behavior at a modest price in terms of lifetime/power consumption.

5   Conclusions

An extensive simulation campaign showed that the adoption of PRIL techniques, including the simpler PRIL-F version, permits the energy wasted due to idle listening to be noticeably lowered (and sometimes almost completely eliminated) in practice. In particular, this is true for typical network configurations (star WSANs/WSNs and two-level WSNs), and when it is possible to predict in advance when the next transmission in a specific TSCH cell will take place. This latter requirement is always met for periodic flows, which are very common in many application contexts (most sensors are parameterized with the sampling rate).

In a representative example of a two-level network composed of 20 leaf motes and 3 relay motes at the intermediate level, power consumption (not counting the gateway/root) was reduced by almost two orders of magnitude thanks to PRIL-F, from $3040\,\mu W$ to $45\,\mu W$. Main future activities will include the development and analysis of more effective PRIL techniques, which can be exploited on networks with more than two levels, and possibly based on intelligent algorithms for inferring automatically the next transmission times.

References

1. IEEE Standard for Low-Rate Wireless Networks. IEEE Std 802.15.4-2015 (Revision of IEEE Std 802.15.4-2011), pp. 1–709 (April 2016). https://doi.org/10.1109/IEEESTD.2016.7460875
2. Mohamadi, M., Senouci, M.R.: Scheduling algorithms for IEEE 802.15.4 TSCH networks: a survey. In: Demigha, O., Djamaa, B., Amamra, A. (eds.) CSA 2018. LNNS, vol. 50, pp. 4–13. Springer, Cham (2019). https://doi.org/10.1007/978-3-319-98352-3_2
3. Hermeto, R.T., Gallais, A., Theoleyre, F.: Scheduling for IEEE802.15.4-TSCH and slow channel hopping MAC in low power industrial wireless networks: a survey. Comput. Commun. **114**, 84–105 (2017). https://doi.org/10.1016/j.comcom.2017.10.004. ISSN 0140–3664
4. Cena, G., Scanzio, S., Seno, L., Valenzano, A., Zunino, C.: Energy-efficient link capacity overprovisioning in time slotted channel hopping networks. In: 16th IEEE International Conference on Factory Communication Systems (WFCS), pp. 1–8 (April 2020). https://doi.org/10.1109/WFCS47810.2020.9114449
5. Utgård, M.: Idle Listening Reduction Mechanism for Overprovisioned Cells in 6TiSCH Tracks. PhD thesis, University of Oslo (2019)
6. Vilajosana, X., Wang, Q., Chraim, F., Watteyne, T., Chang, T., Pister, K.S.J.: A realistic energy consumption model for TSCH networks. IEEE Sens. J. **14**(2), 482–489 (2014). ISSN 2379–9153. https://doi.org/10.1109/JSEN.2013.2285411
7. Cena, G., Scanzio, S., Seno, L., Valenzano, A.: Comparison of mixed diversity schemes to enhance reliability of wireless networks. In: Palattella, M.R., Scanzio, S., Coleri Ergen, S. (eds.) ADHOC-NOW 2019. LNCS, vol. 11803, pp. 118–135. Springer, Cham (2019). https://doi.org/10.1007/978-3-030-31831-4_9
8. Khader, O., Willig, A., Wolisz, A.: Distributed wakeup scheduling scheme for supporting periodic traffic in WSNs. In: 2009 European Wireless Conference, pp. 287–292 (2009). https://doi.org/10.1109/EW.2009.5357978

9. Cena, G., Scanzio, S., Seno, L., Valenzano, A.: Optimal retransmission allocation for EDF-based networked real-time applications. In: 15th IEEE International Workshop on Factory Communication Systems (WFCS), pp. 1–8 (2019). https://doi.org/10.1109/WFCS.2019.8758018

10. Cena, G, Demartini, C.G., Vakili, M.G., Scanzio, S., Valenzano, A., Zunino, C.: Evaluating and modeling IEEE 802.15.4 TSCH resilience against Wi-Fi interference in new-generation highly-dependable wireless sensor networks. Ad Hoc Netw. (2020). ISSN 1570–8705. https://doi.org/10.1016/j.adhoc.2020.102199

11. Tavakoli, R., Nabi, M., Basten, T., Goossens, K.: Topology management and TSCH scheduling for low-latency convergecast in in-vehicle WSNs. IEEE Trans. Ind. Inform. 15(2), 1082–1093 (2019). https://doi.org/10.1109/TII.2018.2853986

12. Zhang, Z., Mehmood, A., Shu, L., Huo, Z., Zhang, Y., Mukherjee, M.: A survey on fault diagnosis in wireless sensor networks. IEEE Access 6, 11349–11364 (2018). https://doi.org/10.1109/ACCESS.2018.2794519

13. Velusamy, B., Pushpan, S.C.: An enhanced channel access method to mitigate the effect of interference among body sensor networks for smart healthcare. IEEE Sens. J. 19(16), 7082–7088 (2019). ISSN 2379–9153. https://doi.org/10.1109/JSEN.2019.2913002

14. Mongelli, M., Scanzio, S.: A neural approach to synchronization in wireless networks with heterogeneous sources of noise. Ad Hoc Netw. 49, 1–16 (2016). ISSN 1570–8705. https://doi.org/10.1016/j.adhoc.2016.06.002

15. Thubert, P.: An Architecture for IPv6 over the TSCH mode of IEEE 802.15.4. IETF Std draft-ietf-6tisch-architecture-28, pp. 1–69 (October 2019)

16. Municio, E., et al.: Simulating 6TiSCH networks. Trans. Emerg. Telecommun. Technol. 30(3), e3494 (2019). https://doi.org/10.1002/ett.3494

17. Boccadoro, P., Piro, G., Striccoli, D., Grieco, L.A.: Experimental comparison of industrial internet of things protocol stacks in time slotted channel hopping scenarios. In: IEEE International Conference on Communications (ICC), pp. 1–6 (2018). https://doi.org/10.1109/ICC.2018.8422899

18. Papadopoulos, G.Z., et al.: Guard time optimisation and adaptation for energy efficient multi-hop TSCH networks. In: IEEE 3rd World Forum on Internet of Things (WF-IoT), pp. 301–306 (2016). https://doi.org/10.1109/WF-IoT.2016.7845475

Towards Long-Lasting Nanoscale Wireless Communications in the Terahertz Band for Biomedical Applications

Vittoria Musa[1,2], Giuseppe Piro[1,2(✉)], L. Alfredo Grieco[1,2],
and Gennaro Boggia[1,2]

[1] Department of Electrical and Information Engineering, Politecnico di Bari,
via Orabona 4, Bari, Italy
{vittoria.musa,giuseppe.piro,alfredo.grieco,gennaro.boggia}@poliba.it
[2] CNIT, Consorzio Nazionale Interuniversitario per le Telecomunicazioni,
Parma, Italy

Abstract. During the last decade, the research on nanotechnology and wireless communications in the terahertz band supported the design of pioneering biomedical applications. To counteract the very scarce amount of energy available for nano-devices, a current challenge is to develop energy-aware and energy harvesting mechanisms enabling long-lasting communications at the nanoscale. Many contributions in this direction envisage exploiting piezoelectric nanogenerators to retrieve energy from external vibrations (i.e., the human heartbeat) and use it for transmission purposes. Indeed, in line with the recent scientific achievements in this context, this paper investigates a power control mechanism based on the feedback control theory. The control law is conceived for managing the communication in human tissues, where nano-devices are equipped with a piezoelectric nanogenerator and transmit information messages through electromagnetic waves in the terahertz band. The amount of energy spent to transmit an information message is dynamically tuned by a proportional controller in a closed-loop control scheme which simultaneously considers harvesting and discharging processes. The whole system is analytically described with a nonlinear state equation. As well, it is presented the acceptable range of values of the proportional gain guaranteeing technological constraints and its asymptotic stability. Finally, a numerical evaluation shows the behavior of the proposed approach in a conceivable biomedical scenario.

Keywords: Terahertz communications · Energy harvesting · Control law · Biomedical application

1 Introduction

The new frontier of nanotechnology is supporting the design of novel and advanced biomedical applications. In fact, nano-devices can be implanted,

L. A. Grieco et al. (Eds.): ADHOC-NOW 2020, LNCS 12338, pp. 145–158, 2020.
https://doi.org/10.1007/978-3-030-61746-2_12

ingested, or worn by humans in order to realize drug-delivering and advanced immune systems, biohybrid implant solutions, pervasive health monitoring, and genetic engineering [1]. The interaction among nano-devices can be enabled by nanoscale wireless communications in the terahertz band [11]. Since the communication process is energy-consuming, the usage of energy-aware and harvesting mechanisms is extremely important to achieve long-lasting communications at the nanoscale [6]. Many scientific contributions in this context assume to harvest energy from the external environment through piezoelectric nanogenerators [4,5,22] and, consequently, to use it in energy-aware communication protocols [2–4,12–14,18,20,21] (see Sect. 2). The idea to tune the transmission power based on the available energy budget has been recently investigated for diffusion-based molecular communications [15], but no works studied similar methodologies in nanoscale wireless communications and biomedical use cases.

To provide a step forward in this direction, this paper investigates a power control mechanism based on the feedback control theory. The control law is properly conceived for managing the communication in human tissues, where nano-devices are equipped with a piezoelectric nanogenerator and transmit information messages through electromagnetic waves in the terahertz band. Specifically, the amount of energy spent to transmit an information message is dynamically tuned by a proportional controller in a closed-loop control scheme which jointly considers harvesting and discharging processes. Here, the harvesting process is modeled as an ideal voltage source in series with a resistor and an ultra-nanocapacitor, while the discharging process is modeled through a current generator in parallel with the ultra-nanocapacitor. The resulting system is described by a nonlinear state equation where the voltage across the ultra-nanocapacitor and the resulting available energy represent the state variable and the feedback variable, respectively. Then, the acceptable range of values for the proportional gain is evaluated by considering 1) technological constraints, including transmission settings due to the Time Spread On-Off Keying (TS-OOK) modulation scheme and minimum energy requirements ensuring an effective communication in a stratified medium, and 2) the asymptotic stability of the system around the equilibrium point. Finally, a numerical analysis is performed to evaluate the impact of the proposed solution on the system behavior in conceivable biomedical scenarios, by considering different communication distances, frame sizes, and message generation statistics.

The rest of this work is organized as in what follows. Section 2 reviews the state of the art on energy harvesting and energy-aware schemes in the terahertz band. Section 3 presents the proposed approach. Section 4 discusses preliminary numerical results obtained in conceivable biomedical scenarios. Finally, Sect. 5 draws the conclusions of the work and summarizes future research activities.

2   Related Works

Traditional harvesting mechanisms (exploiting solar, thermal, and wind sources) are inefficient at the nanoscale. Thus, it is important to introduce new energy harvesting models, like those using mechanical and chemical sources [6,13].

Among the others, piezoelectric nanogenerators composed by lead zirconate titanate [16] or Zinc Oxide [22] nanowires, are widely considered promising solutions for retrieving energy at the nanoscale. Here, the vibrations or motions existing in the surrounding environment bent or compress the nanowires generating an electric current at their ends which charges an ultra-nanocapacitor [17].

Nowadays, several contributions already studied the usage of piezoelectric nanogenerators in nanoscale wireless communications. For example, [8] and [23] model the energy state of nano-devices through Markov chain, while jointly considering the energy harvesting rate and the energy consumption due to the communication process. The study presented in [24] theoretically investigates the achievable throughput of energy harvesting nanonetworks. Other contributions formulate energy-aware mechanisms at different levels of the protocol stack: the energy budget is used to define the time between two consecutive transmissions at the physical layer [4], to control data dissemination in a wireless nano-sensor network [18,20], and to properly manage the Media Access Control protocol [2,3,12–14,21].

At the time of this writing, and to the best of authors' knowledge, the information about the available energy budget has never been exploited for conceiving power control mechanisms in nanoscale wireless communication systems. In [15], the same authors of this paper propose a preliminary energy-aware transmission scheme for diffusion-based molecular communication that dynamically tunes (exploiting the control theory) the transmission power starting from the amount of available energy retrieved by a piezoelectric nanogenerator. This promising approach is applied herein in the context of nanoscale wireless communications enabling biomedical applications, while deeply taking into account the peculiarities of electromagnetic waves transmitted in the terahertz band and the propagation impairments registered in human tissues.

3   The Proposed Approach

This work considers a nano-device implanted in the human body and fed by a piezoelectric nanogenerator. It is able to collect biomedical information (e.g., the presence of sodium, glucose, other ions in blood, cholesterol, cancer biomarkers, and other infectious agents) and communicate them to a receiver positioned on the skin surface by means of electromagnetic waves in the terahertz band. Then, the obtained information can be transmitted to a remote device through traditional communication paradigms. The reference scenario is depicted in Fig. 1.

The main analytical symbols used in this paper are reported in Table 1.

3.1   Application Model and Transmission Scheme

At the physical layer, the nano-device sends messages of M bits by using the TS-OOK modulation scheme. These messages are generated according to a Poisson distribution with parameter λ. The duty cycle of the signal to transmit represents

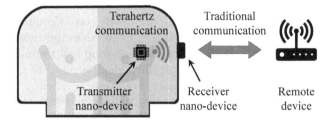

Fig. 1. The reference scenario.

Table 1. List of the main symbols used in this paper.

Symbol	Description
T_p, E_p	Time interval needed to transmit a pulse and resulting consumed energy
M	Number of bit per frame
λ	Average number of frames per second
σ, μ	Standard deviation and mean of the Gaussian pulse
d	Distance between transmitter and receiver nano-devices
f, f_m, f_M	Communication frequency, lower operative frequency, and higher operative frequency
$A_{abs}(f, d)$, $A_{spread}(f, d)$, $A(f, d)$	Absorption, spreading, and total path loss
$S(f)$, $N(f, d)$	Signal power spectral density and noise power spectral density
$\mathcal{C}(d)$	Upper bound of the channel capacity
$\delta(t)$, $\overline{\delta}$	Duty cycle of the signal to transmit and its average value
ρ	Occurrence probability of bit 1
v_h, $i_h(t)$, R_h	Generator voltage, generator current, and resistance of the circuit modeling the harvesting process
h_h	Amount of harvested energy per cycle
t_h	Time duration of the harvesting cycle
C_u	Capacitance of the ultra-nanocapacitor
$i_u(t)$	Current through the ultra-nanocapacitor
$i_d(t)$	Load current modeling the discharging process
g_p	Proportional gain of the controller
$V_u(t)$, $\dot{V}_u(t)$	Voltage across the ultra-nanocapacitor and its variation
E_0	Set point of the closed-loop control scheme
$E(t)$	Available energy budget at the ultra-nanocapacitor
E_{min}	Minimum amount of energy required to transmit bit 1
E_c	Amount of energy consumed per frame at the equilibrium
V_{eq}	Equilibrium point of the closed-loop control scheme

the ratio between the total amount of time spent to transmit the bits 1 of a frame and the frame duration itself. Thus, considering a probability of bit 1 equal to ρ, a pulse duration of T_p, and an average inter-arrival message time $1/\lambda$, the average duty cycle of the signal to transmit is equal to:

$$\bar{\delta} = \rho M T_p \lambda. \tag{1}$$

With TS-OOK, the bit 1 is encoded by means of a short pulse (i.e., $T_p = 100$ fs), and the bit 0 is represented by the silence. The pulse shape is modeled as a derivative of the Gaussian function with mean μ and standard deviation σ: $s(t) = (\sigma\sqrt{2\pi})^{-1}e^{-(t-\mu)^2/(2\sigma^2)}$ [7]. Considering the first derivative of that Gaussian function, the signal power spectral density of the pulse-based signal is:

$$S(f) = \left(\frac{E_p T_p}{\int_{f_m}^{f_M}(2\pi f)^2 e^{(-2\pi\sigma f)^2}df}\right)(2\pi f)^2 e^{(-2\pi\sigma f)^2} \tag{2}$$

where E_p, f_m, and f_M are the energy associated with a transmitted pulse, the lower operative frequency and the higher operative frequency, respectively.

3.2   Propagation Model and Channel Capacity

The propagation of the electromagnetic field in human tissues is modeled by considering a non-homogeneous and dispersive stratified medium, where each layer (stratum corneum, epidermis, dermis and fat) is defined by its dielectric properties and thickness [19]. The total path loss, $A(f,d)$, describes the total attenuation of the signal propagating across the human skin and is computed by summing the absorption path loss, due to the attenuation produced by the vibrations of the transmitted electromagnetic wave (i.e., $A_{abs}(f,d)|_{dB} = 10k(f)d\log e$, where $k(f)$ is the medium absorption coefficient), and the spreading path loss, due to the expansion of electromagnetic waves during the propagation (i.e., $A_{spread}(f,d)|_{dB} = 20\log(4\pi\int_{z_0}^z \frac{dz}{\lambda_g(f,d)})$, where z_0 is the reference section and λ_g is the wavelength of the plane wave propagating in the stratified medium [19]). The noise power spectral density is computed as $N(f,d) = k_B T_{eq}(f,d)$, where k_B is the Boltzmann constant and $T_{eq}(f,d)$ is the equivalent molecular noise temperature due to the molecular absorption.

To evaluate the Signal to Noise Ratio (SNR) and the resulting upper bound of the channel capacity, the total bandwidth B is divided into many narrow sub-bands lasting Δf, where the channel is non-selective. Then, the SNR for the i-th sub-band centered at the frequency f_i at a distance d, can be computed as: $SNR(f_i,d) = S(f_i)/(A(f_i,d)N(f_i,d))$. According to the Shannon theorem and considering (2), the upper bound of the channel capacity is affected by the pulse energy, E_p:

$$\mathcal{C}(d) = \sum_i \Delta f \log_2\left[1 + SNR(f_i,d)\right] =$$

$$= \sum_i \Delta f \log_2\left[1 + \frac{\left(\frac{E_p T_p}{\int_{f_m}^{f_M}(2\pi f)^2 e^{(-2\pi\sigma f)^2}df}\right)(2\pi f_i)^2 e^{(-2\pi\sigma f_i)^2}}{A(f_i,d)N(f_i,d)}\right]. \tag{3}$$

3.3   The Investigated Control Law

As depicted in Fig. 2(a), the nano-device retrieves energy from the vibrations in the surrounding environments by means of a piezoelectric nanogenerator composed by an array of Zinc Oxide nanowires [22], converts the alternating current in a direct one with a rectifier element, and stores the energy within an ultra-nanocapacitor. The retrieved energy is used to feed the communication processes.

The amount of energy available within the ultra-nanocapacitor is computed by jointly considering the harvesting and the discharging processes. According to [8,23], the harvesting process is modeled through an ideal voltage source, v_h, in series with a resistor, R_h, and the ultra-nanocapacitor, C_u. This source generates an amount of charge per cycle, h_h, every t_h seconds. Let $i_h(t)$, $i_u(t)$ and $V_u(t)$ be the generator current, the current passing through the ultra-nanocapacitor and the voltage across the ultra-nanocapacitor, respectively. The discharging process, instead, is modeled as a current source in parallel with the ultra-nanocapacitor with a load current $i_d(t)$. The resulting equivalent circuit describing the harvesting and discharging processes is shown in Fig. 2(b).

The methodology investigated in this paper allows a nano-device to dynamically tune the energy consumed for the transmission of a M-bits long frame starting from the amount of available energy with a feedback control scheme. Accordingly, the load current $i_d(t)$ is dynamically tuned with a proportional controller. The control law is designed with the aim of obtaining a positive value of $i_d(t)$, causing a positive energy consumption during the transmission of information messages. Accordingly, the proportional gain can only be greater than 0 (i.e., $g_p > 0$) and the energy budget available at the ultra-nanocapacitor, $E(t)$, is used as feedback variable. Furthermore, a null set point is considered (i.e., $E_0 = 0$), so that the load current, $i_d(t)$, is proportional to the available energy budget. The resulting feedback control system, depicted in Fig. 3, is analytically modeled by considering the voltage across the ultra-nanocapacitor, $V_u(t)$, as the state variable. Based on the procedure presented in [15], the time variation of the voltage across the ultra-nanocapacitor, $\dot{V}_u(t)$, caused by the aforementioned harvesting and discharging processes is modeled by the following state equation:

$$\dot{V}_u(t) = \frac{v_h}{R_h C_u} - \frac{V_u(t)}{R_h C_u} - \frac{g_p \delta(t) V_u(t)^2}{2}. \tag{4}$$

Since $E(t) = C_u V_u(t)^2/2$, the resulting closed-loop control scheme is nonlinear.

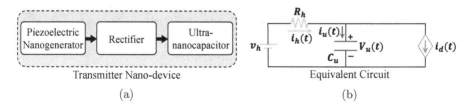

Transmitter Nano-device   Equivalent Circuit

(a)   (b)

Fig. 2. (a) Harvesting mechanism and (b) equivalent circuit modeling harvesting and discharging processes.

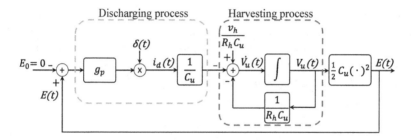

Fig. 3. The investigated closed-loop control scheme.

Equilibrium Point. After a transitory time, the system usually reaches one of the equilibrium points where it will remain for all future time. Analytically, for a continuous-time dynamical system, the equilibrium points are found by assuming a constant input (i.e., the average duty cycle of the signal to transmit, $\bar{\delta}$) and by imposing $\dot{V}_u(t) = 0$. Note that the equilibrium point should be a positive value. A negative equilibrium point, in fact, implies an inversion of the polarization of the voltage across the ultra-nanocapacitor, meaning that the load drains more current than the one generated by the harvesting process. Indeed, the only acceptable equilibrium point for the considered system is:

$$V_{eq} = \frac{-1 + \sqrt{1 + 2\bar{\delta}v_h g_p R_h C_u}}{\bar{\delta}g_p R_h C_u}. \tag{5}$$

Acceptable Value for the Proportional Gain. Besides the initial assumption on the proportional gain (i.e., $g_p > 0$), other technological constraints should be considered in order to evaluate the range of its acceptable values.

First, the equilibrium point in (5) must assume real values. Thus, the squared root and the denominator are set greater and different from zero, respectively:

$$1 + 2\bar{\delta}v_h g_p R_h C_u \geq 0 \text{ and } \bar{\delta}g_p R_h C_u \neq 0. \tag{6}$$

The analytical result of (6) states that $g_p \geq -1/2\bar{\delta}v_h R_h C_u$ and $g_p \neq 0$. Therefore, considering the initial assumption on the proportional gain (i.e., $g_p > 0$), this first condition is always verified.

Second, as highlighted in the derivation of the equilibrium point, it cannot be a negative value (i.e., $V_{eq} > 0$). This condition is always verified when $g_p > 0$.

Third, the equilibrium point cannot exceed the source voltage, v_h, that is $V_{eq} \leq v_h$. Accordingly:

$$V_{eq} = \frac{-1 + \sqrt{1 + 2\bar{\delta}v_h g_p R_h C_u}}{\bar{\delta}g_p R_h C_u} \leq v_h. \tag{7}$$

Also in this case, this condition is always satisfied when $g_p > 0$.

Finally, the fourth constraint states that the load current $i_d(t)$ and, in turns, the amount of consumed energy at the equilibrium, E_c, computed by the closed-loop control scheme should ensure the transmission of one packet entirely composed by 1-bits guaranteeing the target Shannon capacity level: $E_c = i_d(t)V_u(t)\lambda^{-1}|_{V_{eq},\bar{\delta}} \geq E_{min}$, where $E_{min} = ME_p$. Indeed, given that $i_d(t) = g_p C_u \delta(t) V_u(t)^2/2$, it comes that:

$$E_c = \frac{C_u \bar{\delta} g_p V_{eq}^3}{2\lambda} \geq E_{min}.\tag{8}$$

Analytically, (8) is verified if $-\frac{\sqrt{(v_h\lambda^{-1}(3E_{min}R_h - v_h^2\lambda^{-1}))^2 - 4E_{min}^3\lambda^{-1}R_h^3}}{E_{min}^2\bar{\delta}C_uR_h^3}$
$-\frac{v_h\lambda^{-1}(3E_{min}R_h - v_h^2\lambda^{-1})}{E_{min}^2\bar{\delta}C_uR_h^3} \leq g_p \leq \frac{\sqrt{(v_h\lambda^{-1}(3E_{min}R_h - v_h^2\lambda^{-1}))^2 - 4E_{min}^3\lambda^{-1}R_h^3}}{E_{min}^2\bar{\delta}C_uR_h^3}$
$-\frac{v_h\lambda^{-1}(3E_{min}R_h - v_h^2\lambda^{-1})}{E_{min}^2\bar{\delta}C_uR_h^3}$.

To sum up, among all the studied conditions, the fourth constraint determines both the upper and the lower bounds to the acceptable range of values of g_p.

Stability Analysis. The state equation in (4) can be linearized around the equilibrium point, V_{eq}, by using the Taylor series: $\dot{V}_u(t) = f(V_u(t), \delta(t)) \approx f(V_{eq}, \bar{\delta}) + \nabla f(V_{eq}, \bar{\delta}) \cdot [V_u(t)\ \mathcal{D}(t)]^T$, where $f(V_{eq}, \bar{\delta}) = 0$ by definition, $V_u(t) = V_u(t) - V_{eq}$ and $\mathcal{D}(t) = \delta(t) - \bar{\delta}$. Considering $V_u(t)$ as the new state variable, the linearized state equation can be written as:

$$\dot{V}_u(t) = \frac{\partial f(V_u(t), \delta(t))}{\partial V_u(t)}\bigg|_{V_{eq},\bar{\delta}} V_u(t) + \frac{\partial f(V_u(t), \delta(t))}{\partial \delta(t)}\bigg|_{V_{eq},\bar{\delta}} \mathcal{D}(t) =$$
$$= \left(-\frac{1}{R_hC_u} - \bar{\delta}V_{eq}g_p\right)V_u(t) - \frac{g_pV_{eq}^2}{2}\mathcal{D}(t).\tag{9}$$

The asymptotic stability around the equilibrium point of the linearized system in (9) is studied by posing the coefficient of $V_u(t)$ less than 0 [10], that is: $-1/(R_hC_u) - \bar{\delta}V_{eq}g_p < 0$. By substituting (5) in this inequality, it comes $-\sqrt{1 + 2\bar{\delta}v_hg_pR_hC_u}/R_hC_u < 0$ which is always verified. Therefore, considering the initial assumption on the proportional gain (i.e., $g_p > 0$), it comes that the system having the state equation defined in (4) is asymptotically stable around V_{eq} for any $g_p > 0$.

4   Numerical Results

The following numerical analysis aims at evaluating the behavior of the investigated feedback control scheme in conceivable biomedical scenarios, while considering different communication distances, frame sizes, and message generation statistics. The results are obtained through Matlab scripts, modeling the system described in Sect. 3.

Table 2. Summary of simulation parameters.

Parameters	Values	References
T_p	100 fs	[8]
v_h	0.42 V	[8,22]
C_u	9 nF	[5,8,17]
h_h	6 pC	[5,8,17]
t_h	1 s	[8,22]
σ	0.15	[19]
f	[0.5 THz–1.5 THz]	[19]
M	40 bit–100 bit	[5,8]
λ	10^{-2} frames/s–10^{-3} frames/s–10^{-4} frames/s	
d	3 mm–4 mm–5 mm	[8,19]
$\mathcal{C}$	1 Mbps	[11]

Regarding the harvesting process, the proposed study considers the human heartbeat as energy source. According to [8,22], the time duration of the harvesting cycle and the generator voltage are equal to 1 s and 0.42 V, respectively. Given that the size of both piezoelectric nanogenerator and ultra-nanocapacitor strongly affect the capacitance of the ultra-nanocapacitor, C_u, and the amount of harvested energy per cycle, h_h, [5,8,17], when these sizes are equal to $1000\,\mu m^2$, reasonable values for C_u and h_h are 9 nF and 6 pC, respectively. The source resistor is set to $R_h = \frac{v_h t_h}{h_h}$ [8]. Starting from the propagation model presented in [19], the standard deviation of the pulse is set to $\sigma = 0.15$ and the communication frequency spans from 0.5 THz to 1.5 THz. To evaluate the impact of application settings on the system performance, the proposed analysis considers two frame sizes, that are $M = 40$ bit [5] and $M = 100$ bit [8], and an average number of frames per second, spanning from 10^{-2} frames/s to 10^{-4} frames/s. The values of system parameters used throughout the numerical evaluation are summarized in Table 2.

Figure 4 shows the upper bound of the channel capacity obtained according to (3) as a function of the communication distance and the pulse energy. Considering the target Shannon capacity equal to 1 Mbps, different communication distances equal to $d = 3$ mm, $d = 4$ mm, and $d = 5$ mm can be reached by setting the minimum required energy per pulse to $E_{min} = 10$ fJ, $E_{min} = 1$ pJ, and $E_{min} = 100$ pJ, respectively. These quantities are in line with the current state of the art [8,9,11].

Given the constraints presented in Sect. 3.3, Table 3 reports the range of acceptable values for the proportional gain considering the aforementioned parameter settings. It is important to note that the range of acceptable g_p drastically reduces with the frame size, the communication distance, and the average number of frames per second. Moreover, the configuration with communication distance equal to 4 mm, 100 bit per frame, and $\lambda = 10^{-2}$ frames/s has not

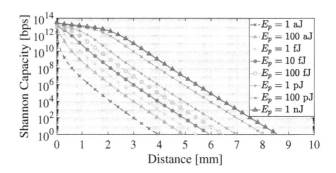

Fig. 4. Upper bound of the channel capacity.

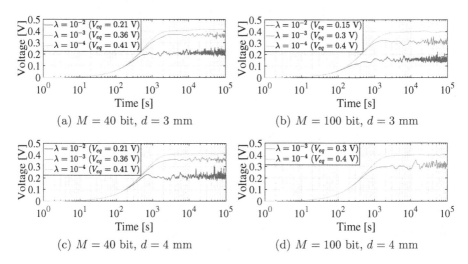

(a) $M = 40$ bit, $d = 3$ mm

(b) $M = 100$ bit, $d = 3$ mm

(c) $M = 40$ bit, $d = 4$ mm

(d) $M = 100$ bit, $d = 4$ mm

Fig. 5. Variation of the state variable, $V_u(t)$, in the time domain.

Table 3. List of the minimum and maximum acceptable proportional gain values.

		$d = 3$ mm		$d = 4$ mm		$d = 5$ mm	
		$M = 40$ bit	$M = 100$ bit	$M = 40$ bit	$M = 100$ bit	$M = 40$ bit	$M = 100$ bit
$\lambda = 10^{-2}$ frames/s	$g_{p\,min}$ [V^{-1}s^{-1}]	6.03×10^8	6.07×10^8	1.16×10^{11}	Unfeasible	Unfeasible	Unfeasible
	$g_{p\,max}$ [V^{-1}s^{-1}]	1.5×10^{17}	9.48×10^{15}	7.74×10^{12}	Unfeasible	Unfeasible	Unfeasible
$\lambda = 10^{-3}$ frames/s	$g_{p\,min}$ [V^{-1}s^{-1}]	6×10^8	6×10^8	6.3×10^{10}	6.8×10^{10}	Unfeasible	Unfeasible
	$g_{p\,max}$ [V^{-1}s^{-1}]	1.5×10^{20}	9.6×10^{18}	1.43×10^{16}	8.46×10^{14}	Unfeasible	Unfeasible
$\lambda = 10^{-4}$ frames/s	$g_{p\,min}$ [V^{-1}s^{-1}]	5.94×10^8	5.99×10^8	6.03×10^{10}	6.07×10^{10}	1.16×10^{13}	Unfeasible
	$g_{p\,max}$ [V^{-1}s^{-1}]	1.5×10^{23}	9.6×10^{21}	1.5×10^{19}	9.5×10^{17}	7.74×10^{14}	Unfeasible

acceptable proportional gain values and it is unfeasible. As well, increasing of the communication distance to 5 mm makes unfeasible all the configurations, except the one for $M = 40$ bit and $\lambda = 10^{-2}$ frames/s. For the following analysis, only the communication distances equal to 3 mm and 4 mm are taken

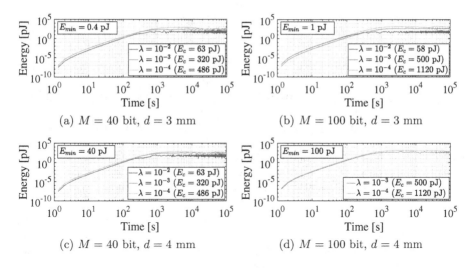

Fig. 6. Variation of the consumed energy in the time domain.

as example and a common intermediate value of g_p (i.e., $g_{p_{int}} = 7.74 \times 10^{11}$ $V^{-1}s^{-1}$) is chosen starting from the resulting acceptable ranges.

Figure 5 depicts the variation of voltage across the ultra-nanocapacitor, $V_u(t)$, in the time domain as a function of the communication distance, d, the frame size, M, and the average number of frames per second, λ. Globally, the equilibrium point, V_{eq}, decreases when λ increases. In fact, given the frame size M and the distance between transmitter and receiver d, a higher λ implies a lower time interval between consecutive message generations. This way, the system has less time to retrieve energy, leading to a lower energy budget and a lower equilibrium point. At the same time, when the transmitter has to transmit a higher number of bit per frame, M, the energy budget decreases, thus reducing the value of the equilibrium point. It is worthwhile to note that, given the value of g_p, the communication distance does not affect the value of the equilibrium point.

The effect of λ, d, and M on the variation of the consumed energy in the time domain is shown in Fig. 6. First of all, the energy consumed at the equilibrium, E_c, is usually higher when M increases. Moreover, the decreasing of the average number of frames per second, λ, implies the increment of E_c. In fact, as demonstrated for the equilibrium point, higher values of λ correspond to lower energy budget. Thus, given the proportional gain g_p, the amount of energy consumed for the communication process is lower. Also in this case, when the g_p is fixed, the communication distance does not affect the value of the energy consumed at the equilibrium. On the other hand, the minimum amount of energy required to transmit a message entirely composed by 1-bits, E_{min}, obviously increases when the number of bit per frame and the communication distance increase. In any case, the amount of energy consumed at the equilibrium is higher than E_{min}.

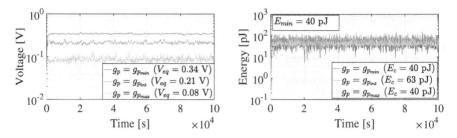

Fig. 7. Variation of (a) the state variable and (b) the consumed energy in the time domain during the transmission of a sequence of packets by considering three different acceptable values of g_p, $\lambda = 10^{-2}$ frames/s, $M = 40$ bit, and $d = 4$ mm.

As shown in Fig. 7(a), the voltage across the ultra-nanocapacitor and the amount of energy consumed for the packet transmission is also affected by the proportional gain, g_p. Given the average number of frames per second, the number of bit per frame and the communication distance, the equilibrium point increases when g_p decreases. In fact, lower values of g_p imply a decrement of the percentage of energy consumed for transmission purposes, allowing the system to reach higher equilibrium point. Combining the voltage across the ultra-nanocapacitor at the equilibrium and the value of the proportional gain, indeed, the maximum amount of energy is consumed when an intermediate value of g_p is used (see Fig. 7(b)).

5   Conclusion

This paper investigated a power control scheme for a nano-device fed by a piezo-electric nanogenerator and willing to communicate in human tissues through wireless communication in the terahertz band. After deriving the state equation of the resulting nonlinear system, the study of technological constraints and asymptotic stability provided the suitable range of values for the proportional gain. Finally, numerical examples showed the behavior of the proposed control approach in biomedical conceivable scenarios. This study demonstrated that the equilibrium point decreases when the inter-arrival message time decreases and the frame size increases, the resulting energy consumed at the equilibrium usually increases when the number of bit per frame and the inter-arrival message time increase, the increasing of the proportional gain implies the decreasing of the equilibrium point, and the maximum energy consumption is obtained when intermediate values of the proportional gain are used. Future research activities will investigate the effects of the conceived control law on the system performance, while jointly considering reception process and various network configurations.

References

1. Abbasi, O.H., et al.: Nano-communication for biomedical applications: a review on the state-of-the-art from physical layers to novel networking concepts. IEEE Access **4**, 3920–3935 (2016)
2. Akkari, N., et al.: Distributed timely throughput optimal scheduling for the internet of nano-things. IEEE Internet Things J. **3**(6), 1202–1212 (2016)
3. Alsheikh, R., Akkari, N., Fadel, E.: Grid based energy-aware MAC protocol for wireless nanosensor network. In: 2016 8th IFIP International Conference on New Technologies, Mobility and Security (NTMS), pp. 1–5 (2016)
4. Canovas-Carrasco, S., Garcia-Sanchez, A.J., Garcia-Haro, J.: A nanoscale communication network scheme and energy model for a human hand scenario. Nano Commun. Netw. **15**, 17–27 (2018)
5. Canovas-Carrasco, S., Garcia-Sanchez, A.J., Garcia-Haro, J.: On the nature of energy-feasible wireless nanosensor networks. Sensors **18**(5), 1356 (2018)
6. Chandrasekaran, S., et al.: Micro-scale to nano-scale generators for energy harvesting: self powered piezoelectric, triboelectric and hybrid devices. Phys. Rep. (2018)
7. Jornet, J.M., Akyildiz, I.F.: Channel modeling and capacity analysis for electromagnetic wireless nanonetworks in the terahertz band. IEEE Trans. Wireless Commun. **10**(10), 3211–3221 (2011)
8. Jornet, J.M., Akyildiz, I.F.: Joint energy harvesting and communication analysis for perpetual wireless nanosensor networks in the terahertz band. IEEE Trans. Nanotechnol. **11**(3), 570–580 (2012)
9. Jornet, J.M., Akyildiz, I.F.: Femtosecond-long pulse-based modulation for terahertz band communication in nanonetworks. IEEE Trans. Commun. **62**(5), 1742–1754 (2014)
10. Khalil, H.: Nonlinear Systems: Pearson New International Edition. Always Learning. Pearson Education Limited (2013)
11. Lemic, F., et al.: Survey on Terahertz Nanocommunication and Networking: A Top-Down Perspective, September 2019
12. Mohrehkesh, S., Weigle, M.C., Das, S.K.: DRIH-MAC: a distributed receiver-initiated harvesting-aware mac for nanonetworks. IEEE Trans. Mol. Biol. Multi-Scale Commun. **1**(1), 97–110 (2015)
13. Mohrehkesh, S., Weigle, M.C.: Optimizing energy consumption in terahertz band nanonetworks. IEEE J. Sel. Areas Commun. **32**(12), 2432–2441 (2014)
14. Mohrehkesh, S., Weigle, M.C.: RIH-MAC: receiver-initiated harvesting-aware MAC for nanonetworks. In: Proceedings of ACM The First Annual International Conference on Nanoscale Computing and Communication, pp. 1–9 (2014)
15. Musa, V., Piro, G., Grieco, L.A., Boggia, G.: A lean control theoretic approach to energy-harvesting in diffusion-based molecular communications. IEEE Commun. Lett. **24**(5), 981–985 (2020)
16. Niu, X.: High-performance PZT-based stretchable piezoelectric nanogenerator. ACS Sustain. Chem. Eng. **7**(1), 979–985 (2018)
17. Pech, D.: Ultrahigh-power micrometre-sized supercapacitors based on onion-like carbon. Nat. Nanotechnol. **5**(9), 651 (2010)
18. Pierobon, M., Jornet, J.M., Akkari, N., Almasri, S., Akyildiz, I.F.: A routing framework for energy harvesting wireless nanosensor networks in the terahertz band. Wireless Netw. **20**(5), 1169–1183 (2014)

19. Piro, G., Bia, P., Boggia, G., Caratelli, D., Grieco, L.A., Mescia, L.: Terahertz electromagnetic field propagation in human tissues: a study on communication capabilities. Nano Commun. Netw. **10**, 51–59 (2016)
20. Piro, G., Boggia, G., Grieco, L.A.: On the design of an energy-harvesting protocol stack for body area nano-NETworks. Nano Commun. Netw. **6**(2), 74–84 (2015)
21. Wang, P., Jornet, J.M., Malik, M.A., Akkari, N., Akyildiz, I.F.: Energy and spectrum-aware mac protocol for perpetual wireless nanosensor networks in the terahertz band. Ad Hoc Netw. **11**(8), 2541–2555 (2013)
22. Xu, S., Qin, Y., Xu, C., Wei, Y., Yang, R., Wang, Z.L.: Self-powered nanowire devices. Nat. Nanotechnol. **5**(5), 366 (2010)
23. Yao, X., Ma, D., Han, C.: ECP: a probing-based error control strategy for THz-based nanonetworks with energy harvesting. IEEE Access **7**, 25616–25626 (2019)
24. Yao, X.W., Wang, C.C., Wang, W.L., Jornet, J.M.: On the achievable throughput of energy-harvesting nanonetworks in the terahertz band. IEEE Sens. J. **18**(2), 902–912 (2017)

New CAP Reduction Mechanisms for IEEE 802.15.4 DSME to Support Fluctuating Traffic in IoT Systems

Florian Meyer[(✉)], Ivonne Mantilla-González, and Volker Turau

Institute of Telematics, Hamburg University of Technology, Hamburg, Germany
{fl.meyer,ivonne.mantilla,turau}@tuhh.de

Abstract. In 2015, the IEEE 802.15.4 standard was expanded by the Deterministic and Synchronous Multi-Channel Extension (DSME) to increase reliability, scalability and energy-efficiency in industrial applications. The extension offers a TDMA/FDMA-based channel access, where time is divided into two alternating phases, a contention access period (CAP) and a contention free period (CFP). During the CAP, transmission slots can be allocated offering an exclusive access to the shared medium during the CFP. The fraction τ of CFP's time slots in a dataframe is a critical value, because it directly influences agility and throughput. A high throughput demands that the CFP is much longer than the CAP, i.e., a high value of τ, because application data is only sent during the CFP. High agility is given if the expected waiting time to send a CAP message is short and that the length of the CAPs are long enough to accommodate necessary GTS negotiations, i.e., a low value of τ. Once DSME is configured according to the needs of an application, τ can only assume one of two values and cannot be changed at run-time. In this paper, we propose two extensions of DSME that allow to adopt τ to the current traffic pattern. We show theoretically and through simulations that the proposed extensions provide a high degree of responsiveness to traffic fluctuations while keeping the throughput high.

List of Symbols

Notation	Description
	DSME Standard Parameters
aUB	aUnitBackoffPeriod (symbols)
BE	CSMA/CA backoff exponent
BI	Beacon interval
BO	Beacon order
CAP	Contention access period
CFP	Contention free period
GTS	Guaranteed time slot
MD	Multisuperframe duration
MO	Multisuperframe order
SO	Superframe order
	Proprietary Parameters
CM	CAPs pe multisuperframe

An extended preprint of this paper is available [9].

© Springer Nature Switzerland AG 2020
L. A. Grieco et al. (Eds.): ADHOC-NOW 2020, LNCS 12338, pp. 159–179, 2020.
https://doi.org/10.1007/978-3-030-61746-2_13

Notation	Description
CTM	CAP's time slots per multisuperframe
GB	GTSs per beacon interval
GS	GTSs per superframe
MB	Multisuperframes per beacon interval
N_{CAP}	Expected number of time slots to send a CAP message
p_{CAP}	Probability of generating a packet during the CAP
SB	Superframes per beacon interval
SbC	Symbols per CAP
SbS	Symbols per superframe
SM	Superframes per multisuperframe
TB	Time slots per beacon interval
T_{CAP}	Expected time to send a CAP message (symbols)
T_{Ch}	Expected channel access time (symbols)
T_{ChCAP}	Expected channel access time for a packet generated during the CAP (symbols)
T_{ChCFP}	Expected channel access time for a packet generated during the CFP (symbols)
TM	Time slots per multisuperframe
TS	Time slots per superframe
α	Smoothing parameter of OpenDSME scheduler
δ	Packets per second
η	Ratio of superframes to CAPs per multisuperframe
τ	Fraction of CFP's time slots a dataframe

1   Introduction

The *Deterministic Synchronous Multichannel Extension* (DSME) [3] extends the
IEEE 802.15.4 standard. It allows nodes to exclusively reserve the resources
time and frequency to prevent interference caused by concurrently transmitting
devices inside of the network. Time is divided into two parts: *contention free
period* (CFP) and a *contention access period* (CAP). The handling of reserva-
tions is done during the CAP, while in the CFP application data is sent during
guaranteed time slots (GTSs).

The objectives of a high agility and a high throughput are conflicting. A
high throughput demands that the CFP is much longer than the CAP. Thus,
the fraction τ of CFP's time slots in a dataframe is a critical value and each
application demands its dedicated fraction. High agility is given if the expected
waiting time T_{CAP} to send a CAP message is short and that the length of
the CAPs are sufficiently long to accommodate the necessary (de)allocations of
GTSs.

Currently, DSME has defined two standard operating modes: CAP reduction,
abbreviated as CR, and no CAP reduction, abbreviated as NCR. The value of τ
in NCR mode is 7/16 and in CR mode increases to $(15 - 8(2^{SO-MO}))/16$. From
these values it is clear that these two operating modes offer extremely different
fractions. This does not allow an optimal usage of resources for a wide spectrum
of applications.

The goal of this work is to extend DSME such that the fraction τ can be
defined with a fine granularity and that it can be dynamically changed, i.e.,

after deployment. We present two new mechanisms that provide more flexibility in setting up τ and therefore provide a better support for dynamically varying traffic. The first mechanism – Alternating CR (abbreviated as ACR) – alternates every *BI* between CR and NCR. This way the actual number of CFP's time slots per *BI* alternates between two values every *BI*. The second mechanism – Dynamic CR (abbreviated as DCR) – allocates GTS in CAPs locally according to the GTS demands of individual nodes. The higher the demand for GTSs the shorter will be the available CAP in superframes. While ACR is far easier to implement and remains within the standard, DCR is more flexible with respect to the fraction of CFP's time slots in a dataframe.

We substantiate through theoretical analysis and simulations, that the two approaches considerably expand the flexibility of DSME. The evaluation considers packet reception rate, mean queue length and the maximum number of allocated GTSs. We show that data collection applications with different demands can be optimally supported by choosing the mode. We believe that this work considerably broadens the range of applications that can be optimally supported by DSME.

2   Related Work

A comparative performance analysis of IEEE 802.15.4 and DSME has been carried out in several works [2,4,6,8]. The analysis in [2] and [6] also covers the *Time-Slotted Channel Hopping* (TSCH) MAC layer. The former work shows that DSME and TSCH outperform IEEE 802.15.4 in scenarios with real-time requirements. The study of DSME shows that CR improves latency and throughput in applications with strict demands. At the same time the energy consumption is higher than NCR mode, since nodes operate in high duty cycles. The latter work remarks the effectiveness of the multichannel feature of DSME in terms of delay. Furthermore, simulation results demonstrate an increased network throughput of about 7% with CR compared to NCR.

Jeon et al. evaluate in [4] single and multihop topologies. In both cases, the reachable throughput in DSME is higher than IEEE 802.15.4. (e.g. in multihop topology is about twelve times when CR is enabled). A scenario under interference from IEEE 802.11b wireless networks is analyzed in [8]. Mainly, given the channel diversity capability of DSME, the adaptability to varying traffic load conditions, and robustness, it is demonstrated a better performance of DSME over IEEE 802.15.4.

A simulative evaluation of DSME is made by F. Kauer in [5]. Results evidence that for an increasing *MO* the network throughput increases when CR is enabled. However, higher values of *MO* represent a severe reduction in total CAPs, which means that the network is unable to handle the amount of managed traffic.

Regarding the impact of CR in DSME, Vallati et al. [11] analyze it from the perspective of network formation. The authors propose an active backoff mechanism and appropriate selection of configuration parameters, that along with CR aim to reduce setup time up to a 60%. In the same direction, a dynamic multisuperframe tuning technique (DynaMO) in conjunction with CR is proposed in [7]. DynaMO was evaluated in openDSME showing a latency reduction up to 15–30% in a large scale networks.

3   Overview of DSME

DSME is a deterministic and synchronous MAC-layer protocol, which guarantees global synchronization and network parameter dissemination through beacon messages. The essential parameters are *beacon order* (*BO*), *multisuperframe order* (*MO*) and *superframe order* (*SO*). Beacons are repeated over time every *beacon interval* (*BI*), with a duration of $BI = 15.36 \times 2^{BO}$ s. A *BI* structures time by grouping superframes (*SF*) into multisuperframes (*MSF*) as illustrated in Fig. 1. The number of multisuperframes in a *BI* and the number of superframes in a *MSF* is calculated as $NMSF = 2^{BO-MO}$ and $SM = 2^{MO-SO}$ respectively. A *SF* is further divided in 16 equally sized slots: the first one is for beacon transmission, the subsequent eight slots form the *contention access period* (CAP) and the remaining seven slots the *contention free period* (CFP).

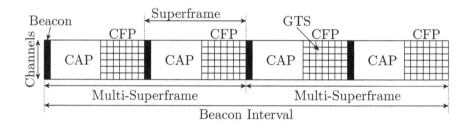

Fig. 1. Frame structure in IEEE 802.15.4 DSME ($BO - MO = MO - SO = 1$).

In the CAP, the PAN coordinator selects one channel, C_{CAP}, that is used by nodes to exchange control messages via CSMA/CA. In the CFP, nodes communicate through GTSs, which are spread over time and frequency providing exclusive access to the medium. A schedule of allocated GTSs is repeated every *MSF* [3].

The available GTS bandwidth per *MSF* in NCR mode is $7 \times (2^{MO-SO})$(GTS). It can be increased by enabling the CR mechanism, in which only the CAP of the first *SF* of each *MSF* is enabled. This is, the reduced CAPs become part of the CFP. Thus, the total number of available GTSs per *MSF* in CR mode equals $7 + 15 \times (2^{MO-SO} - 1)$(GTS) [3].

4   The Proposed CAP Reduction Mechanisms

The use of CR increases throughput at the cost of reducing the number of CAPs per *MSF*. As noted in [5,11], a severe reduction of the CAP reduces the responsiveness of the network to varying traffic demands. This effect is intensified for large-scale networks and higher values of MO since contention is higher and T_{CAP} is prolonged. Additionally, the adaptability of the network to changing conditions (e.g. external interference) is affected. Therefore, it is necessary to provide enough time in the CAPs for exchanging channel states and based on that to schedule GTSs efficiently [10]. We propose two CAP reduction mechanisms to address these problems: Alternating CAP-Reduction and Dynamic CAP-Reduction. In the following both mechanisms will be fully described.

4.1 Alternating CAP-Reduction (ACR)

ACR alternates between NCR and CR every beacon interval. The alternation is not initiated by a central node, e.g., by broadcasting new configuration parameters into the network. Instead nodes know from information encoded in the beacons when to switch mode. The advantage of ACR is a higher GTS bandwidth compared to NCR with the minimum effect on CSMA traffic. That is because switching between CR and NCR is performed systematically, and nodes do not have to exchange additional control messages during the CAP to trigger a change of the operating mode. Moreover, latency does not increase because of the frame structure realignment after each change of the operating mode (i.e., from NCR to CR and vice versa).

As part of the initialization, any node except for the root node (i.e. PAN coordinator), which operates in ACR, starts operating in CR to guarantee that CAP phases will be enabled for CSMA traffic and will not be affected by self-interference given by TDMA traffic from nodes already operating in ACR. Then, after association, nodes receive a beacon from their parents (e.g. PAN coordinator or coordinators), in which the cap reduction field is retrieved to initialize the network's operating mode (i.e. NCR or CR). This is also done in subsequent BIs. Since nodes know when BIs start, the implementation of the alternating behavior is straightforward. Synchronization is guaranteed considering that all beacons transmitted in the network are allocated within in and repeated every BI.

The frame structure of ACR is illustrated in Fig. 2 for the case $MO = SO + 1$ and $BO = MO$. ACR does not increase the potential GTS bandwidth provided by CR. In fact, τ is incremented by the factor $2.14((2^{MO-SO} - 1)/(2^{MO-SO} + 1))$ compared to the fraction τ of NCR.

Scheduling of GTSs. GTSs in ACR are classified according to the type of access period they belong to: contention access period GTSs (CAP-GTS) or contention free period GTSs (CFP-GTS). They can be handled in two ways: by defining separate schedules according to flow priorities or by allocating CAP-GTSs as overprovisioning. The first approach introduces the concept of flows, that enables higher layers (e.g. routing) to manage different schedules depending on the priority of packets, i.e., high priority for flows with a period of $T_{flow} \leq BI$ and low priority otherwise. The second approach schedules CAP-GTS to deliver queued packets or to perform packet retransmissions as soon as possible. In this work, the second alternative is implemented.

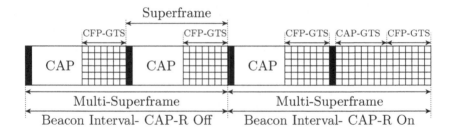

Fig. 2. Frame structure in ACR $(BO = MO, MO - SO = 1)$.

4.2 Dynamic CAP-Reduction (DCR)

DCR starts in NCR mode and is triggered when all GTSs in the CFPs are depleted, i.e., allocated. At this point, DCR allocates additional GTSs during CAPs through the standard DSME 3-way handshake. For this, two allocating nodes, v and w, negotiate a GTS during the last time slot of a random SF's CAP, shrinking it from that moment on. The last slot is chosen because GTS negotiations are triggered at the start of CAPs in openDSME and thus the first slots of a CAP are usually busier than the last slots. Choosing a random CAP ensures that CAPs are reduced evenly and about the same time is available for GTS negotiations during all portions of a MSF. Thereby, DCR does not affect the first CAP of a MSF. The channel C, is chosen so that $C \neq C_{CAP}$. Therefore, communication during the new GTS does not interfere with regular CAP traffic. All nodes, except v and w, can use the CAP normally with the restriction that they cannot communicate with v or w during the allocated GTS. This means, DCR reduces CAPs locally. After an allocation of DCR, v and w have reduced their CAP by one slot, while a third node x can use one less CAP slot for communication with them but all CAP slots for communication with other nodes. The rest of the network remains unaffected. Optionally, x can hold back messages to v or w during the allocated GTS and send those during the next CAP to reduce traffic.

Based on the network's traffic demand, DCR continues allocating additional GTSs during CAPs until CR mode is reached. That means, the first CAP of every MSF is not affected to ensure that GTSs can be deallocated again. This way, up to $8 \times (2^{MO-SO} - 1)$ additional GTSs can be allocated. The resulting frame structure of DCR is illustrated in Fig. 3, where the last GTS of a CAP is allocated first. The deallocation of GTSs works exactly the opposite way. However, CAPs can become fragmented during GTS deallocation, e.g., if the first and third GTS allocation was done by one node and the second GTS allocation was done by another. Then, the deallocation of the second GTS results in a split CAP. A solution is the relocation of the third GTS to a later time slot. This behavior is currently not implemented, but also not mandatory as timers are stopped outside of CAP slots and therefore no timeouts for CAP messages occur.

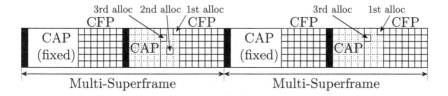

Fig. 3. Frame structure in DCR $(MO - SO = 1)$.

Scheduling of GTSs. DCR provides opportunities for more sophisticated scheduling algorithms. For example, a scheduler could decide to allocate additional GTSs during the CAP if traffic demand is high but deallocate GTSs again if the PRR of the CAP traffic falls below a certain threshold, e.g., during traffic fluctuations. Additionally, a modification of the scheduler has to be done i.e., the scheduler first allocates GTSs during the CFP until they are depleted and then starts allocating GTSs during the CAP.

4.3   An Example of ACR and DCR in DSME

Figure 4 shows an example of how the two proposed CAP reduction mechanisms work. Here two nodes (v and w) send messages to the coordinator (H_C). The GTS during the CFP are already completely allocated, as illustrated in the schedules for the two mechanisms.

With ACR, nodes switch between CR and NCR every BI, and information about the current operating mode is retrieved through beacons received from H_C. As it is shown in this example, during the BI at time t, represented in the first row, nodes operate in NCR. During that BI, a total number of 28 GTSs can be allocated. Then, during the next BI at time $t + BI$, in the second row, nodes alternate their frame structure to CR with a maximum of 44 usable GTSs. This alternating behavior allows nodes to allocate extra GTSs in the extended CFPs. ACR would even work if the beacon from H_C is not heard by, e.g., v because nodes also keep track of time themselves and can switch between CR and NCR autonomously after they heard the first beacon, immediately after the association to the network is completed. Additionally, ACR allows static schedules because the frame structure is completely deterministic (i.e. every BI, the frame structure switches from CR to NCR or vice versa).

For DCR, additional GTS resources are created through the DSME 3-way handshake when all GTSs during CFPs are allocated. Here, v allocates an additional GTS with H_C. For the new GTS, the CAPs of H_C and v are locally reduced and a GTS is allocated on a different channel than C_{CAP}. This way, w can continue using all CAP slots for communication with nodes other than v and H_C (which are not shown here). The benefit is that the number of additionally created GTSs is a direct effect of the traffic load and therefore no unused GTS during the CAP occur.

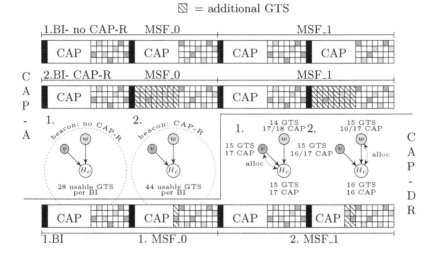

Fig. 4. Example of ACR and DCR making more GTS resources available in a network with 3 nodes $(BO - MO = 1, MO - SO = 1)$.

5   Metrics and Hypotheses

There is a number of relevant metrics for the evaluation of the proposed CAP reduction mechanisms. These include, at an abstract level, the adaptability of DSME with respect to time varying traffic and the fraction of CFP's time slots in a dataframe, i.e., the fraction τ. Adaptability refers the time for (de)allocating a GTS. That is because the proposed mechanims try to increase the potential throughput while maintaining responsiveness and reliability. For the simulative evaluation also the packet reception ratio (PRR), mean queue length, the maximum number of allocated GTS and dwell time are relevant as they indirectly represent adaptability and throughput of DSME.

It can be expected that overall performance of the described CAP reduction mechanisms strongly depends on the difference $MO - SO$, since the two parameters directly control the number of SF per MSF and thus the frequency of the CAPs per MSF. An analysis of this difference can be made considering two cases: Varying MO while fixing SO or varying SO while fixing MO. The former keeps the slot length constant and for each increment of MO, the length of the MSF as well as the number of CAPs per MSF is doubled. The latter preserves the length of the MSF, and each increment of SO doubles the slot length and halves the number of CAPs per MSF.

In case of CR the CAP frequency per MSF is always equals 1. Therefore, for a fixed SO, increasing MO means enlarging the MSF length and thus increasing T_{CAP}. In other words, as the difference between MO and SO increases, CR performs worse as there are not enough CAPs to (de)allocate all GTSs in time. For a fixed MO, decreasing the value of SO increases SM by reducing the length of the SF and therefore the length of CAPs. Thus, as the difference between MO

and SO increases, CR's performance degrades, because the reduction of time in CAPs diminishes the capability of the network to (de)allocate GTSs to adapt rapidly to fluctuating traffic.

On the other hand, differences between MO and SO should not have an strong effect for NCR. This is, because either fixing SO or MO, the number of CAPs per time stays invariant. In some scenarios (e.g. highly varying traffic), MO could be an influencing parameter because it determines the period in which the scheduler updates the number of required GTSs to adapt to traffic changes in the network. Thus, the higher MO the lower the responsiveness of the network to rapid traffic changes over time. In case of the scheduler of openDSME, it uses hysteresis and a smoothing parameter, α, to manage effectively such traffic fluctuations in the network. Therefore, the parameters MO and SO should not have a significant influence on NCR as stated above.

In ACR, the alternation between CR and NCR every BI guarantees that the average amount of time in CAPs is enough to accomplish the required GTS (de)allocations to meet traffic demands. Moreover, the scheduling strategy guarantees stability because it first allocates CFP-GTS and then CAP-GTS, which are less frequent over time. Therefore, as well as NCR, we do not expect higher changes in ACR's performance given by differences between MO and SO. DCR should converge to CR or NCR, depending on which one performs better, and should even exhibit a better performance for a large difference between MO and SO.

6   Theoretical Evaluation

The goal of the new CAP reduction mechanisms is to increase throughput while maintaining adaptability to time varying traffic. We mainly consider two metrics: the fraction τ and the adaptability of DSME expressed by the expected time to send a CAP message, N_{CAP}. Both metrics strongly depend on the average number of CAPs per MSF, CM, and the average number of CAP's time slots per MSF, CTM. For example, CR heavily sacrifices adaptability for a higher throughput, which is especially problematic if not all GTSs are utilized, because they could have been used for CAP traffic. The proposed mechanisms overcome this problem by modifying CM (ACR) and CTM (DCR).

6.1   The Fraction τ of CFP's Time Slots in a Dataframe

The value of τ can be calculated based on CM and CTM as

$$\tau = \frac{TM - CTM - SM}{TM}, \tag{1}$$

where $TM = 16 \times SM$ is the total number of time slots in a MSF. Subtraction of SM is required to account for SM beacon slots per MSF. Therefore, τ increases for decreasing values of CTM, as illustrated in Table 1. NCR is independent of MO, while CR converges towards 93.75% as MO increases. ACR offers a compromise between NCR and CR. Similarly, DCR dynamically adapts the time for sending packets with the lower bound equal to NCR and the upper bound equal to CR.

Table 1. Values of τ of CFP's time slots in a dataframe for increasing values of MO.

	$MO = 4$	$MO = 5$	$MO = 6$	$MO = 7$
NCR	43.75%	43.75%	43.75%	43.75%
CR	68.75%	81.25%	87.5%	90.06%
ACR	56.25%	62.5%	65.63%	67.19%
DCR	43.75%–68.75%	43.75%–81.25%	43.75%–87.5%	43.75%–90.06%

6.2 Expected Time to Send a CAP Message

The adaptability of DSME is characterized by the expected time to allocate a new GTS, i.e., the expected time until a GTS-handshake can be conducted in a CAP. In contrast to τ, which indicates the maximum throughput of a system, adaptability expresses how long it would take to allocate all required GTSs. Since a time slot is a baseline unit in DSME's frame structure, we consider it to estimate adaptability in terms of the expected number of time slots that a node must wait to send a CAP message, i.e. N_{CAP}. This value is calculated per MSF as follows

$$N_{\mathrm{CAP}}(CM, CTM) = \frac{\sum_{i=1}^{\frac{TM-CTM}{CM}} i}{TM}. \tag{2}$$

The expected number of time slots to send a CAP message in NCR is $N_{\mathrm{CAP}}(SM, 8 \times SM)$, which is independent of MO with a value of 2.25 time slots. For CR this value is $N_{\mathrm{CAP}}(1, 8)$. Hence, it dependents on the difference between MO and SO. As shown in Table 2, the expected waiting times to send a CAP message increase exponentially for an increasing MO. For ACR, N_{CAP} is calculated as an average of the expected times for CR and NCR. The value amounts to $0.5 \times (N_{\mathrm{CAP}}(SM, 8 \times SM) + N_{\mathrm{CAP}}(1, 8))$. DCR dynamically adjusts the number of additional GTSs between NCR and CR so that the expected times are bounded by the expected times of these mechanisms.

Expected Channel Access Time on Symbol Level. In the following, a single channel access without contention is considered where the corresponding packet is generated according to a uniform distribution on the interval $[0, MD]$. Two cases have to be considered: packet generation during the CFP and packet generation during the CAP. For the calculation, beacon slots are treated as CFP slots in which no data is sent.

Table 2. Expected time to send a CAP message on time slot level for increasing MO.

	$MO = 4$	$MO = 5$	$MO = 6$	$MO = 7$
NCR	2.25	2.25	2.25	2.25
CR	9.38	24.94	56.72	120.61
ACR	5.81	14.10	29.49	61.43
DCR	2.25–9.38	2.25–24.94	2.25–56.72	2.25–120.61

generating a packet during a CAP is given by

$$p_{\mathrm{CAP}} = \frac{CTM}{TM}. \tag{3}$$

The system can be discretized in time steps, aUB, of $aUnitBackoffPeriod$, the base duration for the CSMA/CA algorithm. If a packet is generated at the end of the CAP, its transmission is more likely to be shifted to the next CAP. Therefore, the expected CSMA/CA backoff duration, $T_b(s)$, for a packet generated during the sth CSMA/CA slot is given by

$$T_b(s) = \frac{\sum_{i=0}^{i \le 2^{BE}-1} B(s,i)}{2^{BE}-1} \tag{4}$$

$$B(s,i) = \begin{cases} i \times aUB & \text{if } aUB \times (s+i) < SbC \\ \begin{aligned} &\eta \times SbS - aUB \times s \\ &+ aUB(i+s) \bmod SbC \\ &+ \eta \times SbS \lfloor \frac{aUB(s+i)}{SbC} \rfloor \end{aligned} & \text{otherwise} \end{cases} \tag{5}$$

where BE is the backoff exponent of the CSMA/CA algorithm, $SbS = 16 \times 60 \times 2^{SO}$ is the number of symbols per SF, $SbC = \frac{CTM}{CM} \times 60 \times 2^{SO}$ is the number of symbols per CAP, and $\eta = \frac{SM}{CM}$ is a stretching factor if $CM < SM$ under the assumption that CAPs are evenly distributed in the MSF. In other words: Eq. (4) calculates the expected backoff from a given slot for all possible CSMA/CA backoff values. The total backoff, B, equals to the CSMA/CA backoff ($i \times aUB$) if there is enough space in the CAP. Otherwise, it includes the wait duration of the CFPs. In this case (Eq. (5), case otherwise), the first summand is the backoff until the next CAP from the time of the packet generation, the second summand is the remaining backoff time in a latter CAP, and the third term adds the backoff for multiple superframes if $i \times aUB$ spans over multiple CAP phases. The expected channel access time, T_{ChCAP}, for a packet generation during the CAP can then be calculated as

$$T_{\mathrm{ChCAP}} = \frac{\sum_{s=0}^{s < CTM/(aUB \times CM)} T_b(s)}{CTM/(aUB \times CM)}. \tag{6}$$

CFP, the expected channel access time is the combination of the expected time to send a CAP message, i.e. T_{CAP}, and the expected CSMA/CA backoff time from slot 0. The expected time to send a CAP message on symbol level is given by $T_{\text{CAP}} = 0.5 \times (T_{\text{CAP}min} + T_{\text{CAP}max})$, where $T_{\text{CAP}min} = 1$ is the minimum time to send a CAP message and $T_{\text{CAP}max}$ is the maximum time to send a CAP message and given by

$$T_{\text{CAP}max} = \eta \times SbS - SbC \tag{7}$$

The expected channel access time, T_{ChCFP}, for a packet generated during the CFP is $T_{\text{ChCFP}} = T_{\text{CAP}} + T_b(0)$.

then given by

$$T_{\text{Ch}} = p_{\text{CAP}} \times T_{\text{ChCAP}} + (1 - p_{\text{CAP}}) \times T_{\text{ChCFP}}. \tag{8}$$

CM and *CTM* is shown in Fig. 5. Here, one can see that ACR achieves a much lower expected channel access time than CR mode. Therefore, the adaptability with ACR is higher. It can be seen that the expected channel access time scales exponentially with a decreasing CAP frequency and ACR operates at the part where a good adaptability is still given. In contrast to that, DCR reduces the number of slots in individual CAPs. Therefore, the expected time to send a CAP message is always quite low. However, in extreme cases all CAP slots might be allocated and DCR performs as CR in terms of expected channel access time.

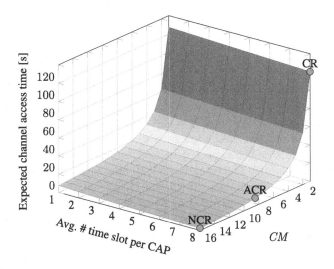

Fig. 5. Expected channel access time in time slots for different values of *CM* and average number of time slots per CAP for $SO = 3$ and $MO = 7$. The performance of the static CAP reduction mechanisms is marked by the green dots. (Color figure online)

7   Scenario Description

We focus on the widely used data-collection scenario using the converge-cast pattern. In this pattern, routing is performed along a rooted oriented tree. In particular we use a rooted binary tree topology with 31 nodes. We abstain from using an unbalanced tree to eliminate the influence of heavily skewed traffic. The chosen topology allows to analyze the behavior of nodes with different loads, because traffic load increases exponentially from the leaves to the sink. All nodes except the sink generate an average of $\delta = \{1, \ldots, 4\}$ packets per second and forward them along the routing tree to the sink. The packet generation follows a Poisson distribution with mean λ and a one second observation interval to model the dynamic behavior of nodes. Two packet generation patterns are considered: generation of packets with $\lambda = \delta$ packets and generation of packets in bursts of size δ and $\lambda = 1$ burst. The first scenario allows the assessment of the network close to saturation because traffic is pretty stable. In the second scenario (bursty traffic), the proposed CAP reduction mechanisms have to (de)allocate GTSs continuously and adjust to the current traffic demand of the network.

We set $SO = 3$ so that a single packet with 127 bytes can be sent per GTS. Furthermore, it insures that all CAPs have the same length for all configurations. If not stated otherwise, we fix $BO = 7$ to guarantee sufficiently many beacon slots in the network for all nodes to associate. The scenario is evaluated for $4 \leq MO \leq 7$. Each node's queue is divided in a CAP queue of length $Q_{CAP} = 8$, and a GTS queue of length $Q_{GTS} = 22$, with a combined total capacity of 30 packets. Table 3 summarizes the setup of the simulation. For each configuration, 20 runs are conducted and results are shown with a 95% confidence level. Simulations are done using OMNeT++ and openDSME.

Table 3. Setup of DSME parameters, traffic generator and TPS scheduling parameters.

Parameter	SO	MO	BO	α	Q_{CAP}	Q_{GTS}	δ
Values	3	$\{4, \ldots, 7\}$	7	0.1	8	22	$\{1, \ldots, 4\}$

8   Simulative Evaluation

In the following, we present a performance assessment of the proposed mechanisms by comparing them with NCR and CR. Performance metrics include the packet reception ratio (PRR), the mean queue length and the maximum number of GTSs allocated. Additionally, the adaptability to time varying traffic metric as explicated in Sect. 6 is also evaluated by simulation. It corresponds to the GTS-negotiation message dwell time. Dwell time is the time between the generation of a message and its transmission, including queuing delay. Therefore, it provides an insight into a system's adaptability, because the system readjusts to changes in traffic faster by (de)allocating GTSs if the respective control messages have a lower dwell time.

8.1 Varying Burst Sizes

Figure 6 shows the average packet reception ratio (PRR) for an increasing δ and different values of MO with a $\lambda = 1$ burst. For all methods, the PRR decreases for an increasing number of packets per burst. This is mainly due to the following reason: especially for smaller values of MO, there are not enough GTSs per second to accommodate all packets generated during a burst, leading to dropped packets as the queues fill up.

For CR, the frequency of CAPs decreases for increasing MO, resulting in more contention during the remaining CAPs. Thus, the required GTSs cannot be allocated in time. This is the case for $MO = 5$, where τ equals 81.25%. From this theoretical value, a high PRR was expected. However our results show that for an increasing number of packets per burst CR is very sensible to high traffic loads.

The performance of NCR is independent of MO, as already indicated by the theoretical analysis in Sect. 6. Therefore, the choice of CR or NCR depends largely on MO, as CR performs better than NCR for $MO = 4$ and $MO = 5$, but NCR performs better for $MO = 6$ and $MO = 7$. If $SO = MO = 3$, all mechanisms perform equally well, since there is only a single SF per MSF, which cannot be reduced by DCR or CR.

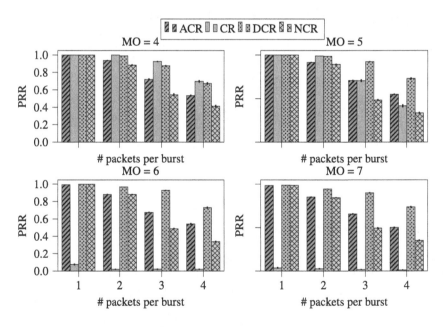

Fig. 6. PRR for varying numbers of packets per burst and different values of MO.

On the other hand, DCR performs similarly to CR for $MO = 4$ and outperforms CR and NCR for $MO \geq 5$. That is because DCR starts with NCR mode and therefore allocates GTSs as fast as possible (e.g., as fast as NCR) for larger values of MO where there is only a small number of CAPs for CR. In addition, it reduces CAPs when all regular GTSs are already allocated so that it converges towards CR. However, the allocation of these additional resources has a slight time overhead, resulting in the performance gap between DCR and CR for $MO = 4$.

Similarly to CR, the performance of ACR depends on MO but its influence is not as strong as for CR. For smaller values of MO, ACR's PRR is about the average between values for CR and NCR. It corresponds to the theoretical analysis regarding τ, with boundaries delimited by CR and NCR (e.g. $\tau = 56.25\%$ for $MO = 4$). For larger values of MO (i.e. $MO \geq 6$), the PRR is less sensible to this parameter, performing even better than NCR. This is because of the alternating behavior every BI, which provides enough CAPs to perform the required GTS negotiations. Moreover, the fact that ACR allocates first CFP-GTS and then less frequent GTSs (i.e. CAP-GTS) is a key aspect in the performance of this mechanism.

All in all, ACR and DCR are attractive alternatives to DSME under varying traffic patterns. The former because it combines the strengths of CR and NCR mechanisms in one approach. The latter because it dynamically adapts to the traffic demands of the network and (de)allocates additional GTSs during CAPs to increase reliability.

8.2 Varying Packet Generation Rates

The following figures show a performance assessment for different packet generation intervals, which correspond to $1/\delta$ seconds. Particularly, Fig. 7 depicts the PRR for different values of MO. As explained in Subsect. 8.1, the choice of CR and NCR largely depends on MO, with CR performing better for $MO \leq 5$ and NCR performing better for $MO \geq 6$. NCR, ACR and DCR provide a good performance for $\delta \leq 1$ and all values of MO. For $\delta > 1$ NCR is operating beyond the maximum capacity and ACR starts to reach the limits of the capacity of available GTSs. Therefore, performance of NCR and ACR is diminished. Contrary to NCR, ACR's PRR is slightly affected by increasing MO. DCR performs significantly better than the other CAP reduction mechanisms, especially for larger values of MO. E.g., it achieves a PRR of 95% for $MO = 7$ and $\delta = 3$, while NCR achieves only about 48%, ACR about 67% and CR less than 2%.

The main reason for lost packets are queue drops. This is also reflected by the average queue length, as shown in Fig. 8. Here, nodes with the same distance to the sink are grouped together, as nodes closer to the sink experience more traffic than nodes further away. With a maximum of 22 packets for Q_{GTS}, it is clearly visible that NCR operates close to the maximum queue capacity at nodes close to the sink for all values of MO. That is because the network is over-saturated for a packet generation interval of 0.33 s and no more GTSs are available. For ACR the network is close to the maximum capacity and therefore the average queue length for nodes closer to the sink is significantly higher and close to the maximum queue capacity (i.e. nodes up to 2 hops away from the sink node). This

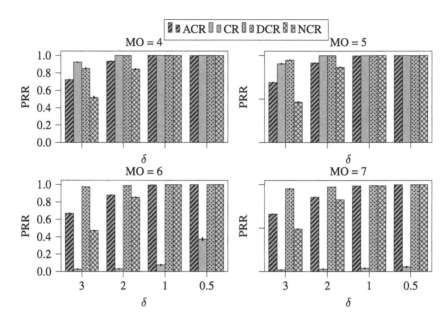

Fig. 7. PRR for different values of *MO* and δ.

funneling effect is intensified for increasing *MO*, which reduces the frequency of CAPs per *MSF* in *BI*s in which ACR operates in CR mode. On the other hand, the average queue length for CR increases with increasing *MO* because there are fewer CAPs per *MSF*. Consequently, the remaining CAPs are more congested and the required GTSs are not allocated in time. The average queue length for DCR is lower than 68% of the maximum queue capacity for all values of *MO*.

The maximum number of RX- and TX-GTSs allocated by the different CR mechanisms for $\delta = 3$ and different values of *MO* is illustrated in Fig. 9. Nodes with the same distance to the sink are grouped together, as more GTSs are allocated closer to the sink. For *MO* = 4, less slots need to be allocated because the *MSF*- and thus the schedule of allocated GTSs - is repeated multiple times per packet generation interval. Theoretically, for *MO* = 7 and $\delta = 3$, the number of required GTSs at the sink node to successfully receive all packets generated in the network is about 180 GTSs per *BI* (assuming that no packet was dropped from any queue). For NCR and CR the highest number of available GTSs per *BI* amounts to 112 and 232 GTSs respectively. For ACR this value corresponds to the average between NCR and CR, which is about 172 GTSs per *BI*. However, given the funneling effect inherent to data collection scenarios, this assumption does not hold. That is, many packets are lost in nodes closer the sink node and therefore the number of allocated GTSs are slightly less than the theoretical value. That is the case for NCR, in which nodes 1 hop further require about 174 GTSs. However, only 112 GTSs can be negotiated. Therefore, about 90 GTSs

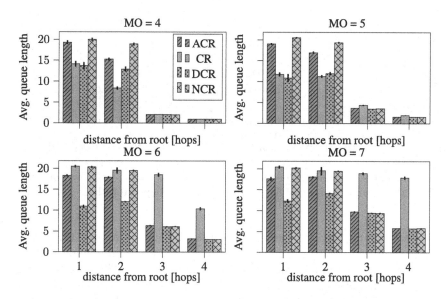

Fig. 8. Average queue length per node for different values of MO and $\delta = 3$.

are allocated at the sink node, which supports the obtained PRR with a value of 47%.

For ACR, one could expect a good performance of the network with these configuration parameters since the average number of available GTSs (i.e. 172 GTSs) should be sufficient to guarantee a low number of packet drops. However, this is not the case because the number of usable GTS varies over time. That is, the number of usable GTSs is limited to 112 in one BI – while operating in NCR – and lifted to a maximum of 232 GTSs in the next BI – while operating in CR. The effect of this drastic reduction of GTSs from one BI to the other is observed in the large value of the average queue lengths for nodes close to the sink. That is, despite the fact that all usable GTSs are allocated, the higher number of queued packets in the BI operating in NCR leads to queue overflows, specially for nodes closer to the sink node.

For DCR, the largest number of GTS is allocated. Theoretically, CR could reach the same performance as DCR but it fails to allocate the GTS in time, as already explained. Still, DCR performs well for $MO \leq 7$ because it can allocate a large number of GTS at the start and then it successively reduces the CAPs to allocate the last remaining GTSs.

Evaluation of the average dwell time, as illustrated in Fig. 10, with one packet per second for messages sent during the GTS negotiation, i.e., *GTS Request*, *GTS Response* and *GTS Notify* shows that CR has the highest dwell time. That is because there is only a single CAP per *MSF*, and GTS commands have to be queued for a long time. The dwell time exponentially increases for an increasing MO as the duration of a MSF doubles when incrementing MO. ACR comes second in this ranking, which has a similar behavior as CR. Although ACR's

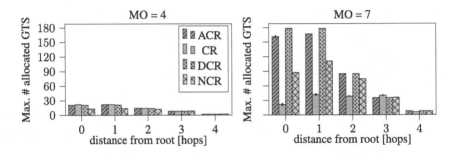

Fig. 9. Maximum number of allocated GTSs per node for $MO = 4$, $MO = 7$ and $\delta = 3$. Nodes with the same number of hops to the root are grouped together.

dwell time is influenced by the length of the MSF given by MO, this effect is diminished during the BIs in which ACR operates in NCR. It should be noted, that although ACR's waiting time is higher than DCR and NCR, it is still enough to guarantee adaptability to fluctuating traffic. The validation of ACR's dwell time by simulations confirm the theoretically estimated value (Sect. 6). This is the case for $MO = 4$ with an average dwell time of 42.80 ms against 44.64 ms from the theoretical model. In this case, the difference between the values comes from the way the estimation in the theoretical model is performed (i.e. average between NCR and CR). That is, the theoretical model does not take into account the scheduling mechanism implemented for ACR, which reduces on a small scale its dwell time.

DCR and NCR perform equally well, e.g., with an average dwell time of 17.08 ms and 18.06 ms, respectively. For NCR this matches with the value of about 17.28 ms from the theoretical models (Sect. 6), which do not consider packet collisions. NCR has a higher dwell time than DCR because nodes are unable to allocate enough GTSs (network saturation) but still can send GTS commands for the required GTSs. This results in more congestion during the CAPs and the nodes backing of more frequently during the CSMA/CA algorithm. Both CAP reduction mechanisms are independent of MO with the dwell time only marginally increasing for an increasing MO because more GTSs are required initially for larger values of MO resulting in more contention. For $MO = 3$ all mechanisms perform the same.

8.3   Summary of Results

The following statements summarize the most significant results from Sect. 6 and 8 without claim to completeness. It is assumed that the configuration parameters MO and SO are fixed before the simulation according to the needs of the application. We evaluated the capability of the proposed CAP reduction mechanisms to support fluctuating traffic in comparison with the NCR and CR modes provided by DSME. To this end, we tested two different packet generation patterns: varying burst sizes and varying packet generation rates with δ packets

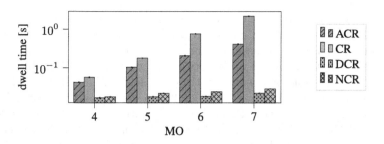

Fig. 10. Average dwell time for GTS-negotiation messages using CR, NCR, ACR and DCR for different values of MO and a packet generation rate of 1 packet per second.

per second. Results are given from a data collection scenario for a binary tree topology with 31 nodes.

- NCR provides good adaptability for all values of $MO - SO$. However, for a large number of packets per second ($\delta > 2$), NCR cannot provide a sufficient number of GTSs for sending all packets. This results in a large number of dropped packets due to full queues.
- CR performs well for $MO - SO \leq 2$. Here, a single CAP per MSF is sufficient to allocate all required GTSs and CR still offers a higher throughput which increases the overall PRR. For $MO - SO \geq 3$, the performance of CR diminishes since it is unable to allocate all GTS in time, resulting in large queues and packet loss.
- ACR offers a compromise between CR and NCR, which is reflected in its performance. For $MO - SO \leq 1$, it performs as a middle ground between CR and NCR. For $MO - SO \geq 2$, ACR starts to outperform the standard modes of DSME because it offers a higher adaptability than CR and a higher throughput than NCR.
- DCR achieves the best overall performance in terms of PRR, dwell time, and queue utilization for all differences $MO - SO$ and different packet generation rates. That is because DCR starts in NCR mode which offers a high adaptability. Then it gradually and dynamically reduces the CAP to allow for a higher throughput. Notably, it manages to achieve a PRR of over 80% regardless of the value of $MO - SO$ in a scenario without bursts and therefore outperforms the standard modes of DSME.

9   Conclusion

One of the pillars of the Internet of Things (IoT) is a robust and reliable wireless communication infrastructure. The IEEE 802.15.4 Deterministic and Synchronous Multi-Channel Extension (DSME) is a MAC protocol that guarantees reliability, scalability and energy-efficiency in WLANs. DSME offers a TDMA/FDMA-based channel access and provides the possibility to assign at run-time the resources time and frequency to individual links in a conflict free way. This allows a continuous distribution of the resources among the network nodes. This way the network can adopt itself to varying communication patterns. The redistribution of resources pursues two conflicting objectives, a high responsiveness towards bursts of packets on the one hand and an efficient utilization of the available bandwidth on the other hand. The first goal calls for a fast channel access for messages that (de)allocate resources. In terms of DSME this calls for long and frequent CAP phases. In contrast the second goal asks for frequent and long CFP phases, such that application packets can be sent with minimal delay and in high number. In DSME the balance between the goals agility and throughput is controlled by τ, the fraction of CFP's time slots in a dataframe. A high value guarantees a high throughput. While a low value ensures that the expected waiting time to send a CAP message is short. Once DSME is configured according to the needs of an application there are only two different possible values for τ and these cannot be changed at run-time. In this paper, we proposed ACR and DCR as two extensions of DSME that allow to adopt τ to the current traffic pattern. We verified theoretically and through simulations that both provide a high degree of responsiveness to traffic fluctuations while keeping throughput high. While the first proposal can be implemented within the original specification the second requires a deeper intervention. We believe that with these extensions more demanding IoT applications, i.e., those with fluctuating traffic including bursts, can be realized with IEEE 802.15.4.

To fully exploit the possibilities of ACR and DCR, a powerful dynamic scheduler is needed. While openDSME already provides such a scheduler which is based on an exponentially weighted moving average filter to estimate the required GTSs with respect to the traffic demand per link, it remains to develop *Minimal Scheduling Functions* (MSF) as defined in [1] by the 6TiSCH standardization group for TSCH. MSF is designed for best-effort traffic, where most traffic is periodic monitoring, with occasional bursts. We believe that the extensions proposed in this paper can be leveraged by future Minimal Scheduling Functions for DSME.

Acknowledgment. This research is partially supported by the German Academic Exchange Service (DAAD).

References

1. Chang, T., Vucinic, M., Vilajosana, X., Duquennoy, S., Dujovne, D.: 6TiSCH Minimal Scheduling Function (MSF). IETF (2019)
2. Choudhury, N., Matam, R., Mukherjee, M., Lloret, J.: A performance-to-cost analysis of IEEE 802.15.4 MAC with 802.15.4e MAC modes. IEEE Access (2020)
3. IEEE Computer Society: IEEE 802.15.4-2015 - IEEE Standard for Local and metropolitan area networks-Part 15.4: Low-Rate Wireless Personal Area Networks (WPANs) (2016)
4. Jeong, W.C., Lee, J.: Performance evaluation of IEEE 802.15.4e DSME MAC protocol for wireless sensor networks. In: First IEEE Workshop on Enabling Technologies for Smartphone and Internet of Things (ETSIoT), pp. 7–12. IEEE (2012)

5. Kauer, F., Köstler, M., Turau, V.: openDSME: reliable time-slotted multi-hop communication for IEEE 802.15.4. In: Virdis, A., Kirsche, M. (eds.) Recent Advances in Network Simulation. EICC, pp. 451–467. Springer, Cham (2019). https://doi.org/10.1007/978-3-030-12842-5_15
6. Kurunathan, H., Severino, R., Koubâa, A., Tovar, E.: Worst-case bound analysis for the time-critical MAC behaviors of IEEE 802.15.4e. In: 2017 IEEE 13th International Workshop on Factory Communication Systems (WFCS), pp. 1–9. IEEE (2017)
7. Kurunathan, H., Severino, R., Koubâa, A., Tovar, E.: Dynamo: dynamically tuning DSME networks. ACM Signed Rev. **16**(4), 8–13 (2020)
8. Lee, J., Jeong, W.C.: Performance analysis of IEEE 802.15.4e DSME MAC protocol under WLAN interference. In: International Conference on ICT Convergence (ICTC), pp. 741–746. IEEE (2012)
9. Meyer, F., Mantilla-González, I., Turau, V.: New cap reduction mechanisms for IEEE 802.15.4 DSME to support fluctuating traffic in IoT systems (2020)
10. Queiroz, D.V., Gomes, R.D., Benavente-Peces, C., Fonseca, I.E., Alencar, M.S.: Evaluation of channels blacklists in TSCH networks with star and tree topologies. In: Proceedings of the 14th ACM International Symposium on QoS and Security for Wireless and Mobile Networks, pp. 116–123 (2018)
11. Vallati, C., Brienza, S., Palmieri, M., Anastasi, G.: Improving network formation in IEEE 802.15.4e DSME. Comput. Commun. **114**, 1–9 (2017)

Secure Communication Protocols and Architectures

Testing and Evaluating a Security-Aware Pub and Sub Protocol in a Fog-Driven IoT Environment

Sabrina Sicari[1][✉], Alessandra Rizzardi[1], Luigi Alfredo Grieco[2], and Alberto Coen-Porisini[1]

[1] Dipartimento di Scienze Teoriche e Applicate, Universitàdegli Studi dell'Insubria, Via O. Rossi 9 - 21100, Varese, Italy
{sabrina.sicari,alessandra.rizzardi,alberto.coenporisini}@uninsubria.it
[2] Department of Electrical and Information Engineering, Politecnico di Bari, Via Orabona, 4 - 70125, Bari, Italy
alfredo.grieco@poliba.it

Abstract. The continuous spreading of innovative applications and services, based on the emerging Internet of Things (IoT) paradigm, leads to the need of even more efficient network architectures/infrastructures, in order to support the huge amount of information to be transmitted in real-time. Hence, new protocols and mechanisms must be conceived to allow the IoT network to be more reactive towards environmental changes and in promptly satisfying the IoT users' requests. Aiming at dealing with the emerged issues, the paper presents an efficient IoT platform, which, thanks to fog computing principles, acts as a middleware layer between data producers and consumers; it adopts a security-aware publish&subscribe protocol, based on MQTT, coupled with a network of brokers, for efficiently sharing the processed information with end-users. Transmitted data are kept secure under an enforcement framework based on sticky policies. A test campaign is conducted on a prototypical implementation of the just mentioned platform, for preliminary evaluating its efficiency, in terms of computing effort and latency.

Keywords: Internet of Things · Fog computing · Security · Testing · Publish&Subscribe

1 Introduction

The diffusion of Internet of Things (IoT) technologies and applications is ever increasing in a large variety of application's domains, ranging from smart buildings, e-health, smart agriculture, industry 4.0, military services, and so on. Such a continuous spreading of the IoT paradigm has a great impact on the network's infrastructure, which must be able to efficiently manage the huge amount of data, continuously provided by IoT devices. Note that heterogeneous technologies are involved, such as Wireless Sensor Networks (WSN), RFID, NFC,

© Springer Nature Switzerland AG 2020
L. A. Grieco et al. (Eds.): ADHOC-NOW 2020, LNCS 12338, pp. 183–197, 2020.
https://doi.org/10.1007/978-3-030-61746-2_14

actuators, and they communicate by means of different standards and protocols (e.g., MQTT, CoAP, ZigBee, BLE, 6LoWPAN). Hence, two main issues naturally emerge: scalability and interoperability. To cope with such problems, many architectures have been proposed in literature in the last years, some of them with a certain distributed nature, other ones semi-centralized, often operating with a cloud [23]. Most of them are conceived as middleware layers or gateways, able to directly interact with IoT devices, and to transmit data to proper servers or clouds, for completing the processing and sharing tasks with the interested parties.

What does not emerge from such approaches is how much such architectures are distributed, in terms of coverage area, number of managed sources, amount of data processed, possible thresholds, and so on. In fact, often the middleware or the gateways are mentioned as single entities, which presumably interact with other similar ones, in a not so clear way. Hence, little attention has been paid, until now, to how to decentralize as much as possible all the network's components (e.g., the middleware's or gateways' modules) and tasks, in order to cover a wider area and make the IoT environment both more pervasive, reliable and powerful.

Following a fog-driven approach [3] should help in facing the raised challenges. In fact, fog computing is pursuing a decentralized networking and computing infrastructure, where data, processing tasks, storage and applications are distributed in an efficient manner towards the edge of the network, in an intermediate layer (e.g., a middleware), which is situated between the data sources and a cloud [9]. Fog computing is promoted by the *OpenFog Consortium*[1], which encourages many initiatives all over the world about its diffusion in the IoT applications.

In such a perspective, the present paper describes how fog computing principles are integrated within a security and privacy-aware IoT-based middleware platform, named NetwOrked Smart object (NOS) [20], which adopts a publish&subscribe protocol, based on MQTT, for disseminating information. Such an architecture has been chosen for two main reasons. On the one hand, the authors own an already existing and running test-bed, which allows to promptly carry out an extensive performance analysis. On the other hand, NOS is already integrated with some relevant security functionalities, which will be described later in the paper. Note that more than one NOS is expected to simultaneously run within the same IoT network. As a consequence, a first fog layer includes the network of such NOSs. Instead, a second fog layer includes a network of brokers, whose role is supporting NOSs in efficiently share the acquired and processed data towards the interested end-users. A scheme of the envisioned infrastructure is sketched in Fig. 1.

The advantages of the just presented vision are the following: (i) avoiding single points of failure, thanks to the presence of multiple distributed NOSs and brokers; (ii) reducing the amount of data transmitted to a central entity, which could represent a sort of bottleneck for the IoT network (e.g., a single NOS or

---

[1] https://www.openfogconsortium.org/.

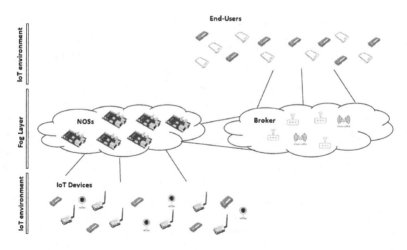

Fig. 1. IoT System composed by a dual fog layer, including multiple NOSs and brokers

a single broker); (iii) reducing the delays of information retrieval, since data are closer to the final consumers, due to the highly distributed nature of the fog layers just defined. Such outcomes are hereby evaluated by means of a test campaign, which is conducted on the just mentioned test-bed. The results reveal that network's latency is reduced, since a better balancing of the data load is achieved.

The rest of the paper is organized as follows. Section 2 presents the state of the art of existing IoT infrastructures and examines how they manage the information dissemination task, which is the main focus of the proposed work. Section 3 describes the background related to NOS's platform and MQTT functionalities, useful to clearly understand the role of the introduced fog layers. Section 4.1 presents the proposed approach, which is then evaluated in Sect. 5. Section 6 ends the paper and draws some hints for future work.

2   Related Work

The IoT environment proposed in this work envisions the coupling of fog computing paradigm and secure mechanisms for data sharing via MQTT protocol; the main purposes of the adopted network infrastructure have been just clarified in Sect. 1. Hereby, some related papers are described, trying to highlight their differences and weaknesses with respect to the work analyzed in the next sections.

With the final aim of improving the quality of service (QoS), the authors, in [14], present *EMMA*, an edge-enabled publish&subscribe middleware; the main weaknesses of such an approach is that it requires a controller and a broker that acts as a server for the client brokers integrated into the gateways, thus introducing a single point of failure into the network architecture.

The work in [4] proposes the adoption of a new kind of broker, named *QEST*, which is able to bridge MQTT primitives and REST interfaces, in order to ease machine-to-machine interactions. With respect to such an approach, the target of the paper proposed hereby is a more heterogeneous and distributed IoT system, not confined to the direct communications among IoT devices, but where interactions among the different involved parties are filtered and mediated by a middleware layer, which is able to perform processing and security tasks.

[22] evaluates the performance of an edge-switch, which implements some basic MQTT broker functionalities, in a Software-Defined Networking (SDN) based system. How the different edge-switches cooperate is not clear as well as it is worth to remark that SDN still presents some centralized features.

Security and privacy requirements are not taken into account by the afore-mentioned solutions. Instead, works which address such issues (e.g., by means of the adoption of enforcement policies) and which make use of MQTT protocol [10,11,15], are based on a centralized broker, which is the obstacle the authors want to overcome in this work.

Concerning fog computing, many solutions are currently inspired to smart health scenarios [8,13,21], or to the Internet of Vehicles (IoV) [1,7], or even to attacks' recognition [6,19]. Despite such approaches deal with end-to-end secure communications, authentication and authorization, a little focus is paid on how information are effectively shared once acquired by the IoT platform.

3   IoT Platform and Information Sharing

In this section, NOS's platform components and interactions are detailed; then, the main MQTT functionalities are explained, in order to clarify the data flow management of the envisioned IoT infrastructure.

Two main entities are typically included in an IoT system: (i) the nodes, conceived as heterogeneous data sources (e.g., WSN, RFID, NFC, actuators, etc.) which send data to the IoT platform; (ii) the users, who interact with the IoT system through services making use of such IoT-generated data, typically accessing them by means of a mobile device (e.g., smartphone, tablet) connected to the Internet (e.g., through WiFi, 4G, or Bluetooth technologies). NOSs are conceived as powerful smart devices, able to manage such entities.

NOSs and the data sources use RESTful interfaces, usually based on the HTTP or CoAP protocols, to communicate. Such interfaces are defined depending on the kind of IoT device. In this way, it is possible to collect the data from the IoT devices and to perform sources' registration. In fact, NOSs deal both with registered and non-registered sources. The registration is not manda-tory, but it provides various advantages in terms of security, since registered sources may specify an encryption scheme for their interactions with NOSs, thus increasing the level of protection of their communications (encryption keys' dis-tribution is made by the algorithms presented in [16]). The information related to the registered sources are put in the storage unit, named *Sources*. Instead, for each incoming data, both from registered and non-registered sources, the follow-ing information are gathered: (i) the kind of data source, which describes the type of node; (ii) the communication mode, that is, the way in which the data are collected (e.g., discrete or streaming communication); (iii) the data schema, which represents the content type (e.g., number, text) and the format of the received data (since heterogeneous IoT devices may be connected); (iv) the data itself; (v) the reception timestamp. Hence, also non-registered sources are known to the system; the main difference with respect to the registered ones, is that non-registered sources does not agree on an encryption schema with NOSs to protect their transmitted data.

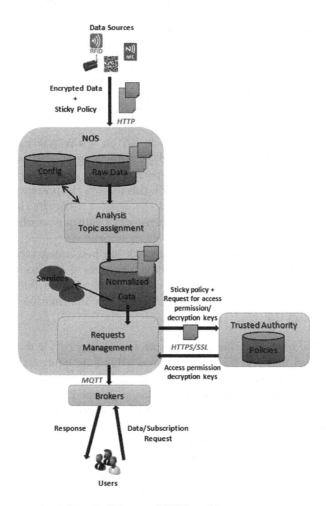

Fig. 2. Scheme of NOS architecture

Since the received data are of different types and formats, NOSs initially put them in the *Raw Data* storage unit. In such a collection, data are periodically processed, in a batch way, by the *Data Normalization* and *Analyzers* phases, in order to obtain a uniform representation and add useful metadata regarding the security (i.e., level of confidentiality, integrity, privacy and robustness of the authentication mechanism) and data quality (i.e., level of accuracy, precision, timeliness and completeness) assessment. Such an assessment is based on a set of rules stored in a proper format in another storage unit, named *Config*, and are detailed in [20]; it allows users who access the IoT data to directly filter by themselves the data processed by NOSs, according to their personal preferences. Figure 2 sketches the NOS's components introduced hereby.

Moreover, NOS offers the following relevant security related functionalities:

- A set of algorithms, as just mentioned, for data quality and security assessment, which are able to perform an automatic evaluation of the information by inferring to the data sources behavior [20]
- Two different key management systems by Dini et al. [5] and Di Pietro et al. [12], which are adopted for protecting the communications among NOSs and data producers/consumers; note that one of them must be chosen (please refer to [16] for further details)
- An enforcement framework, which is based on sticky policies; it provides a set of general-purpose rules, aimed at regulating the access to the IoT resources and controlling the actions performed by NOSs, in order to react towards possible violation attempts [18]; this implies the presence of a *Trusted Authority*, as shown in Fig. 2. Note that the *Trusted Authority* could represent a bottleneck in the system; hence, the presence of multiple coordinated trusted authorities is encouraged
- The enforcement mechanism, just presented, has been integrated with *AUPS (AUthenticated Publish&Subscribe system)*, a protocol able to securely manage publications and subscriptions through Message Queue Telemetry Transport (MQTT)[2] interactions, thus protecting the information sharing with data consumers [15].

Why MQTT has been chosen as the protocol adopted for data dissemination by the NOS platform? Firstly, because MQTT is lightweight event- and message-oriented, and allows the devices to asynchronously communicate across constrained networks to reach remote systems, as happens in typical IoT scenarios. Such a protocol employs a publish&subscribe pattern, where a central broker acts as intermediary among the entities that produce and consume the messages. All the communications among brokers and producers/consumers happen via a publish&subscribe mechanism, based on the *topic* concept. A *topic* is a mean for representing the resources (i.e., the information) exchanged within the system. *Topics* are used by data producers for publishing messages and by data consumers for subscribing to the updates from other producers. A *topic* is assigned by a proper NOS' module to each processed data for regulating the information sharing itself.

---

[2] OASIS, MQTT v5 protocol specification, https://docs.oasis-open.org/mqtt/mqtt/v5.0/mqtt-v5.0.html.

Concerning the MQTT-based AUPS mechanism, it was conceived with the presence of only one broker. Such a choice, initially dictated for simplicity, reveals now to be troublesome, due to the single point of failure and the bottleneck that the broker represents in the current NOS architecture. From such a consideration emerges the proposal to include a network of brokers in the IoT platform. However, such brokers must be properly managed and their tasks must be somehow coordinated, in order to really improve the IoT network's performance. No studies have been specifically conducted in the literature on the performance of the broker involved in an IoT system, as revealed in Sect. 2. Such an aspect will be clarified in Sect. 4.1.

4   Broker's Network

A dual fog layer, composed by NOSs and brokers, respectively, is setup within the IoT network, to reach the following requirements: (i) better balancing the load of the data to be shared with end-users on different brokers; (ii) reducing the delays of information retrieval from the time when information are acquired by NOS, to the time when the same information is received by the end-user; (iii) working in a location-awareness way; (iv) giving more robustness to the whole IoT system, avoiding single points of failure and bottlenecks. These are the main features, characterizing the conceived solution:

- A NOS can be connected to more than one broker and vice versa; hence, a many-to-many relationship can be established among NOSs and brokers
- NOSs and brokers communicate among themselves by means of MQTT protocol, via the MQTT client installed on NOS; such interactions are kept private thanks to the adoption of *AUPS*, as said in Sect. 3
- All the other communications taking place within the presented IoT system are security-aware, because: (i) users/applications receive ciphered data under specific permissions, defined at the subscription phase and implemented as sticky policies [18]; (ii) NOSs, if needed, exchange information among themselves on a HTTPS/SSL channel; (iii) the brokers need not to communicate among each other (in this sense, they are agnostic of each other), since NOSs both supervision on how information is shared and coordinate the brokers' activities
- NOSs and brokers are fully decoupled, in the sense that brokers can also be owned by different organizations/companies, which are interested in exploiting the functionalities made available by NOS platform, to disclose some relevant information to their customers. As a consequence, an organization/company can deploy its own broker and connect it to NOSs; using the MQTT protocol, no issue in terms of interoperability arises. For such a reason, the brokers' instances have not been directly installed within NOSs.

Therefore, a clear separation is created between data acquisition, performed by NOSs (along with processing tasks), and data sharing with end-users, performed by brokers. Summarizing, the authors decided to not integrate one broker for each NOS for three reasons: (i) preserve NOSs' power consumption;

(ii) enabling the participation of third-party brokers; (iii) there's no guarantee that the number of NOSs must be equal to that of brokers. In fact, the proportion between the number of NOSs and brokers within the IoT network should depend on the features of the specific application domain (e.g., number of managed topics, kinds of data producers and consumers involved). In the next section, the interactions among NOSs and brokers will be explained.

4.1 Brokers' Management

Suppose that the different NOSs and brokers involved in the IoT system are identified by NOS_1, NOS_2, ...NOS_n and br_1, br_2, ...br_m, respectively. When a user or an application requires a service/data provided by the IoT system, a session is opened. During such a session, the user/application, identified by $usapp_1$, $usapp_2$, ...$usapp_j$, can obtain the information provided by a NOS, taking into account the accessible resources. The resources can be accessed on the basis of the content of the sticky policies P_{data_1}, P_{data_2}, ...P_{data_k}, defined within the NOS enforcement framework, in the format specified in [18]. An advantage of such an approach is that the brokers can manage the incoming information in compliance with the associated policies, regardless of the NOSs with which they interact, since policies travel along with the corresponding data. However, the brokers must interact with NOSs in order to establish which subscriptions to accept or deny. Hence, brokers do not have a total control on the information disclosure.

At the initial state of the IoT network, NOSs and brokers may be associated in such a way that each broker has at least one connection to a NOS. Moreover, each broker manages the topics related to the data, which are further managed by the connected NOS. This depend on the kind of data transmitted by the sources connected to that NOS. But, what happens when a data acquired by NOS_1, assigned to a certain topic t, and transmitted by NOS_1 itself to the broker br_1, is required (due to another subscription) by a user/application $usapp_2$, connected to broker br_2, which does not receive any data under t? A mechanism for efficiently satisfying such a required information's exchange must be put in action. The simplest solution would be a sort of flooding approach: the broker br_1 notifies all the other brokers br_k of the new published data, so as to make it available in the whole IoT area, covered by the brokers; or, as an alternative, each NOS notifies all the brokers belonging to the IoT network about all the managed information. Clearly, such solutions are power-consuming and redundant, since it can be assumed that the data associated to a certain topic t are not required at all points in the network every time. Hence, a more viable approach follows the steps listed hereby, which also summarized in Fig. 3.

When a user or application $usapp_i$ subscribes to a certain topic t_1 on a certain broker (e.g., br_1), the broker itself inform the connected NOS (e.g., NOS_1), which performs such tasks:

1. NOS_1 checks if $usapp_i$ is authorized to access the data published under the topic t_1 (i.e., the check is executed by contacting the Trusted Authority, which

is able to verify the compliance of the sticky policy associated to the data under topic t_1 with the attributes owned by the requester)

2. If yes, br_1 is enabled to notify $usapp_i$ about the information related to topic t_1; if no, the requested resource cannot be disclosed

3. However, NOS_1 has to check if it directly manages the data assigned to topic t_1; such a check is performed by using a proper table, named *topicsMap*, which is stored in the *Config* collection (see Sect. 3) and contains an entry for each couple topic-NOS in the form (t_i, NOS_i)

   (a) If the couple (t_1, NOS_1) exists, the data acquired by NOS_1 and published under the topic t_1 will be notified by br_1 to the authorized $usapp_i$, but what happens if other NOSs process information related to the topic t_1, instead of NOS_1?

   (b) In such a case or in case the entry (t_1, NOS_1) is not found in NOS_1, then NOS_1 itself must find the couple or the couples (t_1, NOS_i), where i is not equal to 1, and warn the selected NOS_i (for example, NOS_2 in Fig. 3) about the fact that it must begin to publish the data related to the topic t_1 towards br_1. Finally, *topicsMap* must be updated accordingly: as shown in the example of Fig. 3, the couple (t_1, NOS_2) is added to the *topicsMap* on all NOSs; note that such an update is notified to all NOSs for future requests via the proper secure MQTT dedicated channel [17], in order not to compromise the *topicsMap*'s content.

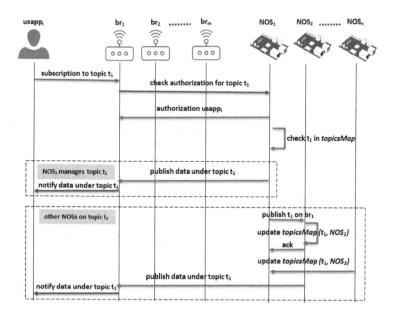

Fig. 3. Scheme of NOSs and brokers interactions

5   Performance Analysis

A test campaign is hereby proposed, in order to preliminary asses the feasibility of the approach presented in Sect. 4.1. Firstly, the employed hardware and software tools are introduced. Secondly, obtained results are discussed.

5.1   Test-Bed Details

A test-bed, whose software is openly accessible at https://bitbucket.org/ alessandrarizzardi/nos.git, is setup to practically perform an analysis about computing effort and latency metrics. The testing environment, sketched in Fig. 4, is composed by four instances of NOS (NOS_1, NOS_2, NOS_3 and NOS_4), running on four Raspberry Pi platforms, and by a variable number of brokers (from two to ten, namely br_1, ..., br_{10}), and data sources, which virtually run on separated virtual machines, installed on a personal computer. The sources use measures from real-world smart home test-bed[3], acquired by means of installed sensors that collect electricity data every minute for the entire home [2]. In particular, data are gathered from smart meter number 2 of *Home A*, which include, among the others, electricity consumption data of: kitchen lights, bedroom lights, duct heater HRV, and HRV furnace, published under the topics *homeA/lights/kitchen* (t_1), *homeA/lights/bedroom* (t_2), *homeA/HRV/ductheater* (t_3), and *homeA/HRV/furnace* (t_4), and so on. Wi-Fi connections are adopted for communications among the data sources, the MQTT brokers, and NOSs (i.e., the Raspberry Pi). NOSs modules interact among themselves through *RESTful* interfaces; such a feature allows the NOSs' administrators to add new modules or modify the existing ones at runtime, since they work in a parallel and non-blocking manner. Moreover, the non-relational nature of the adopted *MongoDB* database allows also the data model to dynamically evolve over the time. *Node.JS*[4] platform has been used for developing NOSs' core operations, *MongoDB*[5] has been adopted for the data management, and Mosquitto[6] has been chosen for realizing the open-source MQTT broker. Information is exchanged in *JSON* format. More details about the implementation can be found in [20].

The parameters used for simulations are summarized in Table 1. The storage overhead will be not investigated in this work, because it has just been deeply analyzed in previous works [17,18]; it is worth to remark NOSs support a non-persistent storage of IoT-generated data, since *Raw Data* and *Normalized Data* collections are emptied as the data are transmitted to the brokers. The same is for the brokers, which do not need to persistently store IoT-data to continue their activity. If the IoT system needs to persistently store the information obtained from the IoT network, a proper infrastructure (e.g., a cloud) must be involved.

---

[3] http://traces.cs.umass.edu/index.php/Smart/Smart.
[4] http://nodejs.org/.
[5] http://www.mongodb.org/.
[6] Mosquitto broker, http://mosquitto.org.

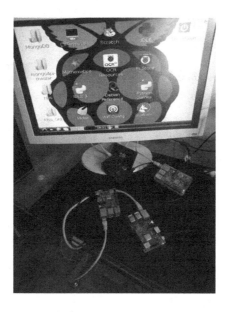

Fig. 4. Test-bed

5.2 Results

Figures 5 and 6 show the average distribution of the CPU load on the analyzed NOSs and brokers, respectively, in three different situations: (i) the IoT system adopting only one broker (i.e., br_1); (ii) running five brokers; (iii) running ten brokers. Such a metric is important for investigating about the computational resources' consumption of the tasks performed at the middleware IoT layer. The simulated scenario is as follows: (i) sources send to NOSs data related to the aforementioned topics at a rate of $10pck/sec$; while data requests (i.e., by hypothetical users) are simulated as well, at the same rate, and imply the notification from the brokers; (ii) at the initial stage, topic t_i is only associated with the topic t_i, but such a setting will vary during the system's running depending on the

Table 1. Test-bed parameters

Parameter	Value
NOSs	4
Brokers	[1, 10]
Sources	4
Topics	10
Data generation rate	10 pck/s
Data request rate	10 req/s
Observation time	24 h

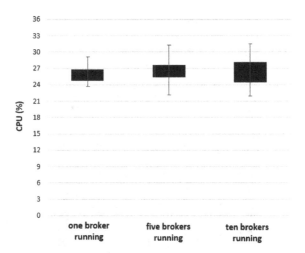

Fig. 5. Whiskers-box diagram: average CPU load on NOSs

random users' requests; (iii) in fact, when an external entity requires, for example, a subscription to t_1 towards br_2, the procedure presented in Sect. 4.1 must be executed.

The obtained results suggest that having more brokers affects, in a relevant way, the performance of the whole IoT system. Instead, the CPU load on NOSs is approximately constant; in the three scenarios, such a behavior is due to the fact that, NOSs process the same amount of data, but, even more important is to note that the resources required by NOSs to manage the *topicsMap* is negligible. Instead, the computing effort on brokers decreases, since they share the data

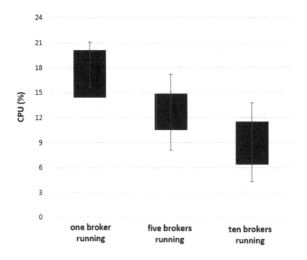

Fig. 6. Whiskers-box diagram: average CPU load on brokers

load, balancing the requests to be managed. Similar considerations can be made for the latency. In fact, the average time required by data from their transmission towards NOS to their reception by the subscribed entities is reduced in the three scenarios, as shown in Fig. 7. This means that, in presence of more brokers, the IoT system is able to satisfy the users' requests in a shorter time, thus improving the efficiency of the whole application.

Summarizing, the presence of more brokers better balances the data load, generated by the IoT system, without demanding all the information sharing task to one centralized broker, than the previous version of the NOS platform.

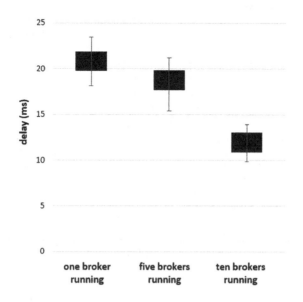

Fig. 7. Whiskers-box diagram: average end-to-end data latency

6   Conclusion

The paper has presented a security-aware fog-driven IoT architecture, composed by a dual fog layer, involving smart powerful devices (i.e., NOSs), responsible of acquiring and processing IoT-generated data, and a network of brokers, responsible for disseminating such elaborated data. Hence, MQTT protocol has been adopted, mainly due to its lightweight primitives, which fit the constraints of IoT devices. The paper has also provided a test campaign with the final aim to assess the advantages brought by the interactions among NOSs and brokers, which are conceived as fully decoupled. The outcomes revealed that network's latency is reduced, since a better balancing of the data load is achieved. Surely, a deeper analysis will be conducted in the near future, taking into account different applications scenarios and the possibility of connecting real IoT-devices as data sources, in order to conduct analysis on the power consumption of both data producers and IoT platform. Moreover, different QoS (Quality of Service) modes, related to the MQTT protocol, can be evaluated, in order to reveal how they affect the system performance.

References

1. Arif, M., Wang, G., Balas, V.E.: Secure VANETs: trusted communication scheme between vehicles and infrastructure based on fog computing. Stud. Inform. Control **27**(2), 235–246 (2018)
2. Barker, S., Mishra, A., Irwin, D., Cecchet, E., Shenoy, P., Albrecht, J.: Smart*: an open data set and tools for enabling research in sustainable homes. In: SustKDD, August 111, 112 (2012)
3. Bonomi, F., Milito, R., Zhu, J., Addepalli, S.: Fog computing and its role in the internet of things. In: Proceedings of the First Edition of the MCC Workshop on Mobile Cloud Computing, pp. 13–16. ACM (2012)
4. Collina, M., Corazza, G.E., Vanelli-Coralli, A.: Introducing the QEST broker: scaling the IoT by bridging MQTT and REST. In: IEEE 23rd International Symposium on Personal, Indoor and Mobile Radio Communications-(PIMRC), pp. 36–41 (2012)
5. Dini, G., Lopriore, L.: Key propagation in wireless sensor networks. Comput. Elect. Eng. **41**, 426–433 (2015)
6. Ionita, M.G., Patriciu, V.V.: Secure threat information exchange across the internet of things for cyber defense in a fog computing environment. Inform. Econ. **20**(3) (2016)
7. Kang, J., Yu, R., Huang, X., Zhang, Y.: Privacy-preserved pseudonym scheme for fog computing supported internet of vehicles. IEEE Trans. Intell. Transp. Syst. **19**(8), 2627–2637 (2018)
8. Moosavi, S.R., et al.: End-to-end security scheme for mobility enabled healthcare internet of things. Fut. Gener. Comput. Syst. **64**, 108–124 (2016)
9. Mouradian, C., Naboulsi, D., Yangui, S., Glitho, R.H., Morrow, M.J., Polakos, P.A.: A comprehensive survey on fog computing: state-of-the-art and research challenges. IEEE Commun. Surv. Tutor. **20**(1), 416–464 (2017)
10. Neisse, R., Steri, G., Baldini, G.: Enforcement of security policy rules for the internet of things. In: IEEE 10th International Conference on Wireless and Mobile Computing, Networking and Communications (WiMob), pp. 165–172 (2014)
11. Niruntasukrat, A., Issariyapat, C., Pongpaibool, P., Meesublak, K., Aiumsupucgul, P., Panya, A.: Authorization mechanism for MQTT-based internet of things. In: IEEE International Conference on Communications Workshops (ICC), pp. 290–295 (2016)
12. Pietro, R.D., Mancini, L., Jajodia, S.: Providing secrecy in key management protocols for large wireless sensors networks. Ad Hoc Networks **1**(4), 455–468 (2003)
13. Rahmani, A.M., et al.: Exploiting smart e-health gateways at the edge of healthcare internet-of-things: a fog computing approach. Fut. Gener. Comput. Syst. **78**, 641–658 (2018)
14. Rausch, T., Nastic, S., Dustdar, S.: EMMA: distributed QoS-aware MQTT middleware for edge computing applications. In: IEEE International Conference on Cloud Engineering (IC2E), pp. 191–197 (2018)

15. Rizzardi, A., Sicari, S., Miorandi, D., Coen-Porisini, A.: AUPS: an open source authenticated publish/subscribe system for the Internet of Things. Inf. Syst. **62**, 29–41 (2016)
16. Sicari, S., Rizzardi, A., Miorandi, D., Coen-Porisini, A.: Internet of Things: security in the keys. In: 12th ACM International Symposium on QoS and Security for Wireless and Mobile Networks, Malta, pp. 129–133, November 2016
17. Sicari, S., Rizzardi, A., Miorandi, D., Coen-Porisini, A.: Dynamic policies in internet of things: enforcement and synchronization. IEEE Internet Things J. **4**(6), 2228–2238 (2017)
18. Sicari, S., Rizzardi, A., Miorandi, D., Coen-Porisini, A.: Security towards the edge: sticky policy enforcement for networked smart objects. Inf. Syst. **71**, 78–89 (2017)
19. Sohal, A.S., Sandhu, R., Sood, S.K., Chang, V.: A cybersecurity framework to identify malicious edge device in fog computing and cloud-of-things environments. Comput. Secur. **74**, 340–354 (2018)
20. Sicari, S., Rizzardi, A., Miorandi, D., Cappiello, C., Coen-Porisini, A.: A secure and quality-aware prototypical architecture for the Internet of Things. Inf. Syst. **58**, 43–55 (2016)
21. Thota, C., Sundarasekar, R., Manogaran, G., Varatharajan, R., Priyan, M.: Centralized fog computing security platform for IoT and cloud in healthcare system. In: Exploring the Convergence of Big Data and the Internet of Things, pp. 141–154. IGI Global (2018)
22. Xu, Y., Mahendran, V., Radhakrishnan, S.: Towards SDN-based fog computing: MQTT broker virtualization for effective and reliable delivery. In: IEEE 8th International Conference on Communication Systems and Networks (COMSNETS), pp. 1–6 (2016)
23. Yaqoob, I., et al.: Internet of things architecture: recent advances, taxonomy, requirements, and open challenges. IEEE Wirel. Commun. **24**(3), 10–16 (2017)

XSS Attack Detection Model Based on Semi-supervised Learning Algorithm with Weighted Neighbor Purity

Xinran Li, Wenxing Ma, Zan Zhou$^{(\boxtimes)}$, and Changqiao Xu

Beijing University of Posts and Telecommunications, Beijing 100191, China
{lxr_bupt,cqxu}@bupt.edu.cn, mwx0519@sina.com, zan.leon.zhou@gmail.com

Abstract. With the popularity of web applications, cyber security is becoming more and more important. The most common web attack is cross-site scripting (XSS), which can be easily constructed in malicious URLs. However, the existing methods of detecting XSS attacks are suffering from the lack of labeled data, and some semi-supervised methods still have the problem of mislabeling. In this paper, we propose a novel XSS attack detection model based on semi-supervised learning algorithm with weighted neighbor purity. Semi-supervised learning can make best use of little labeled data, and a simple mechanism of neighbor purity using weighted-kNN is applied to rectify mislabeled samples, improving classification accuracy. To verify the feasibility of our solution in real-world scenario, we collected real HTTP requests in the China Education and Research Network (CERNET) as training data. The comparison experiment shows that proposed method performs better than a well-known semi-supervised algorithm and a recently published ensemble learning method in different initially labeled rates.

Keywords: XSS attack · Machine learning · Semi-supervised learning · Binary classification

1 Introduction

As the Internet has become an indispensable part in many people's lives, a lot of Internet companies make profit from their web services. However, adversaries can collect information from such a large quantity of Internet traffic and conduct tentative attacks [30]. These attacks have resulted in increasing security incidents like leakage of massive sensitive data [29], causing huge economic losses. The most widespread threat among the top 10 critical web security risks in 2017, according to the Open Web Application Security Project (OWASP) [17], was Cross-site scripting (XSS), which was unfortunately found in about two-thirds of all the web applications. Besides, the data provided by a cybersecurity leader team Imperva [3] showed that - XSS remained as the runner up category of web vulnerabilities in 2019, and probably one of the dominant categories in 2020.

© Springer Nature Switzerland AG 2020
L. A. Grieco et al. (Eds.): ADHOC-NOW 2020, LNCS 12338, pp. 198–213, 2020.
https://doi.org/10.1007/978-3-030-61746-2_15

The great threat of information safety and economic losses warn us to focus on XSS attack detection.

Many web attacks are executed by simply clicking a malicious URL from web browsers, including XSS attacks under discussion. The majority of successful XSS attacks are built by deliberate URLs with malicious code. When victims click an elaborately constructed URL, an evil request is sent to the web server. At the same time, the malicious code is executed on victims' browser, resulting in information leakage, keylogging, dynamic downloads and other serious consequences [18]. Sometimes the evil input sent to the server side will be stored in database, threatening more visitors of this webpage.

To detect XSS attack, this paper focuses on distinguishing malicious URLs with XSS attacks from the benign. In the field of URL detections using artificial intelligence, actually in all the cyber security areas using machine learning, the limited malicious database is a serious problem [16,22], leading many approaches to use not real representative or intentionally generated dataset. Thus, these approaches are lack of empirical evidence against real-world scenarios. Some studies use the semi-supervised learning method to take more advantage of existing labeled data. However, the problems of mislabeling and overfitting in the developed model still need to be solved [12].

In face of the issues above, this paper develops a novel classification model for automatically detecting XSS attacks in malicious URL requests based on a semi-supervised algorithm using weighted neighbor purity. Machine learning method can greatly improve the classification accuracy [20], especially a semi-supervised method based on ensemble learning can eliminate the lack of labeled data. To address mislabeling and overfitting problems in semi-supervised learning, we add two novel restrictions on a well-known algorithm. Also, real-world scenarios are considered by using the real data flows in both training and testing data set.

The main contributions of this paper are summarized as follows:

(1) To improve the classification accuracy of semi-supervised learning algorithm, we ameliorate traditional Co-Training algorithm [1] by calculating weighted neighbor purity as a threshold to reduce mislabeled data, and introducing an excess ratio to address the overfitting problem.
(2) Considering the practical use of real-world application, we train our model by captured URLs from HTTP requests in CERNET and feasible attacks that have caused loss collected by XSSed [4]. To achieve the usability of our detection model, practical data cleaning method is also introduced.
(3) Finally, comparison experiments are conducted to compare our improved method with the original algorithm and another ensemble learning approach published last year, showing that the proposed method outperforms the other two methods.

The rest of this paper is structured as follows: Sect. 2 summarizes the related work about URL detection and semi-supervised learning algorithm. Section 3 explains the overview of proposed detecting model. Section 4 describes the improved semi-supervised algorithm in detail. Section 5 represents the implementation and experimental result of three methods. Section 6 concludes this paper.

2   Related Work

In this section, we introduce the studies of URL attack detection w ith machine learning and semi-supervised learning algorithm. The knowledge in these two respects mostly supports our research.

2.1   Research on URL Attack Detection with Machine Learning

Many web attacks can be simply constructed by embedding or injecting malicious code in URLs [27], and XSS attack is the dominant type among them [19]. Using a machine learning algorithm, we can extract representative static features from URL [20] and train a prediction model to classify benign and malicious samples. Thus, the performance of machine learning depends largely on features. Machine learning methods can detect unknown malicious code, unlike universally used methods based on blacklists. Furthermore, a classifier built by machine learning method consumes little time to predict whether an URL is malicious, that is the reason why more and more web servers choose to use machine learning method for security issues.

Cui et al. [2] designed a feasible feature process procedure. They used gradient learning to perform statistical analysis and their feature extraction is conducted based on a sigmoidal threshold level. Yang [26] created a multi-classifier model for URL with syntax and domain features, indicating that the best performance is achieved by random forest algorithm. Joshi et al. [10] proposed an ensemble classification method with lexical static features to detect malicious URLs, which is currently being used in the FireEye Advanced URL Detection Engine. Zhou et al. [28] also used an ensemble learning method which is based on Bayesian networks, but they combined domain knowledge and threat intelligence with the traditional lexical features, achieving a good result.

The current studies paid more attention to feature extraction, but few of them believes the balanced dataset should be manually checked, though it could consume a large amount of manpower. Instead of using real-world data, most of these studies used generated data. These data could have high-level of identity for training their models, which reduces the reliability of their methods to some extent.

2.2   Research on Semi-supervised Algorithm

In traditional supervised learning, although it's easy to obtain plenty of unlabeled URL samples, it takes a lot of manually labeling time and cost to provide labels for them. To address this challenge, semi-supervised learning is proposed to improve learning performance with mostly unlabeled data. Disagreement-based semi-supervised learning using ensemble learning method is one of the mainstream paradigms in this field [31]. It applies multiple classifiers to utilize unlabeled data, and the disagreement between learners is critical to learning effectiveness. Research on disagreement-based semi-supervised learning began with the work of Blum and Mitchell on Co-Training [1].

There have been many studies on improving Co-Training. Zhou and his collaborators proposed Tri-training [32], which can be seen as an extension of the binary classifier cooperative training. It generated three classifiers from a single-view training set and then used these three classifiers by the rule of majority to generate pseudo-labeled samples and solved the confidence evaluation problem of pseudo-labeled samples. After training, the three classifiers were used as one classifier through a voting mechanism. Li et al. proposed Co-Forest that puts emphasis on the importance of ensemble learning [11]. Gu et al. proposed an ensemble multi-train method of heteromorphic multi-classifiers [7]. The training process of this method is similar to that of Co-Forest but required each base classifier to use a different learning algorithm, and at the same time use different attribute reduction strategies. In this paper, the random forest algorithm is integrated into the semi-supervised learning framework, which can further improve the learning performance of the classifier, and the introduction of multiple classifiers simplifies the calculation of the pseudo-labeled confidence.

In Co-Training, mislabeled data can accumulate during training, which influences diversity and accuracy of the combined classifier. Xiang et al. [24] developed a visual analysis method, which could improve the quality of labeled samples interactively. The quality improvement was achieved through the use of user-selected trusted items and much manual work was required. The study in [12] used data editing in Tri-training [32], which significantly improved the classification performance. Li et al. proposed an improved naive Bayes self-training algorithm based on weighted K-nearest neighbors. Selecting the samples with the similar spatial structure of the labeled samples, the naive Bayes classifier assorted unlabeled samples on a better spatial structure and reduced mislabeled samples effectively [21]. In this paper, the weighted K-nearest neighbor rule is used to rectify the mislabeled data more accurately.

Based on these existing studies, we combine the wisdom of URL attacks detection method and machine learning with a semi-supervised algorithm, for designing a novel detection model of XSS attacks in URL. The lack of labeled data is solved by machine learning, in which real scene and data are considered. Furthermore, to solve the mislabeling problem in semi-supervised learning, we propose a weighted neighbor purity method to rectify pseudo-labeled samples.

3   XSS Attack Detection Model Based on Improved Semi-supervised Learning

This section describes the proposed detection model, as shown in Fig. 1. Following the process lines, raw URL data collected from real world are divided into training set and testing set, and then they are sent into URL processing procedure. The URL processing procedure transfers raw data in training set and testing set, respectively, into practicable feature vectors. Particularly in training process, we add a data cleaning step to eliminate noise in features. After URL processing, the refined data represented as feature vectors from training set are sent to learning process to train a detection model. The detection model is then evaluated by classifying the feature vectors generated from the testing set. If the evaluation result is good enough, the generated detection model can be put into application. Otherwise the control flow goes back to URL processing procedure, trying to extract more representative features.

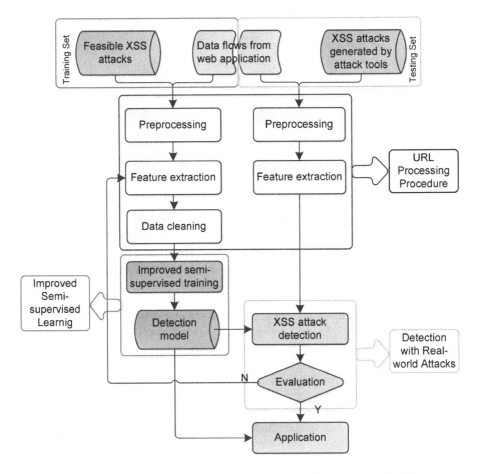

Fig. 1. XSS attack detection model based on improved semi-supervised learning

3.1   URL Processing Procedure

Preprocessing. URLs in HTTP request are often encoded, leading to confusion of both human and artificial intelligence. Many attacks also use encoding method to bypass traditional attack detectors. That is why we need a preprocessing step to check possible attacks. Figure 2 shows the preprocessing procedure, transforming encoded data into human-readable strings. We firstly pick out the URL query section from normal data packet shown in the first box. In the second box, we get the extracted URL query. After URL decoding, HTML entity decoding and lowercasing, URL query is transferred into apprehensible string in the third box.

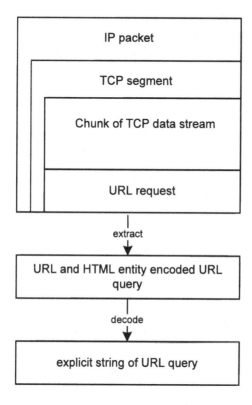

Fig. 2. Preprocessing procedure

Feature Extraction. Feature extraction is conducted on the decoded URL query strings of the last step. According to the previous researches [15,25], we use 70 URL static features as the original attributes. To eliminate the deviation of redundant attributes, we carry out a feature selection algorithm, which is based on correlation between features and its category. After the selection, 14 effective features are selected. These useful features consist of 5 URL structural features, 1 XSS risk level feature, 7 evil char features, and 2 evil keyword features.

Data Cleaning. Considering the adaptation of different practical scenarios, data cleaning is necessary to filter out outliers in training process. The outliers in training set can be regarded as noise, which badly affects the universality of the model to be trained. Feature vectors in training set are projected into a plane space by a dimensionality reduction method t-SNE [14]. Then a density-based clustering algorithm DBSCAN [5] can easily find out the outliers. For test process, as it will omit some real attacks in test data, we do not conduct data cleaning method.

3.2 Improved Semi-supervised Learning

The core algorithm in detection model is a semi-supervised machine learning method improved by weighted neighbor purity. We can describe the target of detecting XSS attacks as a binary classification issue, where positive samples are malicious and negative samples are benign [2]. As for classification, the fundamental assumption is that malicious attacks and benign requests have different features. In this way, the classification model can learn how to predict a new feature vector by adjusting itself according to labeled feature vectors.

Unlike supervised learning method, semi-supervised machine learning can learn from both labeled and unlabeled data, saving a large amount of manpower for labeling. We improve the existing method by introducing weighted neighbor purity and an excess ratio, to ameliorate the accumulating mislabeled error problem and the overfitting problem caused by imbalanced training data. Section 4 describes the improved machine learning algorithm in detail.

3.3 Detection with Real-World Attacks

As attackers usually use attack tools to automatically build XSS attacks, our model is intended to detect newly constructed attacks from normal requests. Therefore, the test set is mixed with XSS attacks generated by attack tools and benign URL requests from life scene in the training set. Although the evil data in training set is collected from real-world XSS attack in website XSSed [4], which is not similar with the test set, our model performs well according to the experiment result.

To evaluate the performance of the detection result, we use classification accuracy as the metric. Classification accuracy is the proportion of correct predictions to all predictions. Equation 1 defines the accuracy, where P and N is the number of positive and negative predictive value respectively, $TP + TN$ is the number of correctly predicted samples, and $P + N$ is the total number of predictions.

$$Accuracy = \frac{TP + TN}{P + N} \qquad (1)$$

4   Improved Semi-supervised Algorithm

This section describes the core algorithm in our detection model. An improved semi-supervised algorithm is proposed similar to Co-Forest [11] for binary classification problems. In the following discussion, we use L to denote labeled samples and U to denote unlabeled samples. $C = \{C_1, C_2, ..., C_n\}$ represents the classification space of labeled samples. First, a labeled training set L is used to build a random forest composed of N base classifiers $H = \{H(1), H(2), ..., H(N)\}$. $H(i)(i = 1, ..., N)$ represents a base classifier in H, and a new ensemble classifier composed of the remaining $N - 1$ classifiers is called the companion classifier of $H(i)$, denoted by $H^*(i)$. During iterations, each companion classifier provides its most confident pseudo label to its base classifier and expand the training set of base classifiers.

4.1 Solution for Overfitting

When building a model for detecting malicious URL, there are often far more samples of normal URL than malicious URL ones. To solve the overfitting problem resulted by extreme imbalance of positive and negative samples, we propose a simple processing mechanism. For each iteration, we measure the proportion of newly added pseudo-labeled samples of different classifications according to the proportion of initially labeled data in different classifications. Suppose the initially labeled samples have N_p positive samples and N_n negative samples, and the ratio of positive and negative samples is r, which is defined in Eq. 2. The allocation of pseudo-labeled samples added to each classifier in each iteration should follow the ratio r, and the excess samples will be put back in U.

$$r = \frac{N_p}{N_n} \tag{2}$$

4.2 Rectification for Mislabeled Data

To reduce the number of mislabeled samples and to improve the performance of the classifier, this paper treats the samples differently according to the marginality of the samples. If the nearest neighbors of a sample mostly belong to the same category, then it has a higher probability of belonging to this category. On the contrary, if the categories of the nearest neighbors are more uniformly distributed, it will be difficult to determine the category according to the neighbors. For each unlabeled sample $x(x \in U)$, we construct a neighbor set $neighbor(x)$ composed of labeled samples. The purity of the neighbors [13] can describe the distribution of neighbor sample categories. This paper proposes weighted neighbor purity, which can more accurately describe the distribution of the neighbors. In order to avoid calculation errors caused of value interval difference in different attributes, it is necessary to normalize each attribute value first. Then, all samples are mapped into points in a multidimensional space, and the distance $dis(x, z)$ between the unlabeled samples x and z refers to their Euclidean distance. The weight of each point w_v is the confidence of the sample, which is defined in Eq. 3. And the weight of each edge $w_e(x, z)$ is defined in Eq. 4.

$$w_v(x) = confidence(x) = \frac{\max\{N_1, N_2\}}{N - 1} \tag{3}$$

$$w_e(x, z) = e^{-\frac{dis^2(x,z)}{8}} \tag{4}$$

Where N_1, N_2 denotes the number of y_1, y_2 labeled by $H^*(x)$ respectively. We use k to denote the number of the nearest neighbors. Then, the weight of the negative samples in k neighbors $W_n(x)$ is defined in Eq. 5. The weight of the positive samples in k neighbors $W_p(x)$ is defined in Eq. 6, where n_i denotes the ith nearest neighbor of x. The weighted neighbor purity is defined in Eq. 7.

$$W_n(x) = \sum_{i=1}^{k} w_v(x) * w_e(x, n_i), y(n_i) = y_1 \tag{5}$$

$$W_p(x) = \sum_{i=1}^{k} w_v(x) * w_e(x, n_i), y(n_i) = y_2 \tag{6}$$

$$wpurity(x) = \frac{W_p(x)}{W_p(x) + W_n(x)} \ln \frac{W_p(x)}{W_n(x)} + \ln \frac{2 * W_n(x)}{W_p(x) + W_n(x)} \tag{7}$$

In this paper, samples with low neighbor purity are called margin samples. The introduction of margin samples is important to improve the generalization ability of the classifier and approximate the ideal hypothesis. We add margin samples that have higher confidence than θ_h to the set of labeled samples, while manually label the samples that have lower confidence than θ_l. For samples with lower marginality, we combine the idea of weighted K-nearest neighbor algorithm to rectify pseudo-labeled samples. That is to say, we sample the k neighbors closest to x, then compare the weights of the positive and negative samples, and the label of the sample is rectified according to the category with larger weight.

The main algorithm flow that applies the semi-supervised learning is given in Algorithm 1. First, N random trees are constructed using labeled samples to build a random forest. For each classifier, we sample some unlabeled data and label them with the companion classifier. If the confidence level and the weighted neighbor purity are high, data editing is employed. On the other hand, if the confidence level and the weighted neighbor purity are low, the sample is manually labeled. Excess samples of a classification are put back in U according to the ratio r. When all classifiers stop updating, training ends.

5   Experiment

This section describes the detailed experiment settings, consisting of data resources, feature selection method, training parameters and comparison experiment results about our method, and other two competitive methods.

Algorithm 1. Improved Semi-supervised Algorithm

Input: L: the labeled set; U: the unlabeled set; θ_h: the high confidence threshold; θ_l: the low confidence threshold; θ_p: the threshold of the weighted neighbor purity; N: the number of random trees; K: the number of the nearest neighbors

Output: classifiers $H = \{H(1), H(2), ..., H(N)\}$;

1: build a random forest consisting N random trees with L
2: **for** $i \in \{1, ..., N\}$ **do**
3:     $\hat{e}_{i,0} = 0.5$
4:     $W_{i,0} = 0$
5: **end for**
6: $t = 1$
7: **repeat**
8:     **for** $i \in \{1, ..., N\}$ **do**
9:         compute the estimated error rate $\hat{e}_{i,0} = EstimateError(H_i, L)$
10:        $L'_{i,t} = \phi$
11:        **if** $\hat{e}_{i,t} < \hat{e}_{i,t-1}$ **then**
12:            sample some unlabeled data $U'_{i,t} = SubSampled(U, \frac{\hat{e}_{i,t-1}W_{i,t-1}}{\hat{e}_{i,t}})$
13:            **for each** $x \in U'_{i,t}$ **do**
14:                **if** $confidence(H_i, x) > \theta_h$ **then**
15:                    **if** $wpurity(x) > \theta_p$ **then**
16:                        compare $W_p(x)$ and $W_n(x)$ to correct the mislabeled data
17:                    **end if**
18:                    add x to the labeled dataset $L'_{i,t} = L'_{i,t} \cup \{(x, H_i(x))\}$
19:                    $W_{i,t} = W_{i,t} + confidence(H_i, x)$
20:                **else if** $confidence(H_i, x) < \theta_l$ and $wpurity(x) < \theta_p$ **then**
21:                    label the data manually and add it to $L'_{i,t}$
22:                **end if**
23:            **end for**
24:            put excess samples back in U according to the ratio r
25:        **end if**
26:     **end for**
27:     **for** $i \in \{1, ..., N\}$ **do**
28:         **if** $e_{i,t}W_{i,t} < e_{i,t-1}W_{i,t-1}$ **then**
29:             update the classifier $h_i = LearnRandomTree(L \cup L'_{i,t})$
30:         **end if**
31:     **end for**
32:     $t = t + 1$
33: **until** none of the trees in random forest changes

5.1   Dataset

To simulate the practical application of our model, we captured 54.8 MB data flows from outgoing traffic of Beijing University of Posts and Telecommunications network as the normal samples. After extracting the investigated URL request from the flows, we obtain 39596 distinct queries. The majority of these samples are used as white data in training set, and the remaining 3770 normal samples are randomly selected into testing set.

The evil XSS attacks in training set are collected from a well-known security website XSSed [4], containing 28776 unique attacks in URL requests. The XSS attacks in testing set are collected from several GitHub repositories, consisting of 3770 distinct attacks. Because of the difference between training and testing data, our model cannot completely learn the feature pattern of testing samples during training procedure, which greatly supports the validity of our evaluation result.

5.2   Feature Selection

Feature selection is an important procedure that determines the efficiency of machine learning algorithm. This part is executed after URL decoding, HTML entity decoding and lowercasing in the preprocessing procedure of training process. After roughly selecting 70 static features according to [15,25], we use a built-in algorithm of Waikato Environment for Knowledge Analysis (WEKA) [23], and finally pick out 14 useful features shown in Table 1, where URL structural features are statistical features for the whole clean strings; XSS risk level feature is calculated by the cumulative number of the XSS keywords occurrence. The evil char and evil keyword features are the respective numbers of certain char and keyword occurrence.

The selection algorithm named CfsSubsetEval [8] calculates the individual predictive ability of each feature in a subset of attributes, the degree of redundancy is evaluated as well. Searched by greedy algorithm, subsets of features having low intercorrelation and high correlation with the category will be recommended.

5.3   Training Parameters

This subsection explains the detailed parameters in our comparison experiments of improved semi-supervised method, original Co-Forest algorithm and the reproduction of an ensemble learning method published last year [28].

In the proposed semi-supervised method, the algorithm benefits from ensemble learning, using Random Tree algorithm as the base classifier, and the N value is set to 10. The other parameters use the default parameters of the random forest package in WEKA. The high confidence threshold θ_h is 0.75 and the low confidence threshold θ_l is set to 0.65. The weighted neighbor purity threshold is set to 0.02. The size of the nearest neighbor set is related to the confidence of the pseudo-label samples and the number of iterations and has no significant impact on the accuracy of classifiers. The nearest neighbor set size is set to 5 in this experiment.

The original Co-Forest [11] algorithm in comparison uses consistent configuration for base classifier with the improved algorithm. Its only confidence threshold of the labeled samples is set to 0.75, as high as our high confidence threshold.

Table 1. Selected features

Category	Feature name	Description
URL structural	URL_length	the total length of a URL query
	digit_percentage	the percentage of digit in a URL query
	letter_percentage	the percentage of letter in a URL query
	parameter_number	number of parameters in a URL query
XSS risk level	XSS_count	accumulative number of XSS keywords occurrence
evil char	"	existence of char "
	<	existence of char <
	\	existence of char \
	,	existence of char ,
	%	existence of char %
evil keyword	img	existence of word *img*
	eval	existence of word *eval*

In the reproduction of another ensemble learning method using Bayesian network as base classifier, we exactly use the same parameters as the paper mentioned [28]. For ensemble learning, bagging and majority voting methods are used to generate different training subsets and predict results. The number of distinguishing base learners is 5. For each base classifier, Tabu [6] search algorithm and BDeu [9] scoring function are applied.

All the approaches are conducted with different initial rates of labeled training sets, which are respectively labeled as 5%, 10%, 20%, and 30%. The average classification accuracy of five tests is finally used for comparison.

5.4   Experiment Result

Figure 3 shows the improved algorithm classification accuracy of different initially labeled proportions. From this figure, it can be seen that in each initially labeled proportion of 5%, 10%, 20%, and 30%, the accuracy increases as the number of iterations increases. Table 2 shows the number of samples that need to be manually labeled as well as exercise classification accuracy for each iteration. Only a few samples need to be manually labeled each iteration, which meets the actual production requirements.

Table 2. The accuracy and manually labeled number of each iteration under different initially labeled proportions. N_{manual} denotes the manually labeled number.

	5%		10%		20%		30%	
	Accuracy	N_{manual}	Accuracy	N_{manual}	Accuracy	N_{manual}	Accuracy	N_{manual}
1	0.875	53	0.901	36	0.933	18	0.942	28
2	0.906	39	0.938	18	0.942	14	0.956	19
3	0.925	48	0.945	61	0.945	27	0.958	20
4	0.936	27	0.953	46	0.956	23	0.965	13
5	0.943	18	0.957	24	0.962	10	0.973	06

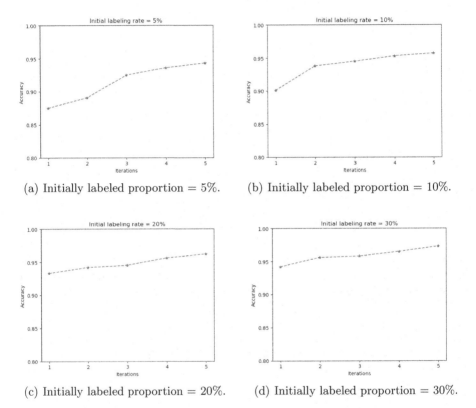

(a) Initially labeled proportion = 5%.   (b) Initially labeled proportion = 10%.

(c) Initially labeled proportion = 20%.   (d) Initially labeled proportion = 30%.

Fig. 3. The improved algorithm classification accuracy of different initially labeled proportions.

Moreover, we compare our work with the Co-Forest algorithm and another ensemble learning algorithm. Table 3 shows the comparison of the accuracy of three algorithms under different initially labeled proportions. As can be seen from the Fig. 4, the improved semi-supervised algorithm has the highest accuracy among the three methods in each initially labeled proportion. The fewer labeled samples, the more obvious the advantages of the proposed algorithm.

Table 3. Algorithm classification accuracy comparison.

Labeled proportion	Improved algorithm	Co-Forest	Ensemble Bayesian Network
5%	94.3%	88.2%	57.6%
10%	95.7%	92.3%	75.7%
20%	96.5%	94.0%	68.9%
30%	97.3%	95.2%	77.5%

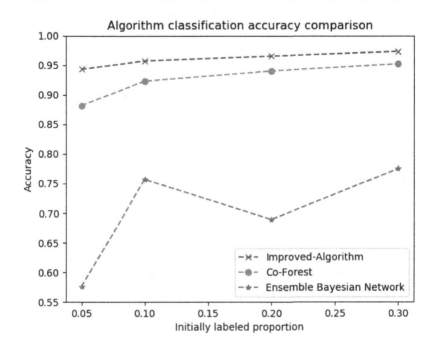

Fig. 4. Algorithm classification accuracy comparison.

Although all of the methods use ensemble learning, the ensemble Bayesian network performs worst in low labeling rates. That is because it does not apply semi-supervised learning to gain more knowledge from limited data, though it actually performs well when learning a fully labeled data set with the classification accuracy of 0.96. In the comparison of two semi-supervised algorithms, the improved one takes the importance of margin samples into account and rectifies mislabeled samples, thereby improving the performance of our classifier.

In general, applying the proposed algorithm to XSS detection has high accuracy and requires little manpower to label the data, proved to have high application value.

6 Conclusion

This paper developed a novel classification model for automatically detecting malevolent URL request with an improved semi-supervised algorithm. To improve the classification accuracy of semi-supervised algorithm, we introduced the weighted purity of edge samples to address the problem of accumulating mislabeled data, and an excess ratio is taken into account for the overfitting problem. In addition, we collected real network traffic in the CERNET and feasible XSS attacks that had caused loss in history for training, achieving practical value of real-world scenario. The experiment showed that our method exceeded a well-known semi-supervised method Co-forest and another competitive ensemble learning method.

In future work, more precise features and the semantic features of the attack can be analyzed and they will greatly improve the universalism of the detection. Furthermore, the proposed method can only detect the evil URLs with XSS attack, and more malicious behaviors in URLs will be taken into consideration, such as code injection, filename attack and so on.

References

1. Blum, A., Mitchell, T.: Combining labeled and unlabeled data with co-training. In: Proceedings of the Eleventh Annual Conference on Computational Learning Theory, pp. 92–100 (1998)
2. Cui, B., He, S., Yao, X., Shi, P.: Malicious URL detection with feature extraction based on machine learning. Int. J. High Perform. Comput. Networking **12**(2), 166–178 (2018)
3. Dima, B., Sarit, Y.: The state of web application vulnerabilities in 2019. https://www.imperva.com/blog/the-state-of-vulnerabilities-in-2019/. Accessed 5 Mar 2020
4. DP, KF: Xssed archive. http://www.xssed.com/archive. Accessed 5 Mar 2020
5. Ester, M., Kriegel, H.P., Sander, J., Xu, X., et al.: A density-based algorithm for discovering clusters in large spatial databases with noise. KDD **96**, 226–231 (1996)
6. Glover, F.: Tabu search: a tutorial. Interfaces **20**(4), 74–94 (1990)
7. Gu, S., Jin, Y.: Multi-train: a semi-supervised heterogeneous ensemble classifier. Neurocomputing **249**, 202–211 (2017)
8. Hall, M.A.: Correlation-based feature selection for machine learning (1999)
9. Heckerman, D., Geiger, D., Chickering, D.M.: Learning Bayesian networks: the combination of knowledge and statistical data. Mach. Learn. **20**(3), 197–243 (1995)
10. Joshi, A., Lloyd, L., Westin, P., Seethapathy, S.: Using lexical features for malicious URL detection-a machine learning approach. arXiv preprint arXiv:1910.06277 (2019)
11. Li, M., Zhou, Z.H.: Improve computer-aided diagnosis with machine learning techniques using undiagnosed samples. IEEE Trans. Syst. Man Cybern. Part A Syst. Hum. **37**(6), 1088–1098 (2007)
12. Liu, R., Verbič, G., Ma, J.: A new dynamic security assessment framework based on semi-supervised learning and data editing. Electr. Power Syst. Res. **172**, 221–229 (2019)
13. Liu, Z., Gao, Z., Li, X.: Co-training method based on margin sample addition. Chin. J. Sci. Instrum. **39**(3), 45–53 (2018)

14. Maaten, L.V.D., Hinton, G.: Visualizing data using t-sne. J. Mach. Learn. Res. **9**, 2579–2605 (2008)
15. Mereani, F.A., Howe, J.M.: Detecting cross-site scripting attacks using machine learning. In: Hassanien, A.E., Tolba, M.F., Elhoseny, M., Mostafa, M. (eds.) AMLTA 2018. AISC, vol. 723, pp. 200–210. Springer, Cham (2018). https://doi.org/10.1007/978-3-319-74690-6_20
16. Mokbal, F.M.M., Dan, W., Imran, A., Jiuchuan, L., Akhtar, F., Xiaoxi, W.: MLPXSS: an integrated XSS-based attack detection scheme in web applications using multilayer perceptron technique. IEEE Access **7**, 100567–100580 (2019)
17. OWASP, T.: Top 10–2017. The Ten Most Critical Web Application Security Risks. OWASP^{TM} Foundation. The free and open software security community (2017). https://www.owasp.org/index.php/Top_10-2017_Top_10
18. Raman, P.: JaSPIn: JavaScript based Anomaly Detection of Cross-site scripting attacks. Ph.D. thesis, Carleton University (2008)
19. Rodriguez, G., Torres, J., Flores, P., Benavides, E.: Cross-site scripting (XSS) attacks and mitigation: a survey. Comput. Networks 106960 (2019). https://doi.org/10.1016/j.comnet.2019.106960
20. Sahoo, D., Liu, C., Hoi, S.C.H.: Malicious URL detection using machine learning: a survey. CoRR abs/1701.07179 (2017). http://arxiv.org/abs/1701.07179
21. Tingting, L., Jia, L.: Improved Naive Bayes self-training algorithm based on weighted k-nearest neighbor. J. Wuhan Univ. (Nat. Sci. Ed.) (2019)
22. Vinayakumar, R., Soman, K., Poornachandran, P., Mohan, V.S., Kumar, A.D.: Scalenet: scalable and hybrid framework for cyber threat situational awareness based on DNS, URL, and email data analysis. J. Cyber Secur. Mobil. **8**(2), 189–240 (2019)
23. Witten, I.H., Frank, E.: Data mining: practical machine learning tools and techniques with java implementations. ACM SIGMOD Record **31**(1), 76–77 (2002)
24. Xiang, S., Ye, X., Xia, J., Wu, J., Chen, Y., Liu, S.: Interactive correction of mislabeled training data. In: 2019 IEEE Conference on Visual Analytics Science and Technology (VAST), pp. 57–68 (2019)
25. Yang, J., Yang, P., Jin, X., Ma, Q.: Multi-classification for malicious URL based on improved semi-supervised algorithm. In: 2017 IEEE International Conference on Computational Science and Engineering (CSE) and IEEE International Conference on Embedded and Ubiquitous Computing (EUC), vol. 1, pp. 143–150. IEEE (2017)
26. Yang, P.: A Study on Real-time Detection of URL Attack Behavior Based on Machine Learning. Master's thesis, Beijing University of Posts and Telecommunications (2018)
27. Yang, W., Zuo, W., Cui, B.: Detecting malicious URLs via a keyword-based convolutional gated-recurrent-unit neural network. IEEE Access **7**, 29891–29900 (2019)
28. Zhou, Y., Wang, P.: An ensemble learning approach for XSS attack detection with domain knowledge and threat intelligence. Comput. Secur. **82**, 261–269 (2019)
29. Zhou, Z., Qiao, Y., Zhu, L., Guan, J., Liu, Y., Xu, C.: Differential privacy-guaranteed trajectory community identification over vehicle ad-hoc networks. Internet Technol. Lett. **1**(3), e9 (2018)
30. Zhou, Z., Xu, C., Kuang, X., Zhang, T., Sun, L.: An efficient and agile spatio-temporal route mutation moving target defense mechanism. In: ICC 2019–2019 IEEE International Conference on Communications (ICC), pp. 1–6. IEEE (2019)
31. Zhou, Z.H.: Disagreement-based semi-supervised learning. Acta Automatica Sinica **39**(11), 1871–1878 (2013)
32. Zhou, Z.H., Li, M.: Tri-training: Exploiting unlabeled data using three classifiers. IEEE Trans. Knowl. Data Eng. **17**(11), 1529–1541 (2005)

A Cross-Layer Intrusion Detection System for RPL-Based Internet of Things

Erdem Canbalaban[(✉)] and Sevil Sen[(✉)]

WISE Lab., Department of Computer Engineering,
Hacettepe University, Ankara, Turkey
ecanbalaban@hacettepe.edu.tr,
ssen@cs.hacettepe.edu.tr

Abstract. The Internet of Things (IoT) is a heterogeneous network of constrained devices connected both to each other and to the Internet. Since the significance of IoT has risen remarkably in recent years, a considerable amount of research has been conducted in this area, and especially on, new mechanisms and protocols suited to such complex systems. Routing Procotol for Lower-Power and Lossy Networks (RPL) is one of the well-accepted routing protocols for IoT. Even though RPL has defined some specifications for its security, it is still vulnerable to insider attacks. Moreover, lossy communication links and resource-constraints of devices introduce a challenge for developing suitable security solutions for such networks. Therefore, in this study, a new intrusion detection system based on neural networks is proposed for detecting specific attacks against RPL. Besides features collected from the routing layer, the effects of link layer-based features are investigated on intrusion detection. To the best of our knowledge, this study presents the first cross-layer intrusion detection system in the literature.

Keywords: Internet of Things · Security · Cross-layer intrusion detection · Routing attacks · RPL · Neural networks

1 Introduction

With the development of technology, the usage of the Internet and smart devices together has become a part of our daily lives. Advances in smart sensors, embedded devices, and wireless communication technologies have led to the emergence of a new concept called the Internet of Things (IoT). The use of IoT has been growing exponentially in different areas such as smart grid, medical care, and smart home systems [15,25]. According to the research conducted by the Statistica Research Department [1], the number of devices connected to IoT will be over 50 billion in 2023 and 75 billion in 2025. The rapid increase in the number of IoT devices has also accelerated research in IoT. Due to attracting attackers' interest, security has become one of the important research areas in IoT.

Many IoT applications collect a large amount of data from various devices. Besides the heterogeneity of these devices, most of them have constraints related

© Springer Nature Switzerland AG 2020
L. A. Grieco et al. (Eds.): ADHOC-NOW 2020, LNCS 12338, pp. 214–227, 2020.
https://doi.org/10.1007/978-3-030-61746-2_16

to power, communication, and computation capabilities. This also brings a challenge for developing complex security solutions. Hence, the existing security solutions might not be suitable for such heterogeneous and complex networks. Therefore, new solutions should be developed, or the existing ones should be adapted to this new environment, which is the main aim of this current study.

New protocols that are less complex and consume less power are introduced for IoT. Routing Protocol for Low-Power and Lossy Networks (RPL) is one of them [4] and designed to provide efficient routing paths especially for resource-constrained devices. Although some security mechanisms are proposed for external attackers in RPL, it is still open to insider attacks such as rank and version attacks, which could affect the entire network. Hence, suitable IDSs for RPL-based IoT should be improved to detect such attacks. As it is stated above, existing IDSs for wired/wireless networks may not be suitable for these networks. Hence, new solutions that consider the specific characteristics of RPL should be proposed.

In this study, a novel cross-layer intrusion detection system based on neural networks is introduced for RPL. Features from both link layer and network layer are employed. The following specific attacks against RPL are targeted: version number, worst parent, and hello flood. The effects of different percentages of attackers are also explored. The results show that the proposed IDS could detect attacks effectively for both binary and multi-class classification. The use of link layer-based features decreased the false positive rate further. The positive effect of link layer features on the detection of version number attacks are also observed in the results. The contributions of the study are summarized as follows:

- A novel neural network-based IDS both for binary and multiclass classification of the version number, worst parent, and hello flood attacks are introduced.
- An attack dataset for RPL-based IoT networks, which covers three attack types specific to RPL with different attacker densities, is introduced and shared with the community[1].
- To the best of the authors' knowledge, this study is the first cross-layer intrusion detection system for RPL-based networks that explores the effect of features obtained from both link and routing layers on intrusion detection.

The study is organized as follows. Section 2 discusses the related studies. Section 3 gives the details of the proposed solution. The targeted attacks and the neural network-based approach for detecting those are explained. Section 4 gives the details of the simulation environment and discusses the experimental results thoroughly. The last section is devoted to concluding remarks.

2 Related Work

Researchers have been exploring the development of suitable IDS for RPL. SVELTE [26] is the first IDS proposed in the literature. It aims to detect sinkhole and selective forwarding attacks by using a hybrid approach of signature

---

[1] https://wise.cs.hacettepe.edu.tr/projects/rplsec/.

and anomaly-based techniques. There are also recent approaches that take the advantage of both techniques. An approach that utilizes 6LoWPAN compression header to detect hello flood, sinkhole, and wormhole attacks are proposed in [20]. The most discriminate features in the header are selected by using a correlation-based feature selection algorithm. Then, machine learning algorithms are applied and shown that the selected features (5 out of 77) outperform previous studies [24, 26].

An anomaly-based IDS for detecting version number and hello flood attacks is given in [29]. They used a small feature set for training a neural network-based model. Recently, another anomaly-based IDS is proposed for detecting version number and hello flood attacks [19]. A feature set consisting the number of topology control messages (DIS/DIO/DAO), the number of different DODAG versions and the UDP forward ratio are used by Kernel Density Algorithm. Another IDS [7] is generated by using genetic algorithm on a rich feature set and located at the root node. The experimental results show that the proposed IDS has high accuracy and low false positive rate on detection of hello flood and version number attacks.

A few specification-based IDSs are proposed in the literature. In [11], the states of RPL and the transitions between these states with corresponding statistics are defined, IDS rules according to them are extracted for detecting rank, neighbor, and sinkhole attacks. The network is divided into clusters to decrease the usage of resources. Each cluster member reports information about itself and its neighbors to the cluster head. Each cluster head runs an IDS agent that analyzes the reports coming from its members and generates an alarm if a node visits a state more than a threshold in a unit period of time. Another specification-based IDS is proposed for sybil attacks. Each node in the network is a monitoring node that cooperates with its neighbors to detect attacks and report them to the border router. Since the nodes in the network need to send a message to the sink node when they detect an inconsistency, it brings extra overhead to the network. Nodes in the network are equipped with a cryptographic co-processor chips to build hardware support identification, store security parameters, and handle cryptography calculations. It also requires a trusted entity for authentication.

There are also prevention and mitigation techniques against RPL attacks. A mitigation method is proposed for version number attacks in [6]. If a version update is coming from leaf nodes is ignored. Otherwise, if most of the neighbors with better ranks agree upon the validity of the version number update, it is accepted. Recently, a mitigation method against DIS flooding attacks is proposed [28]. Here, thresholds for limiting the number of unnecessary trickle timer resets are defined, and hence the number of control message transmissions caused by the attack is controlled. Secure-RPL [9] is a threshold-based detection system based on rank updates and uses hash chain authentication to eliminate illegitimate modification of rank value. SecTrust-RPL [3] is a detection and isolation mechanism against rank and Sybil attacks. The nodes compute the trustworthiness of its neighbors based on direct and recommended trust metrics and each node chooses a parent having higher trust values for routing whereas the nodes with lower trust values are marked as malicious. A distributed monitoring strategy for detecting version number attacks and attackers is proposed in [16]. Monitoring nodes construct a separate network and use it to periodically forward collected information about the version number of DIO messages coming from neighbor nodes to the root, which runs IDS.

A recent survey study [27] reviews the existing security mechanisms proposed for RPL. More than 100 studies are reviewed and shown that there is no cross-layer security solution. It is also emphasized that there is no effective solution against flood attacks. Furthermore, most of the studies use a small number of nodes in their simulation, which can be unscalable and unrealistic for a multi-hop network. The main contribution of this study is to fill this gap in the literature by proposing a cross-layer IDS. Link layer features besides routing layer features are included to distinguish the natural packet losses due to using wireless links from the packet losses caused by attacks. Moreover, the proposed system is simulated on large networks with different settings, which are shared with the community(see footnote 1). Finally, besides developing different algorithms for detecting each attack separately, one algorithm that distinguishes all attack types is developed.

3   RPL and Target Attacks

RPL connects nodes to each other and to border router(s) by creating a destination-oriented directed acyclic graph (DODAG). Three types of nodes can exist in a DODAG. The first one is low power and lossy border router (LBR), which is the root of a DODAG and a collection point for the multipoint-to-point (MP2P) traffic. LBR can create a directed acyclic graph and provides a connection between the Internet and remaining nodes. The second type is routers, which can generate data traffic and forward packets. They can join an existing DAG. The last type is hosts which can only generate data traffic as end-devices. Each node in a DODAG has an ID, a list of its neighbors, a parent node, and a rank value that shows the position of the node itself with respect to the border router. Each node calculates its rank according to the rank of its preferred parent by using the objective function (OF). OF determines the route selection by using different objectives such as ETX, latency.

RPL uses three types of routing control messages namely DAO, DIS, and DIO. In point-to-point (P2P) and point-to-multipoint (P2MP) traffic scenarios, the root node needs to know the path to the remaining devices. Therefore, each node announces its routing path to the root node by sending a Destination Advertisement Object (DAO) messages. DAO propagates upward direction in the DODAG via the parent of each node and the border router becomes aware of the path to each node. DIS (DODAG Information Solicitation) helps new nodes to ask for topology information before joining the network. DIO (DODAG Information Object) helps to set and update the topology. DIO message is sent by each node to inform other nodes about its rank value. RPL uses a trickle algorithm [14] for scheduling DIO message frequency. In this algorithm, to reduce the number of routing control messages, each node holds two parameters: trickle time and DIO counter. Trickle time stands for the time interval that the node waits before sending the next DIO message. If the parameters which cause a topology change in the network are not modified in the incoming DIO message, then the DIO counter will be increased and the trickle timer increases the duration of the idle state. If there is a change in the DIO message, the node will reset the DIO counter and minimize its trigger time.

The main focus of this study is to detect specific attacks against RPL. Three attacks based on their potential effects on RPL are simulated: version number, worst parent, and hello flood attack, which are given in detail below.

Version Number Attack (VNA). The change of version number is triggered only by the root node if the global repair of DODAG is required. When the root node changes the version number, this information is carried with DIO messages to all nodes in the network and a new DODAG is reconstructed. VNA results in unnecessary reconstruction of the DODAG graph and creates overhead. This attack has been analyzed in several studies in the literature [5,17]. In [17], the attacker has been placed in all possible locations via a grid topology. The experimental results show that the effect of attack increases while the attacker is moving away from the root node since the attacker can spread the damage further [17]. In order to help to localize the attacker, loops and rank inconsistencies can be used because they are mainly located in the neighborhood of the attacker. In [5], it is also shown that mobile nodes harm the network with the same impact of far nodes from the root. In the attack scenario, a malicious node illegally changes the version number field before it forwards received DIO message to its neighbors. Here, in the simulations, malicious node increases version number by one in every minute in order to disrupt the network.

Worst Parent Attack (WPA). Rank Attack aims to change the topology of a DODAG. It is one of the most dangerous attacks against RPL. A rank value is calculated by each node in the network and it indicates the quality of a path between the node itself and the root node. The rank value has important roles in RPL such as creating an optimal topology, prevention of routing loops, and managing the overhead of routing control messages. In a rank attack scenario, the attacker falsifies its rank information and sends a DIO message to its neighbors which has a different rank value than its genuine. In WPA, the worst parent (with the highest rank value) is chosen instead of the best one as specified in RPL. As a result of this attack, a child node could find itself in a non-optimal routing path and choose an attacker node as its parent. WPA is implemented for the first time in [12] and the network performance under attack is analyzed by putting the attacker in every possible location in a grid topology. It is shown that the attack cannot be detected easily, since child nodes assume that routing information supplied by their parents via DIO packets are genuine and, they do not have any mechanism to verify the reliability of the parent nodes according to the protocol specification. Here, in the simulations, the malicious node selects the node which has the worst rank value in its neighborhood as its parent. The nodes who select the malicious node as a parent node might find themselves in non-optimal paths.

Hello Flood Attack (HFA). In RPL, a node who wants to join to the network multicasts DIS messages to its neighbors. The new node transmits DIS messages with a fixed interval of time and waits for a reply from nodes in its transmission range. However, RFC 6550 [4] does not specify the time interval for the transmission of DIS messages, and it may vary in different RPL implementations. When the new node receives DIO message(s) as a reply to its DIS messages, it stops sending DIS messages and joins to the network. In P2P and P2MP traffic scenarios, the new node also sends a DAO message to its parent in order to inform the root node. It is shown that HFA is the most influential attack that degrades the performance of IoT network [13]. In this attack scenario, a malicious node pretends to be a new node and multicasts DIS messages periodically to its neighbors. Hence, nodes in the neighborhood of the attacker are forced to reset the trickle timer or to unicast DIS message to a node that has to respond with a DIO message. This can overload RPL nodes by increasing the number of routing control messages and hence might cause network congestion. Here, in the simulations, malicious node multicasts DIS message to its neighbor nodes in every 500 ms. In the simulations, it is observed that if DIS messages are sent more frequently, the network becomes overwhelmed by these messages and unresponsive to legitimate requests.

4   The Proposed Intrusion Detection System

In this section, the proposed neural network-based IDS for RPL-based IoT networks will be given in detail. Firstly, the features used as inputs to the neural network will be presented. For developing an effective IDS, it is important to determine suitable features for training a machine learning system. The selected features should have sufficient information to distinguish malicious activities from benign ones. Furthermore, they are preferred to have non-redundant information, because too many features could negatively affect training. A recent study [7] uses a set that covers most of the features related to the RPL control messages and data packets in the network. In addition to this feature set, the features related to link-layer are employed here, as listed in Table 1.

Data related features include information about data packets received by the root node in a time interval. These features could show whether each node effectively participates in the periodic reporting process to the root node and hence, give indirect information about the stability of a network. Topology related features include information about routing control messages received by the root node. These topology messages could give useful insights for detecting different types of attacks. For example, an abrupt increase in the number of DIS messages could be an indicator of hello flood attacks. However, this situation should be effectively discriminated from the natural increase of DIS messages as a result

Table 1. List of the Features

Feature group	Explanation	Number of features
Data	-Number of data messages -Max/Min/Average length of data messages -Max/Min/Average time difference between data messages	7
Topology	-Number of DIO/DIS/DAO messages -Max/Min of version numbers, the difference between version numbers -Max/Min of rank values, the difference between rank values -Max/Min/Average time difference between DIO/DIS/DAO messages	16
Link-layer	-Number of dropped packets due to collision /neighbor allocation/queueing/packeting	4

of a new node(s)'s participation in the network. Similarly, the features collected about version number and rank value give useful information for detecting version number attack and worst parent attack respectively. Link-layer features give information about the reasons for dropped packets in this layer such as collisions, neighbor allocation, queuing, and buffer management. These features are collected from the root node and its one-hop neighbors. It is assumed that each node periodically forwards these features to the root node. It is shown that while most of the packets are dropped at the routing layer as a result of version number attack, the packet drops in normal networks (under no attack) have mainly resulted from link-layer issues [6]. Therefore, it is believed that link-layer features could help distinguishing normal cases from malicious activities. Hence they are employed for the first time in intrusion detection in RPL. These features are collected periodically at the root node. The time interval for data collection is chosen experimentally by comparing the detection accuracy of the proposed system at different time intervals. The results of this evaluation are presented in Fig. 1. According to these results, the time interval for data collection is set as 5 s to achieve the highest detection rate for the proposed design.

RPL-based IoT networks are generally used for MP2P communication, therefore the data (such as data collected from sensor nodes) flows from leaf nodes to the sink node. The sink node is usually responsible either for forwarding collected data to other applications or analyzing the data locally. Therefore, the root node is generally a more powerful device than other nodes in the network. In addition, it has a better view of the network. Based on these assumptions, a centralized IDS placed in the root node is proposed for applications based on MP2P communication in this study. Moreover, a centralized IDS can fit better

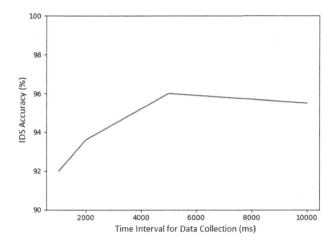

Fig. 1. Accuracy of IDS at varying time intervals for data collection

than a distributed one to the resource-constrained structure of IoT. Here, three attacks are implemented separately on different networks with different percentage of attackers (2%, 6%, 10%, 20%). Each attack is simulated on 5 network topologies for each attacker density. Hence, in total 20 different networks are constructed for each attack. The same simulations are also run in a larger network area in order to observe the effect of node density on intrusion detection. Similarly, 20 networks under no-attack are run for generating benign traffic. The details of simulations are given in Table 2.

As the number of nodes increases, RPL produces lots of routing control messages which are gathered in the root node. In order to process such a large amount of data, a neural network-based IDS is proposed. The aim is to differentiate malicious attempts from normal network behavior with the data collected in the root node. The aim is not only to predict whether there is an attack in the network or not, but also predict the type of RPL attack with high accuracy. Therefore, the problem has been explored as both binary and multiclass classification.

The proposed neural network architecture is demonstrated in Fig. 2. In order to calculate the weights of the input set, 4 fully-connected neural network layer with different output sizes is proposed. As an activation function, the Rectified Linear Unit (ReLU) function is employed. The number of neurons for hidden layers are set as 128, 64, 32, and 16 respectively. There are dropout layers between each fully-connected layer with a 0.5 drop rate to prevent over-fitting. Then, there is a fully-connected layer with a softmax function. The output size of this layer depends on the problem type, namely binary and multi-class classification. So, it has two neurons for binary classification to represent benign and attacked behaviour of the network, and four neurons for multi-class classification. Before training the model, data is pre-processed by applying feature scaling using the standard scaler function of the scikit library [23]. Other libraries used for neural network implementation in this study are Pandas [18], Numpy [21], and Keras [8].

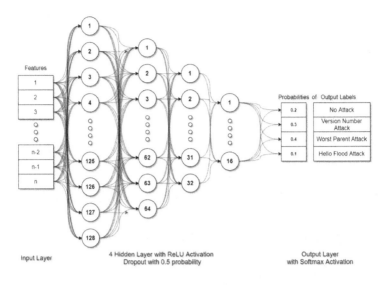

Fig. 2. The proposed neural network architecture

5   Experiments and Results

In this chapter, the simulation environment with its parameters and the performance metrics used in the analysis of the routing attacks in the experiments are detailed. Also, the performance of the proposed IDS solution is analyzed and discussed in this section.

5.1   Experimental Environment

Cooja Contiki Simulator 2.7 [22] is used to simulate IoT networks. Tmote Sky [2] nodes which are low power wireless modules and typically used in sensor networks are used as IoT devices. The sink node is a border router that connects the remaining nodes to the internet. It collects data from other nodes and helps them to create DODAG. The sender node represents an IoT device that sends periodic data messages to the sink node via its preferred parent. When the preferred node has data packets to forward, it sends the packet to its own parent, the packet is forwarded until it reaches the sink node. A malicious node is also a sender node, who manipulates the network and decreases the network performance.

Most of the studies in the literature use a single malicious node in their simulations. Moreover, they are generally simulated with a limited number of devices [17,28]. However, as pointed out in [10], at least 25 or 30 devices are needed to see the multi-hop characteristics of RPL. In these studies, the simulations are also usually run for up to 30 min at most. Considering the time passed for the network to stabilize, this time can be limited to see the real effects of attacks. Moreover, the experiments are always carried out on a grid topology to see the effects of attackers at different locations. However, more realistic scenarios such as the random distribution of nodes and attackers, the partitioning of networks are not discovered in these studies. Therefore, in this study, simulation parameters are selected by considering these critical issues and given in Table 2. As shown in the table, two different networks (small and large) are simulated to see the effects of node density on intrusion detection. Moreover, each attack is carried out with different number of attackers.

Table 2. The simulation parameters

Simulation parameters	
Simulation run time	60 min
Number of nodes	50
Sink node	1
Radio medium	Unit disc graph medium: distance loss
Transmission range	50 m
Interference range	100 m
Seed type	Random seed
Positioning	Random positioning
Simulation area	125 × 125 m (small), 250 × 250 m (large)
MAC protocol	IEEE 802.15.4
Objective function	MRHOF
Traffic type	UDP
Traffic rate	Each node sends 1 packet every 60 s

5.2 Experimental Results

The model for binary classification is trained using two different schemes: 10-fold cross-validation and 60% percentage split. While the percentage split scheme acquires 96.88% DR and 0.13% FPR, the other scheme has 97.11% DR and 0.34% FPR. Therefore, the percentage method is used in subsequent evaluations. The experimental results for each attack type are given in Table 3. It shows that the proposed IDS could detect each attack effectively. Hello flood becomes the easiest attack type to detect even when it is carried out by a few attackers. In general, when the number of attackers increases, their effects on the network become more observable. Since WPA does not become effective until a considerable amount of attackers (10%) participate into the network, these cases were not considered in training/testing. In the large network, the detection rate of WPA is dropped. It is observed that small network is obviously affected by this attack and change parents more frequently. On the other hand, due to low node density in the large network, the clear effects of this attack on the network are less observed. This would cause a decrease in the detection rate.

Table 3. The performance of IDS-binary classification

Attack type	Node density	Small network	Large network
		Detection rate	Detection rate
Version number attack (VNA)	2% Attacker	86.66%	93.99%
	6% attacker	92.99%	92.33%
	10% attacker	98.58%	94.75%
	20% attacker	94.83%	90.99%
	Entire dataset	**93.20%**	**92.96%**
Worst parent attack (WPA)	10% Attacker	96.91%	76.56%
	20% attacker	99.42%	95.75%
	Entire dataset	**98.17%**	**86.16%**
Hello flood attack (HFA)	2% Attacker	99.83%	99.67%
	6% attacker	100%	100%
	10% attacker	100%	100%
	20% attacker	100%	100%
	Entire dataset	**99.96%**	**99.92%**

To see the capability of the proposed method on detection of attacks on networks with different number of attackers, the model is trained only by using networks under high percentage of attackers (10%–20% for VNA, HFA, and 20% for WPA), then tested on networks under low percentage of attackers (2%–6% for VNA, HFA, and 10% for WPA). The results show that the IDS can still detect attacks with high detection rates (VNA: 88.93% WPA: 86.90%, HFA: 99.87%).

To see the effects of routing layer and link layer features, two models are trained with different groups of features and compared in Table 4. Link layer features have caused a decrease in false positive rate since they help to discriminate normal cases from attack case in case of collisions in the link layer. These features have also slightly increased the detection rate of version number attacks since this attack is the main cause of packet drops at the routing layer [6].

Finally, a model is trained for detecting all types of attacks and labeling them. The model has also a high detection rate (97.52%). As shown in the confusion matrix below, in some cases, VNA is confused with attack-free traffic. It is observed that this attack needs some time to affect the network. Hence, at this initial state of the attack, it cannot be distinguished from benign traffic (Table 5).

Table 4. The effects of link layer features

Attack type	Routing layer features		Routing and link layer features	
	DR	FPR	DR	FPR
Version number attack	91.52%	-	93.20%	-
Worst parent attack	99.08%	-	98.17%	-
Hello flood attack	100%	-	99.96%	-
Entire dataset	97.06%	0.61%	96.88%	0.13%

Table 5. The performance of IDS-multiclass classification

True label\predicted as	NA	VNA	WPA	HFA
No attack (NA)	99.7%	0%	0.3%	0%
Version number attack (VNA)	6.94%	92.42%	0.48%	0.17%
Worst parent attack (WPA)	1.42%	0.42%	97.71%	0.46%
Hello flood attack (HFA)	0.04%	0.02%	0.04%	99.9%

6   Conclusion

In this study, a novel neural network-based cross-layer intrusion detection system for RPL-based IoT networks is introduced. Both binary and multiclass classification for the following RPL-specific attacks are covered: version number, worst parent, and hello flood attacks. To the best of the authors' knowledge, the proposed IDS is the first cross-layer intrusion detection system in RPL that explores the effect of features obtained from link-layer on intrusion detection. The experimental results show that the proposed IDS detects each attack type with a high detection rate and an even lower false positive rate using the link-layer features.

Acknowledgements. Thanks to Emre Aydogan and Selim Yilmaz for sharing their experiences during the feature selection and feature extraction process for our neural-network based intrusion detection system.

References

1. IoT: Number of Connected Devices Worldwide 2012–2025—statistica. https://www.statista.com/statistics/471264/iot-number-of-connected-devices-worldwide/. Accessed 18 Jan 2020
2. Tmote sky from moteiv. https://insense.cs.st-andrews.ac.uk/files/2013/04/tmote-sky-datasheet.pdf. Accessed 13 Jan 2020
3. Airehrour, D., Gutierrez, J.A., Ray, S.K.: Sectrust-RPL: a secure trust-aware RPL routing protocol for Internet of Things. Future Gener. Comput. Syst. **93**, 860–876 (2019). https://doi.org/10.1016/j.future.2018.03.021. http://www.sciencedirect.com/science/article/pii/S0167739X17306581

4. Alexander, R., et al.: RPL: IPv6 routing protocol for low-power and lossy networks. RFC 6550 (March 2012). https://doi.org/10.17487/RFC6550, https://rfc-editor.org/rfc/rfc6550.txt

5. Aris, A., Oktug, S.F., Berna Ors Yalcin, S.: RPL version number attacks: in-depth study. In: NOMS 2016–2016 IEEE/IFIP Network Operations and Management Symposium, pp. 776–779 (2016)

6. Arş, A., Örs Yalçın, S.B., Oktuğ, S.F.: New lightweight mitigation techniques for RPL version number attacks. Ad Hoc Netw. **85**, 81–91 (2019). https://doi.org/10.1016/j.adhoc.2018.10.022. http://www.sciencedirect.com/science/article/pii/S1570870518307625

7. Aydogan, E., Yilmaz, S., Sen, S., Butun, I., Forsström, S., Gidlund, M.: A central intrusion detection system for RPL-based industrial internet of things. In: 2019 15th IEEE International Workshop on Factory Communication Systems (WFCS), pp. 1–5 (2019)

8. Chollet, F., et al.: Keras. https://keras.io (2015)

9. Glissa, G., Rachedi, A., Meddeb, A.: A secure routing protocol based on RPL for Internet of Things. In: 2016 IEEE Global Communications Conference (GLOBECOM), pp. 1–7 (2016)

10. Kim, H.S., Ko, J., Culler, D.E., Paek, J.: Challenging the IPv6 routing protocol for low-power and lossy networks (RPL): a survey. IEEE Commun. Surv. Tutor. **19**(4), 2502–2525 (2017)

11. Le, A., Loo, J., Chai, M., Aiash, M.: A specification-based IDS for detecting attacks on RPL-based network topology. Information **7**, 25 (2016). https://doi.org/10.3390/info7020025

12. Le, A., Loo, J., Lasebae, A., Vinel, A., Chen, Y., Chai, M.: The impact of rank attack on network topology of routing protocol for low-power and lossy networks. IEEE Sens. J. **13**, 3685–3692 (2013). https://doi.org/10.1109/JSEN.2013.2266399

13. Le, A., Loo, J., Luo, Y., Lasebae, A.: The impacts of internal threats towards routing protocol for low power and lossy network performance, pp. 000789–000794 (July 2013). https://doi.org/10.1109/ISCC.2013.6755045

14. Levis, P., Clausen, T.H., Gnawali, O., Hui, J., Ko, J.: The trickle algorithm. RFC 6206 (March 2011). https://doi.org/10.17487/RFC6206, https://rfc-editor.org/rfc/rfc6206.txt

15. Maple, C.: Security and privacy in the Internet of Things. J. Cyber Policy **2**, 155–184 (2017). https://doi.org/10.1080/23738871.2017.1366536

16. Mayzaud, A., Badonnel, R., Chrisment, I.: A distributed monitoring strategy for detecting version number attacks in RPL-based networks. IEEE Trans. Netw. Serv. Manag. **14**(2), 472–486 (2017). https://doi.org/10.1109/TNSM.2017.2705290

17. Mayzaud, A., Sehgal, A., Badonnel, R., Chrisment, I., Schönwälder, J.: A study of RPL DODAG version attacks. In: Sperotto, A., Doyen, G., Latré, S., Charalambides, M., Stiller, B. (eds.) AIMS 2014. LNCS, vol. 8508, pp. 92–104. Springer, Heidelberg (2014). https://doi.org/10.1007/978-3-662-43862-6_12

18. McKinney, W., et al.: Data structures for statistical computing in python. In: Proceedings of the 9th Python in Science Conference, Austin, TX, vol. 445, pp. 51–56 (2010)

19. Müller, N.M., Debus, P., Kowatsch, D., Böttinger, K.: Distributed anomaly detection of single mote attacks in RPL networks. In: Proceedings of the 16th International Joint Conference on e-Business and Telecommunications, SECRYPT, vol. 2, pp. 378–385. INSTICC, SciTePress (2019). https://doi.org/10.5220/0007836003780385

20. Napiah, M.N., Bin Idris, M.Y.I., Ramli, R., Ahmedy, I.: Compression header analyzer intrusion detection system (CHA - IDS) for 6LoWPAN communication protocol. IEEE Access **6**, 16623–16638 (2018)
21. Oliphant, T.E.: A Guide to NumPy, vol. 1. Trelgol Publishing, USA (2006)
22. Osterlind, F., Dunkels, A., Eriksson, J., Finne, N., Voigt, T.: Cross-level sensor network simulation with cooja. In: Annual IEEE Conference on Local Computer Networks, pp. 641–648 (November 2006). https://doi.org/10.1109/LCN.2006.322172
23. Pedregosa, F., et al.: Scikit-learn: machine learning in python. J. Mach. Learn. Res. **12**(Oct), 2825–2830 (2011)
24. Pongle, P.: Real time intrusion and wormhole attack detection in Internet of Things. Int. J. Comput. Appl. **121**, 1–9 (2015). https://doi.org/10.5120/21565-4589
25. Ray, P.: A survey on Internet of Things architectures. J. King Saud Univ. Comput. Inf. Sci. **30**(3), 291–319 (2018). https://doi.org/10.1016/j.jksuci.2016.10.003. http://www.sciencedirect.com/science/article/pii/S1319157816300799
26. Raza, S., Wallgren, L., Voigt, T.: Svelte: real-time intrusion detection in the Internet of Things. Ad Hoc Networks **11**(8), 2661–2674 (2013). https://doi.org/10.1016/j.adhoc.2013.04.014. http://www.sciencedirect.com/science/article/pii/S1570870513001005
27. Verma, A., Ranga, V.: Security of RPL based 6LoWPAN networks in the Internet of Things: a review. IEEE Sens. J. **20**(11), 5666–5690 (2020)
28. Verma, A., Ranga, V.: Mitigation of dis flooding attacks in RPL-based 6LoWPAN networks. Trans. Emerg. Telecommun. Technol. **31**(2), e3802 (2020). https://doi.org/10.1002/ett.3802. https://onlinelibrary.wiley.com/doi/abs/10.1002/ett.3802
29. Yavuz, F.Y., Unal, D., Gul, E.: Deep learning for detection of routing attacks in the Internet of Things. Int. J. Comput. Intell. Syst. **12**, 39–58 (2018). https://doi.org/10.2991/ijcis.2018.25905181

Secure Energy Constrained LoRa Mesh Network

Derek Heeger[1,2]([✉]) [iD], Maeve Garigan[3] [iD], Eirini Eleni Tsiropoulou[2] [iD], and Jim Plusquellic[2] [iD]

[1] Sandia National Labs, Albuquerque, NM, USA
[2] University of New Mexico, Albuquerque, NM, USA
{heegerds,eirini,jplusq}@unm.edu
[3] Roper Solutions Inc., Las Cruces, NM, USA
maeve@ropertag.com

Abstract. LoRa (Long Range) is a low-power wide-area network technology well-suited for Internet of Things (IoT) applications. In this paper, LoRa is used in a cattle monitoring application where an ad-hoc mesh network is configured to collect GPS and accelerometer data from cattle-worn sensors and relay the collected data to a base station. Free-range cattle monitoring is a challenging application since the battery-powered sensors must be small and energy efficient, and enable data communications over long distances from unpredictable locations. We propose novel changes to the existing LoRa mesh network protocols that minimize energy consumption by using global time synchronization enabled by GPS sensors and a concurrent transmission property unique to LoRa. The mesh routing phase efficiently occurs during every data collection period, making this approach ideal for networking highly mobile sensors. We integrate efficient authentication and encryption techniques in the data exchange operations to prevent spoofing and to provide confidentiality in the message exchanges between the sensors and the base station. The performance of the proposed secure implementation is compared to an equivalent insecure implementation. Multiple cattle distribution scenarios are constructed and compared to evaluate the energy consumption of the proposed scheme.

Keywords: LoRa · Mesh networks · Cattle monitoring

1 Introduction

In recent years, the Internet of Things (IoT) paradigm has expanded rapidly into commercial, industrial and consumer applications. This expansion has driven a corresponding need for energy efficient battery-powered networked devices. The energy consumed during data communications is a significant fraction of the total energy consumption, and is a particular concern for IoT applications in rural areas, where transmission over long distances is necessary due to a lack of networking infrastructure. Low-power wide-area network (LPWAN) technologies

© Springer Nature Switzerland AG 2020
L. A. Grieco et al. (Eds.): ADHOC-NOW 2020, LNCS 12338, pp. 228–240, 2020.
https://doi.org/10.1007/978-3-030-61746-2_17

such as LoRa (Long Range), Sigfox, and Narrowband IoT (NB-IoT) [1] offer a distinct advantage for rural IoT by providing enhanced energy efficiency and long range data communications.

LoRa uses a proprietary spread spectrum modulation similar to chirp spread spectrum (CSS) modulation to achieve high noise immunity at the expense of low data rates. LoRa has configurable parameters such as spreading factor (SF), bandwidth, and error coding rates, which enable trade-offs between range and noise immunity [2]. LoRa is used as the transport layer for the LoRa Wide Area Network (LoRaWAN) networking protocol in which LoRa-enabled devices communicate directly with LoRa gateways. Given its low cost to build and operate, LoRa has received a great deal of interest from the academic and amateur radio communities, and has been used in various IoT applications, such as smart cities, industrial IoT, agriculture, smart metering, and environmental monitoring [3].

In this paper, we investigate a novel LoRa ad-hoc mesh network architecture for tracking and monitoring the location and activity of free-range cattle. Within the proposed system, battery-powered sensors are attached to the cattle and periodically collect and transmit GPS and accelerometer data to a base station. The long transmission distances and physical obstacles (such as rolling hills, trees and other cattle) require that the sensor network be configured as a mesh, allowing collected data to be relayed from sensor to sensor before reaching the base station. Data transfer between the base station and the sensors is bi-directional and must be accomplished with ultra-low energy consumption. The proposed system introduces a protocol that enables secure and energy-optimized data communication over distances that exceed those specified for LoRaWAN. The proposed framework uses GPS to time synchronize all sensors in the network to precise wake-up times, enabling the configuration of an infrequent, secure, and coherent data exchange network that minimizes energy consumption. Applications that use the proposed system will benefit from the increased data transmission range and improved reliability in packet delivery while experiencing a minimal increase in energy consumption.

1.1 State of the Art and Motivation

A wireless mesh network (WMN) is a network communication paradigm wherein client devices can act as message relays and increase the probability of a successful packet delivery [4]. Mesh network architectures exist for multiple IoT standards, including WiFi, Bluetooth, and Zigbee [5]. Reactive and proactive routing protocols have been proposed within WMNs to define how the system discovers message routing. In proactive routing protocols, the IoT devices maintain routing tables to represent the entire network topology, while in the reactive protocols, a multi-hop route is created on-demand, thus reducing the routing overhead [5]. WMNs have a route discovery phase to generate an internal forwarding table based on the message destination. The routes remain valid until the IoT device status changes (e.g., changes position or goes offline) which initiates a maintenance phase. WMNs can consume significant amounts of energy due to the complexities of maintaining and updating the routing tables.

Various mesh architectures have been proposed for LoRa. A LoRa mesh network is introduced in [6] to monitor underground infrastructure, and consists of stationary sensors that are configured as dedicated relay nodes to LoRaWAN gateways and use GPS time synchronization to minimize energy consumption. The authors develop a LPWAN based on the LoRa physical layer (LoRa PHY) and demonstrate that it overcomes the transmission limitations (i.e., medium-range underground connectivity and time stamping of data packets) of the LoRaWAN standard in underground applications. The LoRaWAN standard supports only single-hop communication, which is addressed in [7] where multi-hop networking between LoRa gateways is proposed as a means of extending coverage. The proposed multi-hop routing protocol integrates Hybrid Wireless Mesh Protocol (HWMP) and the Ad-hoc On-Demand Distance Vector Routing (AODV) technologies into the LoRaWAN specification. Issues related to signal attenuation, particularly those related to obstacles and non-line-of-sight transmission, are addressed in [8], where a mesh network using the LoRa PHY is developed and its packet delivery performance is evaluated. The authors demonstrate that their scheme provides a better packet delivery ratio than an alternative star-network topology, although the proposed scheme lacks security and low power operation.

Concurrent transmissions of IoT devices in multi-hop LoRa mesh networks are investigated in [9] and [10]. In [10], a scheme is proposed for improving packet delivery by introducing timing offsets between the packets. In [9], scalability issues are investigated in large-scale LoRa networks where the authors show that LoRa networks configured with static settings and a single sink are not scalable. They propose a scheme which uses multiple sinks and dynamic communication parameter settings as an alternative. In [11], a network configuration is proposed wherein a forwarder-node is introduced between the IoT device and the gateway to improve the range and quality of LoraWAN communications. That work is extended in [12] using a Destination-Sequenced Distance Vector (DSDV) routing protocol where IoT devices are configured to transmit packets to intermediate relay nodes that forward the packets to LoRa gateways.

1.2   Contributions and Outline

The aforementioned work on LoRa mesh networks focuses on performance and does not address network security within LoRa mesh networks. Moreover, only limited work exists on extending the effective communication range of LoRa devices while minimizing energy consumption. Our work addresses these gaps by introducing a custom ad-hoc network architecture based on the LoRa PHY that provides ultra-low power operation while maintaining advanced capabilities within the network infrastructure, including mesh networking and a framework for authentication and encryption of sensor data using an efficient packet structure.

This work is motivated by a realistic free-range cattle monitoring application that uses battery-powered sensors to collect GPS and accelerometer data and is transmitted via LoRa to a base station [13]. The challenges associated with monitoring free-range cattle using IoT devices are summarized as follows:

1. Cattle are highly mobile and travel long distances to unpredictable locations in rural, off-grid areas, making the communication link unreliable.
2. Cattle act as large dielectrics and can absorb a considerable amount of radio-frequency transmission energy, making the IoT device communications range dependent on cattle orientation.
3. The sensor package must be small and lightweight, requiring a small battery, which creates a highly energy constrained scenario.

We propose a LoRa mesh network that uses adjacent cattle as relays to transmit sensor data to the LoRa base station. Typical mesh network protocols are unsuitable for our cattle monitoring application because they consume significant energy, perform poorly with mobility, and are insecure. Our mesh network architecture overcomes these shortfalls and makes the following novel contributions:

1. Our system leverages GPS time synchronization and LoRa concurrent transmission capabilities to efficiently collect data from ultra-low power sensors distributed over a large geographic area.
2. Our system integrates light-weight encryption and authentication security functions into a LoRa mesh network to prevent packet sniffing, data spoofing, and intelligent denial of service (DoS) attacks.
3. Our system is applied to a novel free-range cattle monitoring application, which introduces significant challenges to ensuring reliable packet delivery and ultra-low energy consumption. The system will be experimentally validated in a cattle ranch environment in the near future using a sensor prototype developed by Roper Solutions, Inc. (Fig. 1).

The remainder of this paper is organized as follows: Sect. 2 describes the mesh network, Sect. 3 provides a detailed performance analysis, Sect. 4 describes the proposed security features, and Sect. 5 concludes the paper.

2   System Overview

The proposed system will be integrated into a cattle monitoring sensor shown in Fig. 1. The custom sensor platform includes a GPS receiver, an accelerometer, and a LoRa module for data communication. The sensor package includes a low capacity battery that is recharged from a solar panel. The current consumption of the battery-powered sensor with the LoRa receiver enabled can exceed 5 mA, creating a significant power drain over time. The sensors can be configured to remain in an ultra-low power mode, however this makes them unable to receive messages. To maintain receptivity and ultra-low power consumption, the sensors are periodically and simultaneously awakened, which requires global time synchronization among all sensors in the mesh network. We use GPS time synchronization with guard bands to achieve this goal and avoid techniques that

Fig. 1. (a) Roper cattle sensor in housing. (b) Graphic of the sensor board PCB.

exclusively maintain time with oscillators as they are prone to error due to drift. We define an *event* as a global awakening of all sensors and a complete data exchange between the LoRa base station and the sensors. Events occur at fixed time intervals, e.g., once every 1–4 h, and the sensors awaken every 0.25 h to collect position and health information and re-synchronize with the global clock.

2.1 System Behavior

The physical location of the cattle determines the number of hops required for the sensor data transmitted during an event to reach the LoRa base station. A series of R rounds is defined within the time frame of an event, with each round subdivided into synchronization (synch) frames and data frames. Each round defines the time interval in which data is collected from a subset of the sensors. For example, during Round 1, the base station collects data from sensors that have a direct communication path (Fig. 2). In Rounds 2 and 3, the base station collects data from sensors that are one and two mesh hops away, respectively. Each round progresses one hop further from the previous round, until all sensors have responded.

The base station is responsible for transmitting synch packets to the sensors in each round, and they respond with data packets that travel back to the base station. An illustration of a packet sequence consisting of synch packets S_x and sensor data packets $Data_x$ is shown in Fig. 3. The synch packet initiates the data transmission operation from the sensors and enables the route-finding algorithm to determine a set of feasible routes. The data frames contain a time slot for each sensor, enabling each of them to communicate their unique GPS and accelerometer data to the base station.

The number of rounds required depends on the distribution of the sensors. For example, if every sensor was within range of the base station, only one round would be required. If there are C cattle spaced equally at the communication

Fig. 2. Illustration of communication pathways within the LoRa mesh network in the context of Events and Rounds.

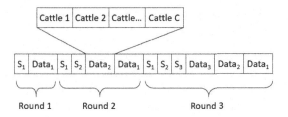

Fig. 3. Example sequence of synchronization and sensor data packets from multiple rounds during an event.

range boundaries, C rounds would be required to collect all the data. An exception occurs when one or more sensors are unable to respond. This scenario can result in empty rounds unless a stop condition is incorporated. Two possible stop criteria are limiting the number of rounds to a fixed upper bound or terminating after a round occurs in which no data is collected.

2.2 Packet Structure

The synch packet formats used in the insecure (top) and secure (bottom) versions of the proposed LoRa mesh network are shown in Fig. 4. The packet includes a Base ID to identify the base station that the packet originated from. The *Round* field is incremented at the end of each round and the *Hop* field is incremented at each mesh hop. The $Bit-mapped\ Response$ field records which cattle have responded, where one bit is allocated for each cow, making the packet size dependent on C. A cyclic redundancy check (CRC) code is appended to the insecure packet to enable detection of packet transmission errors. The secure version includes a digital signature or message authentication code MAC and a time stamp field $Time$, which increase the packet size by 20-bytes over the insecure version. The digital signature is encrypted using a 128-bit version of the Advanced Encryption Standard (AES) algorithm, commonly referred to as AES Cipher-based Message Authentication Code (AES-CMAC). The purpose of the security related components of the packet are discussed further in Sect. 4.

The insecure and secure data packet formats for individual cattle are shown in Fig. 5. The Base ID, Hop Count, and CRC serve the same purpose as described above for the synchronization packet. The Herd ID indicates which cow the data came from. The payload portion of the data packet consists of 25-bytes

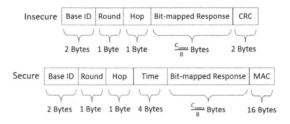

Fig. 4. Insecure (top) and secure (bottom) synchronization packet formats.

of information related to the cow's current location and recent activity. The payload portion of the secure packet is extended to 32-bytes, and includes a 4-byte time stamp and 0-padding as needed, to match the input width of the encryption algorithm, AES-128.

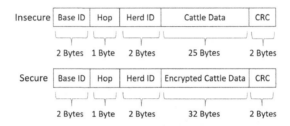

Fig. 5. Insecure (top) and insecure (bottom) data packet formats.

2.3   Transmit and Receive Logic

The LoRa base station enables ad-hoc mesh networking using the following message exchange protocol:

1. Transmit a synch packet containing the bit-mapped response set to 0.
2. Wait for data packets to arrive from the responding cattle sensors.
3. Confirm message authenticity from each data packet (secure version only).
4. Update the bit-mapped response by setting fields to 1 for the cattle sensors that it has received data from and transmit a new synch packet.
5. Repeat Steps 2 through 4 until the stop condition is met.

The behavior of the sensor protocol is described using the example sequence of events in Fig. 6a and 6b, where (a) shows behavior by the receiving portion (Receive logic) and (b) shows the behavior of the transmitting portion (Transmit logic). The figures are annotated with numbers to indicate the time order in which the events occur. The following describes the actions taken by a typical sensor in the network and assumes that the sensor is attached to Cattle 1 which is located 2 hops away from the base station.

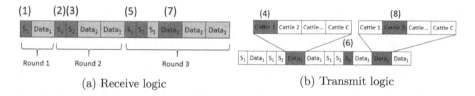

(a) Receive logic   (b) Transmit logic

Fig. 6. Illustrations showing example transmit and receive actions carried out by the proposed protocol.

1. The sensor listens for synch packets until one is received. It listens in Round 1, designated as S_1, but no packet is received so it returns to sleep.
2. The sensor awakens at the beginning of Round 2 and listens for a synch packet (S_1), but again no packet is received. It continues to listen for all synch packets in a given round before returning to sleep.
3. The sensor receives a synch packet in the second time slot of Round 2, designated as S_2, which it received from another sensor one hop away.
4. In response, the sensor transmits a data packet containing its GPS and accelerometer data during the Cattle 1 time slot of $Data_2$ and then returns to sleep mode.
5. The sensor awakens at the beginning of Round 3, and receives another synch packet S_2. The bit-mapped response within the packet contains a 1 in the Cattle 1 field, which indicates that the base station received the data packet. If the bit was not set, indicating a packet loss, it would re-transmit the Cattle 1 sensor data in the $Data_2$ slot. It also acts as a relay node because the round number is greater than the hop count. The sensor deduces the process has not terminated because the bit-mapped fields are not all set to 1.
6. When acting as a relay, the sensor must broadcast the synch packet during S_{h+1}. Figure 6b shows the sensor re-broadcasting the synch packet during S_3.
7. The sensor then listens for broadcasts from other sensors during $Data_{h+1}$ ($Data_3$ in this case) and will act as a relay if it receives any data.
8. If another sensor transmits during $Data_3$, e.g., Cattle 2, it will broadcast this in $Data_2$, during Cattle 2's time slot, which will move the data from Cattle 2's sensor one hop closer to the base station. Note that it is possible for multiple cattle to engage in a (re)transmission operation simultaneously during any given time interval. This condition is referred to as a concurrent transmission which is acceptable because LoRa receivers lock onto the strongest signal.
9. The sensor repeats this process until the synch packet indicates that the data collection process has completed, either because all bit-mapped fields are set to 1 or a stop condition has been met.

3   Analysis

LoRa settings can be changed to increase or decrease communication range with a corresponding penalty or benefit to transmission time. Figure 7a plots the transmission time (T_{Synch}) as a function of the SF and bandwidth to send an insecure and secure synch packet, illustrating the modest overhead associated with the proposed security extension. As discussed earlier, the security extension adds to the length of the network packets and corresponding transmission time, as shown here. Similarly, Fig. 7b shows the time for all C cattle to transmit one data packet (T_{Data}), as a function of herd size, C, under different LoRa settings, with and without the security extension.

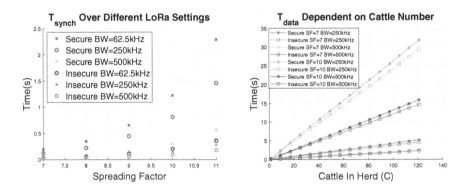

Fig. 7. (a) Transmission time for a synch packet over various LoRa settings, (b) Transmission time for a data window dependent on the number of cattle.

The energy consumption for a sensor to carry out the protocol operations over the time interval defined by a single event is given by Eq. 1, where h is the hop count, R is the total number of rounds, C is the total number of cattle in a herd, and n is the number of sensors with the same or fewer hop counts. P_t and P_r are the transmit and receive power respectively.

$$E_{device}(h, R, n) = (T_{synch}(R - h) + T_{data}(C - n)/C)P_t$$
$$+ (T_{synch}h(\frac{h+1}{2} + R - h) + T_{data}(R - h))P_r \qquad (1)$$

The best case energy consumption scenario is defined by Eq. 2 and occurs when all cattle sensors are within range of the base station.

$$E_{best} = T_{data}P_t + 2T_{synch}P_r \qquad (2)$$

The worst case energy consumption (Eq. 3) occurs for the sensor closest to the base station, in an arrangement where all sensors are spaced equally in a straight line from the base station. Here, the base station must execute C rounds to collect the complete data set.

$$E_{worst} = C((T_{data} + T_{synch})P_t + (T_{synch} + (C - 1)T_{data})P_r) \qquad (3)$$

The total energy consumption for all sensor nodes is defined as the sum of the individual consumption from all the cattle sensors.

To evaluate the performance of our proposed mesh topology, we created a custom simulation model with the cattle sensors distributed in a 1-dimensional space (1-D). Existing simulation tools, such as NS3, could not accurately model the energy consumption performance due to the different states that the sensors operate in. The performance in the 1-D distribution scenario represents the worst case even in an actual 2-dimensional (2-D) scenario. The following parameters are used in our analysis: average $P_t = 330\,\mathrm{mW}$ and $P_r = 15.9\,\mathrm{mW}, C = 128, SF = 9, BW = 250\,\mathrm{kHz}$, and error coding rate 1.25.

We present the energy consumption for the linear distribution of cattle sensors in Fig. 8a, where the number of cows per hop is indicated by the right axis. The transmit and receive energy is plotted as individual curves along with the total energy consumed per device at each hop in the mesh (x-axis). The devices located closer to the base station are tasked with relaying more data and therefore consume more energy. From the graph, the peak energy consumption for sensors located at the first hop is 6 J. This allows for approximately 450 mesh events before recharging is required, assuming a small 2.7 kJ (200 mAh) rechargeable lithium-ion battery is used. An alternative uniform distribution is shown in Fig. 8b where the sensors are distributed equally such that (C/R) cattle are located at every hop. The linear distribution more closely models a real-world cattle distribution. This is true because the base station will typically be placed at the cattle's water source, a location to which the cattle will cluster.

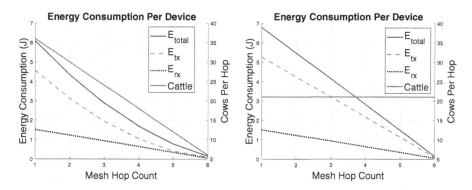

Fig. 8. (a) Energy consumption if cattle have linear distribution, (b) Energy consumption if cattle have a uniform distribution.

We now assess how energy consumption scales as a function of herd size and spreading. Figure 9a shows how the energy consumption scales as the maximum hop count increases. Here, we assume the size of the herd is fixed at 128 and examine increasingly wider distributions among the herd. The average and maximum power consumption of the sensor is plotted under the linear and uniform distribution models. These results indicate that the relationship between energy consumption and hop count is linear, suggesting that a strategy which restricts maximum hop count could conserve energy, but introduces the risk that some sensors may be unable to communicate with the base station. Figure 9b shows that the average and maximum energy consumption scales linearly with the size of the herd. The energy load on the sensors at the first hop, indicated by E_{max}, scales at a higher rate than the average consumption of the herd (E_{avg}).

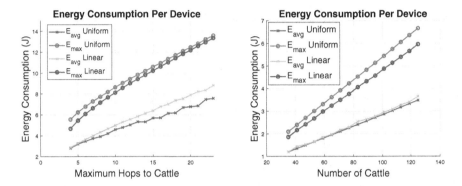

Fig. 9. (a) Energy consumption per device as a function of the number of hops, (b) Energy consumption for six hops as a function of herd size.

4   Security

The primary goals of a secure system are to ensure data privacy and to prevent false impersonation of sensors. The proposed security extension to the cattle monitoring application utilizes two 128-bit keys including a herd key K_h and cattle-specific key K_c for use in AES-based encryption and authentication operations. K_c is unique to every sensor while K_h is common to the entire herd. We assume the base station is able to securely communicate with a server to gain access to the keys.

AES is used to encrypt data using K_c before transmission through the LoRa network. K_c is stored privately in non-volatile memory on each sensor preventing intermediate sensor nodes from decrypting data that they relay to the base station. Each encrypted data packet includes a 4-byte time stamp which serves as a message authentication code (MAC) to enable the base station to detect malicious modifications to the transmitted data. The MAC prevents malicious actors from carrying out spoofing attacks by making it nearly impossible for them to create valid encrypted data packets.

The synch packet is authenticated with a MAC using K_h. Thus, every sensor in the network can validate the authenticity of the fields in the packet. This prevents a simple DoS attack where a malicious actor broadcasts a fake synch packet indicating the base station has received data from all sensors, which in turn triggers all sensors to enter sleep mode until the next event. The 4-byte time stamp makes the MAC unique over successive authentication operations, thus preventing replay attacks where adversaries capture and attempt to reuse previously transmitted MACs.

Encryption prevents malicious actors from eavesdropping on cattle-specific sensor data transmissions if they do not possess the sensor's encryption key. However, an adversary can apply invasive techniques or side-channel analysis methods to extract sensor-specific keys [14,15]. If an adversary is able to extract K_h and K_c using such methods, they would be able to create valid data packets and impersonate the base station. However, because K_c is unique to each sensor, they would be unable to impersonate sensors from other cattle.

In the event that a sensor goes entirely offline because the cow or its sensor moves out of range (for example, in the case of theft), a key update operation would be required to maintain security within the network. The ability to periodically update sensor keys will prevent adversaries who engage in key extraction attacks from compromising network security. Secure re-keying involves selectively updating K_h on every sensor. Distributing $K_{h,new}$ can be accomplished by sending a packet encrypted by the base station with K_c to each device. The key update process requires a distinct packet format and message exchange protocol beyond those defined earlier in this paper.

5   Conclusion

In this work, we propose a novel LoRa secure mesh network architecture designed for battery-powered, GPS-enabled IoT devices and other ultra-low power applications. Our architecture is applied to a cattle monitoring sensor network and addresses unique challenges related to cattle mobility and unpredictability. The design uses device-level GPS to enable time synchronized ad-hoc mesh routing operations performed by all networked devices. We define the packet structure and transmit/receive logic of the proposed protocol, and assess its performance and energy consumption over a variety of cattle distribution models to illustrate its suitability for energy constrained IoT applications. Security extensions are described to provide privacy in data transmissions and authentication between devices in the network. A prototype cattle sensor has been developed and future work will evaluate our secure mesh network architecture using data collected from cattle in a ranch environment.

Acknowledgments. We would like to thank Kevin Nichols for the support and Mike Partridge for the motivation. Sandia National Laboratories is a multi-mission laboratory managed and operated by National Technology and Engineering Solutions of Sandia, LLC, a wholly-owned subsidiary of Honeywell International, Inc., for the U.S. Department of Energy's National Nuclear Security Administration under contract DE-NA-0003525. The research of Dr. Eirini Eleni Tsiropoulou was conducted as part of NSF CRII-1849739.

References

1. Mekki, K., Bajic, E., Chaxel, F., Meyer, F.: A comparative study of LPWAN technologies for large-scale IoT deployment. ICT express **5**(1), 1–7 (2019)

2. SX1276, L.: 77/78/79 datasheet, rev. 4 (2015)
3. Sarker, V., Queralta, J.P., Gia, T., Tenhunen, H., Westerlund, T.: A survey on LoRa for IoT: integrating edge computing. In: 2019 4th International Conference on Fog and Mobile Edge Computing (FMEC), pp. 295–300. IEEE (2019)
4. Hossain, E., Leung, K.K.: Wireless Mesh Networks: Architectures and Protocols. Springer, New York (2007). https://doi.org/10.1007/978-0-387-68839-8
5. Cilfone, A., Davoli, L., Belli, L., Ferrari, G.: Wireless mesh networking: an IoT-oriented perspective survey on relevant technologies. Future Internet **11**(4), 99 (2019)
6. Ebi, C., Schaltegger, F., Rüst, A., Blumensaat, F.: Synchronous LoRa mesh network to monitor processes in underground infrastructure. IEEE Access **7**, 57663–57677 (2019)
7. Lundell, D., Hedberg, A., Nyberg, C., Fitzgerald, E.: A routing protocol for LoRa mesh networks. In: IEEE 19th International Symposium on A World of Wireless, Mobile and Multimedia Networks (WoWMoM), pp. 14–19. IEEE (2018)
8. Lee, H.C., Ke, K.H.: Monitoring of large-area IoT sensors using a LoRa wireless mesh network system: design and evaluation. IEEE Trans. Instrum. Meas. **67**(9), 1–11 (2018)
9. Bor, M.C., Roedig, U., Voigt, T., Alonso, J.M.: Do LoRa low-power wide-area networks scale? In: Proceedings of the 19th ACM International Conference on Modeling, Analysis and Simulation of Wireless and Mobile Systems, pp. 59–67. ACM (2016)
10. Liao, C.H., Zhu, G., Kuwabara, D., Suzuki, M., Morikawa, H.: Multi-hop LoRa networks enabled by concurrent transmission. IEEE Access **5**, 21430–21446 (2017)
11. Velde, B.: Multi-hop lorawan: including a forwarding node (2017)
12. Dias, J., Grilo, A.: Lorawan multi-hop uplink extension. Procedia Comput. Sci. **130**, 424–431 (2018)
13. Roper: Revolutionizing beef production. https://www.ropertag.com/
14. Skorobogatov, S.: Flash memory bumping attacks. In: Mangard, S., Standaert, F.-X. (eds.) CHES 2010. LNCS, vol. 6225, pp. 158–172. Springer, Heidelberg (2010). https://doi.org/10.1007/978-3-642-15031-9_11
15. Zhou, Y., Feng, D.: Side-channel attacks: ten years after its publication and the impacts on cryptographic module security testing. IACR Cryptol. ePrint Arch. **2005**, 388 (2005)

CROSS City: Wi-Fi Location Proofs for Smart Tourism

Gabriel A. Maia⬤, Rui L. Claro$^{(\boxtimes)}$⬤, and Miguel L. Pardal⬤

INESC-ID, Instituto Superior Técnico,Universidade de Lisboa, Lisbon, Portugal
{gabriel.maia,rui.claro,miguel.pardal}@tecnico.ulisboa.pt

Abstract. The ubiquitousness of smartphones, wearables and other mobile devices, coupled with the increasing number of communications infrastructure present in smart cities, has led to the rise of location-based services. Many of these services do not verify the location information they consume and are vulnerable to spoofing attacks. Location proof systems aim to solve this by allowing devices to interact with location specific resources and later prove that they were at the location.

In this paper we describe and evaluate CROSS, a system that performs location verification using techniques compatible with off-the-shelf Android smartphones. We present three strategies to produce location proofs with increasing tamper-resistance. We designed our system with user privacy and security in mind, minimizing the number of connections between devices. We implemented a prototype application to assess the feasibility and reliability of the proof strategies. The application allows rewarding users who complete a touristic route with proofs of visit collected along the way. Our evaluation, which included experiments with 30 users, showed that we can use the system in real-world scenarios, providing adequate security guarantees for the use case.

Keywords: Location spoofing prevention · Location proof · Context-awareness · Security · Internet of Things

1 Introduction

Location is one of the most important pieces of contextual information for Smartphone applications, and is at the core of Location-Based Services (LBS) [3]. These services typically do not verify the location information they use, and are susceptible to *location spoofing attacks*. Developing the means to certify location information is, therefore, of high importance. *Location proof systems* counter location spoofing by providing verifiable location information. One of the use cases for location proofs is in *Smart Tourism* [10]. Tourists can interact with existing or newly-added infrastructure in emblematic city locations, using their personal devices, and record information that can later be used to verify location information.

Wi-Fi can be used as infrastructure for location because most urban environments in modern cities, or other densely populated areas, contain many Wi-Fi

© Springer Nature Switzerland AG 2020
L. A. Grieco et al. (Eds.): ADHOC-NOW 2020, LNCS 12338, pp. 241–253, 2020.
https://doi.org/10.1007/978-3-030-61746-2_18

networks. The overwhelming majority of these announce their presence and can be detected using commodity smartphones.

In this paper we describe and evaluate CROSS (loCation pROof techniqueS for consumer mobile applicationS) with an example application, to ascertain whether the user completed any tourism circuits from a predefined set of routes, as represented in Fig. 1. This paper extends a presentation and security assessment made earlier [11], and adds experimental results and their discussion.

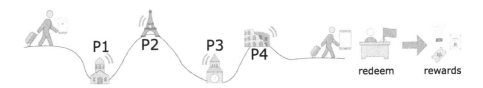

Fig. 1. User flow throughout a tourism route with four locations.

The paper contains the following sections: Sect. 2 presents a brief overview of existing works in the field of location proofs; Sect. 3 gives an overview of our system and its operation; Sect. 4 presents location proof strategies; Sect. 5 discusses experimental results using the prototype implementation; and Sect. 6 concludes the article.

2   Related Work

Wi-Fi technology is widely used in mobile location systems, usually to complement GNSS (Global Navigation Satellite Systems), such as GPS, Galileo or Bei-Dou. Wi-Fi is also used for microlocation, in systems such as Google Indoor [9]. SAIL [12] is an example of a microlocation system which works by combining the Time-of-Flight of Wi-Fi packets with motion sensor data. SurroundSense [2] uses fingerprinting techniques encompassing Wi-Fi, motion sensors, microphones and cameras, to identify the location of the user. Witness-based systems such as APPLAUS [14], LINK [13] and SureThing [8] typically use peer-to-peer communication between witnesses. However, this type of communication is increasingly hampered by mobile operating systems, like iOS and Android, for security reasons. On the other hand, web server communication is usually not restricted. Systems which rely solely on mobile witnesses, without fixed infrastructure, require a minimum amount of diverse users at each location to work. The CREPUS-COLO [4] system solves this problem by introducing trusted witnesses that are installed on specific locations.

User privacy is a primary concern when dealing with exact and certifiable location information. Icelus [1] is a system that locates users and models their movement through IoT devices and uses homomorphic encryption for processing data on third-party servers, that can process but not learn the location of the users.

3 System Overview

The main components of CROSS are represented in Fig. 2: the client application, the server, the Wi-Fi Access Point (for proof strategy described in Sect. 4.2), and the Kiosk (for proof strategy described in Sect. 4.3). The system uses a client-server model with no peer-to-peer communication between clients.

The system operation starts when the tourist installs the smartphone application and signs up for an account. Before starting the trip, the application downloads the catalog of locations. During its use, the application logs visits to locations. The location sensing relies on Wi-Fi exclusively and leverages the scans regularly already performed by the mobile operating system. At the end of the trip, the logging stops, the application submits the collected information to the server, and rewards will be issued.

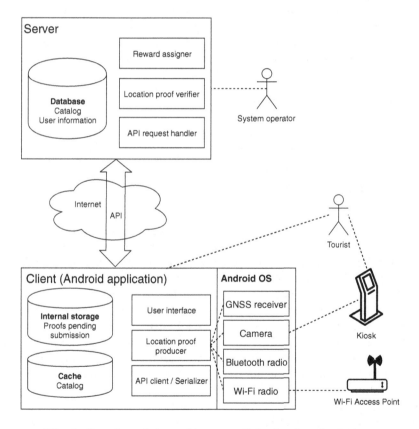

Fig. 2. Overview of the architecture of the developed solution.

The *catalog* stored on the smartphone contains information about the registered locations, tourism routes and respective rewards. It also contains the

BSSIDs[1] for a subset of the Wi-Fi networks that can be found at each location, that we call *triggers*, because they identify at which location it is, and set off the logging of observations for the location proofs. The ability to operate offline is important, as the intended users – tourists – may be roaming without a data plan, or the cellular coverage may not be available. The client communicates with the server, before and after the trip, through a REST API over HTTPS.

The server is responsible for validating the location proofs submitted by the client. For each claimed visit to a location, the server computes a *strength score* based on the set of proofs backing the visit. This value is calculated differently from location to location, depending on the proof strategy used. This score is also modified according to the characteristics of the movement of the user, i.e., it checks if the proofs were collected at a human-like pace.

In the definition of a route, each location is associated with a minimum strength score and a minimum visit duration. The user is eligible to receive the reward for a given route if the collected proofs match or exceed the minimum values acceptable for each point in the route. System operators handle these rewards, and the value of those are dependent of the location proof strategy used. Stronger proof strategies are then more suited for high value rewards.

4   Location Proof Strategies

We propose three different strategies for location proof production and verification, with increasingly stronger guarantees: *scavenging*, *TOTP*, and *Kiosk*.

4.1   Scavenging Strategy

The scavenging strategy, represented in Fig. 3, harnesses the large number of Wi-Fi networks installed by unrelated third parties in urban environments. Location proofs are produced simply by storing Wi-Fi scan results with associated timestamps. We store the SSIDs of networks in plaintext, since they are broadcasted by APs and therefore are public domain. If this were not case, an encryption algorithm would be used before storing the network SSIDs.

On the server side, the set of Wi-Fi networks present in the scan results is compared with the list of known networks for each location. This list is maintained by the system operators. To deal with the volatility of the network list and assist system operators in curating these lists, the server can analyze past location proofs to suggest the addition and removal of certain Wi-Fi networks from the database. The *strength score* is the fraction of client-presented networks over the total number of server-known networks.

The scavenging strategy is simple and has a reduced setup cost, as it just uses existing infrastructure. However, it provides weak guarantee: as soon as the list of networks at a certain location is known, an attacker can forge trip logs.

---

[1] Basic Service Set Identifiers, normally the address of the radio of the Access Point.

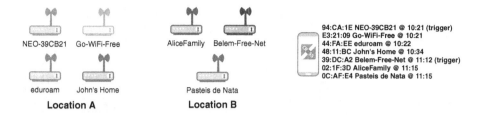

Fig. 3. Representation of the networks and logged information in a visit to two locations, A and B, where the scavenging strategy is used. At each location, one of the networks is known beforehand to trigger the identification.

4.2 TOTP Strategy

The TOTP (Time-based One-Time Password) strategy is illustrated in Fig. 4. This strategy allows for stronger proofs by deploying a customized Wi-Fi access point that is dynamically changing the broadcast SSID[2]. The SSID is used as a low-bandwidth, unidirectional communication channel to transmit a changing value. This strategy is standards-compliant and compatible with existing devices. Note that the device is observing the changing SSID values and does not need to connect to the network.

Time-Based SSID Setting. The SSID should change in a way that is unpredictable to an observer, but which can be verified by the server. We achieve this by including in the SSID a TOTP, similar to the proposed in RFC 6238. Only the Wi-Fi AP and the CROSS server know the secret, to produce and validate the codes. Each AP should use a different secret key, and only the server should know the keys used by all APs. The APs and server must have synchronized clocks with minute granularity, but both components do not need to communicate, which means APs can function as stand-alone beacons in locations without Internet access. Since we are using minute granularity, clock deviation can happen, but does not impact our solution. We expect users to be in range of the APs for longer periods of time and therefore observe multiple changes in the SSID the AP.

We use a time-step size of 120 s, sufficient to provide enough resolution during proof verification, while still fitting within the constraints of most Wi-Fi Stations when it comes to updating scan results. We chose SHA-512 HMAC as the TOTP hash algorithm, with keys as long as the HMAC output, instead of the typically used SHA-1 HMAC. This allows the use of longer keys. These settings were selected to make it computationally complex to infer the secret TOTP key by continuously observing the different SSIDs assumed by the AP. This would amount to a key-recovery attack, where the key is recovered by observing the cipher output for known inputs. To the best of our knowledge, such an attack

---

[2] Service Set Identifier, the user-facing name for a Wi-Fi network.

against SHA-512 HMAC is yet to be conceived [6], unlike HMAC using weaker hash algorithms [5].

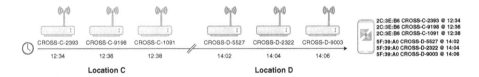

Fig. 4. Representation of the networks and logged information in a visit to two locations, C and D, where the TOTP strategy is used. There is one AP at each location.

Proof Collection and Validation. Clients are programmed to log all the different SSIDs a Wi-Fi network assumes during their visit to a location, along with the timestamps at which each SSID was observed. Clients do not know whether each Wi-Fi network is part of the infrastructure for this strategy, as that is irrelevant to how they collect proofs; only the server needs to know this, to select the correct proof validation strategy. In other words, as far as the client implementation is concerned, the scavenging strategy and the TOTP strategy are the same.

The TOTP strategy, unlike the scavenging one, allows for attesting not just that the user was present at a certain location, but also that he did so at a certain point in time. Therefore, this strategy allows for verifying the visit duration. Here, the strength score corresponds to the fraction of visit time that could be verified, in relation to the total time the client claims to have been present at the location.

Validating the authenticity of Wi-Fi and Bluetooth devices is complex as the hardware identifiers can be trivially spoofed. Because this solution does not involve bi-directional communication with other devices or networks, as in many witness-based proof strategies [14], it minimizes user exposure to attacks. This also protects their privacy, as only the entity operating the CROSS server will be able to know which locations each user visited.

4.3 Kiosk Strategy

The kiosk strategy counters the possibility of claiming multiple rewards for a single trip, by preventing variants of Sybil attacks [7], where a malicious visitor creates multiple user accounts and runs them in parallel using one or more smartphones. This strategy requires interaction with a kiosk device present at the location. The device can have other functionality, including showing information about the location or advertising. Existing tourism information kiosks can be adapted for this purpose. This approach can be an inconvenience for tourists. To mitigate that, we can take advantage of existing ticket machines, so that the process of interaction with a kiosk is done while acquiring tickets for attractions.

Proof Production and Validation. Similarly to Wi-Fi APs in the TOTP strategy, kiosks are required to have their clocks synchronized with the server, also with minute granularity. Each kiosk keeps a private key, which they will use to sign information. The server has the corresponding public key. Kiosks do not need to have a connection to the server.

Location proofs are produced as follows. The client application sends the username of the logged in user to the kiosk, by displaying a QR code[3] that is scanned by the kiosk. The latter, using its private key, signs a message containing the kiosk ID, the username of the user, the current date and time, and a randomly generated large number (a nonce). This message and respective signature is sent back to the client, again using a QR code, which is scanned by the latter.

The smartphone stores this data as a visit proof, part of the trip log. When the trip log is submitted to the server, it verifies this proof by checking the signed message using the public key associated with the kiosk and also that the kiosk ID matches that of a kiosk available at the visit location; the username matches the user account submitting the proof; the date and time is contained within the period of the visit; the nonce was not reused from any other visit proof submitted in the past.

By eliminating the remote network connection to the kiosk, an attacker must be physically present at the location to interact with it. Using QR codes for communication between the kiosk and the smartphone requires physical interaction. This physical interaction can also be inspected by a bystander, e.g., a tourist attraction staff member, to check for suspicious activity like attempting to check-in with more than one device.

This strategy is more inconvenient for the user but it boosts security. It should be used where there are already tourist support kiosks in place, and use the previous strategies in other locations.

5   Evaluation

To validate our solution, we developed prototypes of the client, server and Wi-Fi AP components. This allowed us to evaluate the scavenging and TOTP strategies.

The client prototype is an Android application written in Java, compatible with off-the-shelf smartphones running Android 4.4 and up. The client uses a SQLite database to store the catalog for offline operation, and to store trip logs and respective location proofs. The server exposes a REST API, with JSON payloads, which the client uses to obtain the catalog, and to submit trip logs. The server is written in Go and uses a PostgreSQL database to store information about locations, tourism routes, rewards, and the Wi-Fi networks present at each location, including TOTP secrets. The database is also used to store user credentials and trip logs including the respective location proofs, for auditing. The Wi-Fi AP component for TOTP was implemented using a ESP8266 board,

---

[3] A QR (Quick Response) code is a type of barcode that can be scanned by a smartphone built-in camera.

a low-cost Wi-Fi microchip with full TCP/IP stack. The firmware was written in C++ using the Arduino environment for this microchip.

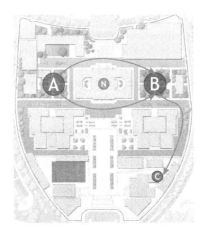

Fig. 5. Campus route used in the experiments.

An evaluation scenario was set up in the Alameda campus of Instituto Superior Técnico, where voluntary participants completed a simulated tourism route, shown in Fig. 5, composed of three locations **A**, **B** and **C**. Additionally, a control location, **N**, was selected to serve as off-limits, and the participants were asked not to visit it.

The simulated route made use of both the scavenging and TOTP strategies. Participants brought their own personal Android phones, which let us reach a large and diverse sample size. A total of 34 Android smartphones were used in the experiment.

5.1 Location Detection Performance

Some factors that reduce the accuracy of the system include: AP transmit power, receiver sensitivity, number of networks and interference sources in an area, and signal propagation patterns. Despite these factors, the expected result in this experiment is that each device should be able to detect all locations except **N**. The results presented in Table 1 correspond to the results after the devices were present for three minutes at each location, except for location **N**, near which every device passed on the way between **A** and **B**.

As expected, no devices detected control location **N**. For other locations, results are satisfactory as well. The lower detection rate of location **A** in comparison with **B** may be explained by the lower number of trigger networks configured for **A**. All devices detected location **C** within three minutes, which may

Table 1. Location detection performance after three minutes at each location (except for **N**, not visited).

Location	Total visits	Total detections	Success rate
A	34	30	88%
B	34	33	97%
C	34	34	100%
N	0	0	100%

be explained by the fact that the single AP was in the same room as the participants, therefore its signal was much stronger and easier to detect than the signals of the APs at **A** and **B**, which were installed in the nearby buildings, at distances between 20 and 80 m from the users.

5.2   Location Proof Performance

In locations **A** and **B**, the Scavenging strategy was used. In this strategy, the confidence score corresponds to the percentage of networks found by the client, compared to the total number of APs registered in the server for each location. In this experiment, we previously registered 21 known APs for location **A**, and 17 known APs for location **B**.

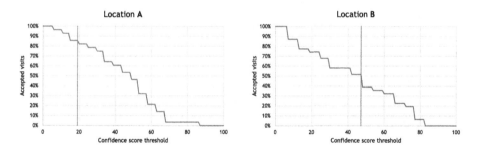

Fig. 6. Percentage of accepted visits in function of the confidence score threshold configured at locations **A** and **B**. (Color figure online)

Figure 6 shows the percentage of accepted visits for locations **A** and **B**, as a function of the confidence score threshold that is set for those locations. When deciding whether to reward an user, all visits must be accepted for the trip to count, but here, each location is being analyzed individually. The vertical orange line in the charts corresponds to the percentage of known networks that are triggers, at each location. We consider that it represents the minimum confidence score threshold acceptable, as only visits proofs with a higher score are guaranteed to contain a non-trigger (secret) network.

Results for this strategy fell short of expectations, as the confidence score threshold has to be set very low – lower than recommended – for a large percentage of visits to be accepted. These results show that most devices did not see a majority of the networks associated to each location, in part certainly due to the short visit duration (three minutes) and the weak network signal levels, whose APs were relatively distant.

In location **C**, the TOTP strategy was used. In this strategy, the confidence score corresponds to the percentage of visit time that could be verified by the TOTP codes present in the scan results collected by the client. Figure 7 shows the relation between the threshold and the accepted visits, for this location.

Results for this strategy were positive. Most devices successfully captured the SSID changes every two minutes; 24 devices (75%) were even able to capture TOTP codes attesting the entirety of the visit period (10 min).

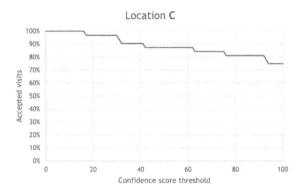

Fig. 7. Percentage of accepted visits in function of the confidence score threshold configured at location **C**.

5.3   Power Consumption

To assess the power consumption of our techniques and compare their consumption with that of alternative solutions, we collected battery usage data on a LG V40 ThinQ smartphone, running Android 9.0.

We compared three different situations: location using both Wi-Fi and GNSS, location using exclusively Wi-Fi scanning, and no location collection at all. For the first case, a modified CROSS application, that also used GNSS to collect location information, was used. In the second case, the unmodified CROSS application was used. In both cases, data was requested every 30 seconds. In the third case, no applications were used - the phone was left turned on, with Wi-Fi enabled, without explicitly using any applications. Table 2 presents the results. p.p. stands for percentage points. *p.p. stands for percentage points.*

Table 2. Battery drain depending on the location collection method.

Method	Polling rate	Total test duration	Average battery drain
No collection	N/A	29 h 05 min	0.58 p.p. / hour
Collection using Wi-Fi	30 s	39 h 30 min	0.61 p.p. / hour
Collection using GNSS and Wi-Fi	30 s	08 h 00 min	1.25 p.p. / hour

CROSS, which exclusively uses Wi-Fi, presents a negligible increase in power consumption relative to no location collection.

5.4 Scavenging Feasibility

One of the concerns with the scavenging strategy, presented in Sect. 4.2, is the need to maintain the lists of Wi-Fi networks for each location where this strategy is used. As time passes, some of the networks may disappear, and new, different networks may appear. Even though the server suggests the addition and removal of networks based on the submitted visit proofs, these suggestions need to be manually vetted. Therefore, it is important to understand how frequently Wi-Fi networks appear and disappear in the real world, to assess whether the current implementation is adequate.

We collected data on the Wi-Fi networks in range, at six locations in Lisbon, in three dates. The second date was ten days after the first, and the third date was 31 days after the first. Five of the locations are well-known tourist attractions and one is a residential area, for comparison with a less busy location. The results, presented in Table 3, correspond to the duplicated network counts after merging the data from the three devices. Across devices and visits, APs were identified by their BSSID to avoid counting renamed networks (such as in our own TOTP strategy) as separate networks. Values for both periods are always relative to the first visit.

Table 3. Wi-Fi networks present at each tourist attraction.

Location	Initial total	After ten days		After one month	
		Present	New	Present	New
Alvalade	86	74 (86%)	13	73 (85%)	31
Comércio	133	8 (6%)	60	7 (5%)	43
Gulbenkian	80	54 (68%)	92	54 (68%)	55
Jerónimos	148	34 (23%)	100	24 (16%)	62
Oceanário	39	22 (56%)	41	24 (62%)	40
Sé	61	25 (41%)	43	22 (36%)	44

The number of networks still present ten days after the first visit is a good indicator of the number of networks that can be considered in the scavenging technique, at each location. Most locations have a sufficiently large set of usable networks, with the notable exception of Comércio, where just 8 APs appear to be permanently installed.

To assess the frequency at which the lists of networks must be updated, we can look at the number of permanent networks that disappeared between the second visit (after ten days) and the third visit (after one month). In most cases, there is only a minor reduction from one visit to another, with Jerónimos being the worst case, but still with a sufficient number of permanent networks.

6   Conclusion

In this paper we presented CROSS, a system that implements location proof techniques for consumer mobile applications. We used smart tourism as a use case, developing a smartphone application where location proofs are used to implement a reward scheme. CROSS includes three different location proof strategies, with trade-offs between strong security guarantees and easier user experience. The system was evaluated in a realistic setting using a diverse sample of devices. The results show the feasibility of location proofs running in current mobile operating systems and hardware without special privileges or configurations.

Acknowledgements. This work was supported by national funds through FCT, Fundação para a Ciência e a Tecnologia, under project UIDB/50021/2020 and through project with reference PTDC/CCI-COM/31440/2017 (SureThing).

References

1. Agadakos, I., Hallgren, P., Damopoulos, D., Sabelfeld, A., Portokalidis, G.: Location-enhanced authentication using the IoT. In: Proceedings of the 32nd Annual Conference on Computer Security Applications - ACSAC 2016. ACM Press (2016). https://doi.org/10.1145/2991079.2991090
2. Azizyan, M., Constandache, I., Choudhury, R.R.: SurroundSense. In: Proceedings of the 15th Annual International Conference on Mobile computing and Networking - MobiCom 2009. ACM Press (2009). https://doi.org/10.1145/1614320.1614350
3. Baldauf, M., Dustdar, S., Rosenberg, F.: A survey on context-aware systems. Int. J. Ad Hoc Ubiquitous Comput. 2(4), 263 (2007). https://doi.org/10.1504/ijahuc.2007.014070
4. Canlar, E.S., Conti, M., Crispo, B., Pietro, R.D.: CREPUSCOLO: a collusion resistant privacy preserving location verification system. In: 2013 International Conference on Risks and Security of Internet and Systems (CRiSIS). IEEE, October 2013. https://doi.org/10.1109/crisis.2013.6766357
5. Contini, S., Yin, Y.L.: Forgery and partial key-recovery attacks on HMAC and NMAC using hash collisions. In: Advances in Cryptology – ASIACRYPT 2006, pp. 37–53. Springer, Berlin Heidelberg (2006). https://doi.org/10.1007/11935230_3
6. Dobraunig, C., Eichlseder, M., Mendel, F.: Security evaluation report on SHA-224, SHA-512/224, SHA-512/256, and the six SHA-3 functions. Technical report, CRYPTREC (2015)

7. Douceur, J.R.: The sybil attack. In: Druschel, P., Kaashoek, F., Rowstron, A. (eds.) IPTPS 2002. LNCS, vol. 2429, pp. 251–260. Springer, Heidelberg (2002). https://doi.org/10.1007/3-540-45748-8_24

8. Ferreira, J., Pardal, M.L.: Witness-based location proofs for mobile devices. In: 17th IEEE International Symposium on Network Computing and Applications (NCA), November 2018

9. Google LLC: Indoor Maps - About. https://www.google.com/maps/about/partners/indoormaps/. Accessed 30 Nov 2019

10. Gretzel, U., Sigala, M., Xiang, Z., Koo, C.: Smart tourism: foundations and developments. Electron. Markets **25**(3), 179–188 (2015). https://doi.org/10.1007/s12525-015-0196-8

11. Maia, G.A., Pardal, M.L.: CROSS: loCation pROof techniqueS for consumer mobile applicationS. In: INForum. Guimarães, Portugal, September 2019

12. Mariakakis, A.T., Sen, S., Lee, J., Kim, K.H.: SAIL. In: Proceedings of the 12th Annual International Conference on Mobile Systems, Applications, and Services - MobiSys 2014. ACM Press (2014). https://doi.org/10.1145/2594368.2594393

13. Talasila, M., Curtmola, R., Borcea, C.: LINK: location verification through immediate neighbors knowledge. In: Sénac, P., Ott, M., Seneviratne, A. (eds.) MobiQuitous 2010. LNICST, vol. 73, pp. 210–223. Springer, Heidelberg (2012). https://doi.org/10.1007/978-3-642-29154-8_18

14. Zhu, Z., Cao, G.: APPLAUS: a privacy-preserving location proof updating system for location-based services. In: 2011 Proceedings IEEE INFOCOM. IEEE, April 2011. https://doi.org/10.1109/infcom.2011.5934991

Wireless Systems

Total Transmission Time Minimization Through Relay Selection for Full-Duplex Wireless Powered Cooperative Communication Networks

Syed Adil Abbas Kazmi, Muhammad Shahid Iqbal, and Sinem Coleri[✉]

Electrical and Electronics Engineering, Koc University, 34450 Istanbul, Turkey
{skazmi14,miqbal16,scoleri}@ku.edu.tr

Abstract. We consider a relay based full-duplex wireless powered cooperative communication network which consists of a hybrid access point (HAP), N users and K decode-and-forward relays with energy harvesting capability. We propose an optimization framework for relay selection with the objective of minimizing the total transmission time subject to energy causality and user traffic demand constraints. The formulated optimization problem is a mixed integer non-linear programming problem, which is difficult to solve for the global optimal solution in polynomial-time. As a solution strategy, we decompose the proposed optimization problem into two sub-problems: time allocation problem and relay selection problem. We derive the optimal solution of the time allocation problem by using convex optimization techniques. For the relay selection problem, based on the optimality analysis, we propose a polynomial-time heuristic algorithm, which minimizes the total transmission time by allocating the best relay to each user. Through simulations, we illustrate that the proposed algorithm outperforms the conventional predetermined relay allocation scheme and performs very close to the optimal solution for different network densities, HAP power values, and initial battery levels.

Keywords: Wireless powered cooperative communication network · Full-duplex communication · RF energy harvesting · Relay selection

1 Introduction

In conventional wireless networks, the network lifetime is limited since the wireless devices in the network are powered by replaceable or rechargeable batteries. Energy harvesting (EH) from various renewable sources, such as wind, solar, and radio frequency (RF), has been proposed as a promising solution to prolong the lifetime of such networks. Among these renewable sources, RF-EH is the most suitable option for future wireless systems due to its controllability,

This work is supported by Scientific and Technological Research Council of Turkey Grant #117E241.

© Springer Nature Switzerland AG 2020
L. A. Grieco et al. (Eds.): ADHOC-NOW 2020, LNCS 12338, pp. 257–268, 2020.
https://doi.org/10.1007/978-3-030-61746-2_19

reliability, and lower cost. In the literature, two main RF-EH network models are proposed: Simultaneous Wireless Information and Power Transfer (SWIPT), and Wireless Powered Communication Networks (WPCN). In SWIPT, information and energy are transmitted simultaneously from the access point (AP) to multiple users, whereas in WPCN, only energy flows in the downlink (DL), and users harvest this energy to transmit their information in the uplink (UL).

Relay nodes are incorporated into the RF-EH networks with the goal of enhancing the throughput and network coverage by assisting the end users in their information transmission [1]. There are two main categories of the relays: decode-and-forward (DF), where a relay node first decodes the received signal and then forwards it to the destination; and amplify-and-forward (AF), in which a relay node amplifies the received signal from the source and forwards it to the destination. Initially, relay selection has been studied in SWIPT systems considering a single source, a destination and multiple EH relays [2–6]. The relay selection is proposed based on the available channel state information (CSI) of the single hop, either of the hop from source to relay or from relay to destination (known as partial relay selection (PRS)), or for both the hops, from source to relay and relay to destination, (known as opportunistic relaying (OR)) [2–4]. [5] and [6] consider EH relays, which are equipped with batteries, and present a relay selection problem based on the available energy level of the relays. All the aforementioned relay based SWIPT systems incorporate half-duplex (HD) transmission mode, in which information transmission and reception takes place in non-overlapping time slots. [7] considers the full-duplex (FD) relay based SWIPT system, where a single or multiple relays can be selected based on the greedy RS method that achieves the maximum capacity, whereas [8] studies a two-way FD SWIPT system, where two relay selection schemes to select a single best relay, to minimize the outage probability and maximize the sum capacity respectively are proposed. [9] extends the work of [8], by incorporating both single relay and multiple relays selection schemes in two-way SWIPT system.

In the context of WPCN, initially researchers analyzed the three node model for the relay based system which consists of a source, a relay and a destination, also referred as the wireless powered cooperative communication network (WPCCN). [10] studies this WPCCN, in which both source and relay need to harvest energy from the HAP in the DL, and work cooperatively in the UL. Authors incorporate the AF relaying scheme and present the closed-form expression of the average throughput. The analysis is also extended to multi-relay scenario and CSI based relay selection. [11] derives an approximate closed-form expression for the average throughput of the proposed adaptive transmission (AT) protocol of the three node WPCCN. In the proposed AT protocol, at the beginning of each transmission block, the HAP transfers energy to the source, and HAP and then, the source performs channel estimation to acquire the CSI. Based on the CSI estimation, the HAP adaptively chooses the source to perform UL information transmission either directly or cooperatively through relay. [12] extends the three node WPCCN model to multiple source/user multiple relay network model and presents a joint relay selection, scheduling and power control problem with the objective of minimizing the total duration of wireless power and information transfer for an HD system. To the best of our knowledge, [10] and [12] are the only works in WPCCN, where the relay selection problem is addressed, but they are limited to HD transmission.

In this paper, we study the multiple relay, multiple users FD-WPCCN, where relays and users are the energy harvesting components and harvest energy from the HAP in the DL. Both the users and the relays incorporate a practical non-linear EH model based on logistic function, whereas all the previous studies incorporated an easy and impractical linear EH model in WPCCN systems. We determine the time allocation and relay selection with the objective of minimizing the total transmission time. The main contributions of our work are as follows:

- We present a new optimization framework for an FD-WPCCN system, incorporating the energy causality and traffic demand constraints by using a non-linear EH model for the first time in the literature.
- We formulate the optimization problem to determine the time allocation and relay selection with the objective of minimizing the total transmission time. The formulated problem is a mixed integer non-linear programming problem (MINLP), which is difficult to solve for global optimal solution.
- We decompose the problem into two sub-problems. First, we formulate a time allocation sub-problem for a given relay selection and after proving its convexity, we propose the optimal solution. Then, we extend the problem to the best relay selection problem and propose a polynomial time heuristic algorithm for the relay selection.

2   System Model and Assumptions

We consider a cooperative WPCN which consists of a HAP, K DF relays and N users, as depicted in Fig. 1. The HAP is operating in an FD mode, whereas the relays and users are operating in HD mode. The HAP is equipped with an FD antenna, which is used for simultaneous wireless energy transfer (WET) in the DL to the relays and users, and wireless information transmission (WIT) in the UL from the users to the HAP via relays. The transmission power of the HAP is assumed to be constant and denoted by P_h. We assume that the channels are block fading and different, i.e., channel gains remain constant during the transmission time and may change independently in the other blocks. DL channel gains from HAP to user i and relay k are denoted by h_i and h_k, respectively. UL channel gains from user i to relay k and from relay k to HAP are denoted by $g_{i,k}$ and g_k, respectively. We assume a practical non-linear energy harvesting model, based on logistic function. The energy harvesting rate of user i is given by

$$C_i = \frac{P_s\left(\Psi_i - \frac{1}{1+e^{a_i b_i}}\right)}{\left(1 - \frac{1}{1+e^{a_i b_i}}\right)}, \tag{1}$$

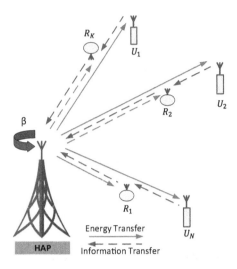

Fig. 1. Architecture for wireless powered cooperative communication network

where $\Psi_i = (1 + e^{-a_i(P_h h_i - b_i)})^{-1}$, and EH rate for relay k is given by

$$C_k = \frac{P_s\left(\Psi_k - \frac{1}{1+e^{a_k b_k}}\right)}{\left(1 - \frac{1}{1+e^{a_k b_k}}\right)}, \tag{2}$$

where $\Psi_k = (1 + e^{-a_k(P_h h_k - b_k)})^{-1}$, P_s represents the maximal power that energy harvester can harvest, a and b are the positive constants related to the non-linear charging rate with respect to the input power and turn-on threshold, respectively.

We consider time division multiple access as medium access protocol for the UL data transmission from the users to the HAP via relays. The total time is partitioned into scheduling frames, which are further divided into variable-length slots, each allocated to a particular user and its selected relay, as depicted in Fig. 2. We assume that the transmission order of the users is predetermined and the relays and users can harvest energy throughout the frame except during information transmission/reception time. The energy harvested after the information transmission can be stored in the battery, resulting in the initial battery level $B_i, i \in \{1, ..., N\}$ and $B_k, k \in \{1, ..., K\}$ for users and relays respectively. We assume that user i and the corresponding relay are transmitting information during time slot i. The transmission time of user i by using relay k is denoted by $\tau_{i,k}$ and transmission time of relay k, to transmit information of user i to HAP, is denoted by τ_k. Therefore, the energy harvesting time of user i till the end of its transmission is given by $\sum_{j=1}^{i-1}\sum_{k=1}^{K} s_{j,k}(\tau_{j,k} + \tau_k)$, where $s_{j,k}$ is a binary variable, which takes value 1 if user j transmits information using relay k and zero otherwise. Then the total available energy for user i is given by

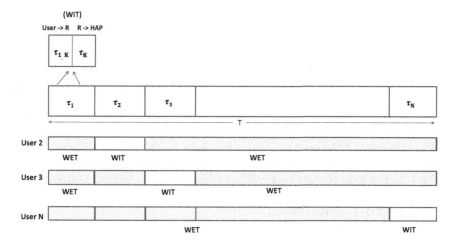

Fig. 2. A time-slotted transmission block for downlink WET and uplink WIT

$$E_i = B_i + C_i \sum_{j=1}^{i-1} \sum_{k=1}^{K} s_{j,k}(\tau_{j,k} + \tau_k) \qquad (3)$$

Similarly, the energy harvesting time before the information transmission of relay k is $\sum_{j \in U} \sum_{k=1}^{K} s_{j,k}(\tau_{j,k} + \tau_k)$, where the set U is the set of users, which are scheduled before user i using their corresponding relays. Note that the set U does not contain the users who have selected the same k^{th} relay to communicate to the HAP. The total available energy of the relay k, E_k is given by

$$E_k = B_k + C_k \sum_{j \in U} \sum_{k=1}^{K} s_{j,k}(\tau_{j,k} + \tau_k) \qquad (4)$$

We assume that user i and relay k must consume all of its available energy in the allocated transmission slot $\tau_{i,k}$ and τ_k, respectively. Then the average transmit power of user i by using relay k is given by

$$P_{i,k} = \frac{E_i}{\tau_{i,k}} \quad \forall i \in \{1, 2, \cdots, N\}, \forall k \in \{1, 2, \cdots, K\} \qquad (5)$$

Similarly, the average transmit power of the relay k is given by

$$P_k = \frac{E_k}{\tau_k} \quad \forall k \in \{1, 2, \cdots, K\} \qquad (6)$$

We assume that user i has traffic demand D_i bits to be transmitted over the scheduling frame. We use continuous transmission rate model and Shannon's channel capacity formula to determine the maximum achievable rate. The instantaneous UL transmission rates from user i to relay k, denoted by $R_{i,k}$ and from relay k to HAP, denoted by R_k, are given by

$$R_{i,k} = \tau_{i,k} W log_2 \left(1 + \frac{E_i g_{i,k}}{\tau_{i,k} W N_0} \right) \tag{7}$$

$$R_k = \tau_k W log_2 \left(1 + \frac{E_k g_k}{\tau_k (\beta P_h + N_0 W)} \right) \tag{8}$$

where βP_h is the power of self-interference at the HAP, arises due to FD mode and $N_0 W$ is the noise power, where W is the bandwidth.

The objective of the optimization is to minimize the total transmission time for an FD WPCCN subject to energy causality constraint and users traffic demand. In the following section, we formulate the optimization problem.

3   Problem Formulation

In this section, we formulate the optimization problem of the relay selection for total time minimization, denoted by $\mathcal{RS} - \mathcal{TTM}$, as follows:

$\mathcal{RS} - \mathcal{TTM}$

$$minimize \sum_{i=1}^{N} \sum_{k=1}^{K} \tau_{i,k} + \sum_{k=1}^{K} \tau_k \tag{9a}$$

$$subject\ to$$

$$\sum_{k=1}^{K} s_{i,k} \tau_{i,k} W log_2 \left(1 + \frac{E_i g_{i,k}}{\tau_{i,k} W N_0} \right) \geq D_i; \forall i \in \{1, ..., N\}, \tag{9b}$$

$$\tau_k W log_2 \left(1 + \frac{E_k g_k}{\tau_k (\beta P_h + W N_0)} \right) \geq \sum_{i=1}^{N} D_i s_{i,k}; \forall k \in \{1, ..., K\}, \tag{9c}$$

$$\sum_{k=1}^{K} s_{i,k} = 1; \forall i \in \{1, ..., N\}, \tag{9d}$$

$$variables$$

$$s_{i,k} \in \{0,1\}; \tau_{i,k}, \tau_k, \geq 0; \forall i \in \{1, ..., N\}, k \in \{1, ..., K\}. \tag{9e}$$

The variables of the $\mathcal{RS} - \mathcal{TTM}$ optimization problem are $s_{i,k}$, the relay selection variable, which is a binary variable taking value 1 if user i transmits information by using relay k and zero otherwise for $i \in \{1, ...N\}$, $k \in \{1, ..., K\}$; $\tau_{i,k}$ transmission time of user i by using the relay k, for $i \in \{1, ...N\}$, $k \in \{1, ..., K\}$; and τ_k, the transmission time of relay k to the HAP for $k \in \{1, ..., K\}$.

The objective of the optimization problem is to minimize the total transmission time duration. Equations (9b) and (9c) represent the constraints on satisfying the traffic demand of the users. Equation (9d) guarantees that only one relay is selected for each user.

The $\mathcal{RS} - \mathcal{TTM}$ is MINLP, which is generally hard to solve for the optimal solution. To solve the problem optimally, we decompose the $\mathcal{RS} - \mathcal{TTM}$ into two sub-problems, namely, time allocation problem and relay selection problem. Next, we formulate the time-allocation problem.

4   Time Allocation Problem

In this section, we discuss the time allocation problem, denoted by $\mathcal{TAP}$. In the $\mathcal{TAP}$ the users are already allocated the relay, i.e., $s_{i,k}$ are known. The $\mathcal{TAP}$ is formulated as follows:

$\mathcal{TAP}$

$$minimize \sum_{i=1}^{N}\sum_{k=1}^{K}\tau_{i,k} + \sum_{k=1}^{K}\tau_k \tag{10a}$$

subject to

$$D_i - \tau_{i,k}Wlog_2\left(1 + \frac{E_i g_{i,k}}{\tau_{i,k}N_0 W}\right) \leq 0; \forall i, \forall k, \tag{10b}$$

$$D_i - \tau_k Wlog_2\left(1 + \frac{E_k g_k}{\tau_k(\beta P_h + N_0 W)}\right) \leq 0; \forall i, \forall k, \tag{10c}$$

$$\tau_{i,k}, \tau_k \geq 0; \forall i, \forall k. \tag{10d}$$

The variables of the problem are $\tau_{i,k}$, the transmission time of the first hop, from user i to relay k, for $i \in \{1, ...N\}$, $k \in \{1, ..., K\}$ and τ_k, the transmission time of the relay k to HAP, for $k \in \{1, ..., K\}$.

Lemma 1. *$\mathcal{TAP}$ is a convex optimization problem.*

Proof. The objective function of $\mathcal{TAP}$ is a linear function of $\tau_{i,k}$ and τ_k. The constraints in Eqs. (10b) and (10c) are convex functions as the hessian of both functions are positive semi-definite. Therefore, $\mathcal{TAP}$ is a convex optimization problem.

Since $\mathcal{TAP}$ is a convex optimization problem, there is a unique optimal solution for the problem. In the following, we provide the optimality conditions of the optimization problem.

Lemma 2. *In the optimal solution of $\mathcal{TAP}$, the constraints in Eqs. (10b) and (10c) should hold with equality.*

Proof. The proof is by contradiction. Suppose that in an optimal solution $\tau = \{\tau_{1,k}^*, \tau_{2,k}^*, \cdots, \tau_{N,k}^*\}$ are the allocated transmission times of users such that $\tau_{i,k}^* Wlog_2\left(1 + \frac{g_{i,k}E_i}{\tau_{i,k}^* W N_0}\right) > D_i$. The function $f(x) \triangleq xlog(1 + z/x)$, where z is a constant, is a monotonically increasing function of x for $x > 0$. Therefore, for any user i, we can always find a $\tau_{i,k}'$ such that $\tau_{i,k}'Wlog_2\left(1 + \frac{g_{i,k}E_i}{\tau_{i,k}'W N_0}\right) = D_i$ and it is clear that $\tau_{i,k}' < \tau_{i,k}^*$. This is a contradiction. In a similar way, we can prove that Eq. (10c) should hold with equality.

Based on Lemma 2, the problem $\mathcal{TAP}$ can be solved for a unique set of transmission times and the solution is presented in Theorem 1.

Theorem 1. *In the optimal solution of* $\mathcal{TAP}$, *the transmission time of user* i *is given by*

$$\tau_{i,k} = \cfrac{1}{\frac{-W}{D_i \ln(2)} \, \boldsymbol{W}\!\left(\frac{-D_i \ln(2)}{W\gamma_{i,k}} \exp\!\left(\frac{-D_i \ln(2)}{W\gamma_{i,k}}\right)\right) + \frac{1}{\gamma_{i,k}}}, \tag{11}$$

where $\boldsymbol{W}(.)$ *is a well known Lambert function [13], and* $\gamma_{i,k}$ *is given by*

$$\gamma_{i,k} = \frac{g_{i,k} E_i}{N_0 W}. \tag{12}$$

Proof. As per Lemma 2, the constraint given in Eq. (10b) should hold with equality, i.e.,

$$D_i - \tau_{i,k} W \log_2\left(1 + \frac{g_{i,k}\gamma_{i,k}}{\tau_{i,k}}\right) = 0. \tag{13}$$

Equation (13) can then be rearranged as follows:

$$1 = \left(1 + \frac{\gamma_{i,k}}{\tau_{i,k}}\right) \exp\left(\frac{-D_i \ln(2)}{W\tau_{i,k}}\right). \tag{14}$$

We rewrite the Eq. (14) in the form of $Y = Xe^X$ as

$$\frac{-D_i \ln(2)}{W\gamma_{i,k}} \exp\left(\frac{-D_i \ln(2)}{W\gamma_{i,k}}\right)$$
$$= \left(\frac{-D_i \ln(2)}{W\gamma_{i,k}} - \frac{-D_i \ln(2)}{W\tau_{i,k}}\right) exp\left(\frac{-D_i \ln(2)}{W\gamma_{i,k}} - \frac{-D_i \ln(2)}{W\tau_{i,k}}\right). \tag{15}$$

Equation (15) is a standard form for $Y = Xe^X$ and its solution is $X = W(Y)$, Then after some simple mathematics, $\tau_{i,k}$ is obtained as given in Eq. (11).

Since, in the decode-and-forward relay network, user and relay transmit their information in non-overlapping transmission times, we can treat both entities separately. The transmission time of the relays is given as presented in the following theorem.

Theorem 2. *In the optimal solution of* $\mathcal{TAP}$, *the transmission time of relay* k *is given by*

$$\tau_k = \cfrac{1}{\frac{-W}{D_i \ln(2)} \, \boldsymbol{W}\!\left(\frac{-D_i \ln(2)}{W\gamma_k} \exp\!\left(\frac{-D_i \ln(2)}{W\gamma_k}\right)\right) + \frac{1}{\gamma_k}}, \tag{16}$$

where,

$$\gamma_k = \frac{g_k E_k}{\beta P_h + N_0 W}. \tag{17}$$

Proof. Theorem 2 can be proved in a similar way as Theorem 1 by solving Eq. (10c) and proof is skipped for brevity.

Now, as we have solved the $\mathcal{TAP}$ problem, the relay selection problem is presented in the following section.

5 Relay Selection

The goal of this section is to determine the relay selection for each user such that the total transmission time is minimized. In Sect. 4, we presented the optimal transmission time allocation for a given relay allocation, i.e., $s_{i,k}$ were known for $i \in \{1, ...N\}$, $k \in \{1, ..., K\}$. On the other hand, the total transmission time can be further minimized by optimizing the relay selection for each user. For instance, allocating a relay to the user with better channel conditions and smaller distance over any random relay will significantly reduce the transmission time of the users. A straightforward approach to this problem can be brute-force search, i.e., enumerate all the possible relay combinations and then pick the combination with minimum transmission time. However, the computational complexity of this approach is exponential due to K^N possible combinations of the relays. Therefore, we propose a polynomial time heuristic algorithm based on the minimization of the total transmission time through the allocation of the best relay to each user. For a single user i, let $\tau_{i,k}$ be the transmission time of the first hop, from user to relay k and τ_k be the transmission time from relay k to HAP. Then $argmin_{k \in \{1,2,\cdots,K\}}(\tau_{i,k} + \tau_k)$ will be the optimal relay that gives the minimum transmission time for the single user. As the users are transmitting data in a sequence, the relay selection is updated online for each user as due to different energy harvesting rates, users may select different relay at different decision times. Based on this we propose the following heuristic algorithm.

Algorithm 1. Minimum Length Relay Selection Algorithm (MLRSA)

1: **input:** set of users $\mathcal{N}$ and relays $\mathcal{K}$
2: **output:** Relay selection $\mathcal{R}$, set of user transmission times $\tau_{i,k}$, set of relay transmission times τ_k, schedule length $t(\mathcal{N})$
3: $\mathcal{R} \leftarrow \emptyset$, $\tau_{i,k}(\mathcal{R}) \leftarrow 0$, $\tau_k(\mathcal{R}) \leftarrow 0$, $t(\mathcal{N}) \leftarrow 0$
4: **for** $i = 1 : |\mathcal{N}|$ **do**
5:     Calculate $\tau_{i,k}, \tau_k, \forall k \in \{1, ..., K\}$
6:     $m \leftarrow argmin_{k \in \mathcal{K}}(\tau_{i,k} + \tau_k)$,
7:     $\mathcal{R} \leftarrow \mathcal{R} + \{m\}$,
8:     $\tau_{i,k} \leftarrow \tau_{i,k} + \{\tau_{i,m}\}$,
9:     $\tau_k \leftarrow \tau_k + \{\tau_m\}$,
10:    $t(\mathcal{N}) \leftarrow t(\mathcal{N}) + \tau_{i,m} + \tau_m$,
11: **end for**

The Minimum Length Relay Selection Algorithm (MLRSA), as given in Algorithm 1, is described in detail next. The algorithm starts by initializing $\mathcal{R}$, $\tau_{i,k}(\mathcal{R})$, $\tau_k(\mathcal{R})$, $t(\mathcal{N})$ to an empty set (Line 3). For each user i of the system, the relay that offers the minimum transmission time is selected (Line 6). Then, the set $\mathcal{R}$ is updated with the selected relay (Line 7). $\tau_{i,k}(\mathcal{R})$ is updated by adding the transmission time of the user i to the selected relay m (Line 8) and $\tau_k(\mathcal{R})$ by adding the transmission time of relay m to HAP (Line 9). Finally, $t(\mathcal{N})$ is updated by adding the transmission times of both the hops i.e, $\tau_{i,m}$

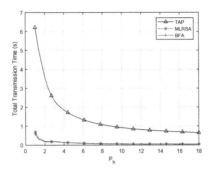

Fig. 3. Total transmission time vs. HAP transmit power P_h

and τ_m (Line 10). Algorithm terminates when all the users in the system are being assigned to the best relays. The computational complexity of MLRSA is $\mathcal{O}(N \times K)$.

6   Performance Analysis

In this section, we evaluate the performance of the proposed algorithm. Simulations are carried out in MATLAB, averaged over 1000 independent random network realizations. The attenuation in the channel is calculated by using both large scale and small scale fading. To model the large scale fading, we used $PL(d, dB) = PL(d_0, dB) + 10\alpha log_{10}(d/d_0) + Z$ where, $PL(d, dB)$ is the path loss at distance d in dB, d_0 is the reference distance and path loss at reference distance $d_0 = 1\,\mathrm{m}$ is taken as $30\,\mathrm{dB}$, the term α is the path loss exponent and is taken as 2.76. Z is a zero mean Gaussian random variable with standard deviation $\sigma = 4$. The parameters used in the simulations are $W = 1\,\mathrm{MHz}$; D_i is 100 bits for $i \in \{1, ...N\}$ and $\beta = -80\,\mathrm{dB}$ [14]. For the non-linear EH model, $P_s = 7\,\mathrm{mW}$, $a = 1500$ and $b = .0022$.

Figure 3 illustrates the total transmission time for different values of HAP transmit power P_h. The total transmission time duration decreases with the increasing transmit power since higher HAP power allows the relays and the users to harvest more energy and complete their transmission in shorter time as long as they can transmit with higher transmit powers. After a certain value of P_h, the total transmission time becomes almost constant due to the saturation region of all the users and relays and any further increase in the HAP power will not improve the energy harvesting rate. The proposed MLRSA outperforms the predetermined relay selection scheme (TAP) and performs very close to the optimal solution (BFA).

Figure 4 illustrates the effect of the network size on the total transmission time. As the number of users increase in the system, the total transmission time increases. When the network size keeps increasing, any further addition of a user results in very small increase in the total transmission time.

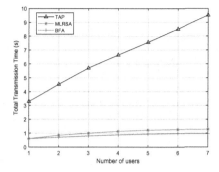

Fig. 4. Total transmission time vs. the number of users in the system

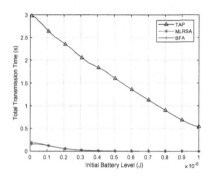

Fig. 5. Total transmission time vs. the initial battery level of the relays and the users

Figure 5 shows the total transmission time for different values of battery levels of the relays and the users. Total transmission time decreases as the energy in the battery of the nodes increases. It is because of the fact that higher initial battery level helps the users to complete their transmissions in shorter time. The MLRSA outperforms the conventional predetermined relay selection (TAP) and performs close to the optimal BFA.

7   Conclusion and Future Work

In this paper, we have investigated the total transmission time minimization of the FD-WPCCN system through relay selection. We formulate an MINLP problem for the subject. To solve the problem efficiently, we decompose the problem into two sub-problems, namely, time allocation and relay selection problem. We derive the optimal solution of the time allocation problem by using convex optimization techniques and present the polynomial-time heuristic algorithm for the relay selection problem. Through simulations, we show that the proposed algorithm performs very close to the optimal solution. We aim to incorporate multi-antenna system in the future.

References

1. Nosratinia, A., Hunter, T., Hedayat, A.: Cooperative communication in wireless networks. IEEE Commun. Mag. **42**(10), 74–80 (2004)
2. Zhao, Y., Li, Q., Huang, L., Feng, S., Han, T., Zhang, J.: Wireless information and power transfer on cooperative multipath relay channels. In: 2016 IEEE/CIC International Conference on Communications in China (ICCC), pp. 1–6, July 2016
3. Sui, D., Hu, F., Zhou, W., Shao, M., Chen, M.: Relay selection for radio frequency energy-harvesting wireless body area network with buffer. IEEE Internet Things J. **5**(2), 1100–1107 (2018)
4. Nasir, H., Javaid, N., Imran, M., Shoaib, M., Anwar, M.: Simultaneous wireless information and power transfer for buffer-aided cooperative relaying systems. In: 2018 14th International Wireless Communications and Mobile Computing Conference (IWCMC). IEEE, June 2018
5. Gu, Y., Chen, H., Li, Y., Liang, Y.-C., Vucetic, B.: Distributed multi-relay selection in accumulate-then-forward energy harvesting relay networks. IEEE Trans. Green Commun. Netw. **2**(1), 74–86 (2018)
6. Wang, F., Guo, S., Yang, Y., Xiao, B.: Relay selection and power allocation for cooperative communication networks with energy harvesting. IEEE Syst. J. **12**(1), 735–746 (2018)
7. Wang, D., Zhang, R., Cheng, X., Yang, L.: Full-duplex energy-harvesting relay networks: capacity-maximizing relay selection. J. Commun. Inf. Netw. **3**(3), 79–85 (2018). https://doi.org/10.1007/s41650-018-0027-0
8. Wang, D., Zhang, R., Cheng, X., Yang, L.: Relay selection in two-way full-duplex energy-harvesting relay networks. In: IEEE Global Communications Conference (GLOBECOM), Washington, DC, pp. 1–6 (2016). https://doi.org/10.1109/GLOCOM.2016.7842211
9. Wang, D., Zhang, R., Cheng, X., Yang, L., Chen, C.: Relay selection in full-duplex energy-harvesting two-way relay networks. IEEE Trans. Green Commun. Netw. **1**(2), 182–191 (2017). https://doi.org/10.1109/TGCN.2017.2686325
10. Chen, H., Li, Y., Rebelatto, J.L., Uchoa-Filho, B.F., Vucetic, B.: Harvest-then-cooperate: wireless-powered cooperative communications. IEEE Trans. Sig. Process. **63**(7), 1700–1711 (2015)
11. Gu, Y., Chen, H., Li, Y., Vucetic, B.: An adaptive transmission protocol for wireless-powered cooperative communications. In: 2015 IEEE International Conference on Communications (ICC). IEEE, June 2015
12. Onalan, A.G., Salik, E.D., Coleri, S.: Relay selection, scheduling and power control in wireless powered cooperative communication networks. arxiv preprint arXiv:2002.00611 (2020)
13. Corless, R., Gonnet, G., Hare, D.E.G., Jeffrey, D.J., Knuth, D.E.: On the LambertW function. Adv. Comput. Math. **5**, 329–359 (1996). https://doi.org/10.1007/BF02124750
14. Iqbal, M.S., Sadi, Y., Coleri, S.: Minimum length scheduling for full duplex time-critical wireless powered communication networks. IEEE Trans. Wirel. Commun. **19**(9), 5993–6006 (2020). https://doi.org/10.1109/TWC.2020.2999130

Energy Aware Epidemic Strategies for Mobile Opportunistic Networks

Floriano De Rango$^{(\boxtimes)}$, Mauro Tropea, and Salvatore Amelio

DIMES Department, University of Calabria, Rende, Italy
{derango,m.trpea}@dimes.unical.it, salvatore.amelio@gmail.com

Abstract. This paper presents a novel data dissemination strategy called Geographic Energy-aware Epidemic Routing (GEER) for Mobile Opportunistic Networks. This routing scheme considers the residual node energy and the node degree to dynamically decide if forwarding or not data to encountered mobile nodes. Moreover, a buffer management policy is applied to preserve buffer space reducing the Time To Live (TTL) of data sent on nodes with higher degree centrality. A node density estimation differentiated for geo-graphic area is proposed to improve the data forwarding and a buffer data discarding policy has been applied to manage packets with different sizes. GEER has been compared with others schemes such as Energy Aware Epidemic Routing (EAER) and EpSoc routing scheme in terms of Data Packet delivery ratio, overhead and energy consumption.

Keywords: DTN · Opportunistic networks · Epidemic routing · Energy

1 Introduction

Delay Tolerant Networks (DTNs) gained a lot of attention in these last years due to its capability to support communication opportunistically also under different mobility conditions and in cases where communication can be intermittent. In distributed wireless systems where mobile phones or IoT devices want to distribute data also in no delay-sensitive way but supporting an hop-by-hop paradigm, DTNs could be a good candidate solution that can differ by the classical network systems supporting end-to-end paradigm. Through the bundle layer and exploiting the contact opportunity of mobile nodes or things, it is possible to design efficient data dissemination strategies that could be useful for many purposes such as the data advertising, the node configurations, viral marketing and so on [1–5]. The opportunistic communication supported by DTN has been extensively studied in these last years and many models related to the social structure of the network, social ties, data replication strategies and data propagation similar to viral infectious have been proposed [6–13]. Considering the last studies in literature, this contribution is focused on an aspect that has been just marginally faced by previously proposed strategies. It is the energy evaluation in the opportunistic networks based on the DTN paradigm. The energy consumption can be a real problem and many performance of classical data dissemination strategies designed for DTN can severely degrade their performance if the energy consumption is not accounted.

© Springer Nature Switzerland AG 2020
L. A. Grieco et al. (Eds.): ADHOC-NOW 2020, LNCS 12338, pp. 269–281, 2020.
https://doi.org/10.1007/978-3-030-61746-2_20

Unfortunately, in real environments, where nodes consume energy in the activation, transmission and reception phases, also very well-known strategies such as Epidemic routing, Prophet, Spray&Wait and so on do not maintain the same performance as in the ideal case, because its "modus operandi" causes excessive energy consumption and, thus, a more frequent death of nodes within the network (a large number of deactivated nodes causes the lowering of the delivery probability) can be observed [14, 15].

In this work we focused on the well-known *Epidemic Routing* (ER) strategies, that have been extensively studied in literature and proposed as benchmarks in many DTN routing approaches [11]. It is well known that ER can improve the data packet delivery ratio and also reduce the latency but its overhead and data replication can be excessive. Other routing strategies has been proposed and compared with ER in order to reduce the control overhead but preserving the data packet delivery ratio (PDR) [11, 17]. In the past, we proposed an improvement to the ER considering the energy issues and showing that when energy is considered as constraints such as buffer, ER performance can severely degrade [13–15]. To overcome this problem the *n*-Epidemic methodology to improve the ER performance reducing the number of nodes involved in the data dissemination has been proposed in [16]. Moreover, the *Energy- Aware Epidemic Routing* (EAER) has been proposed in [15] with the aim to dynamically manage the *n* parameter, improving the performance especially in terms of PDR under energy budget and constraints. However, EAER does not account for other aspects such as preserving the buffer space, reducing much more the energy consumption extending the node lifetime and considering some social properties of the encountered nodes during the movement. At this purpose, it is proposed a novel protocol based on the ER strategy but combined with social aspects of nodes, a smart buffer management policy able to consider also the geographical area where nodes can operate. It is called *Geographic and Energy-aware Epidemic Routing* (GEER). The basic idea is to consider parameters of the networks and nodes related to the geographical area where they operate in order to account about different behaviors that can be related to nodes during part of the day. Considering geographical areas can improve the key parameters estimation such as node density and degree centrality preserving the scalability of the proposed approach.

The paper is organized as follows: Sect. 2 provide a brief description of some related works on DTN routing strategies; Sect. 3 describes the main features of ER, EAER and a recent DTN scheme called EpSoc [18]; in Sect. 4 the data dissemination and management strategy is introduced; performance evaluation and conclusions are summarized respectively in Sect. 5 and 6.

2 Related Work

Many routing strategies have been proposed for opportunistic and DTN networks. Epidemic routing was proposed as a robust routing scheme for such a network, adopting a "store-carry-forward" paradigm: every node acts as a relay for other nodes [3]. All messages are spread in the network to all the nodes including the destination in an epidemic (like disease) manner producing multiple copies of the same message. Due to a large number of redundant messages in the network, this protocol has significant demand on both bandwidth and buffer capacity. Spray and Wait [5] considers a fixed number of replicas allowed in the network during message creation. It tries to reduce the number of replicas to forward in comparison with Epidemic routing. Spray and Wait breaks routing into two phases: a spray phase, where message replicas are disseminated, and a wait phase, where nodes with single-copy messages wait until a direct encounter with the respective destinations. A follow-up protocol called Spray and Focus [6] uses a similar spray phase, followed by a focus phase, where single copies can be forwarded to help maximize a utility function. While both Spray and Wait and Spray and Focus succeed in limiting some of the overhead of flooding-based protocols, their delivery ratios suffer. In PRoPHET [4], each node uses past encounters to predict future best route. Each node maintains Delivery Predictabilities (DPs) in which it stores number of times it has encountered other nodes. When a node encounters another node they exchange their DPs. After receiving DPs, each node updates its DPs and compares them with DPs of the encountered node. Node with lower DPs forwards a copy of a message to the node with higher DPs. Recent approaches tries to get advantage by social relationship that is possible to detect in nodes. In the *Opportunistic Mobile Social Networks* (OMSN), mobile devices are portable by humans so that social features of people can be exploited for networking purposes [12, 17]. Social-based protocols utilize social properties of mobile users such as similarity, centrality, and friendship to improve routing efficiency in the opportunistic mobile social network. This is because social features are more stable and less changeable than other features like mobility patterns. In ML-SOR [10], node centrality (different types of centralities), the similarity between communities, and social ties are all exploited to effectively select the forwarding node. In SORSI [20], network and node overhead is decreased by exploiting social information of mobile users. The authors consider the social community of nodes and utilize it to predict future behavior based on contact history. In addition, they proposed a new mechanism to avoid selfish nodes for more improvements. Social features are utilized widely for buffer management. Liu et al. [21] utilized social features and the congestion level to develop the forwarding strategy that drops the message with the minimum social link rather than random dropping. EpSoc has been proposed in [18] where an improved version of Epidemic able to combine the robust spreading of Epidemic strategy with also social features such as degree centrality has been proposed.

Our proposal is based on the combination of some mechanisms inherited by some protocols such as EAER and EpSoc and some additional features such as explained below. Concerning the energy threshold, it is inspired by EAER strategy [15]; the buffer management of EpSoc but with the addition of a data packet discarding policy that prefer to maintain smaller packets in case of congestion. Moreover, a geographic computation of degree centrality (DC) is applied. In particular, the main contributions of this paper are:

- Buffer management to preserve the buffer space adopting a discarding policy that penalizes larger packets;
- The extension of the EAER protocol through the proposal of a new heuristic based on the dynamic setting of the n parameter differentiated on the basis of the geographical area and based on the degree centrality (DC);
- A dynamic TTL value applied to data packet based on degree centrality; it guarantees a reduction in the data packet propagation.

3   Data Dissemination Strategies in DTN

Many routing protocols over DTN have been proposed in literature. Many of them focused on the routing overhead and packet delivery improvement without caring about energy constraints that can affect the performance in the time. In the last years, one of the work to account about energy consumption on DTN has been proposed in [13–15] and [16] and they were focused on ER. Further works have been presented in [18] where energy considerations have been related also to routing Opportunistic Social Networks such as Bubble Rap [9]. However, these approaches did not combine multiple aspects such as buffer space, packet size, robustness of the ER approach and geographical area knowledge. In the following, some of energy strategies applied to DTN routing considered as benchmarks for our proposal have been recalled.

3.1   n-Epidemic Routing

Considering mobile nodes and assuming that they are powered by batteries, it is not so easy to perform battery recharges and, in the considered scenario, the battery level for each node is a primary and important constraint.

If a node transmits a packet every time it meets another node, battery will be used frequently and unsuccessfully. For this reason, we tried to optimize the possibility of sending messages from node to its neighbors (when node enters in the transmission range of another node, then it can be considered as a neighbor of the latter), taking into account a new scheme, called n-Epidemic Routing (n-ER) [16], for which it is assumed that a node can start to transmit only when it has at least n neighbors. The n-ER strategy is summarized with some snapshots in Fig. 1.

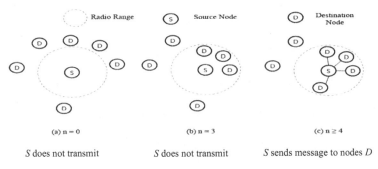

(a) n = 0   (b) n = 3   (c) n ≥ 4

S does not transmit   S does not transmit   S sends message to nodes D

Fig. 1. - n-Epidemic strategy with threshold $n = 4$

3.2   Energy-Aware Epidemic Routing (EAER) Strategy

EAER tries to dynamically set n parameter of n-ER such as proposed in [15]. Let THR be a set of thresholds $\{thr_1, \ldots, thr_K\}$ with $\|THR\| = K$. In this case each $thr_k \in$ THR represents a particular energy level. The idea of heuristic H is to choose a value for n, on the basis of the *Current Energy Level* (CEL) for a particular node. That is to say n is chosen on the basis of the interval that the current value of CEL is belonging to: $CEL_i < \text{CEL} < CEL_j$. In these terms $n = f_H(\text{CEL})$. Each node, in a distributed way and locally, computes the energy level and it can follows the dynamic n-value on the basis of the tables as explained in [15]. It is possible to use also a mixed strategy where node density is combined with the nodes' energy level such as explained in [15] to select how many nodes need to be met to forward the message towards the neighborhood. In this last case $n = f\left(CEL_{N_i}, ANN_{N_i}\right)$ and a message m_{N_i} is sent to neighbors if their number is higher than n. In this case *ANN* represents the *average neighbors nodes* number. More details about the tables' values to apply for computing n on the basis of *CEL* and *ANN* can be found in [15].

3.3 Epidemic Social-Aware Routing (EpSoc)

In the EpSoc, it is used the idea of the degree centrality to reduce the propagation of messages in the time among nodes [18]. The TTL of messages can be decreased on the basis of the degree centrality of the encountered node. It is applied a TTL update as follows:

$$TTL_{N_1} = \frac{TTL_{old}}{DC_{N_2}} \text{ if } \left(DC_{N_2} > DC_{N_1}\right) \tag{1}$$

Where N_1 is the node carrying the message m_{N_1} and DC_{N_i} is the degree centrality associated to the node N_i. For more details about degree centrality please refer to [16–19]. This means that an update to the TTL of message m_{N_1} is applied only if a node meets another node with higher DC. This avoids to propagate to more nodes the message. Moreover, in order to preserve the buffer occupancy, authors propose to use a *block register* to store the message IDs to not process again the message if it comes again from other nodes. This *block register* (BR) is updated with the ID of the new message when a message is sent to a node with higher centrality according to this rule:

$$BR_{N_2} = Include\left(m_{N_1}, BR_{N_2}\right) \text{ if } \left(DC_{N_2} > DC_{N_1}\right) \tag{2}$$

where Include(x, y) is a function that insert x in the data structure y and return the updated data structure y. If a message m_{N_1} has been stored in the BR_{N_2} this means that if this message will be received again by N_2 it will be discarded.

4   GEER for Preserving Buffer Space and Energy Draining

In the following section it is presented the GEER data dissemination and management policy. It is introduced the buffer management with a differentiated discarding policy and buffering, the geo-graphic centrality degree computation and the energy-aware data forwarding.

4.1 Buffer Management Policy

Data forwarding in DTN needs to be effective in terms of data delivery probability. Considering that all nodes present many constraints such as energy, buffer space, computation capability etc., in many cases, these constraints can severely affect the performance also if the data forwarding technique is efficient. This is due to the lack of strategies to apply in the buffer management that can compromise the storage capability of nodes reducing the tolerability to the delay of DTN. In this contribution we analyzed a buffer management policy that considers different packet sizes to be stored and a discarding policy in the case of full buffer that differs by the classical last in first discard (LIFD) policy applied in many DTN context. LIFD policy considers the last packets arrived in a buffer as the first to be discarded because there is a simple LIFO ordering data packet policy. In our case, accounting for different packet sizes, the buffer is ordered for increasing packet size and a discarding policy penalizing the larger packets is applied.

GEER extends the buffer management policy considering packets ordered on the basis of the packet size and this assures that, in case of congestion, the buffer space is left to data that consume less energy (smaller packets) This approach tries to preserve much more the energy in order to maintain more alive nodes supporting a more robust data propagation in a denser network. Thus, the proposed approach is conservative in the data forwarding giving importance to the energy levels of nodes and it is conservative also in the buffer space because the precious data storage resource is preserved for packets that do not consume too much energy. This approach reduces the double risk of data dropping and energy draining. Clearly this conservative approach is applied when critical conditions happen such as congestion and buffer exhaustion or severe energy draining.

4.2 Geographic-Aware Degree Centrality

GEER computes node centrality for a node I, $C_{Cdegree}$, using a long-term cumulative estimate of degree centrality. Degree centrality basically quantifies the number of connections a node has. The advantage in using this measure is that it can be easily computed locally considering only a node's ego network. More specifically, GEER computes the number of unique nodes seen throughout a specific time slot and then average this measure with a set of previous measures. Degree centrality for a node i during a time slot t is computed as follows:

$$C_{degree}(i, t) = \sum_{j=1}^{N} e(i, j, t) \tag{3}$$

Where

$$e(i, j, t) = \begin{cases} 1 \text{ if } i \text{ encounters } j \text{ during time slot } t \\ 0 \text{ otherwise} \end{cases}$$

represents an edge between node i and a node j on the DTN graph corresponding to the time slot considered and N is the number of nodes in i's range. The cumulative degree,

$C_{Cdegree}$, is then computed by averaging the node's degree values over a set of T time slots including the most recent time slot and all the previous ones:

$$C_{DC} = \frac{1}{T} \cdot \sum_{t=0}^{T} C_{degree}(i, T - t) \qquad (4)$$

In that way, GEER provides a fully decentralized approximation for a node's degree centrality, which is easy to be computed. In addition to the C_{DC} computation, it is considered a differentiation of the C_{DC} on the basis of the geographic area where mobile nodes is moving. This means that if N_A areas have been considered in the region, it is associated a C_{DC} for each area in every node. This assures that in the computation it is considered the geographic area effect that can affect the transitory evaluation of the C_{DC}. For example, if a node moves from a high density region, where it met many nodes, to a zone with very low density, the computation of the C_{DC} could be affected by these zone changes in the classical approach. In our proposal, it is maintained a different structure for each considered and pre-defined zone. The extra overhead in the data structure is not excessive because it is related to the number of zones.

4.3 Energy-Aware Data Forwarding

GEER tries to get advantage of the strongest features of EAER and EpSoc. In particular, in the data forwarding it is applied a dynamic tuning of n-Epidemic based on the energy levels and node density such as proposed in EAER. However, it is included also the verification of the *cumulative degree centrality CDC* such as proposed in [12] and recalled in (4) (in order to reduce the data propagation from node with high centrality to many other nodes. It is supposed that higher degree centrality should assure to meet more nodes where to spread a message copy and this means that the TTL could be reduced. This TTL reduction is interesting because it can save buffer space in the time. Moreover, the threshold based forwarding of EAER included in GEER assures that the data forwarding is applied considering also the energy conditions of nodes. In the following it is shown the EAER-like forwarding adopted in GEER but where *CDC* has been applied rather than node density (Fig. 2).

where *fp* (*forwarding probability*) is a randomly selected number uniformly generated in the interval [0,1]. This approach probabilistically allows the reduction of the number of messages forwarded on the network when node residual energy is reduced under a threshold. SNPS strategy considers a data forwarding based on the node density. Some details about this technique can be found in subsection IV.B of the paper [15] (Fig. 3).

In particular, it is applied an association between the average node density computed by a single node on the basis of its encounters and a threshold that tries to reduce the number of data replication among encountered nodes. More details about the threshold values and the mapping with the n parameter for the dynamic tuning of the n-Epidemic can be found in [15].

$f(CEL_i, CDC_i)$: Energy-aware forwarding

IF $CEL_i > 2000mAh$ { //EAER forwarding based on CDC_i
      If $th_1 \leq CDC_i \leq th_2$ $n=2$
      else if $th_3 \leq CDC_i \leq th_4$ $n=4$;
      .   ...
      else if $th_5 \leq CDC_i \leq th_6$ $n=8$;
          else if $DC_i > th_6$ $n=10$; }

ELSE IF $CEL_i < 2000mAh$ {
      If $CEL_1 < CEL < CEL_2$
      If *fp>0,3 apply SNPS* strategy otherwise *no message*
               forwarding
      else if $CEL_2 < CEL < CEL_3$
      if *fp>0,6 apply SNPS strategy*
      else *no message forwarding*
      else if $CEL_3 < CEL < CEL_4$ }
      if *fp>0,8 apply SNPS strategy*
      else *no message forwarding* }

Fig. 2. Pseudo-code for the GEER forwarding strategy

GEER buffer policy and Block Register management

For all $N_i \in N$
    if N_i encounter N_j
        Calculate DC_i, DC_j
        $DC_i \leftrightarrows DC_j$
        For all $m_i \in Buf_{N_i}$
          if $m_{ID} \notin Block_{ID_j}$
            if $f(CEL_i, DC_i)$ // DC_i geographic
                       // estimation
              if $DC_{ij} > DC_{ji}$
              $m_{i_{TTL}} \leftarrow (m_{i_{TTL}}/DC_{ji})$
              $BR_{N_j} \leftarrow m_i$
              end if
              forward m_i to N_j //it is applied EAER or SNPS
                     //according to pseudo-code in Fig.2
              $Buff_{N_i} \leftarrow m_i$ // ordered buffer policy i
            end if
            else
               Discard m_i
        end for
    end for

Fig. 3. GEER Pseudo-code for buffer and block register (BR) management

5 Performance Evaluation

In this section some simulation results obtained by Opportunistic Network Emulator (ONE) simulator [19] are presented. Simulation settings are similar to those presented [15] but fixing the observation time T for the CDC to 30 s and considering a number of nodes equal to 300. Higher observation time T with a fixed time slot t implies an higher number of samples accounted for computing the CDC such as expressed in (4).

5.1 Simulation Scenario

The Working Day mobility model (WDMM) [19] has been considered and data traffic considers three different packet sizes generated by nodes: 500 kB, 1 MB and 1.5 MB. GEER has been compared with EAER and EpSoc in order to evaluate its robustness and adaptability during the time. Data Delivery percentage, Overhead and Average residual energy have been considered in order to see how may data are disseminated in the network and how the energy has been accounted during the data forwarding strategy. Main simulation setting parameters are listed in Table 1.

Table 1. Simulation parameters

Simulation parameters	Value
Transmission rate	2 Mbps
Transmission range	100 m
Buffer size	50 MB
Nodes speed	0.5–1.5 m/s
TTL	300 min
Initial energy	1000–4000 mAh
Activity energy	0.005 mA per minute
Packet transmission energy	0.03 mAh per 10 KB
Radio transmission energy	0.006 mA per meter
Packet receiving energy	0.04 mAh per 4 KB
Packet size	500 kB, 1 MB, 1.5 MB
Observation time T	30 s
Time slot t	5 s

Values reported above have been considered after some simulations where different values has been considered. We reported here only some values that can represent very common IEEE 802.11b card parameters such as transmission range and channel capacity, some common low mobility speeds (pedestrian) and an initial energy value of some battery that could be found on the market. Concerning packet transmission and reception energy consumption, some values have been achieved by some wireless products datasheets. Due to space limitations, other values that could be considered for performance evaluation purpose have been omitted. However, the goodness of the proposal is still maintained. Simulation metrics considered in our evaluation are:

1. **Data Delivery:** it represents percentage of delivered data at the destinations.
2. **Overhead:** it indicates the number of replica forwarded on the network in order to deliver data to destinations. More efficient data dissemination can reduce the number of replica for delivered data.
3. **Average Residual Energy:** it represents the average final node energy expressed in mAh at the end of the simulation. It is useful to see how much energy can be saved applying a specific data dissemination strategy.

5.2 Simulation Results

It is possible to see as GEER outperforms EpSoc in terms of Data Delivery in Fig. 4. This means that GEER is able to get advantage of the buffer preserving mechanism of EpSoc through the TTL update but it is able also to involve a better number of nodes to spread the data. Moreover, overhead and energy consumption, such as shown in Fig. 5 and Fig. 6 are reduced in GEER during a day because it is able to account the energy consumption adopting a more conservative data forwarding policy that reduces the number of nodes involved in the spreading especially when the energy is drained out. EpSoc performs better than GEER in terms of overhead in the first hours of the day, but it reduces its performance after because it does not consider a reduction of the data forwarding on the basis of the energy status.

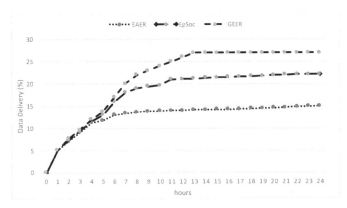

Fig. 4. Data Delivery (%) vs time (in hours) for EAER, EpSoc and GEER in a network with 300 nodes.

On the other hand, GEER is able to change dynamically the data forwarding threshold value used for the spreading and is able also to reduce the spreading when energy levels are under some thresholds. GEER improves also the data delivery because it is able to better manage the buffer under different packet size conditions.

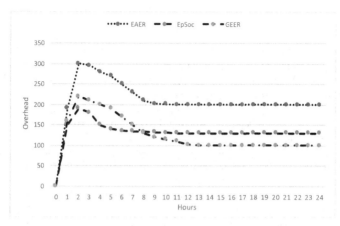

Fig. 5. Overhead vs time (in hours) for EAER, EpSoc and GEER in a network with 300 nodes.

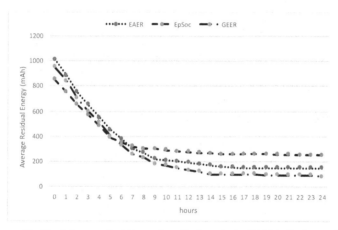

Fig. 6. Average Residual Energy (mAh) vs time (in hours) for EAER, EpSoc and GEER in a network with 300 nodes.

6 Conclusions

In this paper a novel routing strategy GEER for DTN has been proposed. It considers degree centrality computed per areas where nodes can move. Moreover, GEER makes use of an energy aware threshold mechanism to dynamically choose the minimum number of nodes to meet for forwarding the data replicated packets. A buffer management policy is also proposed under different packet sizes forwarding, proposing to discard larger packet size in case of congestion preserving energy. GEER performs better than other well know strategies such as EpSoc and EAER in terms of Data Delivery Rate and Energy Consumption presenting also a good protocol overhead.

References

1. Fall, K.: A delay-tolerant network architecture for challenged internets. In: Proceedings of ACM SIGCOMM, pp. 27–34, August 2003. http://doi.acm.org/10.1145/863955.863960
2. Gao, L., et al.: Multidimensional routing protocol in human-associated delay-tolerant networks. IEEE Trans. Mob. Comput. **12**(11), 2132–2144 (2013)
3. Vahdat, A., Becker, D.: Epidemic routing for partially-connected ad hoc networks, April 2000
4. Lindgren, A., et al.: Probabilistic Routing Protocol using History of Encounters and Transitivity (PRoPHET). In: RFC 6693, IETF Document (2012)
5. Spyropoulos, T., Psounis, K., Raghavendra, C.S.: Spray and wait: an efficient routing scheme for intermittently connected mobile networks. In: Proceedings of the 2005 ACM SIGCOMM Workshop on Delay-Tolerant Networking, pp. 252–259, August 2005
6. Spyropoulos, T., Psounis, K., Raghavendra, C.S.: Spray and focus: efficient mobility-assisted routing for heterogeneous and correlated mobility. In: 5th Annual IEEE International Conference on Pervasive Computing and Communications Workshops, pp. 79–85, March 2007
7. Henderson, T., Kotz, D., Abyzov, I., Yeo, J.: CRAWDAD Trace Set Dartmouth/Campus/Movement (v. 2005-03-08), Marzo 2005. http://crawdad.cs.dartmouth.edu/darmouth/campus/movement
8. Fan, J., et al.: Geocommunity-based broadcasting for data dissemination in mobile social networks. IEEE Trans. Parallel Distrib. Syst. **24**(4), 734–743 (2013)
9. Hui, P., Crowcroft, J., Yoneki, E.: Bubble rap: social-based forwarding in delay tolerant networks. IEEE Trans. Mob. Comput. **10**(11), 1576–1589 (2011)
10. Socievole, A., Yoneki, E., De Rango, F., Crowcroft, J.: ML-SOR: message routing using multi-layer social networks in opportunistic communications. Comput. Netw. **81**, 201–219 (2015)
11. Socievole, A., De Rango, F., Coscarella, C.: Routing approaches and performance evaluation in delay tolerant networks. In: Wireless Telecommunications Symposium (WTS), pp. 1–6 (2011)
12. Socievole, A., Yoneki, E., De Rango, F., Crowcroft, J.: Opportunistic message routing using multi-layer social networks. In: Proceedings of the 2nd ACM Workshop on High Performance Mobile Opportunistic Systems, pp. 39–46 (2013)
13. De Rango, F., Amelio, S., Fazio, P.: Enhancements of epidemic routing in delay tolerant networks from an energy perspective. In: The 9th International Wireless Communications & Mobile Computing Conference, IWCMC 2013, pp. 731–735, July 2013
14. De Rango, F., Amelio, S.: Performance evaluation of scalable and energy efficient dynamic n-epidemic routing in delay tolerant networks. In: 2013 International Symposium on Performance Evaluation of Computer and Telecommunication System, SPECTS 2013, pp. 167–173, July 2013
15. De Rango, F., Amelio, S., Fazio, P.: Epidemic strategies in delay tolerant networks from an energetic point of view: main issues and performance evaluation. J. Netw. **10**(1), 4–14 (2015)
16. Lu, X., Hui, P.: An energy-efficient n-epidemic routing protocol for delay tolerant networks. In: IEEE 5th International Conference on Networking, Architecture and Storage (NAS), pp. 341–347, July 2010
17. Han, B., Hui, P., Kumar, V.S.A., Marathe, M.V., Shao, J., Srinivasan, A.: Mobile data offloading through opportunistic communications and social participation. IEEE Trans. Mob. Comput. **11**(5), 821–834 (2012)
18. Lenando, H., Alrfay, M.: EpSoc: social-based epidemic-based routing protocol in opportunistic mobile social network. Mob. Inf. Syst. **2018**, 1–9 (2018)

19. Keränen, A., Ott, J., Kärkkäinen, T.: The ONE Simulator for DTN Protocol Evaluation, Helsinki University of Technology (TKK), Department of Communications and Networking, March 2009
20. Socievole, A., Caputo, A., De Rango, F., Fazio, P.: Routing in mobile opportunistic social networks with selfish nodes. In: Wireless Communications and Mobile Computing (WCMC), pp. 1–15 (2019)
21. Liu, Y., Wang, K., Guo, H., Lu, Q., Sun, Y.: Social-aware computing based congestion control in delay tolerant networks. Mob. Netw. Appl. **22**(2), 1–12 (2016). https://doi.org/10.1007/s11036-016-0759-8

Integrating an MQTT Proxy in a LoRa-Based Messaging System for Generic Sensor Data Collection

Kiyoshy Nakamura[1], Pietro Manzoni[1(✉)], Marco Zennaro[2],
Juan-Carlos Cano[1], and Carlos T. Calafate[1]

[1] Universitat Politécnica de Valéncia, Valencia, Spain
minapin@posgrado.upv.es,
{pmanzoni,jucano,calafate}@disca.upv.es
[2] ICTP, Trieste, Italy
mzennaro@ictp.it

Abstract. In this paper we use a "frugal innovation approach" to propose an efficient and generic solution to provide support to the deployment of IoT system in rural areas. Our proposal includes an MQTT (Message Queuing Telemetry Transport) proxy to integrate generic low-cost and low-power sensor devices in a messaging system based on LoRa (Long Range) technology. MQTT allows these data to be provided to external "data lakes" so that they can be used for tasks such as reporting, visualization, advanced analytic, and machine learning. LoRa technology provides long wireless links that can be used to connect villages and towns.

Through a REST-based interface and using JSON as a lightweight data-interchange format, we show how our platform can be used to distribute generic sensor information from rural communities. Finally, we demonstrate through experimental evaluation that this solution provides stable data transfers over links of various kilometers with a minimal utilization of resources.

1 Introduction

According to ITU's (International Telecommunication Union) latest statistics [1], the world has reached an important milestone regarding connected people. At the end of 2018, 51.2% of the global population, or 3.9 billion people, had access to the Internet; in developing countries, growth has shown an increase from 7.7% in 2005 to 45.3% at the end of 2018. Despite this, and basically due to economical reasons, there are still large areas of poorly or not-connected at all zones, not only in developing countries, but also in the countryside of Europe and the USA [2].

Community networks are a successful attempt to solve this situation. They are built by citizens and organizations who join together and share resources and efforts to build network infrastructures. The employed technologies span a very

© Springer Nature Switzerland AG 2020
L. A. Grieco et al. (Eds.): ADHOC-NOW 2020, LNCS 12338, pp. 282–294, 2020.
https://doi.org/10.1007/978-3-030-61746-2_21

wide range, from low-cost, off-the-shelf wireless (e.g., WiFi) routers to expensive optical fiber equipment. A few examples are: Broadband for Rural North (B4RN)[1], in Lancashire, UK, the Nepal Wireless Networking Project (NWNP)[2], or the GUIFINET in Spain [3].

In a previous work [4], we defined the architecture for a messaging system that combined very cheap and flexible devices and the LoRa technology to establish links that can cover wide areas with an easy-to-use interface using the "frugal innovation approach" [5,6]. This term comes from the initial focus on poorest socio-economic users in emerging markets, but is nowadays moving away from the idea of "cheap" innovations to become a more "efficient" approach in terms of minimal utilization of resources such as electricity, time etc. and sustainable innovations, where sustainable means developed to be long–lasting and environmentally responsible [7].

Our messaging application could serve, for example, to arrange for a specific appointment with a remote doctor, or to ask for the price of some goods in a far away market, thus allowing the user to save time and resources. We centered our solution on the use of LoRa [8], a promising solution for long range and low power Internet of Things (IoT) and machine to machine (M2M) communication application. In mountainous regions one can leverage the terrain topography to accomplish line-of-sight transmissions at very long distances with really low power devices.

In this work we propose a solution to ease the deployment of IoT systems by integrating in this platform the support for ordinary sensing applications, based on any type of sensors like environmental sensors for weather forecasting, chemical sensors, level sensors, images sensors, and so on. Locating these devices close to our system's "hubs", enables them to send data across long distances and to be integrated in a Publish–Subscribe (Pub/Sub) system based on MQTT. MQTT [9] is a machine-to-machine connectivity protocol currently widely used in the Internet of Things world. It was designed as an extremely lightweight publish/subscribe messaging transport and it is therefore extremely useful for connections with remote locations where a small code footprint is required and/or network bandwidth is at a premium. Finally, the use of JSON (JavaScript Object Notation) provides a lightweight data-interchange format to the data.

Summing up, in this paper, we propose a system that can collect data from remote sensors, transmit this data over long distances using LoRa, and automatically integrate it into a pub/sub system based on MQTT.

The paper is organized as follows. First, Sect. 2 comments some of the related work in the area. Section 3 presents the overall architecture and functioning of the messaging system. Section 4 describes the integration of the MQTT proxy in the messaging system. Section 5 shows the performance evaluation of a prototype of our proposal. Finally, Sect. 6 presents the conclusions.

---

[1] http://b4rn.org.uk/.

[2] http://www.nepalwireless.net/.

2   Related Works

The general scope of this work is to offer solutions to provide IoT technologies in poorly or not-connected at all scenarios. A very active Internet Research Task Force (IRTF) group in this context, the "Global Access to the Internet for All Research Group (GAIA)" [10] focuses its activities to provide increased visibility and interest among the wider community on the challenges and opportunities to enable global Internet access, in terms of technology as well as in the social and economic drivers for its adoption.

GreenLinks [11] is a platform that provides mobile services reliable and resilient to intermittent links. It was designed to support applications in rural contexts in extreme operating environments with little power and no cellular coverage. The basic element of a GreenLinks network is a so-called Virtual Cell Node (VCN) that is basically an open cellular base station. The VCNs are supposed to be connected. Each VCN requires access to a core network and operates in a licensed spectrum band.

Messaging systems like WhatsApp, Telegram, or the "classical" SMS (short message service) have been and are among the most widely used applications for mobile devices worldwide since they offer an open communication channel among people or the members of a community. Clearly, the possibility to offer this service between villages, and between villages and main cities is highly demanded either for purely personal use or for commercial purposes in rural area, too.

For example, Martinez et al. offer [12] an analysis of the communication needs in rural primary health care in developing countries. They found that one very simple application originally implemented over HF voice-only radio communication proved quite successful: scheduling doctor's appointments for patients. It was found that patients in isolated areas had to spend significant time and resources to reach the nearest hospital, and often they could not be treated immediately, but given an appointment at a time that implied a second trip from home. In the literature there are already other works that specifically address the combination of these two technologies, like in [13–19].

In [20] the authors describe the design of an Internet of Things based platform having as main objective the real-time management of energy consumption in water resource recovery facilities and their integration in a future demand side management environment. In [21] the authors proposes the design of LoRa-MQTT gateway device for supporting the sensor-to-cloud data transmission in smart aquaculture IoT application. In this work the authors focus on the integration of the collection data from sensor devices and to transmit them to a cloud based data storage server.

A very interesting solution is presented in [22] where a low-cost remote monitoring system for dangerous areas based on drones is described that again takes advantage of LoRa and MQTT as the basic technologies. Also, in [23] an open-source earthquake and weather monitoring system is presented based on a Long Range (LoRa)-based star topology with a fully energy-autonomous sensor node.

The goal of this work is to create a frugal smart object that could be used to provide IoT solutions in challenging scenarios [24]. This paper describe the efforts and result of integrating MQTT in our platform. We consider that the combination of LoRa and MQTT adding the flexibility provided by our platform and the use of a JSON interface provides a powerful and yet flexible architecture that can adapt to many various scenarios.

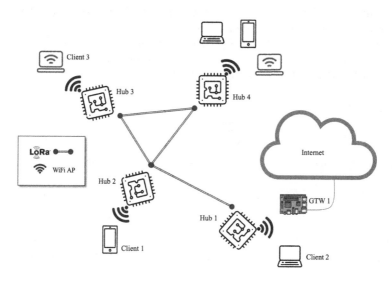

Fig. 1. Overall structure of the messaging platform.

3   The LoRa Messaging System

Figure 1 presents the overall architecture proposed in [4]. At the core there are dedicated devices, called *hubs*, that create the connectivity spot inside an area. The hubs must have both a WiFi (IEEE 802.1b/g/), and a LoRa transceiver.

The hubs work as standard WiFi access point to provide connectivity to closeby devices. The interface with the messaging application is a web based system. The user can decide whether to send a text message to either a specific destination or to all reachable users, or to check for incoming messages stored in the hub. The hubs offer a REST interface to the connected devices to either send a message, or return previously received and locally stored ones.

Every user needs to "register" before exchanging any message. Registration is required to allow the system to localize end-points. When a user sends a message, the local hub "learns" that user is connected through it, and creates an entry in a table. The first step is to discover where the destination user is located. To this end, the hub sends a broadcast message to all the surrounding devices and waits for the searched one to respond. A special *broadcast* user was included for messages that are to be delivered to all the registered users.

At this point, using a reliable unicast protocol, messages are transferred and stored in the destination hub. Once the user checks for available messages, he or she will receive the one stored in the local hub. The unicast protocol is based on a stop-and-wait ARQ (Automatic repeat request) approach with a dynamic and adaptive value for the re-transmission delay. The protocol ensures that information is not lost due to dropped packets and that packets are received in the correct order.

The packet header structure is shown in Fig. 2. We must point out that the maximum application payload depends on the selected data rate. For example, assuming the European 863–870 MHz band, the maximum packet size used was set according to the spreading factor used, i.e. 25 bytes for SF12, and 200 bytes for SF7, with a fixed 24 bytes header.

1	Source addr (8 bytes)			
2	Dest. Addr. (8 bytes)			
3	Seqnum (2B)	Acknum (2B)	flags	Checksum (3B)

Fig. 2. Structure of the header of a packet used by our stop-and-wait ARQ.

Finally, to better integrate our system with standard Internet applications, we designed a *gateway-hub* to link it with Telegram[3], a widely used messaging application, using "Bots". In short, the gateway-hub receives via LoRa messages directed to a Telegram user, registered through the Bot, and forwards them to the user's phone via the Internet. The gateway-hub of our prototype was implemented using a Raspberry Pi board.

More details of the messaging system can be found here [4].

4   Integration of the MQTT Proxy

Data sensor collection is integrated within our platform through a dedicated service that is attached to the system as a specific client. The general idea is that sensors will collect the data, pack them as a structured piece of information, and send them to this service as a message. The receiving device, where the service is executing, will then (1) unpack the message, (2) build a proper MQTT message, and (3) publish it to the broker being used. The set-up required is the one shown in Fig. 3. The sensor is attached to the hub using the WiFi link, as any other client. The device that will execute the *MQTTproxy* service has also to be connected to a hub using WiFi and must clearly have a connection to the used broker, either through the Internet or through a direct TCP/IP link.

Sensors are integrated in this platform using the REST interface. The sequence is basically the same used by regular clients: there is a first register phase followed by a "Push" phase. Figure 4 graphically describe this operation.

---

[3] https://telegram.org/.

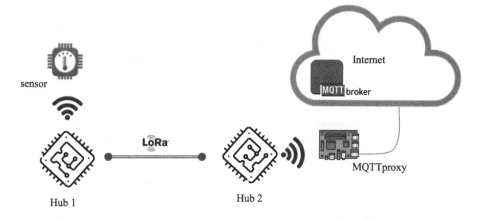

Fig. 3. The required set-up for the sensors and the MQTTproxy integration.

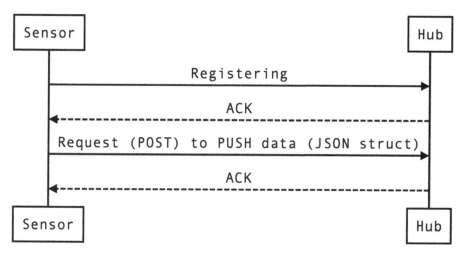

Fig. 4. The data flow when a sensor data is pushed to a hub.

The transferred data is stored in a JSON object with the structure indicated in Listing 1.

```
1  {
2      'DEV_ID': 'lopy_374534',
3      'QOS': 0,
4      'TOPIC': 'sensor1/luminosity',
5      'VALUE': 25
6  }
```

Listing 1. JSON structure of the sent message.

The data contained in the JSON object can have a variable size limited only by the slow data rate that we can obtain from a LoRa channel. Topics average length can range between 10 to 50 bytes, while values can be anything from a few bytes, to hundreds of kilobytes, like with photo-pictures (e.g., taken by a camera supervising a crop) or a short video or audio registration. Multimedia content has to be previously encoded with anything as simple as the *Base64* algorithm. In the evaluation Section we will present the results with messages of up to 100 kbytes to include all these cases.

The provision of the MQTTproxy is based on an "anycasting" approach. This means that there can be various MQTTproxys available in the area covered by any hub. As for regular clients, the hub that received the JSON message will start the search for an MQTTproxy as if they were regular end users; if multiple replays are received the first one is selected. Other strategies could be adopted, based for example on the detected load of a certain MQTTproxy device. The hub will packetize the JSON message sent to it to the selected MQTTproxy hub using the standard procedure used by the messaging system. The MQTTproxy, using the REST interface, will periodically interrogate the hub it is connected with to obtain the data. Figure 5 graphically describes this operation.

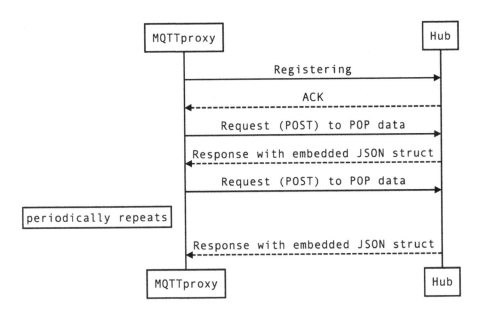

Fig. 5. The MQTTproxy getting data from the hub.

Once the message is obtained, the MQTTproxy will extract the JSON and create a proper "publish" message to the connected broker.

5   Experimental Results

This Section presents the results obtained with the proposed system by varying the distance between the hubs and the size of the sent messages; moreover, we compared the performance while using two different spreading factors, namely SF7 and SF12.

The devices we used as hubs were LoPy4 by Pycom[4]. The LoPy4 are a quadruple bearer MicroPython enabled development board with: IEEE 802.11b/g/n, Bluetooth v4.2 BR/EDR and BLE, LoRa (Semtech SX1276), and Sigfox with an Espressif ESP32 chipset (Xtensa dual–core 32–bit LX6), 520 KB + 4 MB of RAM, and 8 MB of external flash. It has a dual processor and two antenna connectors: one for the 868 MHz band used by LoRA and another one for the 2.4 GHz band used by WiFi and Bluetooth. This allows fitting the antenna best suited for the application. For instance, high-gain directional antennas can be used to connect a rural village to a city that could be at a very long distance, using very small power by leveraging the spread spectrum features of LoRa modulation. The network processor handles the WiFi connectivity and the IP stack, while the main processor is entirely free to run the user application.

This device is energetically very efficient, with an average consumption of 30 mA when idle and of 105 mA during a LoRa transmission A prototype of the complete hub, made of a LoPy node with an omnidirectional antenna, and a 5 W solar panel, is shown in Fig. 6.

Fig. 6. A prototype of a complete hub.

To execute the MQTTproxy we used a Raspberry Pi 3 Model B+ that has a 64-bit quad core processor running at 1.4 GHz, dual-band 2.4 GHz and 5 GHz wireless LAN, Bluetooth 4.2/BLE, and an Ethernet port.

We considered the following distances between the two hubs: 1 m, 100 m, 750 m, and 6000 m. The 1 and 100 m tests where performed in the facilities of the University. The 750 m tests where performed in Valencia, in the "Ciudad de las Artes y las Ciencias" area, see Fig. 7, while the 6km test where performed

---

[4] https://pycom.io/.

between two viewpoints in Chiapas, México. These latter locations are in areas high enough not to have obstacles in between; Fig. 8 shows the scenario where we the tests were done; there is a clear line of sight between the two points that are 6 km away, as shown in Fig. 8b.

(a) View from the right-side hub.

(b) View from the left-side hub.

Fig. 7. Location in Valencia for the 750 m tests.

(a) Map view of the link trajectory. (Image obtained using Google Earth, ©2019 DigitalGlobe)

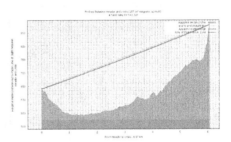
(b) Terrain profile between the two locations.

Fig. 8. The 6 km tests location in Chiapas, México.

We measured the performance of the system using a metric called "successful transfer time (STT)". It measures the transfer time of a message from the point of view of the sender, and it is computed from the moment at which the first fragment of the message is sent, to the moment when the last ACK of the last fragment of the message is received. All the tests were performed using both a Spreading factor of 7 (SF7) and a Spreading factor of 12 (SF12).

Bursts of 10 messages were sent to determine the stability of the system. The system performance was stable and almost identical to that of the tests at shorter distances. Retransmissions were rare events in the long-range experiments, having a negligible impact on the SST. We have to consider that delays are in the order of hundreds of seconds, and therefore a few more seconds do not affect the usability of the system. No effect was detected on message delivery.

Figure 9a allows to better view the evolution of the STT as a function of the message size using a spreading factor SF7. As we can see, the STT clearly grows as the message size increases, while it is evident that the impact of distance is negligible. As expected, the overall throughput that LoRa offers us is quite low, in the order of 250 bps.

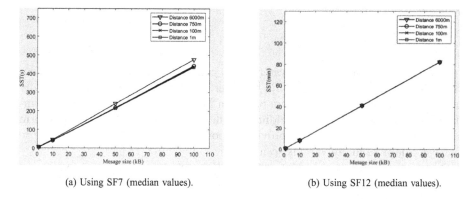

(a) Using SF7 (median values).   (b) Using SF12 (median values).

Fig. 9. Behavior of the STT when varying the message size.

The following figures show the behavior of the STT by varying the distance between the two nodes. The average values are displayed. Figure 10a is obtained using a spreading factor SF7 and Fig. 10b using a spreading factor SF12, in both cases messages of 1 kB, 10 kB, 50 kB, and 100 kB are sent. Almost constant behavior can be observed in the results, although the STT clearly grows as the message size increases. The system is quite stable at increasing distance and very few retransmissions were required during the experiments.

From the above results we can conclude that our solution is an effective and stable solution to integrate data from long distances using LoRa and MQTT.

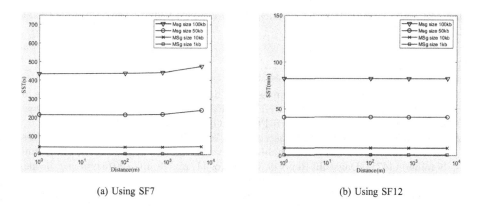

(a) Using SF7   (b) Using SF12

Fig. 10. Behavior of the STT versus distance between two nodes.

For example, with messages of 100 kBytes and SF7 the maximum delay obtained was 457,56 s, and the minimum 451,49 s; with SF12 the maximum delay obtained was 82,545 min, and the minimum 82,513 min. Clearly, the worst aspect is the low throughput that we can obtain due to the use of LoRa. We consider, anyway, that this is compensated by the long range obtained and by the low energetic cost that these devices requires, thus making this a frugal solution to a clear problem.

6   Conclusions

In this paper we presented a system that can collect data from remote sensors, transmit this data using LoRa to cover long distances, and automatically integrates it into a pub/sub system based on MQTT. We consider that the combination of LoRa and MQTT adding the flexibility provided by our platform and the use of a JSON interface provides a powerful and yet flexible architecture that can adapt to many various scenarios.

The goal was to provide support for IoT systems in rural areas connecting any type of sensor, like environmental sensors for weather forecasting, chemical sensor, level sensors, images sensors and so on. This system is embedded in a LoRa-based messaging system to conform a novel "frugal" IoT platform. We focused on the use of "frugal innovation approach" that aims to become a more "efficient" approach in terms of minimal utilization of resources such as electricity, time etc. and sustainable innovations, where sustainable means developed to be long–lasting and environmentally responsible.

We evaluated our solution varying the size of the packets and the spreading factor, and compared the performance over various distances, showing that our solution is effective and stable, allowing us to integrate data from long distances using LoRa and MQTT. The current version of the used code is available at: http://bit.ly/msnlora.

Acknowledgment. This work was partially supported by the "Ministerio de Ciencia, Innovación y Universidades, Programa Estatal de Investigación, Desarrollo e Innovación Orientada a los Retos de la Sociedad, Proyectos I+D+I 2018", Spain, under Grant RTI2018-096384-B-I00.

References

1. ITU/UNESCO Broadband Commission for Sustainable Development: The state of broadband 2019. On-line, ITU/UNESCO, Report, September 2019. https://www.itu.int/dms_pub/itu-s/opb/pol/S-POL-BROADBAND.20-2019-PDF-E.pdf
2. Crowcroft, J., Wolisz, A., Sathiaseelan, A.: Towards an Affordable Internet Access for Everyone: The Quest for Enabling Universal Service Commitment (Dagstuhl Seminar 14471). Dagstuhl Reports, vol. 4, no. 11, pp. 78–137 (2015). http://drops.dagstuhl.de/opus/volltexte/2015/4971
3. Micholia, P., et al.: Community networks and sustainability: a survey of perceptions, practices, and proposed solutions. IEEE Commun. Surv. Tutor. **20**(4), 3581–3606 (Fourthquarter 2018)

4. Cardenas, A.M., Pinto, M.K.N., Pietrosemoli, E., Zennaro, M., Rainone, M., Manzoni, P.: A low-cost and low-power messaging system based on the LoRa wireless technology. Mobile Netw. Appl. **25**, 961–968 (2019). https://doi.org/10.1007/s11036-019-01235-5

5. Agarwal, N., Brem, A.: Frugal innovation-past, present, and future. IEEE Eng. Manag. Rev. **45**(3), 37–41 (Third 2017)

6. Rao, B.C.: Advances in science and technology through frugality. IEEE Eng. Manag. Rev. **45**(1), 32–38 (First 2017)

7. Ottosson, S., Moldavska, A., Ogorodnyk, O., Skogsrød, T.: What is and how to develop sustainable innovation? In: Benlamri, R., Sparer, M. (eds.) Leadership, Innovation and Entrepreneurship as Driving Forces of the Global Economy. SPBE, pp. 191–209. Springer, Cham (2017). https://doi.org/10.1007/978-3-319-43434-6_16

8. Chaudhari, B.S., Zennaro, M.: LPWAN technologies: emerging application characteristics, requirements, and design considerations. Future Internet **12**(3), 46 (2020)

9. Banks, A., Briggs, E., Borgendale, K.,Gupta, R.: MQTT Version 5.0. On-line, OASIS Standard, Technical report, March 2019. https://docs.oasis-open.org/mqtt/mqtt/v5.0/mqtt-v5.0.html

10. Saldana, J., Arcia-Moret, A., Braem, B., Pietrosemoli, E., Sathiaseelan, A., Zennaro, M.: Alternative Network Deployments: Taxonomy, Characterization, Technologies, and Architectures. Internet Requests for Comments, RFC Editor, RFC 7962, August 2016. https://www.rfc-editor.org/rfc/pdfrfc/rfc7962.txt.pdf

11. Ahmad, T., Afutu, A., Adjaho, K., Nyarko, Y., Subramanian, L.: Technical report: design, implementation and deployment of intermittency-aware cellular edge services for rural areas. arXiv preprint arXiv:1604.05355 (2016)

12. Martinez, A., Villarroel, V., Seoane, J., del Pozo, F.: Analysis of information and communication needs in rural primary health care in developing countries. IEEE Trans. Inf. Technol. Biomed. **9**(1), 66–72 (2005)

13. Bharadwaj, A.S., Rego, R., Chowdhury, A.: IoT based solid waste management system: a conceptual approach with an architectural solution as a smart city application. In: IEEE Annual India Conference, INDICON 2016, pp. 1–6 (2016)

14. Spinsante, S., Ciattaglia, G., Del Campo, A., Perla, D., Pigini, D., Cancellieri, G., Gambi, E.: A LoRa enabled building automation architecture based on MQTT. In: AEIT International Annual Conference 2017, pp. 1–5 (2017)

15. Penkov, S., Taneva, A., Kalkov, V., Ahmed, S.: Industrial network design using low-power wide-area network. In: 2017 4th International Conference on Systems and Informatics (ICSAI), pp. 40–44 (2017)

16. Niswar, M., et al.: IoT-based water quality monitoring system for soft-shell crab farming. In: IEEE International Conference on Internet of Things and Intelligence System, IOTAIS 2018, pp. 6–9 (2018)

17. Huang, A., Huang, M., Shao, Z., Zhang, X., Wu, D., Cao, C.: A practical marine wireless sensor network monitoring system based on LoRa and MQTT. In: 2019 IEEE 2nd International Conference on Electronics Technology (ICET), pp. 330–334 (2019)

18. Paolini, C., Adigal, H., Sarkar, M.: Upper bound on LoRa smart metering uplink rate. In: 2020 IEEE 17th Annual Consumer Communications Networking Conference (CCNC), pp. 1–4 (2020)

19. Lachtar, A., Val, T., Kachouri, A.: Elderly monitoring system in a smart city environment using LoRa and MQTT. IET Wirel. Sens. Syst. **10**(2), 70–77 (2020)

20. Nunes, M., Alves, R., Casaca, A., Póvoa, P., Botelho, J.: An internet of things based platform for real-time management of energy consumption in water resource recovery facilities. In: Strous, L., Cerf, V.G. (eds.) IFIPIoT 2018. IAICT, vol. 548, pp. 121–132. Springer, Cham (2019). https://doi.org/10.1007/978-3-030-15651-0_11

21. Bhawiyuga, A., Amron, K., Primanandha, R., Kartikasari, D.P., Arijudin, H., Prabandari, D.A.: LoRa-MQTT gateway device for supporting sensor-to-cloud data transmission in smart aquaculture IoT application. In: International Conference on Sustainable Information Engineering and Technology, SIET 2019, pp. 187–190 (2019)

22. Angrisani, L., et al.: An innovative air quality monitoring system based on drone and IoT enabling technologies. In: IEEE International Workshop on Metrology for Agriculture and Forestry, MetroAgriFor 2019, pp. 207–211 (2019)

23. Boccadoro, P., Montaruli, B., Grieco, L.A.: Quakesense, a LoRa-compliant earthquake monitoring open system. In: 2019 IEEE/ACM 23rd International Symposium on Distributed Simulation and Real Time Applications (DS-RT), pp. 1–8 (2019)

24. Ciuffoletti, A.: Low-cost IoT: a holistic approach. J. Sens. Actuator Netw. **7**(2), 19 (2018)

A Fault Tolerant LoRa/LoRaWAN Relay Protocol Using LoRaWAN Class A Devices

Olivier Flauzac[1] , Joffrey Hérard[1]([✉]) , Florent Nolot[1] , and Philippe Cola[2]

[1] University of Reims Champagne Ardennes, CReSTIC, 51097 Reims, France
{olivier.flauzac,joffrey.herard,florent.nolot}@univ-reims.fr
[2] Bouygues Telecom, 75008 Paris, France
pcola@bouyguestelecom.fr

Abstract. One of the most widely used communication protocol in the Internet of Things, for collecting information in cities, are LoRa and the LoRaWAN protocol. Thanks to star topologies, operators can, therefore, collect electricity, water or gas consumption remotely and automatically. Unfortunately, some equipment is placed in difficult environments such as tunnels, cellars or wastewater drains. In this paper, we present the 1st fault-tolerant LoRa LoRaWAN relay solution working in LoRaWAN class A and our experimental results that we have been running for almost 1 year on SPOT (https://spot.objenious.com/) and The Things Network platforms. This solution solves the problem of sensor access to a gateway with our relay while respecting the LoRaWAN standard. The access to the medium is managed by our solution in order to avoid collisions.

Keywords: LoRa · LoRaWAN · Uniform relay protocol · Internet of Things

1 Introduction

Sensors networks are widely used to collect environmental data, to monitor infrastructures such as buildings, roads or bridges. One of the most wireless sensor network (WSN) architecture used is Linear Sensor Networks (LSN) or Semi-Linear (SLSN). This network topology puts sensors in a linear form. The Linear sensor networks have gained much attraction of the researchers due to their several positive aspects, including easy deployment for linear structures and robustness in different environments. But with this architecture, if a node, which we will call isolated node (IN), is outside the coverage area of the gateway, it cannot send its data. We therefore propose to add a node, called a relay, between the gateway and the isolated node, as shown in Fig. 1. This relay node will allow the isolated node to exchange with the gateway. In our solution, the

Supported by Objenious and Bouygues Telecom.

relay node also has the ability to send its own information and so be considered as a classic LoRaWAN node.

Our relay communicates in LoRa RAW with the isolated node and in LoRaWAN class A with the gateway. One of the main problems is to synchronize the isolated nodes and the relay to respect the duty cycle imposed by the ETSI EN300.220 and to reduce energy consumption.

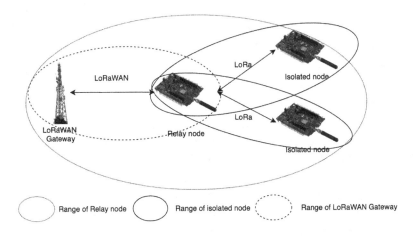

Fig. 1. Case of a remote LoRa device

In this paper, we first present the related works, followed by our LoRa-LoRaWAN uniform relay protocol. In the last part, the experimental results are explained before the conclusion.

2   Related Works

In [1] the authors propose a communication scheme with relays to improve the reliability of LoRa sensor network. Simulations show that relaying is very beneficial, even though the nodes are not coordinated and duty cycling limits the number of sensor measurements that can be forwarded. In [2] the authors propose a multi-hop communication setup based on LoRa. Results demonstrate that the multi-hop communication setups can provide up to 13 times higher packet delivery ratio and up to 60% lower energy consumption compared to the LoRaWAN communication setup and its recommended communication setting. Fault tolerance of a system mainly depends on the characteristics and architecture of the system. The main characteristics of WSN are cross-layer design, energy harvesting, resilience, mobility, scalability, withstand harsh environment, ease of use, dynamic network topology, unattended operation, heterogeneity and homogeneity. The wireless sensor network's basic characteristics, architectural specifications, and classifications are presented in this work [6] and summed up in this Table 1.

Table 1. Summary of fault-tolerant techniques

Class	Method
Time	Curative
	Preventive
Objective	Flow management
	Data Management
	Coverage/connectivity management
Size	For small scale
	For large scale
Implementation method	Redundancy based
	Clustering based
	Deployment base
Fault region	Link-based
	Node based
	Malfunction nodes

The management of fault tolerances depends on the duration of the fault, the impact of the fault on data recovery or the connectivity of the nodes. Fault management also depends on the size of the network. Fault management also depends on the size of the network, whether it is small or large. There are solutions based on redundant or clustered methods. These faults are listed in 3 cases: the link between two nodes is broken, a node does not work properly anymore (Byzantine) and a node stops working.

In [4], a distributed approach is used to detect the fault of Cluster Heads to detect fault in a network. FDFC is a proficient algorithm to detect failed Cluster Heads by using a distributed algorithm and resolves this issue by replacing the new Cluster Head. Simulation results show that the suggested work is more efficient than DFCA in terms of energy consumption by the faster recovery of failed Cluster Head. Simulation is performed on three different networks (small, medium and large). The details of each simulations performed are in the Table 2.

In [5], the authors studied the energy and time costs to recover failures depending on the failure density and the surface density in the Multilevel and EDCR protocols. According to their assessments, they found that the energy and time costs increase with the increase of failures and surface densities. They showed that the redundancy of the nodes if it does not increase the failures recovery time when the number of failures in the path of data transmission is increased, it can significantly reduce the network lifespan when the number of the failure is quite significant.

Table 2. Comparison table of [4]

Type of network	Initial energy level (Joule)	No. of sensor nodes	No. of clusters	Impact
Small	50	100	4	Good
Medium	50	300	12	Better
Large	50	500	20	Best

3   The Fault-Tolerant LoRa-LoRaWAN Uniform Relay Protocol for LoRaWAN End Node in Class A

It is assumed there is at least one isolated node, a relay node, and a LoRaWAN gateway, as in Fig. 1 and 2.

With our protocol [3], the relay node only needs to be compatible with the LoRaWAN protocol and can be reached by the LoRaWAN gateway of the provider. In our work, the specification version 1.0.3 is respected. The isolated node only needs to be able to communicate in LoRa and be in the coverage of the relay node. The relay node communicates in LoRaWAN Class A in Over-The-Air (OTA). The OTA procedure use 2 type of messages, Join request initiate by any

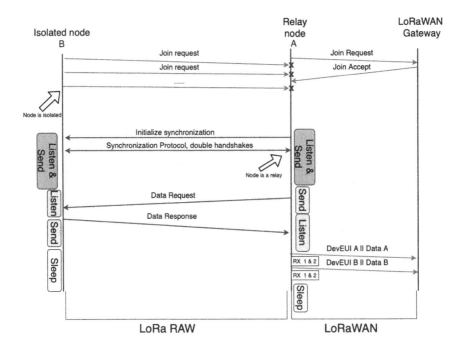

Fig. 2. Global mechanism

end nodes and the response from the antenna the Join Accept. Next, the relay node initializes a local synchronization system with the isolated node. Realized with different timer provided by the relay and different message integrated in the system [3]. The drawback of this first version of our relay protocol is energy consumption. The relay and the isolated node are not synchronized and the relay node works in class C, i.e. it is always in a waiting state (RX state) of messages. As a reminder, class A is the class with the lowest energy consumption. When the equipment has data to sent it does so without control. Class B is a compromise between energy consumption and the need for bi-directional communication. Class C has the highest power consumption but allows bi-directional communication that is not programmed. The equipment has a permanent listening window. So, some times, when the relay node sends data to the gateway, a message sent by the isolated node can be lost. The isolated node and the relay node have to be synchronized with each other. When the relay node sends the information up to the LoRaWAN Gateway, it must be possible to identify the source of the data. The identity of the sender is included in the payload sent by the relay node, as illustrated in Fig. 2. A new Join procedure must not be initiated to limits the calculation of session elements and encryption costs. The different steps of our algorithm at the relay node are in Table 3.

Table 3. Steps of the algorithm

Relay node	Isolated node
Initiate the Join Request procedure	Detect its role: whether it is isolated
Listen and transmit in LoRa to synchronize with an isolated node	Listen and transmit in LoRa to synchronize with a relay node
Transmit the information collected via DataRequest procedure by the isolated node to LoRaWAN	Transmit the information to the relay when the node is requested
Transmit the information collected by the relay node	Awake at the next RX window
Start over at the next RX window	X

3.1 Fault Tolerance Aspect

Several different faults can occur like a node failure (isolated node or relay node), a gateway failure or a transmission corruption. We can also have apparitions of new isolated nodes, new gateways or new relays. Table 4 summarizes all faults that our protocol takes into account and the solutions proposed. It is possible to consider the generation of faults from each node present in the Fig. 1. An isolated node, a relay node as well (1 as a gateway can generate faults. The faults considered here are the disappearances of one of these nodes. It is also

considered the dynamicity in the system, i.e. the addition of additional nodes
such as isolated nodes, relays or gateway. Here is a Table 4 that summarizes the
possible actions to restore a stable state with respect to a change to a non-stable
state. Each actions proposed was tested in the experimentation part.

Table 4. Fault in the system and solutions proposed

	Fault	Additional node	Solution proposed Isolated Node side	Solution Proposed Relay Node side
IN paired	Empty battery/ Physical problem	X	X	Detect by not collecting the node after a long time
IN not paired	Empty battery/ Physical problem	New deployment	X	Detect by not collecting the node, after a long time/No impact due to our protocol
RN with paired IN	Empty battery/ Physical problem	X	Not collected during a long time	X
RN without IN paired (End Device)	Empty battery/ Physical problem	New deployment	Not collected during a long time/No impact due to our protocol	X
LoRaWAN Gateway	Problem with the Network Server/Maintain	New deployment	Make a new Join Request after a time. If it's a success the IN signal it to the RN	X

3.2 Experimentations

Our fault-tolerant LoRa - LoRaWAN uniform relay protocol is implemented on
ST Micro Discovery Kit[1]. These tests started on July 17, 2019 by first deploying
two isolated nodes and a relay node. The scenario outlined here is as follows: the
relay node started to relay the informations of the two isolated nodes and then
the isolated nodes will be detected a Bouygues Telecom antenna. The number of
messages relayed is shown in the following Figs. 3, 4, 5 for 8 months. Each column
represent a week. The graphs in green are the number of uplink messages. The
nodes are programmed to send a data message every hour. Nodes have detected
their role by the response or lack of response to the Join Request. Phase A in
Fig. 3 represents the number of messages sent by the relay without having an
isolated node. This is the classic behavior of an end device. About 200 messages
per week or about 1 message per hour. Phase B represents the relaying of two
isolated nodes. This explains the increase in the number of messages which is

---

[1] https://www.st.com/en/evaluation-tools/b-l072z-lrwan1.html.

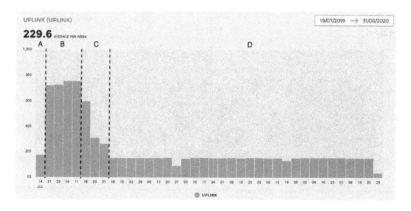

Fig. 3. Messages sent by the relay node (Color figure online)

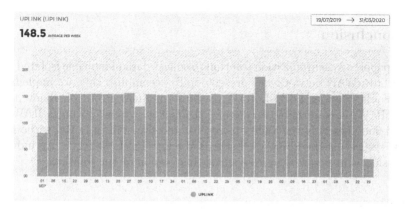

Fig. 4. Messages sent by the first isolated node (Color figure online)

700 messages. The number of messages is high because message aggregation is not used. We observe a loss of message possibly due to radio collisions. Phase C is the moment when an isolated node has successed to become a relay. There remains one isolated node still paired to the relay. Phase D is a return to phase A where both isolated nodes have become relay nodes. This explains the significant drop to about 200 messages per week. These graphs show when an isolated node become a relay did not impact the operation of the starting relay node. Convergence is slow due to the fact that the nodes became out of sync as it was no longer relayed over time. In addition, LoRaWAN coverage is unreliable in the experimental environment, which is what is wanted.

We also observe that some messages are missing on some weeks in the phase D. In terms of the number of messages sent from isolated nodes, it is equal to a classic end-device role as shown in[3]. Indeed this corresponds to data loss due to a failure on the network server or the LoRaWAN gateway of the operator.

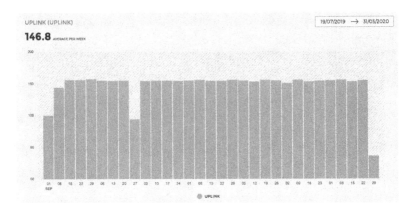

Fig. 5. Messages sent by the second isolated node (Color figure online)

4 Conclusion

In this paper, a synchronization solution to collect data of multiple isolated nodes from a LoRaWAN network was presented. To accomplish this, we implemented a new Fault Tolerant LoRa-LoRaWAN Uniform Relay Protocol. Relay node is fully LoRaWAN compatible, in spite of the fact it switches to LoRa RAW. The isolated node has only the ability to receive and transmit in LoRa, without necessarily respecting the LoRaWAN standard and ETSI EN300.220. An industrial partnership is in progress to implement this version of our solution.

References

1. Borkotoky, S.S., Schilcher, U., Bettstetter, C.: Cooperative relaying in LoRa sensor networks. In: 2019 IEEE Global Communications Conference (GLOBECOM), pp. 1–5 (2019)
2. Farooq, M.O.: Introducing scalability in LoRa-based networks through multi-hop communication setups. In: 2019 IEEE Global Communications Conference (GLOBECOM), pp. 1–6 (2019)
3. Flauzac, O., Hérard, J., Nolot, F., Cola, P.: A low power LoRa-LoRaWan relay function with a single input, single output device. In: International Conference on Embedded Wireless Systems and Networks, EWSN 2020, pp. 283–288 (2020)
4. Katre, V., Chauhan, S.: Cluster head failure detection and correction algorithm for WSN. In: 2018 Second International Conference on Intelligent Computing and Control Systems (ICICCS), pp. 1859–1862 (2018)
5. Moussa, N., El Belrhiti El Alaoui, A.: Statistical study of energy and time costs of fault tolerance in multilevel and EDCR protocols. In: 2019 International Conference on Wireless Technologies, Embedded and Intelligent Systems (WITS), pp. 1–4, April 2019. https://doi.org/10.1109/WITS.2019.8723778
6. Shyama, M., Pillai, A.S.: Fault tolerance strategies for wireless sensor networks - a comprehensive survey. In: 2018 3rd International Conference on Inventive Computation Technologies (ICICT), pp. 707–711 (2018)

IETF Reliable and Available Wireless (RAW): Use Cases and Problem Statement

Georgios Z. Papadopoulos[1]($\boxtimes$) (iD), Fabrice Theoleyre[2](iD), Pascal Thubert[3](iD), and Nicolas Montavont[1]

[1] IMT Atlantique, Irisa, Rennes, France
{georgios.papadopoulos,nicolas.montavont}@imt-atlantique.fr
[2] University of Strasbourg/CNRS, ICube Lab, Strasbourg, France
[3] Cisco Systems, Mougins Sophia Antipolis, France
pthubert@cisco.com

Abstract. Due to uncontrolled interferences, including the self-induced multi-path fading, deterministic networking is difficult to achieve on wireless links. The radio conditions may change much faster than a centralized routing paradigm can adapt and reprogram, in particular when the controller is distant and connectivity is slow and limited. Reliable and Available Wireless (RAW) separates the routing time scale at which a complex path is recomputed from the forwarding time scale at which the forwarding decision is taken for an individual packet. RAW operates at the forwarded time scale. The RAW problem is to decide, within the redundant solutions that are proposed by the routing plane, which will be used for each individual packet to provide a Deterministic Networking (DetNet) service while minimizing the waste of resources. A solution would consist of a set of protocols that evaluate the media in real time and another that controls the use of redundancy and diversity attributes that are available along the path. In this paper, we first introduce the motivation behind this approach along with the industrial use cases that requires RAW characteristics. We then give an overview of the ongoing related works at the Internet Engineering Task Force (IETF). Finally, we present the RAW problem statement.

Keywords: Reliable and available wireless · RAW · DetNet · LLNs · PAREO functions · Industrial wireless networks

1 Introduction

Wireless networks operate on a shared medium where uncontrolled interference, including the self-induced multi-path fading, adds another dimension to the statistical effects that affect the packet delivery. Scheduling transmissions can alleviate those effects by leveraging diversity in the spatial, time, code, and frequency domains, and provide a Reliable and Available service while preserving energy, and optimizing the use of the shared spectrum.

© Springer Nature Switzerland AG 2020
L. A. Grieco et al. (Eds.): ADHOC-NOW 2020, LNCS 12338, pp. 303–314, 2020.
https://doi.org/10.1007/978-3-030-61746-2_23

Bringing determinism in a packet network means eliminating the statistical effects of multiplexing that result in probabilistic jitter and loss. This can be approached with a tight control of the physical resources to maintain the amount of traffic within a limited volume of data per unit of time that fits the physical capabilities of the underlying technology, and the use of time-shared resources (bandwidth and buffers) per circuit, and/or by shaping and/or scheduling the packets at every hop.

Deterministic Networking (DetNet) is an attempt to mostly eliminate packet loss for a committed bandwidth with a guaranteed worst-case end-to-end latency, even when co-existing with best-effort traffic in a shared network. This innovation is enabled by recent developments in technologies including IEEE 802.1 TSN (for Ethernet LANs) and IETF DetNet (for wired IP networks). It is getting traction in various industries including manufacturing, online gaming, professional A/V, cellular radio and others, making possible many cost and performance optimizations. The DetNet architecture [9] is composed of three planes: a (User) Application Plane, a Controller Plane, and a Network Plane. Reliable and Available Wireless (RAW) [6] extends DetNet to focus on issues that are mostly a concern on wireless links, and inherits the architecture and the planes. A RAW Network Plane is thus a Network Plane inherited by RAW from DetNet.

RAW networking aims at providing highly available and reliable end-to-end performances in a network with scheduled wireless segments. Uncontrolled interference and transmission obstacles may impede the transmission, while techniques such as beamforming with Multi-user MIMO (MU-MIMO) can only alleviate some of those issues. This uncertainty places limits on the computation of the amount of traffic that can be transmitted on a link while conforming to a RAW Service Level Agreement (SLA) that may vary rapidly. Moreover, the wireless and wired media are fundamentally different at the physical level, and the methods to achieve RAW will differ from those used to support time-sensitive networking over wires, as a RAW solution will need to address less consistent transmissions, energy conservation and shared spectrum efficiency. However, recent efforts at the Electrical and Electronics Engineers (IEEE) and 3GPP indicate that wireless is finally catching up at the lower layer and that it is now possible for the Internet Engineering Task Force (IETF) to extend DetNet for wireless segments that are capable of scheduled wireless transmissions.

The intent for RAW is to provide DetNet elements that are specialized for short range radios. From this inheritance, RAW stays agnostic to the radio layer underneath though the capability to schedule transmissions is assumed. How the PHY is programmed to do so, and whether the radio is single-hop or meshed, are hidden for the IP layer and are not part of the RAW abstraction. Still, in order to focus on real-world issues and assert the feasibility of the proposed capabilities, RAW will focus on selected technologies that can be scheduled at the lower layers: IEEE Std. 802.15.4 Time-Slotted Channel Hopping (TSCH), 3GPP 5G Ultra-Reliable Low Latency Communications (URLLC), IEEE 802.11ax/be where 802.11be is Extreme High Throughput (EHT), and L-band Digital Aeronautical Communications System (LDACS) [26].

The establishment of a path is not in-scope for RAW. It may be the product of a centralized Controller Plane as described for DetNet. As opposed to wired networks, the action of installing a path over a set of wireless links may be very slow relative to the speed at which the radio conditions vary. Moreover, it makes sense in the wireless case to provide redundant forwarding opportunities at the IP level. RAW distinguishes the longer time scale at which routes are computed from the shorter forwarding time scale where per-packet decisions are made. RAW operates at the forwarding time scale on one flow over one path that is pre-established and installed by means of techniques which are outside of the scope of RAW. The scope of the RAW Working Group (WG) comprises Network plane protocol elements such as Operations, Administration, and Maintenance (OAM) and in-band control to improve the RAW operation at the Service and at the forwarding sub-layers, e.g., controlling whether to use packet replication, Hybrid ARQ and coding, with a constraint to limit the use of redundancy when it is really needed, e.g., when a spike of loss is observed. This is discussed in more details in Sect. 4 and the next sections.

This paper is organized as follows. In Sect. 2, we present a number of wireless use cases that demonstrate the need for RAW capabilities. Then, Sect. 3 exposes the related work that has been done at the IETF. We describe in Sect. 4 the terminology that RAW uses. In Sect. 5, we detail the RAW approach, describing first the difference between the routing and forwarding time scales, and then exposing the RAW problem statement, i.e., the WG charter. Finally, Sect. 6 concludes the paper.

2 Use Cases

Many Industrial Applications rely on a deterministic industrial network [11]. However, enabling wireless communications also multiplies the possibilities [17]. We detail here a few use cases that may benefit from a RAW solution.

2.1 Industry 4.0 and Robotics

Industry 4.0 represents the next industrial revolution [15]. The objective consists in collecting a huge volume of data in real-time to adapt dynamically the industrial process. Thus, we need big data tools to handle the huge volume of data, and to extract interesting features.

However, to enable Cyber Physical Systems (CPS), we need also a network infrastructure able to forward critical flows, guaranteeing both ultra reliability and small and bounded end-to-end latencies. The DetNet working group has provided pioneering piece of work to standardize the communication stack, so that resources can be allocated end-to-end [10]. It relies mostly on the IEEE 802.1 Time Sensitive Networking (TSN) features [29]. Each switch on the path is able to pre-reserve a port to a specific flow: periodically, a flow has the full priority to send its packets through a physical port. This way, TSN removes the competition, and thus transforms the Ethernet network into a fully deterministic infrastructure. While industrial networks are expected to integrate wireless communications in the future, wireless transmissions are known to be time-variant, and lossy [18–20]. In these conditions, providing ultra high reliability, and a low latency is particularly challenging.

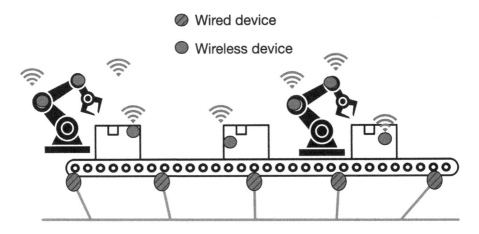

Fig. 1. Wireless industrial networks.

A typical use case mixes both wired and wireless parts (Fig. 1). While some sensors on the manufacturing line may be directly connected to the wired infrastructure using e.g., DetNet, some wireless devices are also present. For instance, robotic arms are mobile and wires tend to cause premature wear and malfunctions. In such infrastructure cohabit very different flows: a geofencing application with an accuracy of a few seconds, or robots with almost real time control. For instance, human and robotic safe integration needs 15 to 36 ms end-to-end latencies [22].

2.2   Gaming and Multimedia

Current home consoles consist of a single computational device, and a few wireless remote controls. However, we face to increasingly complex interactions, that integrate virtual reality devices, smartphones, other home consoles, headsets, etc. [14].

While some displays and the gaming server may be connected through a high bandwidth network (Fig. 2), some devices need wireless communications. Remote control and virtual reality headsets typically cannot function properly with cables since they would negatively impact the user experience. Moreover, multi camera techniques for motion capture [8] generate a huge volume of data to process in real-time. Last but not least, multiple wireless technologies may cohabit to fit the different requirements (motion capture vs. remote controls). A

Fig. 2. Home gaming scenario.

unified way to manage the wireless infrastructure is required to allocate properly the radio resources, and to limit co-interferences.

Artistic applications that exploit gaming technologies have started to emerge. By creating installations that react to the audience, modern art tends to now abolish the frontiers between the real and digital, imaginative worlds. In particular, digital fulldomes provide a full 360° experience [23], where the digital worlds may react dynamically to the actions of the audience and the artists. For this purpose, we need wireless communications with a very small latency to provide natural interactions. Digital walls would represent also a promising futuristic Human-Computer Interface [12], using partly wireless devices to personalize the user experience. Using wireless part allow a more flexible reconfiguration, assembling the different blocks very easily.

2.3   Smart Building and Home Automation

Smart buildings pave the way for a reduction of the carbon footprint, and for a better usage of offices and homes. In particular, energy management seems a key enabler: the objective is to dynamically adapt the heating or HVAC system to the building occupancy [7]. A collection of sensors detect the presence of occupants, or may even identify uniquely each individual bodies to adapt the behavior of the room to the users. To maximize the reconfigurability, most sensors and actuators may use wireless transmissions. Moreover, deploying kilometers of cables in existing buildings seems unreasonable, and a clean slate approach is unrealistic as well.

Many flows may cohabit in the same infrastructure with very different characteristics. Temperature sensors generate small packets periodically, every e.g., minute, while Closed-Circuit TeleVision (CCTV) generate multimedia streams

Fig. 3. Smart building scenario.

toward the video servers. Smart buildings require to interconnect the different applications (cf. Fig. 3), so that the different sensors send their data to multiple controllers, to make *smart* decisions. Thus, we need a global solution able to jointly optimize all the transmissions, with different co-interfering wireless technologies.

3   Related Work at the IETF

RAW intersects with existing protocols or practices in development at the IETF. In particular, the Dynamic Link Exchange Protocol (DLEP) [21] from Mobile Ad Hoc Networks (MANET) [1] can be leveraged at each hop to derive generic radio metrics (e.g., based on Link Quality Indicator (LQI), Received Signal Strength Indicator (RSSI), queueing delays and Expected Transmission Counts (ETX)) on individual hops. These metrics are typically useful for RAW since the radio link quality is time-variant in radio networks, and have to be carefully estimated to size correctly the amount of bandwidth to reserve for a flow.

In the same way, OAM for DetNet [16] allows to observe the state of the IP Data Plane. Typically, it monitors MultiProtocol Label Switching (MPLS) and IPv6 pseudowires [28], in the direction of the traffic. RAW needs feedback that flows on the reverse path and gathers instantaneous values from the radio receivers at each hop to inform back the source and replicating relays so they can make optimized forwarding decisions.

In RAW, we need also to be fault tolerant. In particular, Bidirectional Forwarding Detection (BFD) [2] detects faults in the path between an ingress and an egress forwarding engines, but is unaware of the complexity of a path with replication, and expects bidirectionality. BFD considers delivery as success while RAW has also to consider the end-to-end latency.

SPRING [5] and BIER [3] define in-band signaling that influences the routing when decided at the head-end on the path. A draft [27] already addresses this problem, and more may follow. RAW will need new in-band signaling when the decision is distributed, e.g., required chances of reliable delivery to destination within latency. This signaling enables relays to tune retries and replication to meet the required SLA.

The Common Control and Measurement Plane (CCAMP) [4] defines protocol-independent metrics and parameters (measurement attributes) for describing links and paths that are required for routing and signaling in technology-specific networks. RAW would be a source of requirements for CCAMP to define metrics that are significant to the radios networks.

4   Definitions

RAW defines the following terms:

PAREO (Packet Automatic Repeat reQuest, Replication and Elimination, and Ordering (PAREO)) [13] is a superset of DetNet's Packet Replication, Elimination, and Ordering Functions (PREOF) that includes radio-specific techniques such as short range broadcast, MU-MIMO, constructive interference and overhearing, which can be leveraged separately or combined to increase the reliability.

Flapping corresponds to a radio link with a very time-variant quality. Typically, the wireless connectivity drops abruptly for a short period of time, for e.g., a few hundreds of milliseconds, or even a few seconds.

Reliability measures the probability that an item will perform its intended function for a specified interval under stated conditions. For RAW, the service that is expected is delivery within a bounded latency and a failure is when the packet is either lost or delivered too late. RAW expresses reliability in terms of Mean Time Between Failure (MTBF) and Maximum Consecutive Failures (MCF).

Availability measures the relative amount of time where a path operates in stated condition, in other words (uptime)/(uptime+downtime). Because a serial wireless path may not be good enough to provide the required availability, and even two parallel paths may not be over a longer period of time, the RAW availability implies a path that is a lot more complex than what DetNet typically envisages (a Track).

a Track abstracts the underlaying technology, and represents a set of resources along the path from the source to the destination. RAW specifies strict and loose Tracks depending on whether the path is fully controlled by RAW or traverses an opaque network where RAW cannot observe and control the individual hops.

5   RAW Approach

A prerequisite to the RAW work is that an end-to-end routing function computes a complex sub-topology along which forwarding can happen between a source and one or more destinations. This represents a *Track*, as specified in the 6TiSCH Architecture [25]. Tracks provide a high degree of redundancy and diversity and enable DetNet PREOF, end-to-end network coding, and possibly radio-specific abstracted techniques such as ARQ, overhearing, frequency diversity, time slotting, and possibly others.

How the routing operation computes the Track is out of scope for RAW. The scope of the RAW operation is one Track, and the goal of the RAW operation is to optimize the use of the Track at the forwarding timescale to maintain the expected service while optimizing the usage of constrained resources such as energy and spectrum.

Another prerequisite is that an IP link can be established over the radio with some guarantees in terms of service reliability, e.g., it can be relied upon to transmit a packet within a bounded latency and provides a guaranteed BER/PDR outside rare but existing transient outage windows that can last from split seconds to minutes. The radio layer can be programmed with abstract parameters, and can return an abstract view of the state of the Link to help forwarding decision (think Dynamic Link Exchange Protocol (DLEP) from MANET). In the layered approach, how the radio manages its PHY layer is out of control and out of scope. Whether it is single hop or meshed is also unknown and out of scope.

5.1 Routing Time Scale vs. Forwarding Time Scale

With DetNet, the end-to-end routing can be centralized and can reside outside the network. In wireless, and in particular in a wireless mesh, the path to the controller is expensive to maintain, consuming both air time and energy. Reaching the routing steady state can also be slow in regards to the speed of events that affect the forwarding operation at the radio layer. Due to the cost and latency to perform a route computation, the controller plane is not expected to be sensitive/reactive to transient changes. The abstraction of a link at the routing level is expected to use statistical operational metrics that aggregate the behavior of a link over long periods of time, and represent its availability as shades of gray as opposed to either up or down.

In the case of wireless, the changes that affect the forwarding decision can happen frequently and often for short durations, e.g., a mobile object moves between a transmitter and a receiver, and will cancel the line of sight transmission for a few seconds, or a radar measures the depth of a pool and interferes on a particular channel for a split second, see Fig. 4.

There is thus a desire to separate the long term computation of the route and the short term forwarding decision. In such a model, the routing operation computes a complex Track that enables multiple Non-Equal Cost Multi-Path (N-ECMP) forwarding solutions, and leaves it to the forwarding plane to make the per-packet decision of which of these possibilities should be used.

This concept is already widely used in wired networks, where traffic engineering exploits multiple alternate paths, using e.g. OAM in MPLS-TP or BFD over a collection of SD-WAN tunnels. RAW brings this concept in the wireless world, where the forwarding time scale is an order(s) of magnitude shorter than

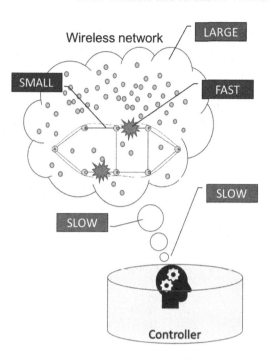

Fig. 4. A multi-hop RAW network that may represent potential delays on routing and forwarding decisions due to the network instabilities.

the controller plane routing time scale. It separates the protocols and metrics that are used at both scales. Routing can operate on long term statistics such as delivery ratio over minutes to hours, but as a first approximation can ignore flapping. On the other hand, the RAW forwarding decision is made at packet speed, and uses information that must be pertinent at the present time for the current transmission.

5.2 Problem Statement

Within a large routed topology, the routing operation builds a particular complex Track with one source and one or more destinations; within the Track, packets may follow different paths and may be subject to RAW forwarding operations that include replication, elimination, retries, overhearing and reordering.

The RAW forwarding decisions include the selection of points of replication and elimination, how many retries can take place, and a limit of validity for the packet beyond which the packet should be destroyed rather than forwarded uselessly further down the Track.

The decision to apply the RAW techniques must be done quickly, and depends on a very recent and precise knowledge of the forwarding conditions within the complex Track. There is a need for an observation method to provide the RAW forwarding plane with the specific knowledge of the state of the Track for the type of flow of interest (e.g., for a QoS level of interest). To observe the whole Track in quasi real time, RAW will consider existing tools such as L2-triggers, DLEP, BFD and in-band and out-of-band OAM [24].

RAW forwarding decisions may be implemented at the ingress and piggy-backed, in-band, in the packet, which requires new loose or strict Hop-by-hop signaling. To control the RAW forwarding operation along a Track for the individual packets, RAW may leverage and extend known techniques such as Det-Net tagging, Segment Routing (SRv6) or BIER-TE such as done with BIER-PREF [27].

An alternate way is to enable each forwarding node to make the RAW forwarding decisions for a packet on its own, based on its knowledge of the expectation (timeliness and reliability) for that packet and a recent observation of the rest of the way across the possible paths within the Track. Information about the service should be placed in the packet and matched with the forwarding node's capabilities and policies. In either case, a per-flow state is installed in all intermediate nodes to recognize the flow and determine the forwarding policy to be applied.

6   Conclusions

Industrial wireless networks promise to enable reconfigurability while still providing strict guarantees concerning the reliability and the end-to-end delay. We presented several use cases, that may benefit from a wireless infrastructure, to send even critical flows. We presented here the RAW working group, that aims to design the network protocols able to exploit multiple wireless technologies. Since radio links are known to be lossy, RAW proposes to separate the routing (long) timescale from the forwarding (short) timescale. While RAW is in charge of constructing end-to-end redundant paths to cope with packet losses, the lower layers are in charge of taking the forwarding decisions, so that e.g., temporary link flapping may be combatted.

In the future, we expect to design the routing algorithms able to construct accurately the different paths (independency, complementary, load-balancing), adapted for the wireless forwarding plane. We also plan to explore how existing OAM tools are adapted for wireless networks, and to propose protocols and algorithms to cope with their specificities, for instance, to detect flapping links, or temporary and permanent route breaks.

References

1. Charter IETF MANET WG, Mobile Ad hoc Networking, July 2016
2. Charter IETF BFD WG, Bidirectional Forwarding Detection, March 2018
3. Charter IETF BIER WG, Bit Indexed Explicit Replication, March 2018
4. Charter IETF CCAMP WG, Common Control and Measurement Plane, January 2018
5. Charter IETF SPRING WG, Source Packet Routing in Networking, October 2018

6. Charter IETF RAW WG, Reliable and Available Wireless, January 2020
7. Agarwal, Y., Balaji, B., Gupta, R., Lyles, J., Wei, M., Weng, T.: Occupancy-driven energy management for smart building automation. In: ACM Workshop on Embedded Sensing Systems for Energy-Efficiency in Building (BuildSys), pp. 1–6 (2010). https://doi.org/10.1145/1878431.1878433
8. Baytaş, M.A., Yantaç, A.E., Fjeld, M.: LabDesignAR: configuring multi-camera motion capture systems in augmented reality. In: Proceedings of the 23rd ACM Symposium on Virtual Reality Software and Technology (2017). https://doi.org/10.1145/3139131.3141778
9. Finn, N., Thubert, P., Varga, B., Farkas, J.: Deterministic NetworkingArchitecture. IETF RFC 8655, October 2019
10. Finn, N., Thubert, P.: Deterministic Networking Problem Statement. RFC 8557, May 2019. https://doi.org/10.17487/RFC8557
11. Grossman, E.: Deterministic Networking Use Cases. IETF RFC 8578, July 2019
12. Klemmer, S.R., Everitt, K.M., Landay, J.A.: Integrating physical and digital interactions on walls for fluid design collaboration. Hum. Comput. Interact. **23**(2), 138–213 (2008). https://doi.org/10.1080/07370020802016399
13. Koutsiamanis, R.A., Papadopoulos, G.Z., Jenschke, T.L., Thubert, P., Montavont, N.: Meet the PAREO functions: towards reliable and available wireless networks. In: Proceedings of the IEEE International Conference on Communications (ICC) (2020)
14. Lai, Z., Hu, Y.C., Cui, Y., Sun, L., Dai, N., Lee, H.: Furion: engineering high-quality immersive virtual reality on today's mobile devices. IEEE Trans. Mobile Comput. **19**, 1586–1602 (2019)
15. Lu, Y.: Industry 4.0: a survey on technologies, applications and open research issues. J. Ind. Inf. Integr. **6**, 1–10 (2017). https://doi.org/10.1016/j.jii.2017.04.005
16. Mirsky, G., Chen, M., Black, D.: Operations, administration and maintenance (OAM) for deterministic networks (DetNet) with IP data plane. Internet-Draft draft-mirsky-detnet-ip-oam-02 [work-in-progress], IETF, DetNet WG, March 2020
17. Papadopoulos, G.Z., Thubert, P., Theoleyre, F., Bernardos, C.: RAW use cases. Internet-Draft draft-bernardos-raw-use-cases-03 [work-in-progress], IETF, RAW WG, March 2020
18. Papadopoulos, G.Z., Gallais, A., Schreiner, G., Jou, E., Noel, T.: Thorough IoT testbed characterization: from proof-of-concept to repeatable experimentations. Elsevier Comput. Netw. **119**, 86–101 (2017)
19. Papadopoulos, G.Z., Gallais, A., Schreiner, G., Noel, T.: Importance of repeatable setups for reproducible experimental results in IoT. In: Proceedings of the 13th ACM International Symposium on Performance Evaluation of Wireless Ad Hoc, Sensor, and Ubiquitous Networks (PE-WASUN) (2016)
20. Pavkovic, B., Theoleyre, F., Barthel, D., Duda, A.: Experimental analysis and characterization of a wireless sensor network environment. In: ACM PE-WASUN, pp. 25–32 (2010). https://doi.org/10.1145/1868589.1868595
21. Ratliff, S., Jury, S., Satterwhite, D., Taylor, R., Berry, B.: Dynamic LinkExchange Protocol (DLEP). RFC 8175, June 2017
22. Robla-Gómez, S., Becerra, V.M., Llata, J.R., González-Sarabia, E., Torre-Ferrero, C., Pérez-Oria, J.: Working together: a review on safe human-robot collaboration in industrial environments. IEEE Access **5**, 26754–26773 (2017)
23. Schnall, S., Hedge, C., Weaver, R.: The immersive virtual environment of the digital fulldome: considerations of relevant psychological processes. Int. J. Hum. Comput. Stud. **70**(8), 561–575 (2012). https://doi.org/10.1016/j.ijhcs.2012.04.001

24. Theoleyre, F., Papadopoulos, G.Z., Mirsky, G.: Operations, Administration and Maintenance (OAM) features for RAW. Internet-Draft draft-theoleyre-raw-oam-support-02 [work-in-progress], IETF, RAW WG, April 2020

25. Thubert, P.: An Architecture for IPv6 over the TSCH mode of IEEE 802.15.4. Internet-Draft draft-ietf-6tisch-architecture-28 [work-in-progress], IETF, 6TiSCH WG, October 2019

26. Thubert, P., Cavalcanti, D., Vilajosana, X., Schmitt, C., Farkas, J.: Reliable and Available Wireless Technologies. Internet-Draft draft-thubert-raw-technologies-05 [work-in-progress], IETF, RAW WG, July 2019

27. Thubert, P., Eckert, T., Brodard, Z., Jiang, H.: BIER-TE extensions for Packet Replication and Elimination Function (PREF) and OAM. Internet-Draft draft-thubert-bier-replication-elimination-03 [work-in-progress], IETF, BIER WG, March 2018

28. Varga, B., Farkas, J., Berger, L., Malis, A., Bryant, S.: DetNet Data Plane Framework. Internet-Draft draft-ietf-detnet-data-plane-framework-04 [work-in-progress], IETF, DetNet WG, February 2020

29. Varga, B., Farkas, J., Malis, A.G., Bryant, S.: DetNet Data Plane: IP over IEEE 802.1 Time Sensitive Networking (TSN). Internet-Draft draft-ietf-detnet-ip-over-tsn-02, Internet Engineering Task Force, March 2020

Author Index

Printed in the United States
By Bookmasters